Bengal in Global Co

CHICAGO STUDIES IN PRACTICES OF MEANING

Edited by Jean Comaroff, Andreas Glaeser, William Sewell, and Lisa Wedeen

ALSO IN THE SERIES

Producing India: From Colonial Economy to National Space
by Manu Goswami

Parité! Sexual Equality and the Crisis of French Universalism
by Joan Wallach Scott

Logics of History: Social Theory and Social Transformation
by William H. Sewell Jr.

Inclusion: The Politics of Difference in Medical Research
by Steven Epstein

*The Devil's Handwriting: Precoloniality and the
German Colonial State in Qingdao, Samoa, and Southwest Africa*
by George Steinmetz

*Bewitching Development: Witchcraft and the
Reinvention of Development in Neoliberal Kenya*
by James Howard Smith

Peripheral Visions
by Lisa Wedeen

Bengal in Global Concept History

Culturalism in the Age of Capital

ANDREW SARTORI

The University of Chicago Press

CHICAGO AND LONDON

ANDREW SARTORI is assistant professor of history at New York University. In addition to being the author of numerous journal articles, he is coeditor of *From the Colonial to the Postcolonial: India and Pakistan in Transition.*

The University of Chicago Press, Chicago 60637
The University of Chicago Press, Ltd., London
© 2008 by The University of Chicago
All rights reserved. Published 2008
Printed in the United States of America

17 16 15 14 13 12 11 10 09 08   1 2 3 4 5

ISBN-13: 978-0-226-73493-4 (cloth)
ISBN-13: 978-0-226-73494-1 (paper)
ISBN-10: 0-226-73493-5 (cloth)
ISBN-10: 0-226-73494-3 (paper)

Library of Congress Cataloging-in-Publication Data

Sartori, Andrew, 1969–
    Bengal in global concept history : culturalism in the age of capital / Andrew Sartori.
        p.   cm. — (Chicago studies in practices of meaning)
    Includes bibliographical references and index.
    ISBN-13: 978-0-226-73493-4 (hardcover : alk. paper)
    ISBN-13: 978-0-226-73494-1 (pbk. : alk. paper)
    ISBN-10: 0-226-73493-5 (hardcover : alk. paper)
    ISBN-10: 0-226-73494-3 (pbk. : alk. paper)
    1. Culture—social aspects—India—Bengal. 2. Culture—Economic aspects—India—Bengal.
3. Bengal (India)—Civilization. 4. Bengal (India)—Historiography. I. Title.
DS485.B44S345 2008
954'.14—dc22

2007041822

⊗ The paper used in this publication
meets the minimum requirements of the American National
Standard for Information Sciences—Permanence of Paper
for Printed Library Materials, ANSI Z39.48-1992.

Contents

Acknowledgments • vii

CHAPTER ONE • 1
Bengali "Culture" as a Historical Problem

CHAPTER TWO • 25
Culture as a Global Concept

CHAPTER THREE • 68
Bengali Liberalism and British Empire

CHAPTER FOUR • 109
Hinduism as Culture

CHAPTER FIVE • 136
The Conceptual Structure of
an Indigenist Nationalism

CHAPTER SIX • 176
Reification, Rarification,
and Radicalization

CONCLUSION • 230
Universalistic Particularisms and
Parochial Cosmopolitanisms

Notes • 235
Index • 269

Acknowledgments

DIPESH CHAKRABARTY adopted me while I was still a shy undergraduate wandering the halls of the University of Melbourne in search of a major. He introduced me to the study of South Asia and to the world of subalternist and postcolonialist historiography and theory, and his teaching fired the enthusiasm that led me into graduate studies in South Asian history at the University of Chicago. I thank him for his avuncular care and an intellectual generosity that has given me the space to carve out my own theoretical path.

In my first year at the University of Chicago I encountered the second major influence on my intellectual development, Moishe Postone. His seminar on the first volume of *Capital* captivated me thanks to the rigor of his pedagogy, the critical power of his reinterpretation of Karl Marx's work, and the sheer profundity of Marx's writings. I want to thank Moishe for the unwavering support he has given me, especially through some rocky moments in my graduate school career. Not only has he had a considerable impact on my approach to teaching, but it was also his influence that set in motion a long (and perhaps interminable) process of intellectual revision on my part as I tried to work through the extended implications of his remarkable reconstruction of Marx's approach for the kinds of theoretical issues that I was grappling with in South Asian history.

One inevitable correlate of working with Moishe is participation in the Social Theory Workshop that he and Bill Sewell have been cosponsoring for many years at the University of Chicago. This has been an exceptional intellectual environment that approaches works in progress with a rare combination of incisive criticism and constructive engagement, and I want to thank all the participants who have given me feedback over the years. Bill Sewell in particular has a most remarkable ability to think through, and with, other people's arguments and intentions, and his criticism has been both invaluable intellectually and exemplary pedagogically. Bill was responsible for bringing my manuscript to the Editorial Board of the Chicago Studies in Practices of Meaning, who in turn provided me with extremely helpful suggestions about finding the right voice for the persuasive presentation of my argument. Bill personally provided stringent and irreplaceable line-by-line criticism of the two introductory chapters.

While this book grew out of general theoretical concerns, the specific focus on "culture" as a problem of intellectual history emerged out of a seminar on the history of anthropology that George Stocking led, and subsequently an especially stimulating qualifying exam reading list that I compiled with Jan Goldstein on the concept of civilization in modern European intellectual history. Jan has been particularly generous with her time and advice over the years, and that has been much appreciated. Clint Seely taught me Bangla with preternatural patience. Manu Goswami has been unfailingly enthusiastic about and supportive of my work. She also gave me very helpful advice on the framing of my opening chapters. Gautam Bhadra provided helpful archival advice and helpful comments while I was in Calcutta. Ralph Austen has been a provocative and generous interlocutor in several forums over the years. I have benefited from exchanges of ideas with Chris Bayly and Shruti Kapila, both of whom have been wonderfully encouraging of my aspirations to a global intellectual history. Sheldon Pollock gave me helpful advice early on in the development of this project. Ron Inden, although unsympathetic to my approach, nonetheless was a committed teacher and insightful reader during the first three years of graduate school. I have been happily entangled in Paul Magee's thought processes for many years now, even though an ocean has separated us for more than a decade. I also benefited enormously from the conversation, debate, and company of various friends at the University of Chicago over the years, especially Dave Como, Atiya Khan, Spencer Leonard, Mark Loeffler, Rochona Majumdar, Kwai Hang Ng, Sunit Singh, and Hylton White. The Hunts and Danny Sullivan were incredibly hospitable during my research stint in London. Thanks to Dawn Hall for her patience and care in editing the manuscript. And last but certainly not least I would like to thank David Brent and the University of Chicago Press for backing this book.

The research for this book was completed with support from the Social

Sciences Research Council and American Council of Learned Societies International Dissertation Field Research Fellowship Program, the Woodrow Wilson National Fellowship Foundation Charlotte W. Newcombe Doctoral Dissertation Fellowship Program, the Committee on Southern Asian Studies at the University of Chicago, and the Society of Fellows in the Liberal Arts at the University of Chicago. I have also benefited from the kindness of many people, not only at the University of Chicago but also from the American Institute of Indian Studies, the Centre for Studies in Social Sciences, Calcutta (my host institution in India), the National Library of India, the National Council of Education, Bengal, and Dhaka University.

Parts of chapter 2 have been previously published by Cambridge University Press as "The Resonance of 'Culture': Framing a Problem in Global Concept-History," *Comparative Studies in Society and History* 47, no. 4 (2005): 676–99. Chapter 5 draws on material previously published by Duke University Press in "The Categorical Logic of a Colonial Nationalism: Swadeshi Bengal, 1904–1908," *Comparative Studies of South Asia, Africa, and the Middle East* 23, nos. 1 and 2 (2003): 271–85 (Copyright 2003. Used by permission of the publisher), and by Cambridge University Press in "Beyond Culture-Contact and Colonial Discourse: 'Germanism' and Colonial Bengal," *Modern Intellectual History* 4, no. 1 (2007): 77–93.

None of this could have happened without the patience, love, and generosity of my family. Special thanks to Mum and Dad, Barb and Lee, and Ed.

This book is dedicated to Amy and Izzie, who are gorgeous, fabulous, funny, and amazing.

Andrew Sartori
November 2007

———— ✳ ————

CHAPTER ONE

Bengali "Culture" as a Historical Problem

IN 1952, the Bengali filmmaker Satyajit Ray dragged his cameras into a rural landscape, known to him only through the conventions of Bengali literature, to begin pitching the lauded humanism of his famous Apu trilogy.[1] *Pather Panchali* (1955), *Aparajito* (1956), and *Apur Sansar* (1959) follow the development of a young Brahman boy (Apu) from his impoverished childhood in a small village through separation from his family, school, marriage, tragic loss, and finally to maturity. Together they form an eloquent cinematic vision of the resolution of parochial tradition—the village from which Apu emerges as a small child in the first film and to which he returns to claim his abandoned son at the end of the last—into the broad framework of a cosmopolitan humanism (the trajectory first introduced by a globe that Apu is awarded at school as a small boy).[2] But we can also already sense alongside the ideals of culture encoded in the bildungsroman structure of the Apu narrative a troubling anxiety about the aesthetic and ethical rootlessness of a materialistic modernity symbolized most strikingly by the recurrent intrusion of the locomotive, whose headlong, clamorous rush is variously awe-inspiring, threatening, oppressive, and the recurrent instrument of emotionally painful separations.[3] Ray ascribed Nehruvian sympathies to his early work, and Nehru, the socialist advocate of industrialization and modernization, had conversely lent his personal support to the completion of the trilogy.[4] Yet one need only notice the complete absence of the dams, irrigation projects, and machinery characteristic of the modernist aesthetic of technology so evident in contemporary postindependence Hindi cinema (for example, Mehboob Khan's 1957 film, *Mother India*)

✱ Aesthetic and ethical rootlessness in a materially modern society

to recognize a distinctly "Bengali" cast both to his self-conscious humanism and to the anxieties that haunted it.

Anxieties that remained the slightest of hints in the Apu trilogy would already stand out as the central theme of his 1958 film *Jalsaghar* (*The Music Room*). Produced between the second and third installments of the trilogy and originally conceived to be a more broadly popular "musical" project, this film unexpectedly transmuted in the course of production into one of his most broodingly serious works.[5] An aging *zamindar* (landlord) who has lost his fortune and his family to an immoderate passion for Hindustani classical music leads a life of isolation, enervation, and deepening insolvency, immersed in memories of the magnificent musical soirées that were once his hallmark. As he sits smoking his hookah surrounded by the crumbling relics of an increasingly anachronistic cultural prestige, we hear in the background an intrusive, irritating drone emanating from the new electrical generator of his nouveau riche neighbor. Having mounted his horse in a final desperate grasp at past glory, the zamindar falls to a death that is surely inevitable from the perspective of the feudal historical resonances that Ray seems to have intended. Yet that death is also saturated with the pathos of tragic heroism.

With *Jalsaghar*, Ray evinced an acute sense that the modern onslaught of materialistic vulgarity necessarily rendered aesthetic and ethical value deeply fragile.[6] By the 1970s, this anxiety had become the dominant mood of his films. In *Jana Aranya* (*The Middleman*, 1975), he gives us an unremittingly bleak portrayal of the descent of an idealistic and bright young student into total ethical collapse as, in the face of unmerited unemployment, he takes up the business of a commercial middleman (*dalal*) on the streets of a Calcutta reduced to sordid interests and the brute struggle for survival. And in *Ghare-Baire* (*The Home and the World*, 1984), he would directly contrast the humanistic ideals represented by the lonely voice of the enlightened and cosmopolitan zamindar, Nikhilesh, against the self-serving, chauvinistic rabble-rousing of the charismatic nationalist agitator, Sandip. The mood of these films was clearly inseparable from a more general political disillusionment: "All the political parties have been disappointing," he would comment in 1970, noting the "corruption on all levels of public and private work, and a certain laziness and lack of values and nothing to guide." Faced with this universal corruption, it was in his own artistic practice that he found redemption: "That's why I love to lose myself in my work."[7]

Ray was as literary a filmmaker as it is perhaps possible to be, drawing heavily on classic Bengali novels and stories for many of his best-known films. In fact, *Ghare-Baire* was based on a 1916 novel by the Bengali Nobel Prize winner Rabindranath Tagore; and Tagore had clearly intended Nikhilesh, the doomed moral authority of Ray's film, to stand in as his own fictional alter ego in the original novel. So it is perhaps not so surprising to realize that Ray's Janus-vision of aesthetic self-cultivation and everyday corruption had deep resonances with Tagore's own sensibilities. It was indeed with much the same preoccupations in mind that Tagore, the ultimate icon of Bengali culture, had in the 1930s launched a rather extraordinary campaign to raise *sanskriti*, the Bengali term conventionally used today to translate *culture*, to its contemporary position of sole supremacy in conventional usage, and to downgrade to marginality its chief rival, *krishti*.[8] Krishti (derived from *cash*, meaning "cultivation" in its literal sense) was tied, Tagore argued, by its Sanskrit root and usage to the practice of tilling the soil, a mundane association at profound odds with the rarified significance of culture in its higher sense. English usage might conflate the two meanings in one term, but that was no reason for Bengali to follow suit.[9]

> There exist various skills and endeavors for filling our stomachs and fulfilling the requirements of livelihood; but to fill man's emptiness and awaken the man of the mind in various ways to a variety of sensibilities, he has literature and art. How exalted and immense is this in the history of man. If it could be extinguished in some civilizational armageddon, what a vast emptiness would open out like a black desert in the history of man. Man has the field of *"krishti"* for his agriculture, for his offices and factories; literature is the field of his *sanskriti*, here occurs the *sanskriti* of his own self, through it he raises himself in every respect, he becomes his own self. As the Aitareya Brahmana has said, "Arts indeed are the *sanskriti* of the soul."[10]

Tagore's aversion to krishti was a function of a philosophy of literature according to which, in Niharranjan Ray's words, "the creation of art and literature occurs from within a space beyond necessity and outside the limits of the requirements of human livelihood."[11] Since agriculture was essentially an instrumental function of mundane necessity, krishti was necessarily the negation of culture. In contrast, sanskriti was understood to mean something like *purification*, the extraction of man's spiritual self from the phenomenal attachments of the grossly material, and as such it better expressed the spiritual striving for free autonomy that was at the very heart of man's cultural activity. The human aspiration to free self-cultivation was formed in a space sharply demarcated from the petty interests and material necessities that Tagore saw as driving the world more generally.

That alternative *sanskritik* space might be precariously situated in the interstices of the modern city itself, where even the most penniless of the educated could snatch beauty and meaning out of an anonymous and dehumanizing environment through the practices of reading, writing, and reciting poetry, or of singing Tagore's much loved devotional songs (*rabindrasangit*).[12] "From one Calcutta sidewalk to another, from sidewalk to sidewalk / As I walk along, my life's blood feels the vapid, venomous touch / Of tram tracks stretched out beneath my feet like a pair of primordial serpent sisters," wrote the poet Jibanananda Das in a 1938 meditation on the very Calcutta streets where sixteen years later he would be run down by a tram on his evening walk. "A soft rain is falling, the wind slightly chilling. / Of what far land of green grass, rivers, fireflies am I thinking?"[13] Jibanananda snatched transcendence from his impoverished immersion in the banalities of everyday life, but as the form of his musings here also implies, the sanskritik space of freedom could also be elsewhere in a more literal sense—out in the villages that some continued to imagine as a haven from the sullying touch of Western modernity. And more especially still, it could be in Shantiniketan (the Abode of Peace), a community whose "founding ideal" was voluntary civility and cooperative self-cultivation, where communal and caste differences were to be forgotten, and where Tagore's university, Visva-Bharati, self-consciously pitched itself as an "all-embracing institute of universal cultural exchange" that would work to subordinate to the "ever-expansive unison-fostering amity of man's mind," both the "self-protective, possessive animal passion" of our individual creaturely existence, and the "devastating possibilities of the physical dimension of life heaping up unrestrictedly in venomous animosity."[14]

For most of the twentieth century, a problematic of culture has provided the framework both for the optimistic pride and the anxious pessimism of modern Bengali identity, as well as for Bengal's ambivalent relationship to conceptions of national and global modernity. But this Bengali peculiarity also resonates strikingly with forms of culturalism in, for example, the Indian region of Maharashtra, Germany, Japan, and Russia. Indeed, in the course of the nineteenth and twentieth centuries, culture achieved the status of a truly global concept. We find discourses of culture emerging to prominence in the German-speaking world during the second half of the eighteenth century; in the English-speaking world starting in the first half of the nineteenth century; in Eastern Europe, East Asia, and South Asia starting in the second half of the nineteenth century; and just about everywhere else in the course of the twentieth century. Culture began to circulate far beyond the European sites of its modern genesis, sometimes through the direct transfer of lexical items from Western European languages (Russian *kul'tura;* the use of *kalcar* in various South Asian languages); and more often through the construction of new translative equivalencies with preexisting words or concepts most often signifying purification, refinement, or improvement (Japanese *bun-ka;* Chinese *wen-hua;* Bengali, Hindi, and Marathi *sanskriti;* Urdu *tamaddun*).[15]

This book sets out to give an account of the emergence of Bengali culturalism in a manner that can grasp at once its local specificity and the global resonance of its major themes. Even the most determinedly nationalist forms of cultural discourse, I will show, took form within the profoundly transnational context of the circulation of ideological forms. Rather than attempt to marginalize the significance of this transnational dimension of culturalist discourse, this work will instead attempt to locate Bengali culturalism within a global framework. After all, a cosmopolitan audience would enthusiastically embrace Rabindranath Tagore's poetry and Satyajit Ray's films precisely to the extent that the universalistic spirit of their humanism was embodied in the concrete exoticism of their imagery.[16] The history of the culture concept in Bengal can be treated neither as a local deviation from nor as a late reiteration of an essentially Western intellectual form, but will rather be investigated as a spatially and temporally specific moment in the global history of the culture concept.

While this book is certainly intended primarily as an exercise in intellectual history, it will not stop at the narration of a history of ideas or the successive constellations of discourse formations. Rather, my account *of* Bengali culturalism will also be an attempt to account *for* Bengali culturalism—to understand why the logic of culturalism's most fundamental organizing categories were plausible within a particular historical milieu. In other words, I will not root Bengali culturalism in the ethnic particularity of regional culture or in the timeless "nature of things"; I will root it in the complex structure of social practices that, I argue, renders the culturalist imagination meaningful as a lens for thinking about self and society. I shall insist on seeing this constellation of social practices as constituted, *in its specificity,* within the global structures of capitalist society. And I shall read Bengali culturalist discourse as grounded in a systematic misrecognition of these structures. By *misrecognition,* I do not mean to imply that Bengalis were either stupid or duped. I mean that they mistook the *forms of appearance* through which these structures manifested themselves for their actuality—a mistake grounded in the very nature of modern capitalist society, which systematically presents itself in forms that cloak its deeper logic. I hope to show that, within the logic of culturalist ideology, the underlying practical structures that have constituted its historical plausibility can still be recognized—and, *precisely for this reason,* Bengali culturalism can be understood, with neither condescension nor credulity, as a meaningful response to the particular historical context within which it has been articulated.

The culture concept with which this study grapples is not primarily a lexical item, but rather a particular way of linking, implicitly or explicitly, the freedom of human subjectivity with practical activity—a point to which I shall return in more detail in the following chapter. In this book, I will focus primarily on the relative coherence of the conceptual logic of Bengali culturalism. This logic is certainly not given full articulation in every text or speech that has invoked it; and indeed, more often than not it is simply taken for granted. To render this logic visible then, and to distinguish it from other competing ideological structures, is the first task. In what follows, I argue that Bengali culturalism emerged in the 1880s as a reaction against a liberal ideological paradigm that had emerged to dominance in the early nineteenth century. I thus elaborate culturalism and liberalism as distinct ideological paradigms. I am aware that, in any specific context-bound textual or discursive artifact, both paradigms might be found side by side, producing either a synthesis or merely an incoherent jumble. But my aim is to take a step back from such concrete complexity to try to grasp the constellation of arguments being drawn upon in such ambiguous articulations. This in turn is to understand the rationality and plausibility of particular ideological paradigms in terms of the practical determinations of historically specific forms of subjectivity—to follow both Hegel and Marx in moving from the abstract determination to the concrete instance rather than vice versa.[17] In doing so, I will focus overwhelmingly on some of the "great men" from the pantheon of the so-called Bengal Renaissance, the succession of nineteenth- and early twentieth-century men of letters, beginning with Rammohun Roy and culminating in Rabindranath Tagore, who developed modern Bengali linguistic and literary forms and gave the most prominent expression to Bengali visions of national renewal. But if I do this, it is certainly not because I embrace a "great man" theory of history turning on notions of influence and inheritance. It is rather because I see their iconic status as indicative of their capacity to articulate a (relatively) coherent formulation of specific modes of social reflection and ethico-political argument that either had emerged or would soon emerge to prominence in colonial Bengal. They are studied as voices that condense the deeply social and historical forces that gave rise to their iconicity, and not for their ineffable genius or enlightened insight.

My narrative will emphasize discontinuity over continuity, but in a way

"Culturalism and liberalism as distinct ideological paradigms"

that is perhaps unusual in the practice of colonial history. The discontinuity I will emphasize lies not along the axis of a colonizer/colonized distinction, but rather within the narrative of colonial political discourse in Bengal, as a distinction between liberal and culturalist ideological paradigms. The continuity of the conventional narrative of the Bengal Renaissance where Indian tradition is revived by its nineteenth-century colonial encounter and synthesis with Western thought, will be fundamentally disrupted in the account that follows, with the liberal paradigm of the early through mid-nineteenth century being sharply interrupted by the emergence in the later nineteenth century of a distinct ideological paradigm that I call culturalism. In fact, the colonizer/colonized distinction will throughout this study be understood as having been more fundamentally *constituted* within the changing constellations of nineteenth- and twentieth-century colonial society than it was *constitutive* of a composite social formation comprised of colonizer and colonized, European and Indian, two enduringly distinct (but hierarchically ordered) forms of cultural particularity. This is not to suggest that there were not real differences between the ways that Britons and Bengalis lived their everyday lives, but that these differences were in a constant process of reconstitution within the larger structuring framework of a colonial society that was embedded within a larger imperial-cum-global context. I shall privilege what literary theorist Homi Bhabha has called "cultural difference" the act of articulating differences between cultures and construing them as meaningful, over "cultural diversity," where cultures are understood to be simply "out there" as empirical objects of inquiry.[18] But at the same time, I shall also shift the terrain of study from Bhabha's examinations of the performative ambiguities that arise when cultural discourses are articulated in concrete contexts, to an investigation into how specific practices have constituted the conditions of possibility for both the specific form and the historical plausibility of discourses of culture.

The choice of Bengal as the focus of this study is at one level largely contingent on circumstances. To the extent that I argue that the specificity of Bengali culturalism is grounded within global structures of social practice, the history of the culture concept in Bengal can only be a moment in the global history of the dissemination and circulation of that concept. And indeed, that is one of the advantages I claim for my approach: that it can account for Bengali culturalism in a manner that recognizes its specificity as an ideological formation, and yet also recognizes that as a form of modern culturalism it is far from singular in its logical structure or thematic content, and is readily translatable across geographical or linguistic boundaries. If I choose Bengal rather than Maharashtra or China or Japan or Russia as the focus of my study, it is simply because that is my primary area of scholarly competence. And if I choose one historical location rather than undertaking a broader survey of the circulation of cultural discourses, it is because I want to show just how profoundly the categories of capitalist modernity have shaped the thought worlds of non-Western historical actors in one particular place, rather than suggesting a more general but less comprehensive set of formal family resemblances among several different places.

But for anyone familiar with the cultural politics of nineteenth- and twentieth-century South Asia, it will be immediately apparent that the choice of Bengal is utterly overdetermined. In modern South Asia, Bengal is the emblem of a certain model of culture—the "high culture" of a peculiarly colonial provenance whose prestige in the nineteenth and early twentieth centuries was gradually compromised in the twin contexts of the emergence of a modern popular culture industry in the 1920s and 1930s, and of the increasing political marginalization of Bengal in the nationalist and independence eras.[19] Of course, we should be careful here from the start: the name *Bengal* is a regional signifier, but it also condenses an entire set of assumptions about who is Bengali. Used without qualifiers, the term *Bengalis* refers not, it turns out on closer inspection, to the inhabitants of Bengal generally (including the Muslim peasants or the low-caste laborers who numerically predominated), but rather to the Bengali *bhadralok*—the respectable classes that spanned the range of social positions from lowly clerks and village priests through intermediate tenure holders and professionals to magnates and quasi-aristocrats like the Tagores; who, broadly speaking, combined high Hindu caste with nonmanual employment; and who were responsible for the production of new political, ethical, and literary forms that would overwhelmingly define the self-conception of the region in the colonial and postcolonial eras. This identification of the Bengali would even be true, albeit in much more complicated and contested ways, for East Pakistan/Bangladesh, where the Bengali alphabet and language, and the poetry and songs of Rabindranath Tagore, would assume enormous significance as icons of Bengali-Muslim identity; where efforts to construct a Bengali-Muslim literature were deeply shaped by (even when they sometimes explicitly disavowed) the canonicity of a body of literature produced by predominantly Hindu authors; and where to this day "Bangladeshi" identity more readily articulates its "Bengaliness" as a qualifier (Bengali Muslims) than as a substantive (Bengalis, Hindus who live on the other side of the border).

Many historians of South Asia now complain that the centrality of Bengal (and especially of that bhadralok Bengal of rarified, colonially inflected tastes) has figured too prominently in the historiography of colonial South Asia, providing too narrow a template for our understanding of the dynamics of South Asia's experience of colonialism and modernity. But if we are to take this complaint seriously, we will need not only to complicate our understanding of the dynamics at work in different sites in the subcontinent but also to grasp the historical configuration that produced Bengal's privilege as the historiographical center. This study is thus an attempt, as much as anything else, to offer a history of Bengal's historiographical privilege as the model of a certain kind of cultural modernity, and to account for the endurance of that privilege at a more profound level—the constitution of the conceptual resources that shape our understanding of South Asian society and history.

THE HISTORIOGRAPHICAL IMPASSE

The dominant theoretical frameworks in the existing literature on South Asian intellectual and cultural history have arrived at dilemmas that provide an instructive point of departure for the kind of historiographical intervention to be undertaken in this work. Approaches to the constitution of an ideological terrain in colonial South Asia have been broadly defined around the binary of colonizer and colonized. An understanding of the colonial relationship in terms of an identification of the West as the vehicle of modern universality and of the non-West as the repository of anachronistic particularisms was as normative in this field of area studies as it was in any other for most of the twentieth century (even if South Asia had no Joseph Levenson to systematically conceptualize and narrate encounter and transition[20]). In this discourse, concepts are orderable into universal and particular, modern and traditional. Yet nationalism, inevitably one of the major focuses of developmentalist concerns, proved a recalcitrant term in this dyadic paradigm, representing an intractable condensation of the aspiration to universality and the specter of particularistic atavism.[21] Two major traditions have sought to complicate the transparency of developmentalist historicism: first, the objectivistic attempt to historicize ideological forms by grounding them in particular social interests; and second, a subjectivistic attempt to displace the problem of universality by rewriting the encounter between colonizer and colonized as the meeting of two incommensurable, but politically unequal, forms of particularism.

[margin annotations: Marxist reading of anticolonial discourse in Indian subcontinent; Non-Marxist State]

There is a long tradition within both Marxist and non-Marxist historiography that has sought to interpret the emergence of anticolonial discourse in the Indian context as a function of social location and the competition of interests. On the non-Marxist side, the early writings of Anil Seal and his circle of students sought, often brilliantly, to show how nationalist politics emerged from the specific ways in which ambitions were channeled and shaped through the interconnections of structures of power and governance at the local, provincial, and all-Indian levels.[22] Yet for all the many insights of this literature, a crucial remainder stood unexplained, and indeed unexamined: the core conceptual content of nationalism itself, including that most fundamental "feeling of national solidarity against imperialism, an alien political and economic force that stood against the interests of the population of the Indian subcontinent *as a whole*," a sentiment that "could not be reduced to a catalogue of rivalries between Indian and Indian vying for government patronage."[23] Meanwhile, the Gramscian turn in Marxist historiography was in its turn refining the older Marxist interpretation of Indian nationalism as the expression of the ambitions of a national bourgeoisie. Yet even within this Gramscian-Marxist tradition, for which "material forces are the content and ideologies are the form," it would hardly be a novelty to observe that the conceptual content of nationalist ideologies cannot be deduced from the configurations of a "historical bloc" of class interests.[24] Writing on Bengal's Swadeshi movement (discussed at length in chapter 5) in a study that was seminal to the Gramscian turn in the scholarship of modern South Asia, Sumit Sarkar had been driven to conclude more than thirty years ago that "economic distress"—for which, I submit, one might as easily read "economic interests" in the broadest sense—"could lead to nationalist politics only via the 'mediation' of an ideology."[25] Yet Sarkar offered few clues as to how the historical availability of this "ideology" was to be explained if it was not the universalization of some particular bloc of social interests.

The instrumental emphasis of these approaches, both non-Marxist and Marxist, has produced some remarkable historical insights—but only by marginalizing the historicity of the actual conceptual content articulated in discourse through an overwhelming focus on the pragmatic problematic of the intents and purposes for which concepts have been deployed. Quentin Skinner's influential rendition of intellectual history, for example, corrects the transhistoricizing and reifying tendencies of traditional approaches to political theory and intellectual history by locating the historicity of political theory not in the conceptual content of those theories (their "locutionary" dimension), but rather in the ways in which concepts were deployed in particular textually defined contexts (their "illocutionary" intention).[26] An analysis of the specific ends to which some concept is being invoked is indeed central to the interpretation of concretely situated discourse. But faced with Skinner's stark dichotomy between the transhistoricity of reference and the radical contingency of practice, how might we approach the historically determinate character of the conceptual content of ideological discourse if we are not once again to resort immediately to the categories of class, interest, positionality, or utility? How, in other words, might we approach the social constitution of cultural discourses in such a way as to forestall a consideration of social interests until after we can explain the conceptual terrain in which those interests are capable of being formed, conceptualized, and articulated?

To some extent in response to this impasse, a new generation of postcolonialist historians and literary critics in the 1980s and 1990s set out to supplement, and ultimately even to displace, modes of sociological objectivism through an emphasis on the cultural specificity of forms of subjectivity. Seminal texts like Benedict Anderson's *Imagined Communities* explained the history of the assimilation of certain key concepts possessing a Western intellectual genealogy (and the category of modernity with which that history is inextricably associated in the developing world) in terms of the discursive effects of the global replication of certain institutional forms—most notably the nation-state itself.[27] From a perspective made famous by Edward Said's *Orientalism*, modern forms of subjectivity—the conceptual apparatus through which we apprehend the world and form intentions—are peculiarly Western categories that have been imposed upon the rest of the world as one of the means by which the West dominated—indeed, even produced— its Others.[28] The Bengali adoption of a concept like *culture*—the banner of Eurocentric universalism and of the critique of Eurocentric universalism— would have to be viewed as derivative, the result of a process of epistemic violence or cultural colonization that coercively subordinates the culturally particular thought worlds of colonized peoples to the authority of Western forms of thought and knowledge.[29] The colonizer's monopoly over legitimate truth claims has served to produce two apparently quite contrary effects: a direct identification with the colonial Master (Westernization, civilization, modernization); and a contrary particularizing impulse that has served to "consolidate the Self of Europe by obliging the native to cathect the space of the Other on his home ground."[30] In its starkest formulations, this kind of argument risks reducing any deviation from a precolonial cultural norm to an instance of cultural colonization operationalized institutionally either

[handwritten margin notes: "consolidate the Self of Europe" ; "Western concept of civilization came to be contested & the dominant authority"]

through the direct application of colonial pedagogy or through the indirect effects of practices of colonial knowledge production (such as the census) that introduce new forms of identification in the subject population.[31] Such approaches understand the agency of the transmission of new concepts to colonial contexts in terms of a Western will to power that imposes Western norms of subjectivity on indigenous subjects through coercive practices of representation. The indigenous realm—the subaltern—thus becomes a horizon to Western modernity, linked to it only through its counterfeiting in Orientalist discourse or its hybridization with a series of deceptively isomorphic Western concepts (so that, for example, it comes to seem as if *dharma* simply "means" religion, whereas it in fact bears a host of older connotations and meanings that this too-easy equation erases).[32] Either way, this mode of critique struggles to constitute a standpoint outside of a universalistic, hegemonic model of subjectivity characterized as "Western," even as it inevitably articulates its claims about this external standpoint in a scholarly language that is ineradicably tied to the very norms of subjectivity that it denounces.

In his classic work *Nationalist Thought and the Colonial World,* Partha Chatterjee undertook a brilliant attempt to combine these two approaches so as to achieve a richer description of the complexity of nationalist discourses. On the one hand, to make sense of what he called the *thematic* of the discourse—the way in which it sought to justify its claims as legitimate and authoritative—Chatterjee adopted a poststructuralist analysis of the dependence of nationalist truth claims on Western epistemic norms. On the other hand, to motivate its *problematic*—the historical possibilities that nationalists identified, and the practical political, social and/or ethical projects to which these gave rise—he adopted a Gramscian analysis of the ambitions of an "emergent bourgeoisie" to "moral-intellectual leadership" over the peasantry. Accounts that made sense of the emergence of colonial nationalisms through recourse to forms of "sociological determinism and functionalism" effectively devalued the specifically subjective moment of nationalism's ideological dimension by reducing it to a by-product of objective historical structures. Chatterjee's account of the imposition of Western epistemic norms on colonized subjects, in contrast, was intended to highlight the irreducibility of the emergence of new forms of subjectivity for the possibility of nationalist consciousness. Meanwhile, the emphasis on class interests was intended to remedy the reduction of colonial nationalism to a merely derivative reiteration of its Western original by locating it as a specific kind of political project developed in peculiar historical circumstances that were unlike those prevailing in the West.[33] In the colonies, the modern and the

Subaltern to be colonized by Western modernity

national necessarily presented themselves as disjunctive: in a context where the advent of modernity was a direct result of colonial domination, the modern would necessarily assume the guise of the Western, while the national correlated with the indigenous and the traditional. Faced with this dilemma, the colonial elite would appear to have attempted a partial appropriation of the popular energies of the peasant masses (the national) in order to displace the colonial Master in the name of that Master's own form of rationality (the modern).[34] The result was ultimately the ascendance of a "marriage between Reason and capital" (thematic and problematic) as the governing logic of a postcolonial polity that endlessly deferred the actual realization of national-popular (subaltern) sovereignty through its subordination to, and absorption into, a statist, elitist politics of national development.[35]

The emphasis on colonialism as the agency underlying elite subject constitution—and hence ultimately determining the ideological agendas of the dominant nationalist tradition even throughout its necessary political engagement with the disjunctive realm of the national popular—left open that vast residual space of subaltern culture that lay beyond the limits of colonial discourse. It was to this terrain that Chatterjee would subsequently turn in *The Nation and its Fragments*. Dissatisfied with the lack of creative, autonomous agency that his earlier analysis had ascribed to colonial nationalists, he shifted the line of demarcation between the colonial and subaltern lifeworlds from the more conventional distinctions of social stratification into the constitutive fabric of nationalist discourse. Long before they formulated nationalism as a strictly political demand, Bengali nationalists were already "dividing the world of social institutions and practices into two domains—the material and the spiritual." The former of these represented the utilitarian, "external" domain of Western political, economic, scientific, and technological rationality. The latter represented "an 'inner' domain bearing the 'essential' marks of cultural identity" in which the subjective agency of the colonized was preserved from the effects of the concession of Western superiority in the material domain. It was in this autonomous "spiritual" domain, Chatterjee argues, that the work of "imagining" the nation was first undertaken.[36] He thereby sought to reject the Eurocentric privileging of Western subjectivity by establishing the formal equivalency of Western and Indian subjects as autonomous historical agents.

While at first glance Chatterjee might appear to be merely characterizing the claims made by this (proto)nationalism, in fact his analysis proceeds from a critical ethico-political agenda. His project is to salvage the subjective agency—the "freedom of imagination," as he puts it—of the nationalist elite that his earlier work had done so much to compromise.[37] As the site of "creativity" and "agency," this "inner domain" of spiritual autonomy thus becomes, through a key conceptual slippage, the autonomous, externalized, and ultimately valorized standpoint for a critique of the derivativeness of nationalist discourse.[38] Indian nationalism confronted the derivativeness of colonial political and civil institutions with those "autonomous forms of imagination of the community" that constituted the "inner domain of culture" as "the sovereign territory of the nation."[39] "Community," a concept systematically elided by the modern Western emphasis on associational life, becomes the standpoint for an "antimodernist, antiindividualist, even anticapitalist" discourse that holds out the possibility of a political imagination that exceeds the limits of Western reason and the normative models of universal history.[40] The nationalist quest to "fashion a 'modern' national culture that is nevertheless not Western" remains motivated ultimately only by a return to the class-interest model of his earlier Gramscianism, leaving the question of the actual forms of consciousness (rather than the purposes to which they are put) once again unaddressed.[41] An intellectual history of the constitutive concepts of "national culture" could in the end only really be a process of identifying their roots in the precolonial conceptual universe, because where else could native intellectuals find the conceptual elements of an "original," that is, non-Western, thought system?

For Chatterjee, "community" confronts the institutions of state and civil society that underpin capitalist society as a "subterranean, politically subversive" counternarrative that capital, according to its immanent logic, should have successfully banished, but that "refuses to go away" because it represents a perduring truth about human society.[42] Colonial and nationalist narratives of development have indeed accorded in locating community as a category of premodernity. But Chatterjee's implicit acceptance that community is a category of social organization that is rooted in the premodern, and hence can only represent the persistence of premodernity in the age of modern capital, leads him into some murky waters. His argument proceeds from an understanding of modernity as a fundamentally discursive form constituted ultimately by its antithetical relation to the non- or premodern. Even his invocation of capitalism as an explanatory category oscillates uncertainly between "capital" and "the narrative of capital," with capital functioning as a form of social analysis with explanatory purchase in the first instance, but only as a Western discourse of power in the latter.[43] Approaching these basic categories of modernity from what Manu Goswami has termed a sociohistorical perspective, in contrast, would open up a quite different possibility: "Instead of either presupposing an autono-

(margin annotation: Different conceptions of community)

mous socio-cultural domain exempt from colonial and capitalist mediation or positing indigenous practices as untranslatable in any but local terms," one would have to recognize "that colonial and nationalist forms, though distinguishable, were not separable."[44] Such an approach leads to the radical displacement of any conception of modernity that is constituted solely within the transition dyad of tradition/modernity. Goswami's important intervention, *Producing India,* proceeded from the insight that the modern, individualist, and capitalist discourses that are most conventionally understood to embody the overall project of colonial modernity express only one side of a more complex social dynamic that simultaneously has the capacity to generate "antimodern, antiindividualist, even anticapitalist" discourses that, despite their ostensible anticapitalism, still draw their meaning from specifically modern, and constitutively capitalist, social practices. Such an approach, furthermore, allows us to grasp these antinomic effects on both sides of the colonial divide, paying closer attention to the homology that links the protonationalist delineation of a sovereign "inside" with the contemporary colonialist affirmation of the proper role of native custom in ordering and governing the colonial polity in the age of indirect rule.

Chatterjee does have moments when he comes close to suggesting something more dialectically critical, pointing beyond the strictly discursive theoretical framework that governs his work more generally. Concluding his analysis of the discourse of caste, for instance, he explains that he has been concerned to unearth "a level of social life where laboring people *in their practical activity* have constantly sought in their 'common sense' the forms, mediated by culture, of [a kind of] community" in which "a more developed universal form of the unity of separateness and dependence" is posited as the foundation of a process of "democratization."[45] Here Chatterjee reverses his particularizing strategies to address head-on the problem of universality that must be the necessary premise of the ethico-political concerns of equity and justice that underpin both the passion and the conceptual structure of his writings. But if (as his method of reading most often suggests) universalistic claims are merely contingent forms of discourse, what is the theoretical justification for grounding the presumably real political universals that he himself endorses (equity, justice, democracy) in specific repertoires of discursive practice? How, in other words, do we derive ethical universality from institutional contingency or cultural particularity? Must we resort to an irrationalist politics of will to motivate the transformation of universal*isms* into ethico-political universals? Or, alternatively, to a UNESCO-style dogma of underlying cultural commonality founded on the eternal verities?

To derive universal claims from concrete practices of everyday life requires that we first understand those concrete practices as mediated by global structures of social practice that, because they are not moored in local institutional complexes or ephemeral conjunctures, are capable of grounding such a universalistic truth value. This maneuver might in turn open up the possibility of resituating the practical constitution of the subjective forms of colonizer and colonized, of the colonial and the national, and of the modern and the antimodern within the same global temporal and social horizons. To do this, however, we must first find a way to displace the practical agency of colonial discourse from the position of explanatory primacy that it holds in the literature of postcolonialism. In the wake of the achievements of postcolonialist criticism, the aim cannot be to deny the constitutive effects of discourse. Rather, this book attempts to address a logically prior problematic: the historical constitution of the conditions of possibility for the power of specific discursive repertoires in specific historical contexts. Only by setting out from this level of analysis will it be possible to generate an account of Bengali culturalism that respects the specificity of the colonial context of its articulation and yet simultaneously locates that specificity within a historically determinate form of conceptual universality (not culture as a transhistorical truth, but culture as a modern global concept). Maintaining this double agenda should in turn make it possible to interpret the history of Bengali culturalism in the colonial era through categories also capable of speaking to the wider context of the dissemination of cultural discourses within the semi- and noncolonial locations of, for example, East Asia and Eastern Europe.

Such an approach would open up an entirely new way of interpreting the "inherent contradictoriness in nationalist thinking" that Chatterjee had so perspicaciously identified in his early work. Colonial nationalism "reasons within a framework of knowledge whose representational structure corresponds to the very structure of power nationalist thought seeks to repudiate." But Chatterjee has taken this paradox as an invitation to *transcend* the horizons of the global modern in the name of a subaltern indigeneity that lies "beyond" its limits.[46] And indeed, the contradiction that drives nationalist thought appears to be grounded in the difference between, on the one hand, the predatory capitalism and abstract rationalism of "Western" civilization and, on the other hand, an Indian cultural or civilizational order external to it. But if we then go on to understand this appearance as grounded in contradictions *internal* to capitalist social forms (as expressed in the particular context of this kind of colonial society), we can instead recognize that the double bind of nationalist thought is really only a specific

* Does nationalism have to be a rejection of modernism?

instance of the more general condition of criticism in the age of capital. In other words, anticolonialism's organic connection to colonial categories of thought should be read as an invitation or provocation to *immanent critique,* where critique's condition of possibility is generated from within the social order that it takes as the object of its criticism.

A NEW APPROACH

In 1902, Okakura Tenshin, the great Japanese art historian, arrived in Calcutta on a mission to study the famous Buddhist caves at Ajanta and Ellora. Once there, he helped inaugurate Bengal's new enthusiasm for all things Japanese (an enthusiasm that would peak, not surprisingly, during the Japanese victories over Russia in 1904 and 1905) by befriending members of Calcutta's social and cultural elite (such as the Tagore family), and of Calcutta's new political radicals. It was one of these radicals, Sister Nivedita, who helped Okakura compose in English his major pan-Asianist statement, *The Ideals of the East,* a work that outlines the global spiritual mission of a renascent Asia through a history of its aesthetic self-expression. We might already recognize here the creative intersection of new theological, historicist, and political conceptions emerging in modern Japanese Buddhist and Shinto discourses with the developing discourses of Indian nationalism and Hindu revivalism. But the story is even more complicated than that, for Nivedita was an Irishwoman by birth who had in the 1890s converted to Hinduism as one of the most prominent disciples of the late nineteenth-century protonationalist religious guru, Swami Vivekananda, and had subsequently identified herself with the most radical elements of the nationalist movement for Indian independence.[47]

How are we to make sense of the complex transnational conjunctures that played so ubiquitous a part in the elaboration of Bengali cultural discourse? How can we conceptualize the remarkable translatability and transmissibility of key modern concepts like culture? That the genealogical roots of the culture concept lie in the intellectual traditions of the West is not really in dispute. And indeed, it is undeniable that local genealogies necessarily inflect local usages of global concepts, and that linguistic mediation produces forms of connotative trace that are irreducibly particular (a point to which I shall return in the next chapter). But what is surely more striking is the degree to which culture has assumed a global status, such that the conceptual content of culture can no longer be usefully identified as Western—and it is this translatability and transmissibility that remains inadequately explained. The meaning of the culture concept is certainly to be found in each context of its articulation. This in itself is no longer a particularly controversial proposition—though it is generally taken to imply that the meaning of concepts must therefore differ according to the different contexts of their articulation. But how can the meaning of a concept like culture be reduced to the contingency of local contexts when the concept seems to traverse such wildly diverse locations?

If the socially grounded approach I take up in this work does not, as I contend, imply the dissolution of the culture concept into the fragmented existence of mere family resemblance, it can only be so because some fundamental structures of social practice span the real and enormous differences that separate diverse regional and local lifeworlds. In the next chapter I will elaborate the theoretical outlines of a kind of Marxian approach to intellectual and cultural history that has been largely unexplored in the historiography of South Asia—one that bypasses base-superstructure models, eschews teleological accounts of world history as a fixed succession of modes of production and their respective class conflicts, and rejects the one-dimensional identification of capitalism with market exchange, instead attempting to grasp capitalism as an epochally particular constellation of social practices.[48] I think this approach is best able to grasp the global dimensions of Bengali culturalism without effacing its specificity.

The approach I take to the history of Bengali culturalism breaks fundamentally with some of the major hypotheses that have produced the historiographical impasse discussed above. First, it suspends a consideration of the role of social positionality or interest in the constitution of ideologies until *after* the constitution of the actual thought forms, within which both position and interest must necessarily be construed, can be explained. This is something whose necessity both the Marxist tradition of ideology critique and the non-Marxist tradition of the sociology of knowledge have in their most sophisticated formulations recognized. Norbert Elias, for example, began his great classic, *The Civilizing Process,* with an analysis of the concepts of civilization and culture in terms of social positionality (the inclusion of the French bourgeoisie in courtly life in France, their exclusion in Germany); but he proceeded in the core of his analysis to argue that civilization and culture took as their condition of historical possibility large-scale transformations in structures of social practice that were responsible for constituting the practical content of the civilization and culture concepts, and also mediating the salient social positions from which they could be construed as divergent.[49] And while Marx has been widely read as reducing capitalism

[Handwritten margin note left: Does not take into account the role of social positionality in the formulation of ideas]

to a function of class domination, a closer reading makes it clear that he was really arguing that class domination is a function of forms of capitalist social relations that produce the "economic categories" that "bourgeois" and "proletarian" are taken to "personify" in *Capital*.[50] This sociohistorical approach to concept history opens up the space for the core of this project: grounding the Bengali discourse of culture in Marx's analysis of the commodity as the "cell-form" of modern society.[51]

Second, my approach displaces the centrality of epistemic or symbolic violence by interpreting colonial discourse in the historical context of its articulation as if it were not derivative of an earlier European tradition of thought. I thereby deemphasize the specifically pedagogical moment of colonialism so as to foreground the role of borrowed concepts in allowing Bengalis to begin to make sense of a new object of thought: namely, forms of social abstraction that will be discussed further in chapter 2. The consignment of the native intellectual to the irremediable status of native informant has largely turned on a misplaced anxiety about identifying Western intellectual influences. But surely there is no moment in intellectual history that is not derivative in some fundamental sense. How would one formulate an argument or an analysis without drawing from a preexisting repertoire of concepts? As such, there seems no prima facie reason to treat an act of intellectual appropriation as substantially different from an act of conceptual innovation. To appropriate a Western thought form in nineteenth-century Bengal was itself effectively an act of conceptual innovation that necessarily must have had its roots in moments of social transformation that explain its new plausibility as a way of interpreting the world. In this sense, the history of a European concept's appropriation in Bengal should be analyzed in the same manner as the history of the generation of that concept in Europe in the first place—in terms of the practical structures that render that concept a compelling lens through which to make sense of the world.[52] Modern Bengali intellectual history does not stand in relation to modern European intellectual history as reception stands to production. If Raymond Williams could (in this respect uncontroversially) read the history of British cultural criticism without substantial regard to the fact that its themes and terms were largely borrowed from German classical thought, I am not sure that there is any compelling reason to treat the case of Bengali culturalism any differently—even if we might want to be a little more self-conscious than Williams was about what the fact of such substantial yet selective borrowing might teach us.

Finally, my approach also diverges fundamentally from the kind of historicist-developmentalist Marxism whose narrative of the evolution from feudalism to capitalism has featured so prominently (and, it should be added, eminently) in the historiography of South Asia. Following Dipesh Chakrabarty and the postcolonialist tradition, I repudiate the kind of historical transition narrative that takes conventional understandings of the evolution of modernity in European history as a model for modern history in general, and which reads non-Western histories as more or less flawed reiterations of that historical model.[53] While I do insist on a radical epochal break from the forms of nonmodern social relations that characterized premodern South Asia, I do so to emphasize the historical specificity of the global social structures into which these older institutions have come, in an inevitably transformative manner, to be embedded, and not to negate the concrete continuities of particular social practices. There can be no question of reading the particularistic social forms of Bengali society as direct concrete analogies of the abstract categories of Marx's critique of capitalist society. But nor can there be any question of imagining that locality and particularity constitute an "outside" unmediated by the formal structures of capitalist society.

Ranajit Guha has answered the question, "Where does criticism come from?" with the emphatic response: *"From outside the universe of dominance which provides the critique with its object, indeed from another and historically antagonistic universe."*[54] In this instance, he meant subaltern consciousness, the consciousness of an uncolonized Indian mind that has survived because Western colonial dominance never achieved hegemonic control over the subcontinent. Yet by the end of the same essay, Guha was led by his discussion of the hybridization of Western and Indian concepts to conclude that *"as a new and original entity, none of the elements"* of colonial discourse *"is a replica of its corresponding idiom in either of the paradigms"* that constitute it.[55] Despite his own apparent self-understanding, Guha implicitly recognized that once incorporated into capitalist social relations, the conceptual apparatus of precolonial South Asian society had been contextually resituated in such a way that the meanings of its key terms must necessarily have changed, even when their ostensible positive content might not have. At the same time, he also recognized that the nature of this transformation was far too complicated to be reduced to any straightforward assimilation to a Western norm or model, implicitly making the notion of capitalist modernity irreducible to the normativity of Western institutional models. It is this impulse to rethink the universalistic category of modernity beyond the Western model that I take up in the analysis that follows.

The approach I take by no means invalidates in principle the construction of genealogies of locally specific practices or conceptual categories obscured by the ascendancy of European sociological or conceptual categories. In the face of the very different norms of thought, sensibility, and behavior prevalent in different parts of the world, the role of indigenous practices and concepts in shaping the concrete historical experiences and dispositions of colonial subjects is certainly undeniable. But at the same time, it is also necessary to emphasize that, even when particular practices or concepts endure through time (such as family-based smallholding peasant agriculture, or caste-based marriage and property organization[56]), the continuity of their transmission has been necessarily fractured by their incorporation into capitalist structures of social interdependency. In other words, the acknowledgment of continuity remains crucially incomplete until we also acknowledge that the reproduction of those indigenous repertoires of practice and thought was necessarily mediated in turn by wider historical transformations, as those same colonial subjects were drawn into the complex global structures of interdependence that characterize the modern world. This is not to dispute the Foucauldian and hermeneuticist position that specific concepts exist in an intimate relationship with specific, concrete repertoires of practice. It is rather to insist that these concrete practices must always in turn be located within the structures of practice that embed specific social locations within a global context. From this perspective then, the relative indigeneity of any particular practice or concept would seem to matter less than the transformation of its significance within the changing historical contexts of capitalist modernity. Only in this way can historical critique ground the adequacy of its analytical categories.

THE NARRATIVE OF THIS WORK

In the course of the nineteenth and twentieth centuries, culture achieved the status of a truly global concept. In the next chapter, I attempt to think through a sociohistorical framework for treating it as such. I begin by returning to the *loci classici* of European culturalism to argue that the modern culture concept represents a unified conceptual field that traverses the boundaries of linguistic difference and the specific discourse formations of its humanistic and anthropological usages. The culture concept, I suggest, has articulated a claim about the fundamental "underdeterminedness" of human subjectivity—the freedom of subjectivity from determinations of objective necessity such as biology, nature, economy, or society. I argue that the only way to make sense of the global reach of the appeal and compelling plausibility of a specifically modern concept like culture is to ground it in structures of subject-constituting practice that are themselves global. I then contend that the only such structures that meet the double criteria of dynamic expansion (demanded by the globalizing reach of the culture concept) and historical specificity (demanded by the modernity of the culture concept's dissemination) are the abstract structures of social interdependence that characterize modern capitalist society. I thus ground the appearance of subjective underdetermination in what I consider to be the most fundamental organizing category of modern life, the commodity form.

The narrative I then unfold begins during the half-century before the rise to prominence of a culturalist ideological formation in Bengal, when the intellectual initiative was held by a Bengali liberal reformism that struggled polemically against forms of social conservatism in the name (at least in principle) of the emancipation of the rational, self-interested individual from the bondage of custom and discrimination. I begin my story in chapter 3 by showing how this discourse was implicitly grounded in the ideal of free exchange in civil society propounded by classical political economy. From this vantage, I then chart the gradual drift of this ideological formation into crisis and contradiction in the second half of the nineteenth century, as eastern India's socioeconomic formation underwent a structural bifurcation whereby a Calcutta-centered sphere of circulation was increasingly reified as inherently and essentially "white," and the sphere of production in the hinterlands increasingly epitomized the authentic characteristics of "native" society. By the 1870s, the promise of liberal ideals of free exchange in civil society could only be salvaged through a counterintuitive appeal to an agenda of protectionism and state-sponsored development. At the same time, however, the enunciation of this liberalism by a Western-educated service class became increasingly problematic as the sphere of circulation in which its ideals were grounded assumed the racialized appearance of an alien social form exploitatively superimposed upon native society. In such a context, the sphere of circulation's universal promise of emancipation and autonomy could only be experienced as domination and alienation.

In the 1880s, Bankimchandra Chatterjee, Bengal's most renowned man of letters of the later nineteenth century, unequivocally renounced the increasingly uncertain, and yet quite radical, liberal propensities he had expressed throughout the 1870s. Using this iconic figure to explore a wider generational shift, I show in chapter 4 how Bankim adopted the concept of "culture" to rebuild a philosophical foundation for ethical and political action.

Drawing upon nineteenth-century British cultural criticism and Auguste Comte's science of sociology, Bankim sought to restore what he understood to be the immanent rationality and dynamism of Hindu tradition. The new indigenism of Bankim's Hindu revivalism asserted, on the authority of the Bhagavad Gita, the universal centrality of practices of culture to human self-realization. The new regulative principle of ethical conduct was to be the harmonious cultivation of human capacities in society as a form of pure action without regard to its outcome. This practice of cultivation would render possible an authentic form of self-realization that the desiring, self-interested subject of civil society could never achieve, and also the organic integration of a coordinated collectivity unriven by individual desires and empowered to negate the alien forces of colonial civil society.

In chapter 5, I turn my attention to the Swadeshi movement of early twentieth-century Bengal, the first attempt at nationalistic mass mobilization under India's new colonial middle class. Striving to elaborate a political ideology grounded in popular Indian social forms, Swadeshists yoked together Bankim's ethical critique of the interest-seeking, rights-bearing subject of civil society with a neomercantilist political economy focused on the coordinated development of productive capacities and the accumulation of capital through renunciatory practice. Swadeshi ideology adopted a Hegelianized Vedanta to posit a form of nationhood whose existence was grounded in the logic of self-constituting practice—at the individual level (the constitution of spiritual freedom through desireless practice) and at the national level (the historical appropriation of nature to spirit). Working within the antinomic logic of the commodity form, Swadeshi discourse superimposed a political-economic critique of British rule, an ethical critique of commercial and civil society, an idealist critique of materialism, and a historicist critique of abstraction. It thereby located the constitutive essence of the nation within the dynamic and concrete temporality of the nation's history. History thereby became the determinate negation of the homogeneous empty time that the (allegedly) Western subject of civil society inhabited.

The ultimate collapse of the Swadeshi movement, as experienced through the refractive lens of Swadeshi ideology, deeply impacted the subsequent career of the culture concept in Bengal. Swadeshi's collapse was widely interpreted as the result of a profound moral failure on the part of the Bengali people to live up to the cultural principles that Swadeshi discourse had identified as the core rationality of indigenous tradition. Since Swadeshi ideology had posited this immanent cultural impulse as the very condition of possibility for its agenda, the identification within "the people" of a "Western" propensity for the pursuit of self-interest represented a profound ideological crisis. In chapter 6, I show how this materialistic propensity came to be linked specifically with a stereotype of the selfish, fanatical, and alien Muslim that was a condensation of multiple histories. In the face of the distancing of "Hindu culture" from the realm of what I call the "Muslim popular," post-Swadeshi Bengali intellectuals increasingly displaced the ideal of culture from its Swadeshi ambition of transfiguring national life onto practices pursued within more circumscribed social spaces—notably, the village community, the reforged Hindu community of elite communalism, and the aesthetic and literary practices of cosmopolitanism most famously associated with Rabindranath Tagore. Culture was thus conceptually extracted from and opposed to the material life of the people as a perduringly distinct dimension of human existence. The proliferation of concepts of culture in twentieth-century Bengal is ultimately understood as the result of its displacement and involution in the wake of the self-diagnosed failure of Swadeshi, and not of the triumph of culturalist ideology.

In the post-Swadeshi period, then, the discourse of culture was increasingly assimilated to a language of distinction and prestige that expressed the social isolation and collective interests of the (mostly high-caste Hindu) bhadralok. But the heterotopic strategies of disavowal discussed in this last chapter were not left unchallenged. Against the generalized critique of democracy that was at the heart of post-Swadeshi discourses of culture, there emerged a broadly leftist project of reclaiming the very popular energies that had undermined the Swadeshi movement to a democratic project that at once sought to transcend culturalism and yet remained haunted by its shadow. I examine the emergence of a Marxist left in Bengal, its more-than-fortuitous genealogical links with the Swadeshi movement, its explicit repudiation of culturalist nationalism, and the subsequent ambivalence of its relationship with culturalist conceptions. Marxism in Bengal has long enjoyed a troubled intimacy with the culturalist tradition that renders transparent simultaneously the practical foundations of Bengali culturalism and the conceptual limitations of that form of Marxism.

CHAPTER TWO

✳

Culture as a Global Concept

Whatever the subject of debate, the dialectical method is concerned always with the same problem: knowledge of the historical process in its entirety. This means that "ideological" and "economic" problems lose their mutual exclusiveness and merge into one another. The history of a particular problem turns into the history of problems. *The literary or scientific exposition of a problem appears as the expression of a social whole, of its possibilities, limits and problems. The approach of literary history is the one best suited to the problems of history. The history of philosophy becomes the philosophy of history.*

GEORG LUKÁCS, "THE MARXISM OF ROSA LUXEMBURG"[1]

THIS BOOK grapples with the implications of the ready transmissibility of one of the key concepts of the modern world. The global dimension of this project is likely to provoke the most immediate resistance from historians, so before launching into the substance of my narrative, I want to begin by lingering over the problem of definition. When I write of a global history of the culture concept, what kind of concept do I have in mind? What was this concept, culture, that people in the most disparate of places were adopting as a lens for construing their world? This chapter will begin by reconstructing a broad history of the culture concept in the West to show how it is possible to construe that concept as a unitary, if differentiated, object of analysis. It then proceeds to show how the categories of Marx's analysis of capitalist society can be used to grasp the formation of this conceptual field.

Proceeding from the prima facie case that the culture concept was found powerful, resonant, and useful in numerous and diverse historical contexts

[handwritten margin note: "Global history of the culture concept"]

as the appropriate thought form for certain kinds of social analysis and critique, I shall challenge the disaggregative instincts of contemporary intellectual historians to begin with by identifying a single, broadly pan-European modern culture concept that has traversed the boundaries of the specific discourse formations of pedagogy, aesthetics, anthropology, and so on. This culture concept, I suggest, has articulated a claim about the fundamental underdetermination of human subjectivity, and has done so fairly consistently since its emergence into philosophical importance in the eighteenth century. From the perspective of this analysis, the global dissemination of the culture concept consequently becomes susceptible to a more systematic historical analysis than is suggested by fragmentary histories of the transmission of intellectual influences or the reproduction of discursive apparatus. Reading the global history of the culture concept as the dissemination of a category of autonomous agency does not foreclose the investigation of the specific conditions of its reception in particular times and places. After all, this work represents just such a project. Rather, it forms the starting point for an investigation into the ubiquitous centrality of discourses of culture to critiques of alien bureaucracy, of colonial domination, and of the anarchic and anomic tendencies of commercial society.

PART ONE: FRAMING AN OBJECT OF INQUIRY

Culture and Civilization

Matthew Arnold's well-known espousal of the term culture in the 1860s immediately identified him in the eyes of his contemporaries as a spokesman for what the Victorians termed *Germanism*.[2] *Culture* and *cultivation* were two mostly synonymous English words that were closely bound throughout the nineteenth century to two German words, *Kultur* and *Bildung*, which at least until the end of the eighteenth century still had fuzzy enough contours to be sometimes used interchangeably: Immanuel Kant, for example, used them more or less interchangeably, while Moses Mendelssohn's pragmatic juxtaposition of the two terms was necessarily self-conscious.[3] *Bildung* began its career as a translation from Latin: *Bild* = *imago* (*dei*). In the course of the eighteenth century, however, it shed its Pietist roots and instead came to signify the process of active self-cultivation envisioned by the philhellenist neohumanists.[4] The term *Kultur* was assimilated into German from an earlier French usage (*la culture*), which also had an early English offshoot (culture), all of which were in turn ultimately derived from Latin (most famously,

Cicero's stoic conception of *cultura animi*). In early usage, *culture* was typically accompanied by a genitive phrase (*of the spirit, of the mind, of literature,* or even *of the body*) in keeping with its foundation in the agricultural metaphor. But from as early as the late sixteenth century we find it gradually emerging as a freestanding concept. Samuel Pufendorf's juxtaposition of a *status naturalis* and a *status culturae* (identified in turn with the *status civilis*) may be the first important instance of such a usage; and this early formulation of the nature/culture opposition already seemed to presage the later importance of the concept.[5]

Culture has had a long and intimate relationship with the more expansive concept of *civilization,* a term that emerged in mid-eighteenth-century French (and English very soon thereafter) with the aspiration to unite the disparate themes of *police, politesse, civilité,* and *doux commerce* under the single heading of an overarching social process.[6] To say *Kultur* in German has most often meant implicitly to translate the French word *civilisation* or its English complement; for *Kultur* was most often understood on a collective scale to name the degree to which some specific people or nation had progressed in overcoming their subjection to nature—in other words, the overcoming of scarcity, the development of technical capacities, the institution of a rule of law and/or rational administration, the progress of knowledge and the softening of manners that were at the core of the various narratives of *civilization*.[7] Conversely, both the British and the French would translate the word *Kultur* as *civilization* wherever the usages seemed consonant, including in some rather prominent instances: Jacob Burckhardt's *Die Kultur der Renaissance* was translated into English as *The Civilization of the Renaissance,* and into French as *La civilisation de la renaissance* soon after its publication in 1860; and Freud's 1930 essay, *Das Unbehagen in der Kultur,* became *Civilization and Its Discontents* and *Le malaise dans la civilisation.*

But the concept has also been slipperier than such an easy translative equation might suggest. "The German word *Kultur,*" explained W. D. Robson-Scott in a footnote to his 1928 translation of Freud's *Future of an Illusion,* "has been translated sometimes as 'culture' and sometimes as 'civilization,' denoting as it does a concept intermediate between these and at times inclusive of both."[8] In fact, *culture* could be distinguished from *civilization,* to begin with, through a simple juxtaposition of part (the spiritual, intellectual, and moral dimensions of human development) to whole (the total process of social development). However, to disembed culture in this way could already be the first step to making a more radical claim about the autonomous activity of the human subject within or against the objective historical processes of civilizational development, which could in turn be figured in broadly Rousseauian terms as a corruptive descent back into external or material determinations (selfish interest, materialistic desire, structures of social interdependence). The *Bildungsideal* assumed its centrality in German intellectual discourse in the late eighteenth century precisely as a critique of Enlightenment rationalism's reduction of human beings to functional utility within a (bureaucratic) division of labor, from the standpoint of the natural self's "unconditional right to self-determination."[9] Anthony La Vopa's emphasis on the role of "poor students" in this discourse echoes, even as it complicates, Norbert Elias's classic sketch of the origins of the modern German culture-civilization dichotomy in the exclusion of the middle-class intelligentsia from the (francophone) courtly society of the eighteenth century.[10] Elias's longer *durée* history must be tempered with the recognition that the famous *lexical* opposition between the terms *Kultur* and *Zivilisation* was essentially a product of the late nineteenth century, and that the specifically nationalistic understanding of this lexical opposition (as a distinction between Germany and France) became commonplace only from around the period of the First World War.[11] Yet in the end, Elias's analysis was seeking to derive the later emergence of the lexical opposition from an earlier, eighteenth-century *conceptual* opposition between external institutions and inner life that was the precondition for nationalistic homologies.[12] In any case, it is quite clear that from the 1870s at least, German writers like Heinrich von Treitschke were increasingly matching stereotypes of France's glossy and formalistic show of *civilisation* with critiques of Britain's allegedly sudsy conception of *civilization*, and German academics were beginning to grapple with conceptual oppositions that substantially prefigured the later, more systematic lexical opposition of *Kultur* (authentic subjectivity free from the material determinations of utility and self-interest) and *Zivilisation* (material progress).[13]

Conversely, writers in English, drawing directly on these German intellectual influences, would adopt the words *culture* or *cultivation* whenever a distinction from *civilization* was implied.[14] Thus, in 1829, Samuel Coleridge, erecting his political theory on a solid foundation of German classical idealism, had already identified "the permanent *distinction,* and the occasional *contrast,* between cultivation and civilization," adding the observation that "a nation can never be too cultivated, but may easily become an over-civilized race."[15] Arnold himself would echo this formulation forty years later when opposing culture (the "idea of perfection as an inward condition of the mind and spirit") to "the mechanical and material civilization in esteem with us."[16]

Similarly, while the French might commonly translate *Kultur* as *civilisation*, they could also, working under German intellectual influences that were at least as powerfully felt in nineteenth-century France as in nineteenth-century Britain, reinvigorate the marginalized term, *culture*, where a lexical distinction from *civilisation* was called for, as for instance during the reception of Friedrich Nietzsche in the 1890s.[17] In fact, francophone authors had already in the eighteenth century developed their own terminological opposition between *true* and *false* civilization, the latter being characterized by the superficialities of *civilité*, lacking any real underlying moral substance.[18] This theme would be further elaborated in the early nineteenth century, as the eminent philosopher Victor Cousin worked to establish philosophically, and cultivate practically, the efficacious integrity of a *moi* grounded in the power of volition. Through a critique of the sensationalist doctrines of John Locke and Étienne Condillac, which threatened to dissolve the self into discrete moments of sense perception, Cousin sought to elaborate a "self-possessed" form of personhood capable of rational reflection and moral responsibility against the relatively "unselved" form of personhood that functioned merely as the passive instrument of "spontaneous suggestions of consciousness."[19] Even in the French intellectual world, the distinction between inner and outer development had been significant since the eighteenth century.

For a liberal like François Guizot, the distinction between the moral and material dimensions of human progress, while clearly conceived, was nonetheless contained within the larger process of *civilisation*, which was the higher synthesis of its two equally necessary subordinate elements.[20] This French faith in the coherence of a unitary civilizational narrative synthesizing both moral and material progress could fairly be described as the norm in both English and German for most of the modern era.[21] The culture concept has never been incompatible with liberal thought, even when that liberalism grounded itself in the objective historical processes of civilizational development. Culture could supplement the more classically liberal, negative conception of *emancipation from* the illegitimate exercise of state authority, with the positive conception of subjective freedom as a *capacity to*. John Stuart Mill, for instance, shared with other liberals the belief in individual liberty both on grounds of principle and general social utility, and he was hardly eccentric in linking the historical emergence of a liberal society to major transformations in the structure of economy, society, and polity. But what Mill added to the framework of his liberal and utilitarian forebears was the notion that such freedom from external constraint was justified not only because it allowed for the generalized pursuit of material pleasure (Jeremy

Bentham's *happiness*) that underpinned the logic of political economy, but also because it provided the opportunity for the cultivation of each individual's innate potential through the pursuit of the higher pleasures of the spirit or mind.[22] Here, the positive freedom that was at the core of the culture concept was being nested within a liberal conception of negative freedom.

Yet one can see how easily this kind of liberal culturalism could slip into a culture/civilization opposition: while Mill would on the one hand posit liberty and culture as mutually reinforcing and complementary principles, he could on the other hand call for the cultivation of higher virtues on the part of university elites to *counter* the dangerous leveling effects of the democratized mass society that civilization had called forth.[23] Arnold would make broadly the same argument in his manifesto for a "better liberalism" that would eschew "the pedantic application of certain maxims of political economy in the wrong place" in favor of the cultivation of a "best self." By bringing men into harmony under the guidance of an impersonal "right reason," "culture" would provide a "principle of authority" to "counteract the tendency to anarchy which seems to be threatening us." That principle directly implied "the idea of *the State*," that is, the "organ of our collective best self, our national right reason," "entrusted with stringent powers for the general advantage."[24] At such moments, we see culture becoming entangled in a wider project that would use the idea of disinterested self-cultivation to construct an extrapolitical, extraeconomic space homologous with the universal collective interest represented ideologically by the state.[25] But what this in turn meant was that the ethical state was being positioned, through the language of culture, as the preeminent organ of the nation's collective spiritual life, so that it served as a force antithetical to the material determinations of petty self-interest that drove civilization.[26] In the end, even though culture could be posited as a complementary or even metonymically subordinate moment of civilization, wherever the progressive course of history was understood to entwine human subjects heteronomously in ever-tighter networks of materialistic desire and instrumentalization, culture could always be invoked as a Rousseauian counterprinciple of internality, authenticity, and autonomous self-formation.

Culture and Autonomy

Seen from this wider perspective, we might suggest that the culture concept enjoyed a precarious universality at least within a European cosmopolis constituted by the heritage of Latin cosmopolitanism and the subsequent

[margin handwritten note: Culture as a "civilizing" force that would bring a "Principle of authority"]

history of modern vernacular interpenetration. Yes, this universality was shot through with different emphases, degrees of prominence, discursive functions, homological transformations, and ideological implications within particular national and linguistic arenas. And certainly the instabilities of two centuries of usage render any single and exhaustive definitional generalization outrageous at a strictly lexical level. Yet in the end it seems difficult to deny that the concept's major fault lines have followed less the contours of different languages than certain semantic differentiations internal to the concept's translingual history.

The well-known "review" of the history of the culture concept undertaken by Alfred Kroeber and Clyde Kluckhohn identified two of the most prominent of these semantic fault lines. To begin with, the distinction between culture and civilization in Germany seemed, they not unreasonably noted, to correlate with "the spirit-nature dichotomy—*Geist und Natur*—that so deeply penetrated German thought from the eighteenth to the twentieth century."[27] But the exact nature of this correlation was, they observed, fraught with ambiguity. It might seem obvious to those familiar with the discourses of German and English cultural criticism that culture would line up unproblematically with *Geist*. Yet, as Kroeber and Kluckhohn observed, some forms of usage also suggested the very opposite alignment. *Kultur* had often been used, since the late eighteenth century, to refer to the development of man's technical capacities to control nature, much in keeping with the agricultural metaphor at the etymological core of the concept. In contrast to the instrumentalism of *Kultur* then, it would be *Zivilisation* that would bear the burden of both moral and social improvement. This would seem to align culture with nature and civilization with spirit. It would also seem to imply that the nineteenth-century usage of the term *Kultur* was so puzzlingly broad as to encompass conceptual polarities.

"*Civilization*," explained Wilhelm von Humboldt, Kroeber and Kluckhohn's most important exemplar of this alternative tradition, "is the humanization of peoples in their outward institutions and customs, and the inner attitudes pertaining thereto. *Culture* adds science and art to this refinement of the social order."[28] Yet only a certain lexical literalism could have led Kroeber and Kluckhohn to ignore the fact that, despite this apparent downgrading of *Kultur* in a definitional passage ripped from its context, Humboldt was indeed still working from within a more familiar form of the culture/civilization dichotomy. He did so, however, by contrasting both *Zivilisation* and *Kultur*, as "outward" forms, to *Bildung*, the kind of cultivation that is "something at the same time higher and more inward, namely the disposi-

[margin note, handwritten:] Kultur used to discuss man's technical capacities to control nature

tion that, from the knowledge and feeling of the entire mental and moral endeavour, pours out harmonious upon temperament and character."[29] Zivilisation names the social interconnections that link human beings with each other "in their *outer institutions and customs* and in their inner attitude *pertaining thereto.*" It has no necessary connection with inner cultivation, but can be a wholly external imposition.[30] Inner cultivation begins with the subordination of an inchoate creative energy to organic form:

> Even in his earlier circumstance, man transcends the *present* moment, and does not remain sunk in mere sensual enjoyment. Among the roughest tribes we find a love of adornment, dancing, music and song, and beyond that forebodings of a world to come, the hopes and anxieties founded on this, and traditions and tales which commonly go back to the origin of man and of his abode. The more strongly and brightly does the *spiritual power,* working independently by its own laws and forms of intuition, pour out its light into this world of the past and future, with which man surrounds his existence of the moment, the more purely and variously does the mass [of his creative energy], simultaneously, take shape. Thus do *science* and *art* arise, and the goal, therefore, of mankind's developing progress is always the fusion of what is produced independently from within with what is given from without, each grasped in its purity and completeness, and bound into the subjection which the current endeavour by its nature demands.[31]

For Humboldt, "contact with the *world*" and "communication of outer exertion and inner perceptions" turn out to be irreducibly necessary for the actual "*formation of character*" that *Bildung* names.[32] Neohumanists like Humboldt understood *Bildung* to be, in La Vopa's words, a form of "self-cultivation [that] throve on constant and ever varied interaction between the subject and objective reality. Subjectivity acquired substance for its inner articulation in its very self-projection into external forms."[33] This positions *Kultur*—the technical capacity to subordinate nature to inner force that Humboldt defined through a direct reiteration of the terms *science* and *art* in the definitional passage with which we began—as the necessary outward expression of the free and spontaneous agency that characterizes human consciousness.[34] The distinction between civilization and culture can thus be understood as a distinction between human beings embedded in relationships with other human beings and human beings in their relationship with (inner and outer) nature. It is in their relationship with nature rather than with one another, Humboldt seems to be saying, that human beings are able to give practical expression and meaning to subjective freedom. Yet, as the truly protoanthropological passage cited at length above makes abundantly clear, this alignment has never precluded the relationship to nature being understood at the level of the collectivity, so long as collectivity is grasped organically rather than in terms of individual interaction.

Humboldt's emphasis on *Kultur* as the practical expression of subjective freedom was fundamentally inspired by Kantian idealism. Kant had defined *Kultur* in his *Critique of Judgment* as the process of "producing in a rational being an aptitude for purposes generally (hence [in a way that leaves] that being free)," where such "aptitude for purposes generally" included both "man's aptitude in general for setting himself purposes," and his aptitude "for using nature (independently of [the element of] nature in man's determination of purposes) as a means [for achieving them] in conformity with the maxims of his free purposes generally." Such a practice of culture necessarily founded humanity's acquisition of technical prowess (skill) upon a prior "culture of discipline" that served to constitute a rational "will" capable of casting off the "despotism of desires" (which might otherwise condition or limit the freedom of rational thought to select the ends to which a human being might direct such skills).[35] In the *Critique of Pure Reason*, Kant was juxtaposing discipline and culture as negative to positive: the restraint and extirpation of our natural inclination to contravene the dictates of reason, versus the acquisition of skills that can be used to any given end, whether or not in accordance with reason.[36] In the third critique, however, Kant recognized that an aptitude could only be considered a form of culture (a properly *human* aptitude) if it was grounded in the "culture of discipline," that is, in the free subjectivity of a rational will. But while distinguishing freedom from nature, Kant had read too much Rousseau to confuse culture with a mere denatured artifice: "The ideal [*Idee*] of morality belongs to culture," he famously declared; "its use for some simulacrum of morality in the love of honor and outward decorum constitutes mere civilization [*Civilisierung*]."[37] Culture was not the mere artificiality of human sociality, which would ultimately have to derive from the element of nature (specifically, desire and self-love) in man's determination of purposes. Rather, it specifically named those forms of nature-commanding activity that practically realized the rational self-determination of the human subject. Culture, in other words, was from the beginning bound tightly to the category of labor—a point to which we will return at greater length further on in this chapter.

Culture in Kant's usage might seem, as Raymond Geuss has argued, a profoundly individualized, and even utterly asocial, category.[38] Yet Kant made it clear in his writings on education that it is the pedagogical application of discipline (*Disziplin, Zucht*) that, by making possible the subsequent internalization of self-discipline, lays the foundation for the regular exercise of subjective freedom (skill directed to freely and rationally chosen ends). Unlike the beast, "man requires his own reason. He has no instinct, and must himself construct the plan of his own behavior. Since he is not however immediately capable of doing this . . . others must do it for him. . . . *One generation educates the other.*"[39] Culture is, in other words, something that is formed *within* the realm of the social, and always tends toward the construction of a social framework that encourages conduct in accordance with the moral principles of practical reason.[40] If the passage of human history can be seen as a transition from "an uncultured, merely animal condition to the state of humanity, from bondage to instinct to rational control—in a word, from the tutelage of nature to the state of freedom"—then it was the role of culture to "bring about such a development of the dispositions of mankind, considered as a *moral* species, as to end the conflict between the natural and the moral species . . . until such time as finally art will be strong and perfect enough to become a second nature" and thus complete "the genuine education of man as man and citizen."[41]

Seen from this perspective, the relationship between what Kroeber and Kluckhohn identified as "contrary" currents of usage appears much less opaque: both Kant and Humboldt agreed that technical prowess could be the logical extension of the critical constitution of the self as a self-determining (autonomous) subject. Even when it seemed to name an instrumental relationship to *res extensa*, culture ultimately, and crucially, retained its affiliation with the "spirit" side of the classic antinomy. But more importantly, we can already identify in Kant's discussion of culture the key problematic that has consistently defined the culture concept: the practical realization of free subjectivity.

Anthropological Culture

Kroeber and Kluckhohn, however, viewed this first genealogical puzzle as an anachronism that could be largely consigned (as "mainly an episode in German thought") to the prehistory of the "scientific" culture concept that was at the heart of their concerns.[42] This previous (apparent) inconsistency in nineteenth-century usage remained firmly within what they termed a *humanistic* understanding of culture—the individual or collective cultivation (understood as either a process or an achieved state) of the "human" or "spiritual" or "rational" or "higher" or "universal" qualities, and extending from there to include the objectified results of such cultivation (literature, art, music, and so on). This was the older usage, and for most of the culture concept's history it remained the more commonplace. Yet it is true that there has long been an alternative set of meanings to culture that would seem to exceed the terms of the discussion above—what is commonly referred to as the anthropological understanding of the concept. Where the humanistic concept would appear to express an achieved degree of emancipation from natural determinations ("the despotism of desires"), anthropological culture would instead accord to all human collectivities the fundamental character- istic of self-determining agency, "a set of attributes and products of human societies, and therewith of mankind, which are extrasomatic and transmis- sible by mechanisms other than biological heredity."[43]

Analytically, it would be quite straightforward to assume, as so many have, that the humanistic and anthropological conceptions are in a straightforward sense definitionally distinct. *Culture,* in other words, was simply a homonym. But a properly historical investigation cannot afford to leap directly to this analytical premise without first lingering over some important questions: Why have these two analytically distinct dimensions of the culture concept been so ubiquitously conflated in actual usage (hence provoking the need for recurrent analytical clarifications, of which Kroeber and Kluckhohn's review merely stands as the best known)? And if the humanistic meanings of the word *culture* long predate its ethnological meanings, what was it about that earlier usage that made the word available for its new role as the foun- dational concept of an emergent discipline of cultural anthropology?

Genealogies of anthropological culture most commonly begin with Ger- man Romanticism, and more particularly with Johann Gottfried Herder's pluralistic organicism as the antithesis of Kant's abstract universalism. They all too rarely take stock of the fact, however, that Herder's pluralism revolved around the concept of *Volk,* not *Kultur.*[44] The latter term occurs exclusively in the singular. Each people had its own distinct instantiation of *culture,* but culture itself remained a process of unfolding the inner propensities of each people, who were in turn bound within the single world-historical process of the organic development of a unitary principle of humanity as the ultimate end of human nature. Such humanity would find its proper realization in the establishment of *"reason and equity in all conditions, and in all occupations of men,"* defined "not through the will of a sovereign, or the persuasive power of tradition, but through natural laws, on which the essence of man reposes."[45] "Every addition to the useful arts secures men's property, diminishes their labour, extends their sphere of activity, and neces- sarily lays therewith the foundations of farther cultivation and humanity. . . .

[margin handwritten note:] Herder pluralism centered around Volk

Let us thank the Creator, that he conferred *understanding* on mankind, and made *art* essential to it."[46] While Herder embraced the diversity of peoples, this pluralism seems to have been inextricably bound to his providentialist attachment to a broadly Kantian understanding of culture. "God made man a deity upon Earth; he implanted in him the principle of *self-activity*, and set this principle in motion from the beginning, by means of the internal and external wants of his nature."[47] This attachment to a universalistic conception of "humanity" was equally characteristic of other late eighteenth-century Romantics like Johann Adelung, who sought to extend the semantic range of culture to include a properly *social* meaning: "Culture is the transition from a more sensual and animal condition to the more closely knit interrelations of social life," and "consists of the sum of defined concepts and of the amelioration and refinement of the body and of manners."[48] Such moments underline once again the continuity between—indeed, the near coevalness of—humanistic usages and usages that even Kroeber and Kluckhohn were able to recognize as protoanthropological.

Whether used in the singular as a horizontal conceptual distinction within social process (for example, culture rather than economics), or as a vertical distinction between different social groups (for example, Nuer culture), anthropological culture has always taken plurality and diversity as its defining object. As Jörg Fisch has argued, one can trace through the course of the nineteenth century the gradual "reification" of the culture concept, along with the word's consequent pluralization.[49] But while the term's assimilation as a constitutive element of new historical and ethnological discourses in the second half of the nineteenth century represented a significant moment in the evolution of the concept, we need to beware of overstating the degree to which the consequent extension of its range of reference constituted a fundamental break in its history. Of course, one might well suspect Kroeber and Kluckhohn of having something of a disciplinary interest in trying to demarcate such a sharp break: they were seeking to ground the integrity of a specifically "cultural" anthropology in a creation myth that would prophylactically seal its core concept from the sullying touch of its predisciplinary, humanistic past. But anthropological culture enjoyed no immaculate conception. As George Stocking has observed, despite Kroeber and Kluckhohn's nomination of E. B. Tylor as the Zeus to anthropological culture's Athena, "the history of the culture idea in English and American anthropology suggests that it did not leap full-blown from Tylor's brow in 1871." On the contrary, "close consideration of Tylor's definition in the context of his work and time does in fact suggest that his idea of culture was perhaps closer to that of his humanist near-contemporary Matthew Arnold than it was to the modern anthropological meaning."[50] For Tylor, *culture* named the progressive evolution of human moral, intellectual, and technical capacities in society, in contrast to *custom*, which could include regressive holdovers of the past. It is quite clear that, as a concept that named the gradual emancipation of human life from the despotism of nature, Tylor's *culture* remained firmly within the humanistic tradition, even as that tradition was being stretched to incorporate a relatively new object of investigation. In other words, "knowledge, belief, art, law, morals, custom, and any other capabilities and habits acquired by man as a member of society" (all categories long-established in the study of human societies) were now being reconceptualized, rearticulated, and redefined as a "complex whole" that, insofar as it represented a progressive agent of the emancipation of human subjectivity, could be called *culture*.

Whether we are talking about culture as such, or the various cultures that differ from one another, the category has emerged as a term of social analysis in constitutive contradistinction to objective determinations. Sigmund Freud, for instance, would define both functions of *Kultur*—"to protect men against nature and to adjust their mutual relations"—in terms of the imposition of the restriction and sublimation of the primordial instinctual drives of the individual.[51] "Where id was, there ego shall be. [Psychoanalysis] is a work of culture—not unlike the draining of the Zuider Zee."[52] If his interpretations of the actual symbolic fabric of consciousness were in terms of its over- rather than underdetermination, this was in spite of culture's effectiveness, the result of the irremediable incompleteness of a cultural process that could never truly eliminate the element of nature from man's determination of purposes. Of course, culture can be defined to include *all* elements of a social organization, but it names the elements of such an organization specifically as forms distinct from direct biological determinants, at least in the very minimal sense that, even if culture were understood as a form of animal behavior, it must remain a form of learned behavior whose most obvious index would be variability within a biologically homogeneous species. The Boasian adoption of the culture concept served to assert the autonomy of even "primitive" systems of social action and meaning (what Kroeber and Kluckhohn called the *superorganic*) from racial and biological determinations.

Alternatively, culture has been analytically juxtaposed to other dimensions of the social that are organized by what are understood to be objectively necessary abstract laws, such as the economy or society. Adam Kuper has argued that Talcott Parsons's disaggregation of the structure of social action into economic, political, social, and cultural determinations was not only central to laying the foundations for anthropology's claims to disciplinary autonomy, but also in so doing it further underwrote the autonomy of culture itself as a distinct determination of social action.[53] And conversely, as Carl Pletsch observed, in the developmentalist discourse of the 1950s and 1960s the construction of culture as a residual determinant after social and ideological factors had been subtracted could lead to a negative characterization of cultural subjectivity as an obstacle to the "natural" process of economic growth.[54] Even that notorious arch-determinist Claude Lévi-Strauss used the concept of culture to mark out an autonomous function for the intellectual process of transforming percepts into signs, radically distinguishing the logic of classificatory systems from the "social" determinations of infrastructural "praxis" and demographic change.[55] From this perspective, the critique of structuralist culture as a reification that effaces individual human agency (following the terms of the structure/agency debate) assumes secondary importance to a more fundamental (and thoroughly Kantian) move to establish the intellectual process of meaning-making as a self-positing agency constitutive of, rather than constituted by, structures of practice; for as a relatively autonomous sign system, culture is a form of subjectivity whose only determinations (inflexible as these may be) are "cultural."

Following from such substantive contrasts between collectively constituted subjectivity and objective structures of social organization, anthropological culture can also by extension be opposed as a theoretical or methodological category of analysis to the "brute and disinterested objectivism" of sociological abstractions, providing a richer subjectivistic emphasis on the "rich description" of "human thought, achievement, consciousness, pain, stupidity and evil" that, because of its irreducibility to objective structures of determination, "cannot be anticipated on the basis of some theoretical premise."[56] This is nothing other than a restatement of the antireductionist tradition stretching from Wilhelm Dilthey into American cultural anthropology.[57] This methodological dimension of the culture concept emerged in late nineteenth-century German thought as a direct reaction against the rise of positivistic science, and after something of a lull in the concept's centrality during the period of Hegelianism's intellectual ascendancy.[58] It needs to be positioned, then, in the context of the resurgence of a neo-idealist defense of subjectivity from reductionist determinism in later nineteenth-century philosophy and social inquiry—alongside, in other words, the neo-Kantian turn in epistemology that culminated in Heinrich Rickert's redefinition of the

Geisteswissenschaften (a term that could include the deterministic knowledge of lawlike regularities characteristic of psychology, for example) as the *historischen Kulturwissenschaften* (a term that specifically designated a form of knowledge that applied to unique phenomena the significance of whose singularity was grounded simultaneously in the value-orientations of historical actors and in the historian's own subject-centered judgments of value).[59]

The issue is not, as Stocking sometimes seems to imply, one of shifting the moment of the transition from humanistic to anthropological conceptions of culture from Tylor in the later nineteenth century to Franz Boas in the early twentieth. For Kroeber and Kluckhohn, the key issue on which the difference between anthropological and humanistic cultures turned was value neutrality. But while the shift from viewing culture as a condition achieved through a history of human improvement to viewing it as a universal condition of human social existence is certainly of great significance for the history of the social sciences, the two cultures are still defined by a single problematic. Anthropological culture still indexes the relative autonomy of human subjectivity from natural or objective determinations. This is not to deny that there can be a theory of culture that attempts to identify forms of social or biological determination. On the contrary, Bronislaw Malinowski's analysis of "basic needs" is just one eminent attempt within the modern anthropological tradition to identify such forms of determination. But for the object of such an analysis to be initially identifiable as culture is what first requires historical explanation. While culturalism—a discourse that assumes the standpoint of culture as a category of human underdetermination—was required for the identification of certain kinds of objects or practices (for example, custom, symbolic representation) as culture, once the identification of such objects as forms of culture was disciplinarily conventionalized, culture became immediately susceptible to analysis in terms of external determinations, whether in terms of needs, interests, or practices. Yet the deeper history of the constitution of the cultural object of knowledge remains evident symptomatically even in the writings of an ethnologist with such distinctly reductionist leanings as Malinowski. In *Argonauts of the Western Pacific,* for instance, he used culture as a standpoint from which to attack the stereotype of the "Primitive Economic Man," the fabricated projection of classical political economy who was "prompted in all his actions by a rationalistic conception of self-interest." Even "man on a low level of culture," Malinowski sought to demonstrate, was driven to "work and effort"—far beyond the merely necessary, and, indeed, even as "an end in themselves"—"by motives of a highly complex, social and traditional nature,

[handwritten margin note: "Analysis in terms of external determinations"]

and towards aims which are certainly not directed towards the satisfaction of present wants, or to the direct achievement of utilitarian purposes."[60] The Trobriand Islander was, as a cultural subject, necessarily underdetermined by the despotism of desires—by his immediate wants, needs, or self-interest. The collective culture of the islanders became for Malinowski the medium through which basic needs were fulfilled while at the same time releasing human beings from their immediate subjection to the demands of merely organic existence.

The anthropological conception of culture, stripped of its implication of evolutionary improvement so as to accord underdetermined subjectivity to all social collectivities, replicates the Kantian understanding of human subjectivity at a collective level. In other words, *culture* still names the emancipation of human reason (now grasped as variable systems of meaning-making, but still constituted subjectivistically in keeping with Kant's "Copernican revolution") from the natural determinations of utility maximization or biological necessity ("the despotism of desires"). The community thus comes to stand in as the arena for the realization of human worldly agency (skill) that this fundamental freedom is supposed to ground. This transformation of the subjectivistic standpoint from the individual to the collective level may not be admissible in the strictly philosophical terms of Kant's argument, but this should not blind us to the broader structural logic.

PART TWO: TOWARD A THEORY OF
CONCEPT FORMATION

In Defense of Raymond Williams

None of this is to say that these different forms of cultural discourse—anthropological and humanistic—are simply the same. After all, the specific modalities in which subjective autonomy has been conceived—as a characteristic of the individual or the social, the community or the state—must surely be significant when we turn our attention to particular historical contexts. My point is rather to suggest that, from a historical standpoint, the proliferation of meanings should be considered within a single, internally differentiated conceptual history structured by a single, more or less internally consistent, modern understanding of human subjectivity as underdetermined and thus self-positing. Culture, humanistic and anthropological, has with remarkable regularity operated within a repertoire of related antinomies: inside-outside, authenticity-appearance, content-form, organism-mechanism, mind-body, meaning-thing, subject-object, freedom-necessity, autonomy-heteronomy, and spirit-nature. As a method of investigation, it will be indisputably important to specify the historical transformations the concept has undergone at particular points in time and space. Yet it will simply not do to dissolve this remarkable regularity into the pluralized discursive formations connected to particular institutional practices—to deny that culture is a concept whose generality has exceeded its articulation as a specific form of discourse within particular institutional contexts. Such a strategy will get us no closer to understanding the central antinomic logic that has with such remarkable consistency marked the concept across its different major forms of usage.

A concept that is historically modern cannot be derived from metaphysical truth; not, at least, without explicitly addressing the question of why an eternal verity had to wait so long for a systematic elaboration. Recognizing this has driven many intellectual historians to critique the more traditional "history of ideas" from the standpoint of a genealogical approach to the history of discourse formations. Yet it remains unclear whether the explanatory power and compelling plausibility of any concept to which can be ascribed the kind of universality that culture has enjoyed (in the dual sense of the regularity of its reproduction across two or three centuries and its disregard for geographical and linguistic boundaries) can be derived from the specific institutional contingencies of discursive practice. The Foucauldian argument has certainly been made. Ian Hunter has argued that British cultural discourse in the second half of the nineteenth century took its significance from the pedagogical arrangement of the classroom: the presentation of the teacher as a model for ethical emulation shifted cultural discourse from its earlier valence of reflexive self-formation to a form of power knowledge whose normalizing function was strategically directed to the production of a manageable population. For Hunter, the history of cultural discourse is not a "tradition" of thought, but rather a discourse formation generated "piecemeal" out of an "ensemble of historical surfaces and forces" that was a "purely contingent and provisional configuration or 'programme,' whose emergence is not governed by any overarching historical purpose or theoretical goal" such as might be figured by the concept of "man."[61] Yet the only way to sustain this kind of argument is to radically disaggregate discourses of culture into their particular institutional contexts. Such a turn to concrete repertoires of practice seeks to unveil the process of the hypostatization of historically determinate concepts; but in the process, it leaves the larger regularities and the eminently transmissible nature of the culture concept ultimately unmotivated.

David Lloyd and Paul Thomas share Hunter's suspicion of the figure of "man" at the heart of cultural discourse, but they balk at this crypto-positivist reduction of discourse to institutional contingency.[62] They instead argue that cultural discourse is an ideology whose "regulative idea" is that of the "modern state," which is as much as to say, the state not "as a contingently linked assemblage of institutions which have emerged over time in *ad hoc* response to political and social pressures" on the Foucauldian model, but rather "as the fully developed and unifying representative of a national people." Culture, in the terms of this discourse, serves to "mediate between a disenfranchised populace" who represent fractious interests, and "a state to which they must in time be assimilated" because it represents a truly universal interest that must sublate the competing fractious interests within the nation.[63] In the hands of ideologues like Matthew Arnold and John Stuart Mill, culture was constituted as an "extrapolitical, extraeconomic space" beyond the limits of civil society and thus homologous with the state.[64] This is an ideological project, Lloyd and Thomas have suggested, that far exceeds the limitations of discipline formation with which Hunter was concerned; literary education might be an "instrument" of cultural ideology, but it was certainly not coterminous with the "concept."[65]

Yet surely the devastating critique that Lloyd and Thomas direct at Hunter could just as easily be laid at their own feet. Does the fact that the ideological project of Victorian state consolidation appropriated a discourse of culture (as they convincingly demonstrate it did) necessarily mean that the concept can be derived from or reduced to such functionality? In this sense, Hunter as well as Lloyd and Thomas fundamentally fail to come to terms with one of the core insights of the classic text against which they have commonly positioned their arguments. In *Culture and Society,* Raymond Williams had sought to show, in a thoroughly nonfunctionalistic manner, how the concept of culture had emerged in modern British thought "as an abstraction and an absolute." The delineative axis of the concept's significance was grounded in "the recognition of the practical separation of certain moral and intellectual activities [and ultimately, these conceived in turn as "a whole way of life"] from the driven impetus of a new kind of society"—which is as much as to say, the positing of a peculiarly modern subject-object dichotomy, and its subsequent alignment with a culture-society dichotomy. The evaluative axis then involved "the emphasis of these activities, as a court of human appeal, to be set over the processes of practical judgment and yet to offer itself as a mitigating and rallying alternative" (that is, the assumption of cultural subjectivism, whether individual or collective, as the standpoint for a critique of the abstract, coercive, and destructive forces of modern industrial society).[66] Lloyd and Thomas's critique of Williams's fundamental inability to recognize the historical complicity of the cultural trope of "man" with Victorian statist ideologies seems fair. But their approach nonetheless falls short of the deeper insight of Williams's text. Williams located the emergence of the culture concept in a specifically modern experiential bifurcation (admittedly only posited rather than really analyzed or explained) of two zones of social existence: one constituted by subjects inhabiting meaningful lifeworlds, the other constituted by an abstract field of heteronomous forces. He thereby generated a framework that, by eschewing functionalistic explanations for the culture concept's importance, remains the most promising starting-point for developing a truly historical account of the constitution of the concept itself, as distinct from its deployment within any particular discursive apparatus.

Beyond the West

Yet Williams was, of course, writing about industrial Britain, which leaves wide open the larger question of what such a noninstrumentalist historical account would look like when considered at the level of the global dissemination and circulation of the culture concept as a category variously of colonial cosmopolitanism, anticolonial nationalism, pan-Asianism, and anti-Western anticapitalism.

The emergence of an assertive culturalist politics in colonial Bengal followed the broad structural contours of the British juxtaposition of subjective agency to the heteronomy implicit in objective structures. Bengali critics like Bankimchandra Chatterjee bemoaned the deleterious characterological, ethical, and political consequences of the absorption of Indian bureaucratic and clerical functionaries into the structures of civil society: the reduction of society to a "giant marketplace" where effeminate, hypocritical, verbose, and ineffective "babus" lived a travesty of "independence" in the practical reality of a mere "habit of heartless isolation."[67] Conceiving a stark dichotomy between either debasing oneself through the bestializing pursuit of material self-interest, or debilitating oneself through an otherworldly pursuit of spiritual detachment, Bankim would (as we shall see in more detail in chapter 4) draw from British cultural criticism, Comtean sociology, and the teachings of the Bhagavad Gita to elaborate a third way: a "doctrine of culture" (*anushilanatattva*) according to which the cultivation of innate human capacities would give birth to a new model of humanity capable of disavowing slavery to material attachments at the same time as enhancing the (this-worldly) rational agency of both the individual and collective-national subject. In Bengal, Bankim's intervention stood at the head of a vibrant culturalism that would flourish, albeit in subtly shifting forms, throughout the twentieth century—the history that forms the narratival core of this study.

Culturalism was not confined, however, to Britain's colonial territories. Starting in the later nineteenth century, the concept of culture was widely adopted to challenge Western civilizational domination through an identification of authentic indigenous tradition as the practical and intellectual foundation for the recuperation of an autonomous subjectivity from slavish imitation. In the 1850s, the slavophile Ivan Kireevsky was clearly in search of a concept with which to articulate a distinction between Europe's alleged propensity for rationalist formalism and Russia's Christian commitment to the "higher and living unity" of "inner wholeness." His contrast turned on the difference between Western and Russian modes of *prosveshchenie* (enlightenment), a term that powerfully evokes the notion of a subjectivity liberated from external constraint, but whose usage in this context to express the notion of discrete collective value orientations stretched its conventional meaning to the limits of intelligibility.[68] By the 1860s, Nicolai Danilevsky had found a better term with which to articulate the autonomy of Russian values and institutions from the superficial universalistic judgments of Western civilization: *kul'tura*.[69] And just as Bankim was identifying "the principle of culture" as the foundational doctrine of a revived Hinduism, so too would his contemporary Konstantin Leont'ev identify the "love of culture" as the "central idea" of "true Slavophilism."[70]

Civilization and *enlightenment* (*bunmeikaika*[71]) were the watchwords of the Meiji project to overthrow the burden of the past and establish Japan as a viable and independent national subject in the modern world order. But already by the 1870s some Japanese and Chinese intellectuals were juxtaposing the formalism and materialism of Meiji reformist thought to the authentic cultivation of subjective autonomy.[72] To this end, they adapted the concept of *wen* (writing)—the classical antithesis of *wu* (military prowess) and the basis for what would become the Chinese and Japanese translative equivalents of civilization (*wen-ming, bunmei*) and culture (*wen-hua, bunka*)—as a key platform from which to "organize an opposition to the present," that is, to the "tide of Westernization [that] promised to flood Japanese society with immoral and inhuman practices like 'economy.'"[73] In both Japan and China, national culture, a concept that condensed both humanistic and ethnographic discursive functions, would become a fundamental element of state-building and empire-building ideologies; while the idea of the global redemptive mission of "eastern" or "Asian civilization" would sweep through East and South Asia well before the East Asia Co-Prosperity Sphere appropriated its rhetoric.[74] It is true that these ideological projects would as often ride under the banner of "civilization" as "culture," but this was explicitly understood to be a specifically "eastern" or "Asian" form of "civilization"—a "cultural" or "spiritual" civilization whose guiding principles were antithetical to the materialism of Western civilization (a formal replication of the twentieth-century German understanding of the antithesis of *Kultur* and *Zivilisation* that surely cannot be reduced to a question of "influence").[75]

But if we are to accept the claim that a concept like culture can be translingual in this wider global sense, we will have to account for the very possibility of a translingual, and indeed transcivilizational, concept—in the face of a reception of Ferdinand de Saussure that understands the signified to be inextricably and constitutively bound to the linguistic contingencies of the signifier. Furthermore, if we are to accept the claim that a modern culture concept has remained broadly coherent despite its dissemination across the quite different discourse formations of its various humanistic and anthropological usages, we must account for the capacity of certain determinate objects of specific discourse formations (education, custom, sign systems) to be translated into instances of some other conceptual matter that we are calling *culture.* The concept of culture, in other words, must serve to translate certain discursive objects into instances or concrete manifestations of some other kind of conceptual object that, in turn, is apparently not restricted to the signifying capacities of any particular language.

The post-Saussurian tradition of semiological inquiry has generated a sophisticated and highly elaborated analysis of the connotative trace. On the basis of this connotative dimension of the sign, we would have to recognize that even the German words *Kultur* and *Bildung,* for example, inevitably set in motion linguistically specific structures of intralinguistic and intertextual connotation whose parameters are less than fully congruent with those implied by the English words, *culture* and *cultivation.* As such, the semantic content of these particular words is always entangled in a specifically lexical, and hence linguistically contingent and particular, structure. Postcolonialist scholarship has emphasized this fragility of translations, especially translations that transgress the limits of the West.[76] Perhaps most notably, Dipesh Chakrabarty has analyzed the role of rough translations in effacing the continuing subterranean life of connotative traces that furtively invoke unassimilated indigenous conceptual structures, thereby assimilating the opaque lifeworlds of non-Western societies to familiar and transparent Western abstractions while correlatively reducing non-Western histories to the status of flawed or incomplete recapitulations of a Western master narrative.[77]

But as Roman Jakobson insisted (and certainly not without due attention to the significance of the connotative effects of sign usage), "all cognitive experience and its classification is conveyable in any existing language."[78] Jakobson was aware that one cannot conflate the semantic content of a word (the signified, or concept) with a concrete referent. But his insight into the irreducibility of the semantic capacity of language remains crucial: to use a sign is to generate a generalized "meaning," even if it is also necessarily to set in motion more specific traces of contextually bound and historically accrued determinations of connotation or sense.[79] It may be true, as Saussure argued, that the capacity to articulate a concept depends on the definition of that concept through an entire ecology of differentiation and association, but this falls far short of a demonstration of the nominalist contention that the linguistic sign is the irreducible vehicle of concept formation.[80]

What constitutes transformations in the parameters of a specific sign's semantic value? Is the material world really an inert domain awaiting linguistically diverse forms of conceptual apportioning? Or does it get implicated in forms of historicity that exceed the linguistic or representational? And if so, how might we thematize this historicity? There are strong traditions of dissent from the Saussurian hypostatization of sign systems within the field of sociolinguistics. A slew of literature in linguistic anthropology now draws on Charles Sanders Peirce's semiotics and/or Valentin Voloshinov's sociolinguistics to show how context and materiality can both become implicated in, affect and circumscribe structures of meaning in culturally determinate ways.[81] But the problem I am addressing in this work does not quite fit here either. The conventional pragmatist approach effectively remedies Saussure's marginalization of actual sign usage through recourse to a focus on concretely situated semiosis to emphasize the heterogeneity and practical contingency of meanings. But if the basic contention of this book is correct, then the concept of culture is not constituted at the level of contingency any more than it is at the level of linguistic structure. If the meaning of the culture concept is not reducible in either of these more familiar ways, then where might the historicity of the semantic content of this concept be constituted? In the answer to this question lies the key to an understanding of translingual equivalence that neither effaces linguistic specificity, nor conflates concept with concrete referent, nor establishes a metaphysical conception of the pure idea through an implicit appeal to natural language.

The kind of approach I have in mind here can only proceed on the basis of some notion of a historically specific yet universal concept—a concept that emerges in the modern epoch, yet which transcends the boundaries of linguistic and cultural specificity to achieve global plausibility as a means of construing the world. *Culture* will therefore be understood in terms of a historically specific form of semantic universality, contingent upon the operation of capitalist social forms that at once reconstitute the preconditions for the continuance of everyday life, and yet exceed the institutional and conventional limits of any one locality—including the locality of Western Europe. As such, the crucial task of "provincializing Europe" in which Chakrabarty invites us to join will necessarily take on a different guise in this work. I will contend that the dynamic impulse to global expansion that is characteristic of capitalist social forms has not only served to "Europeanize" the conceptual universe within which the rest of the world operates, but, and perhaps more fundamentally, it has also served to de-Europeanize the concepts that constitute the now global thought forms of modernity.

Abstract Mediation

While there may well be good reason to quibble over the terms in which Raymond Williams grasped the formation of the culture concept, I shall directly pursue his larger methodological agenda. I shall proceed from the proposition that, before we can argue that culture represented a new category of thought in the modern world, we need first of all to recognize that a new kind of object must have come into existence demanding a new concept through which it could be thought. This book will proceed from the conviction that an adequate account of the historicity of the concept of culture must focus first and foremost on the concept's object orientation—its denotative capacity—rather than on its connotative traces. But the object of cultural discourse—its meaning—cannot be grasped adequately in terms of the series of (more or less) cognitively apprehensible objects that instantiate culture in its diverse discursive usages. Rather, and more fundamentally, this object is a historically determinate form of human subjectivity whose self-understanding is one of underdetermination and autonomous agency. To describe this structure of subjectivity as historically determinate is implicitly to argue that the emergence of this new conceptual object must be grounded neither in nature nor in human nature, but rather in structures of social practice. This was implicit in Williams's analysis of experiential bifurcation, even if the explicit theorization of the causes and practical modalities of that bifurcation were not the main focus of his work.

At the same time, however, insofar as it traverses the limits of locality and language, the culture concept must be grounded in structures of practice that are socially general rather than linked either to specific language communities or to concrete institutional apparatus or practical conventions that necessarily vary from place to place. The structures of practice that fulfill these dual criteria of historical specificity and social generality are best described as practices of abstract social mediation. By this I mean the essentially impersonal relationships that, as the most fundamental conditions for the reproduction of individual and collective life, saturate the practical structures of modern life and link complete strangers in mutual objective interdependence through the mediation of both exchange and production by a historically specific form of social totality that Marx called *capital*.[82] Adam Smith was perhaps the first to grasp in a relatively systematic way the peculiarity of modern social formations—that their cohesion was based most fundamentally not on structures of affective solidarity or on intentional or conventional modes of relating, but on the objective systemic effects of the production and exchange of value-bearing commodities operating beyond the conscious intentions of historical actors.[83] For Smith, however, modern "commercial" or "civilized society" was a direct outcome of an immutable human nature that included the "propensity to truck, barter, and exchange one thing for another" as a means to maximize individual utility.[84] As such, he could have no real conception of the historicity of human subject constitution.

It was Marx who would transform the Smithian account of the relationship between individual subjectivity and social-structural objectivity in his radical critique of the transhistorical assumptions of political economy. Marx's category of value must be understood, not as a category of primitive premarginalist economics, but rather as a way of grasping determinate forms of social interdependence that marginalist economics has simply taken for granted. To the extent that the production process is subsumed to the reproduction of capital, individuals in capitalist society must correlatively produce for others as a means to provide for their own concrete needs; which is to say, following Smith, that they use labor primarily as a means to acquire the products and services of others, paradigmatically through the medium of the wage, the sale of labor to capital. One peculiarity of this social system is that human beings are thereby bound to one another most fundamentally through the (essentially anonymous) exchange of labor rather than by concrete institutional or sentimental bonds. But Marx further complicated this Smithian insight by arguing that what regulates these exchanges is the

[margin note: Culture concept must be grounded in structures of practice that are socially general]

peculiar mode that characterizes wealth when it has been subsumed to the reproductive cycle of capital, rather than the concrete need of individuals. Wealth in capitalist society assumes the form of value, a measure that is quantitatively determined in terms of a homogeneous substance, abstract human labor. Abstract labor represents the average amount of socially necessary labor time required for the production of a given quantity of that commodity. It thus determines the relative exchange value of qualitatively different products of human labor in terms of the relative amount of socially necessary labor time they represent.

Every act of commodity exchange in capitalist society practically presumes that all particular labor is really but a moment of the total labor of society, and the exchange value of the product measures the share of its contribution by implicit reference to the expenditure of a peculiarly homogeneous form of activity, abstract labor. In capitalist society, each occasion for the exchange of labor is always mediated by reference to the total reproduction of society. For Marx, the peculiarity of capitalist society is that the relationships that bind human beings to one another are at once radically impersonal (in the sense that one depends on the labor of a myriad of people one will never meet, a dependence that takes on the quasi-objective form of abstract functions like the market), and at the same time are always mediated by the totality of social labor (which determines the exchange value of a given commodity).[85] The real mediation that structures the objective interdependence among individuals in capitalist society is thus most fundamentally labor itself. For while labor necessarily continues to function as a means of appropriating nature to human ends (qualitatively distinct forms of concrete practical activity that produce qualitatively distinct use values), as the concrete incarnation of abstract activity it is indifferent to the qualitative distinction of the product and the activity that produces it. Rather, labor under capital produces a substance that can be grasped in terms of proportionate measures (one pen costs the same as, say, one hundred paper clips), and which thus serves as the medium of social exchange in the manifest form of money, the universal equivalent. The laborer works specifically in order to receive the means of purchasing commodities in general (again, money), and not to receive a qualitatively distinct set of use values. This argument in turn depends on an analysis of capital as self-positing and self-expanding value—that is to say, an accumulation of value (abstract labor time) that is forwarded as an investment into the production process with a view to the recovery of a larger quantity of value at the end of the cycle (M [money]-C [commodity]-M′ [more money] [M-C-M′]), the additional value thereby produced being termed *surplus value*. In this process, the concrete particularity of the actual commodity being produced is subordinated as a mere means to the further accumulation of the abstract substance, value. This is what Marx meant when he suggested that the peculiarity of capitalist society was fundamentally that human beings come to be dominated by the product of their own labor as an alien power. The "product" at stake here is not hammers or paper clips, but "value," the constitutive substance of capital.

While abstract labor mediates social relations, the relationship between individuals in the sphere of circulation where commodities are exchanged is one that takes the apparent form of "a social relation between the products of labour," that is, in the relative exchange values of those products. As such, the commodity form "reflects the social relation of the producers to the sum total of labour as ... a relation which exists apart from and outside the producers."[86] The socially mediating function of labor, in other words, does not appear transparently as labor, but rather assumes a form of appearance that cloaks the real nature of social interdependence behind the appearance of an objective value property (the commodity's "price"[87]) that regulates the exchange of the products of labor. Exchange relations between individuals are always mediated by abstract labor, that is to say, by the totality of value-producing labor (and so, Marx goes on to show, will their productive activities increasingly be too, the more they are geared to the production of value). This regulative, mediating function of labor thus appears to stand outside of the individuals who exchange their product as a form of objective necessity (concepts like "the economy," "the market," and "society" all seek to grasp this condition).

This in turn establishes an antinomy between individuals (who are free to seek their own interests through acts of commodity exchange) and society (which confronts the individual as something separate and alien). Yet abstract labor is itself continuously reconstituted by the generalized practice of exchanging quantities of labor that necessarily take concrete, qualitatively distinct forms. Juxtaposed to the atomized individuals who appear to stand disembedded from external social determinations is the homogeneous substance, value (abstract labor time), by which their relationships with one another are at the most fundamental level abstractly mediated, and yet which their own laboring activities collectively (re)constitute as an alien, objective power. In a society organized on the basis of the production and exchange of commodities, then, the individual subject can assume two very broad but quite distinct ways of construing the significance of practical activity, one that I will call *liberal*, and the other that I will call *culturalist*.

In the case of liberalism, practical activity is paradigmatically understood to be an instrument to the pursuit of the private interests of individuals in civil society—and society emerges either as a contractual or associational correlate of free exchange in the sphere of circulation; as the agent of forms of regulation, coercion, or restriction of individual action; or as the realm of objective necessity expressed in the form of exchange value. In the case of culturalism, practical activity constitutes the very substance of the social whole; the subject of practical activity who transforms nature to social ends (creates use values) achieves emancipation from natural determinations; and it is in the concrete forms of that nature-appropriating activity that the individual achieves a higher subjective unity with the social totality (abstract labor). Liberalism does not intrinsically confront culturalism as bourgeois to proletarian or as capitalist market to socialist planned economy; on the contrary, insofar as both of these conceptions of subjective autonomy proceed from the historically specific structures of capitalist society, they must both be understood in terms of an antinomy internal to the logic of capitalist social forms.

Capitalism in a Peasant Society

Approaching Marx in these terms opens up new ways of grasping the salience of the categories of his analysis of capitalist society to an ostensibly underdeveloped economy like colonial Bengal's. It has never been difficult to understand how Bengal's bhadralok were inhabitants of a modern capitalist society. While great families like the Tagores had built their wealth out of the social upheavals of the eighteenth and early nineteenth centuries, even those in the educated middle class who received some income from intermediate tenures in the rural land hierarchy (revenue streams that would be more and more constricted from the 1860s in any case[88]) were overwhelmingly dependent on salaried employment for their survival. "Your primary duty is to keep your job," Bankimchandra Chatterjee warned his nephew. "Otherwise there will be nothing to eat."[89] But most historiography follows the self-understanding of this educated middle class in seeing their existence in colonial civil society as an externally imposed surface phenomenon overlaying an agrarian society that remained resistant to capitalist transformation. And while there is an important element of truth to the notion that the social structure of agrarian Bengal resisted capitalist transformation (if by *capitalist transformation* one specifically means industrialization), foundational to the argument of this book is that the structures of social interdependence in Bengali society as a whole, not just the *babu* classes, were increasingly mediated by the structural logic of capital in the nineteenth and twentieth centuries. The issue is not whether Bengal industrialized, or to what extent market functions came to operate unconstrainedly in the rural economy. I will argue that rural Bengal's connection with the structures of capitalist society was intrinsic to the forms of its social organization rather than being externally constituted through a colonial superimposition or through the articulation of discrete modes of production. It is on this rejection of any kind of semifeudalism thesis about Bengali society that my Marxian reading of the intellectual history of colonial Bengal turns. To make this claim is not to suggest, however, that smallholding peasant agriculture is an organic form of capitalist production in the same way that, say, proletarian industrial labor is. It is rather to say that, while peasant family labor is certainly a productive institution that long precedes capitalism's penetration of the subcontinent, the endurance of its concrete forms cloaks the transformation of its significance and function in the larger context of capitalist integration.

Marx is infamous for (among many other sins) having argued that the global expansion of capital was posited by its own immanent logic and accordingly tended to "drive beyond national barriers and prejudices as much as beyond nature-worship, as well as all traditional, confined, complacent, encrusted satisfactions of present needs, and reproduction of old ways of life. It is destructive towards all of this, and constantly revolutionizes it." Yet Marx warned against viewing the expansion of the world market as producing any simple homogenizing effect: "from the fact that capital posits every such [particularistic] limit as a barrier and hence gets *ideally* beyond it, it does not by any means follow that it has *really* overcome it, and, since every such barrier contradicts its character, its production moves in contradictions which are constantly overcome but just as constantly posited."[90] One might well, in the terms of Marx's own argument, question the conventional assumption that the expansion of a global system of circulation and production can only result in a direct struggle between universalistic capital and local particularity, between the systemic logic of Western capitalist society and the fragile lifeworlds of non-Western cultures. First, even if capital does confront particularistic "barriers" of custom and convention as externally posited impediments, the continued existence of "old ways of life" is still fundamentally transformed by the sheer fact of their being embedded within the new social context of a capitalist social formation—and thus of their being rearticulated as barriers to capital's social process rather than as the constitutive fabric per se of a premodern social formation. But we can go fur-

[margin note, handwritten:] Bengal's connection to capitalism was intrinsic to its social organization

ther than this by recognizing that revolutionizing old ways of life might also mean their "destruction" in the same way that the *"historic presuppositions"* of capital (among which Marx explicitly included money, commodities, and capital accumulation) "disappear as real capital arises"—which is as much as to say, "disappear" as independent forms by being subsumed into a social formation that "posits the conditions for its [own] realization" and thus reconstitutes these preexisting forms as moments of its own reproduction.[91] Overcoming "old ways of life" might just as easily be understood to include the reconstitution of what were once "mere *local developments,*" as "barriers" that instead become the "creation of capital itself."[92] What this argument amounts to is the recognition that, operating within the constraints posed by preexisting political, social, and cultural arrangements, capital takes hold of existing forms of the organization of production (notably in Bengal, small-holding peasant agriculture) and transforms them into vehicles for the production of surplus value without necessarily abolishing the concrete forms themselves—a process that, as Jairus Banaji has pointed out, was grasped by Marx in terms of "the formal subsumption of labor to capital."[93]

It is a too-often-forgotten fact that Bengal was of interest to the East India Company in the seventeenth and eighteenth centuries not for the legendary natural bounty of the Gangetic delta, but rather as one of the most significant centers of textile manufacturing in the world. The Company and its servants would become increasingly engaged in taking control of weavers' labor in the *arangs* (manufacturing centers) clustered along the shores of the river systems of lower Bengal. But a combination of supply bottlenecks, the Company's need to keep wages low in an era of relative labor shortage, and, after its assumption of direct political control, the Company's increasing emphasis on agriculture as a source of desperately needed revenue to fund its promises of booty to the metropole and also its expanding military operations in the subcontinent would see the marginalization of this manufacturing industry by the early nineteenth century.[94] As a result of larger processes of deindustrialization and peasantization through the later eighteenth century and first half of the nineteenth century, what developed in place of Bengal's failing textile industries was a regressive form of rural social order in which the extraction of surplus took often-brutal forms that failed to encourage the productivity gains that had driven the Company to grant zamindars a private-property right in their estates in the late eighteenth century.[95]

But as Rajat Datta has argued, "while the early eighteenth century textile-based commerce set the tone of a long-wave of commercialization, it was the late eighteenth century which provided the distinctive departure by

[margin handwritten note: Bengal important as a textile manufacturing center]

bringing about the commercialization of the province's *rice producing economy and of the social relations which were embedded in it*"—transformations indexed by the rapid proliferation of sharecropping peasantry and the increasing intervention of the grain merchant in agricultural production.[96] By the end of the eighteenth century, Datta persuasively shows, Bengal already had a highly monetized and integrated regional market in agricultural commodities grounded in the exploitation of the labor of cultivators with insufficient land for reliable subsistence, especially in an era of recurrent famine. With the land:labor ratio gradually shifting to the former's favor, and with zamindars armed with greater legal powers over their tenants as well as the legal right to unlimited rent enhancement, intensification of rent demands in the first half of the nineteenth century spurred on the dependence of cultivators on some combination of credit, seasonal wage labor and commercial crops.[97] If Bengal's peasantry were "subsistence farmers," it was certainly not in the sense that they were growing their own subsistence as autarchic producers. "The majority of peasants," Rajat Ray writes of later nineteenth-century rural Bengal, "lived at the subsistence level because their surplus produce was alienated in the form of taxes for the government, rent for the landlords, interest for the moneylenders and, less obviously, low purchasing prices obtained by the peasants from [monopsonistic] traders who bought their produce at less than market value."[98]

The reproduction of peasant households relied ever more deeply on forms of commodity exchange.[99] We can see this firstly and most generally in the form of rent: whether mediated by money (cash-rent) or by the direct appropriation of a portion of the crop (sharecropping), economic rents ultimately represented an exchange of agricultural labor for access to privately controlled land. Second, where cultivators lacked sufficient land to provide for their subsistence, they regularly sold their labor for cash to supplement their income. This often took the overt form of seasonal wage labor on other people's land; but, as we shall see below, it could also assume the covert form of paying interest on credit advanced as productive capital. Third, the cash to cover both the interest on advances and the cash-rents that British policy consolidated as a newly inflexible and uncompromising foundation of the revenue system in the later eighteenth century was itself generated through an increasing reliance on a general extension of commodity production premised on the extension and integration of regional and international markets: the selling of cash crops and the purchase of food, cloth, seed, and other goods. Eastern India's agrarian sector was already in the 1820s implicated deeply enough in global structures of commodity exchange to be vulnerable to metropolitan economic crises, "prospering or decaying according to fluctuations in the London market."[100] As Sugata Bose has underscored, any form of "'dualism' which views western capitalism as an alien enclave in a traditional economy" can only serve to "obscure the keen sensitivity of Bengal's regional economy to external fluctuations."[101]

Before 1860, aside from the trade in food grains, indigo stood out as the most important commercial crop produced by smallholders, mostly in central and western Bengal.[102] Indigo planters generally preferred to have smallholding peasants grow the crop on their own tenurial holdings rather than hiring labor to cultivate lands under their direct possessory dominion. This evasion of a direct wage relation had the advantage of forcing peasants to deploy unpaid family labor to meet the demands of their indigo contracts.[103] Indigo may possibly have initially appealed to cultivators as a convenient way to get their hands on the cash they increasingly needed to survive, but from around 1825 (when previously soaring indigo prices began to fall) indigo was consistently unremunerative for those who actually grew it. It continued to be grown largely as a result of two forms of coercion practiced by the European planters who ran the industry: firstly, since colonial law increasingly reduced cultivators to tenants-at-will, the threat of rent enhancement to which cultivators who held their tenures directly from the planters themselves (whether acting as zamindars or as intermediate tenure holders) were subject; and secondly, a system of advances that cultivators were often forced to accept, that reduced their recipient to "little better than a bond-slave to the factory" in a cycle of inescapable debt-bondage, that gave the planters a legally recognized interest in the plants grown therewith, and that legally obliged the cultivator to make payment in kind at the end of the season at risk of imprisonment.[104] Planters showed little enthusiasm about having cultivators pay off their debts or collecting on defaulted loans; what they wanted was to use debt as an instrument to keep cultivators growing indigo.

Indigo would be driven out of the Bengal countryside by the 1859–60 Blue Mutiny, a series of peasant protests (often backed by zamindars) fueled by the short supply of planter credit after 1848, and compounded by rising prices of commodities, wages, and rents running up against the planters' need to keep labor costs low.[105] After 1860, two major shifts would occur in the agrarian economy. Firstly, there would be a further surge in cash-crop agriculture in rural Bengal, especially in the central and eastern parts of the region. The leading crop was jute, the export volume of which jumped forty-fold between 1838 and 1843 and 1868 and 1873, and the export value of which increased fivefold in the 1860s alone.[106] The cultivators who rebelled against indigo in 1859–60 saw the crop, with its attendant structure of humiliation and violence, as an irremediable affront to their personal dignity.[107] Cash crops like jute, tobacco, and food grains, meanwhile, were cultivated freely by peasants who recognized in remunerative (if sometimes unstable) cash crops a new basis for securing subsistence from smallholdings. Already in 1857 the *Hindu Patriot* was complaining that the cultivation of jute, along with the extension of railways, had led to both a new prosperity among some of the cultivators and a new assertiveness more generally: "The ryot [cultivator] who only a few years ago could not find courage to talk to a well-dressed person except with downcast eyes and folded hands now knows the value of his position."[108] Jute became a cornerstone of the new assertiveness of cultivators who would contest zamindari dominion as free commodity producers. In the words of the Joint Magistrate of Barasat (not far from Calcutta) in 1856, rebellious cultivators would "not sow indigo for this very sound reason that they find tobacco and other crops far more profitable."[109]

Through a combination of *ryot* resistance and new legal restrictions on rent enhancement pushed through by a colonial state looking closer to the ground for new agents of capital accumulation and agricultural improvement to enhance dwindling revenues, the 1860s also saw the beginnings of the retreat of rent as the primary form of surplus appropriation.[110] The reinforcement of cultivators' tenurial rights went hand in hand with the extension of their participation in commercial cultivation: "If the land belonged to the Queen, and the *Sahib* had nothing to do with it, but dealt with us as a mere merchant and paid for the plant in cash right down, we should be satisfied," Santosh Mundal, a ryot who also dabbled in minor trade and money lending, declared to the Indigo Commission in 1860.[111] But while peasant production of cash crops was primarily undertaken by smallholding agriculturalists with stronger legal claims in a tenurial structure increasingly redefined out of the domain of supply and demand by new pro-ryot legislation, this should not be taken to mean that these cultivators straightforwardly constituted an "independent" peasantry.[112] The cultivators' widespread and longstanding reliance on credit for both production and consumption made them susceptible to mounting burdens of debt. Especially from the 1880s, an increasingly indebted peasantry was tied to the moneylender rather than the zamindar as the primary master of its product.[113] As one author put it in the *Calcutta Review* back in 1874, while the "social structure" of rural Bengal "for want of a better term must be called feudal," the "*motive power* by which it is kept working is the *mahajan,* or village capitalist. . . . whose sole object is to realize his money as advantageously as possible."[114]

It was arguably not until the 1930s that the drying up of credit would lead to the widespread dispossession of smallholding peasants and the formation of a large-scale rural proletariat of landless labor—the result not of an aggressive project of expropriation that would have risked dangerously destabilizing rural society, but rather of the collapse of credit mechanisms through which creditors had effectively preserved smallholding agriculture in order to extract surplus value from peasant labor.[115] But there is good reason to see the century and a half preceding the Great Depression as an era when Bengal's peasant labor was coming to be increasingly subject to the logic of capitalist society.

Firstly, and at the most obvious level, we can recognize that the production of cash crops like indigo and jute implicitly represented a form of production in which the producer was indifferent to the qualitative specificity of the product.

Secondly, as Jairus Banaji has argued in detail, money advanced or loaned to cultivators could represent an obscured form of "wage" under circumstances where the loan served to guarantee the capacity of the cultivator to continue producing their subsistence at the same time as returning a surplus in the form of interest. In the case of the rice market in the late eighteenth century, cultivators were already dependent on both production and consumption loans from merchants (*byapari*) who thereby increasingly extended their control into the very heart of agricultural production.[116] As the peasants of Burdwan frankly explained: "it is only because of the merchants that we have the means of purchasing our subsistence and preserving our lives."[117] In the case of indigo in the first half of the nineteenth century, whether or not cultivators initially turned to the crop for reasons of their own convenience, the cultivation of the crop was certainly coerced on a widespread basis. But its underlying "wage-labor" character can nonetheless be glimpsed in laws that not only prescribed imprisonment for peasants who were unable or unwilling to fulfill their "contracts," but actually recognized the planters' "lien or interest" in plants tended by peasants who had received advances.[118] The cultivators were thus already positioned de facto as wage laborers producing surplus value out of the capital of the planters. Advances functioned as wages foisted upon the cultivator through either force of necessity (want of cash) or direct coercion (the threat of dispossession through rent enhancement or naked violence), and forcibly depressed to such a low level as to ensure that the product so secured would return surplus value. In the case of cash crops after 1860, what began as a form of relatively independent production for the market by a smallholding peasantry drawing on moneylender capital rapidly became for more and more cultivators a means to maintain interest payments on mounting debts. A deepening dependence on credit represented the mediation of peasant subsistence by capital. Here again, the credit received from moneylenders served the function of a wage (the means to subsistence), and the interest paid to the moneylender served as a form of surplus value. As Banaji has argued, insofar as the structure is M-C-M', what takes the outward form of interest is better understood as surplus value generated through exploitation of productive activity.[119] In this case, peasant subsistence can only be secured through the sale of labor to capital, even if that sale does not take the overt form of a labor contract on the model of classic proletarianization. The development of commodity exchange in Bengali rural society had been inseparable since the later eighteenth century from the extension of the dependence of producers on capital for the reproduction of their subsistence.

Thirdly, as Sugata Bose has compellingly argued, peasants' cultivation of cash crops for the world market "rested heavily on the forcing up of labour intensity within family units actually tilling the land," turning especially on the intensification of labor by women and children. Where women did broadly participate in hired labor to subsidize household income (notably in the poorer, drier districts of western Bengal), their contributions tended to be systematically devalued because of the seasonal and sporadic nature of their employment, the displacement of many of their traditional occupations by cheaper imported manufactures, and their tendency to enter the market only under conditions of duress when the demand for labor was at its lowest.[120] But in Dinajpur in northern Bengal (where sharecropping families produced cash crops under the explicit direction of rich farmers, or *jotedars,* who had possessory dominion of the land and controlled both the credit and product markets[121]), it was reported in 1888 that "females do not work for their livelihood, but for their own household and cultivation work"; and even among agricultural laborers women "are not allowed to work for hire."[122] In the fertile eastern districts of Bengal, the heartland of small-holding cash-crop agriculture, however, women appeared to constitute the smallest percentage of the agricultural workforce.[123] Whereas women were in reality heavily involved in agricultural production (weeding, transplanting and husking rice, stripping jute, picking cotton), they appeared as a "very low proportion of the agricultural workforce of Bengal . . . because unpaid labour, which formed the bulk of women's contribution to production, was by and large left out of account" in colonial censuses and surveys.[124] With the rise of smallholding cash-crop agriculture from the 1860s, the increasing reliance on unpaid family labor led to "less easily fathomable but highly significant" transformations in the organization of rural society—albeit along lines of gender and generation rather than class.[125] Although this intensification was clearly driven by the exigencies of a process of commodification (labor-intensive cash-crop cultivation), the labor of women and children was blocked from commodification because, although it certainly entered into the production process as productive labor, it at no point appeared as part of the ultimate exchange relation. That is to say, to the degree that they were integrated into the smallholding system of household-based commodity production, women and children did not sell their labor in the way that the male peasant householder (implicitly) did. The marginalization of women within commodified productive labor increasingly consigned women to the apparently noneconomic role of household reproduction rather than economic production; and it arguably became a constitutive factor in the constitution of ideologies of domesticity in the nineteenth and twentieth centuries by reinforcing the disassociation of women and productive labor that would underpin the social prestige associated with female seclusion (*purdah*).[126] But perhaps more importantly for the argument of this book, the centrality of the peasant household to commodity production opens up two quite different (but insufficient) ways of conceiving rural Bengali society: on the one hand, as a society of (male) individuals engaged in exchange; and on the other hand, as the social space that lay below the surface of a superimposed domain of exchange, and hence as a productive organism where activity was organized on principles that had little or nothing to do with the sphere of circulation. We shall see both these social imaginations at work in the chapters that follow.

Smallholding family-based peasant cultivation may have endured as the dominant form of production, but we must not therefore be blind to the deeper changes at work beneath the surface of this apparent continuity. The peasant household becomes not a location external to capitalist society, but rather a moment in its reproduction. Obviously, the actual organization of production remained external to the logic of capital in the sense that the kinds of familial institutions around which production was structured were drawn from precapitalist repertoires of practice. As instances of formally subsumed labor, capitalist abstraction does not enter overtly into the production process (as it does, say, on the factory floor). Yet the household was also being restructured precisely because of its deepening implication in capitalist social relations. The ostensible failure of India to complete a transition to capitalism does not imply the persistence of the premodern past alongside the functions of the market. Rather, it marks the development of a specific social configuration in which the predominance of a smallholding peasantry prevents the dynamic of relative surplus value (surplus value gained through revolutionizing production processes) from taking hold and restricts capital to the exploitation of peasant family labor for the production of absolute surplus value (surplus value gained through the prolongation and intensification of labor). In this argument, the very backwardness of India's smallholding economy is grasped intrinsically as a moment of capitalist social relations. Capitalism in Bengal did not sit atop noncapitalist cultivation like a lid on a jar; it mediated social relations within agrarian society at a profound level.

Beyond Marxist Culturalism

Marx argued that the practices of commodity production and exchange constituted and reconstituted simultaneously the abstract social forces within which concrete human lifeworlds were historically situated, and the subjective dispositions and potentialities of the individuals who inhabited those abstractly mediated lifeworlds, transforming the relationship of human beings not only to nature but also to one another and to themselves. "Consciousness can never be anything other than conscious existence, and the existence of men is their actual life-process."[127] Subjects, in other words, are the agents of action but are also constituted by their actions; and through their actions they in turn reconstitute social structures that constrain the repertoire of actions that they can then undertake. Consequently, the formation of subjectivities necessarily varies with the different repertoires of practice characteristic of the different sociohistorical contexts in which they are formed. The commodity form thus comes in the modern world to mediate both objective circumstances (which constrain the range of possible actions available to individuals) and subjective propensity (the ways in which individuals construe and value aspects of their environment and themselves, and form projects on this basis)—as well as serving to constitute the radical phenomenological disjuncture that, as Williams recognized, experientially appears to separate conflicting subjective and objective domains from each other. Furthermore, since what we are talking about here are practices that serve to mediate relationships among individuals, between individuals and institutions, among institutions, and between individual or institutional agents and nature, the commodity form may be said to perform this constitutive role across the boundaries that differentiate concrete lifeworlds. The concrete institutions and practices of some particular corner of the world will certainly be transformed by their insertion into capitalist society, but, as we have seen in the case of peasant agriculture in Bengal, that by no means implies that they will be straightforwardly erased or homogenized to conform to a Western model.

This book sets out to reground postcolonial critique within the Marxian tradition by demonstrating the power of Marx's categories for the historical interpretation of the culture concept's emergent intelligibility and compelling plausibility in the modern world as much as in modern Bengal more specifically. The constitution of the concept as a category of practice demands that we fundamentally disrupt the insulated temporality of the history of subjectivity that the category of culture has historically served to help constitute. This is not to reduce the culture concept to the epiphenomenal condition of superstructure, because the structure of subjectivity that culture names is a real moment of social reproduction that, insofar as it is brought into conflict with external constraints, can have consequential, and potentially transformative, effects.[128] It is rather to posit practical activity as the constitutive groundwork of both *objectivity* and *subjectivity*, and to recognize that each of these terms is therefore necessarily and irreducibly mediated by the other. We will then have to grasp the implicit claim to subjective underdetermination that the culture concept encodes in terms other than the self-positing subjective freedom that culturalism articulates.

"The separation of subject and object is both real and illusory," Theodor Adorno argued in a brilliant Marxian reformulation of the Hegelian critique of Kantian subjectivism. "True, because in the cognitive realm it serves to express the real separation, the dichotomy of the human condition, a coercive development." In other words, there is a real separation of subject and object constitutive of a "human condition"—albeit a "human condition" whose historically determinate existence as an aspect of capitalist modernity is already marked here by its identification as a "coercive development." Thus, it follows that the dichotomy is also false, "because the resulting separation must not be hypostatized, not magically transformed into an invariant." Real, but not transhistorically true, the falsity of the dichotomy lies not in the possibility of subject and object being "thought away" in the name of some underlying identity between them, but rather in the fact of "their being mutually mediated—the object by the subject, and even more, in different ways, the subject by the object." Both the truth and falsity of the dichotomy are posited in the philosophical problematics of epistemology, wherein the separation is established "directly, without mediation"—as "a product of the wrong abstraction, already a piece of reification." In other words, the epistemological problematic of how the subject can know the object takes the radical antinomy of subjectivity and objectivity as ontologically given rather than socially formed. This hypostatization of subjectivity as a radically separate dimension of human existence makes possible the mind's "claim of independence" and, subsequently, "claim of dominance. Once radically parted from the object . . . the subject swallows the object, forgetting how much it is an object itself." To say that the dichotomy of subject and object is a "separation" rather than merely a distinction, Adorno insisted, was not to hearken back to a primal identity, but rather to show how the dichotomy assumed determinate forms under the influence of historically specific social mediations.[129]

To say that concepts, as the determinate thought forms of subjectivity, contain within themselves traces of the object to which they refer is not simply to return to an objectivistic understanding of concepts as positive referents. That would be to take for granted the very antinomy of subject and object that Adorno was critiquing. The object at stake here—the social itself—is of a very specific kind, being composed of the structured forms of relationship that connect subjects both to each other and to nature in historically determinate ways, and not of the pure exteriority of *res extensa*.[130] To the extent that concepts have as their object a social fact, and to the extent that the historical constitution of the specific mode of subjectivity that is capable of thinking a specific set of concepts is itself mediated by social determinations, such concepts must already contain within themselves a capacity to represent the object that enters into their own constitution. (This still leaves open the possibility, or even likelihood, of this representation being inadequate if this act of representation is grasped not reflexively as the result of practical mediation, but rather as a transparent moment of positive reference.)

Reinhart Koselleck has argued that there is a productive tension between the use of concept history as an index of social-historical changes (and hence in turn as a form of source criticism), and the recognition that concepts constitute an autonomous domain that defines the horizons of intelligible experience for historical actors through the condensation of historically accrued layers of meaning ("the contemporaneity of the noncontemporaneous"). It is in recognition of this latter dimension of the intertextual and semiotic trace that we might characterize the modern culture concept as possessing a multiform universality: a universality of meaning that is always qualified by the contextual contingency of sense. The argument of this book, however, is that the former, referential dimension—reconceived in terms of the constitution of concepts within mediating structures of practice—is the condition of possibility for the latter, hermeneutic dimension—their capacity to render historical experience intelligible to particular subjects. Only by maintaining this logical sequence in historical explanation can we understand the emergence of new, specifically modern concepts whose plausibility and power are at once real, persistent over time, globalizing in reach, and yet specifically modern.[131]

The theoretical approach of this book sets itself squarely in the non-economistic tradition of Hegelian Marxism, drawing particular inspiration from Lukács's extraordinary analysis (and appropriation) of the history of German classical idealism in *History and Class Consciousness*. It was Lukács who realized that the core of Marx's dialectical approach was Hegel's conception of the self-moving activity of spirit (as the practical mediation of subject and object), which was in reality the reflection in thought of the structured determinations of human activity in capitalist society.[132] For all its insights, however, a closer look at the foundations of this tradition shows that Lukács's critical theory ultimately stopped short of grasping the profound historicity of the culture concept because (perhaps ironically given its own self-conception) of its profound complicity with the subjectivism that the culture concept articulates. If I situate myself within the tradition of Western Marxism, it cannot be uncritically. The systematic critique of subjectivism that I have been outlining above necessitates a more circumspect relationship to the affirmation of the figure of "man" that both Hunter and Lloyd and Thomas have so acutely criticized in Williams's work. The humanistic referent of critical theory must be brought more firmly into the analysis of historical determinacy as an object of immanent critique (in other words, as grounded in the categories of capitalist society) rather than as an external standpoint from which a transcendental judgment can direct its critique of capitalist society. There can be no question of opposing the concrete figure of productive "man" to reified abstraction once it is recognized that the concrete figure of man is itself dialectically bound to the social abstraction that is its apparent antithesis in the complex condensation that is the commodity form.[133]

Lukács's central aim in "Reification and the Consciousness of the Proletariat," the centerpiece of *History and Class Consciousness*, was to establish the proletariat as the "identical subject-object" of history, the historical subject whose revolutionary praxis could overcome the irresolvable conceptual antinomies of reified consciousness by dissolving the contradiction in capitalist society between the mode of distribution (the market) and the forces of production (proletarian labor) that, he believed, gave rise to the determinate form of those antinomies in capitalist society.[134] Lukács's history of classical German philosophy in the second section of his essay served to illustrate how the fundamental contradiction of capitalist society—the contradiction between the qualitative specificity of use value and the commodity as a measure of uniform value, between the rationality of production and the irrationality of the market and private property, and ultimately between the proletariat and the bourgeoisie—had been posed in classical philosophy, at the level of pure thought, in terms of a *hiatus irrationalis* that separated content and form in the face of all attempts to resolve it in the name of the transcendental subject of knowledge. In Kant's first critique, for instance, the formal apparatus of phenomenal knowledge leaves an irresolvable, noumenal residue of pure, unknowable content. The impossibility of concrete knowledge in Kant's system is for Lukács a direct symptom of a form of consciousness organized around the formal equivalence established by the value form of the commodity, and the consequent erasure of the qualitative specificity of use value and the concrete human activity with which it is aligned. In struggling to resolve the form/content antinomy, the classical tradition of German philosophy had in effect set about thinking "the deepest and most fundamental problems of the development of bourgeois society through to the very end—on the plane of philosophy. It is able—in thought—to complete the evolution of class."[135]

The main current of philosophy has consistently proceeded from a formalist analysis, "acknowledg[ing] as given as necessary the results and achievements of the special sciences and assign[ing] to philosophy the task of exhibiting and justifying the grounds for regarding as valid the concepts so constructed."[136] That, however, leaves to one side a marginalized tradition of antiformalist philosophy that could "radically question the value of formal knowledge for a 'living life.'"[137] In this "irrationalist" tradition one finds what we might call the first (philosophical) conception of the proletariat. Jean-Jacques Rousseau had argued "that social institutions (reification) strip man of his human essence and that the more culture and civilization (i.e. capitalism and reification) take possession of him, the less able is he to be a human being."[138] This in turn pointed the way forward to a new argument, elaborated by Friedrich Schiller, which linked the original essence of humanity to its recuperation through the cultivation of the inner person. "'Nature' here refers to authentic humanity, the true essence of man liberated from the false, mechanising forms of society: man as a perfected whole who has inwardly overcome, or is in the process of overcoming, the dichotomies of theory and practice, reason and the senses, form and content; man whose tendency to create his own forms does not imply an abstract rationalism which ignores concrete content; man for whom freedom and necessity are identical."[139] Thus Schiller's emphasis on individual aesthetic cultivation becomes a crucial anticipation of Hegel's higher resolution, at the level of the social, of the antinomies of bourgeois thought: *"man having been socially destroyed, fragmented and divided between different partial systems is to be made whole again in thought."*[140] Whereas culture (as a synonym of civilization) appears initially in Lukács's discussion of Rousseau as part of capitalist civilization (as part of what takes away from humanity), it reemerges immediately thereafter in his discussion of Schiller as "cultivation," that which restores the humanity that has been lost. The philosophical figure of "man" at the heart of Schiller's cultural ideal is thus the idealist double of the sociological figure of the proletariat. From Lukács's standpoint, what "culture" does individually in Schiller, the proletarian revolution does socially in Marx: restore the wholeness and autonomy of the human subject. That Lukács's understanding of the proletariat as identical subject-object remains grounded fundamentally in an ontology of "man" is clear from his own reiteration of Rousseau's and Schiller's narratives of lost and fractured human essence, both in this essay and even more explicitly in his essays on Goethe.[141] In what amounts to an implicit conceptual recapitulation of his own biographical trajectory from idealism to Marxism, it is not Schiller's conception of man that he challenges, but rather the idealist confinement of human realization to a socially residual realm of thought, play, and art.[142]

Following Lukács then, one could reformulate the relationship between philosophical man and the proletariat to say that the critique of reification becomes the critique of the historically specific relations of production under capitalism (the market and private property) from the standpoint of the transcendental humanity posited by the discourse of culture—a humanity that is in turn most adequately realized historically by the practical activity of the proletariat (labor). Lukács was superimposing a critique of capitalism from the standpoint of culture (humanity) onto the critique of capitalism from the standpoint of labor. The historicity of the culture concept was understood to lie only in the way it divorced its referential domain from the wider realm of social determinations, not in its role in constituting the category of humanity itself. The structure of Lukács's analysis of capitalist society led him to the implicit reinscription of culture as a metaphysical ideal. Culture might seem to be the idealist antithesis of Marxist materialism; but it might well be better understood as its philosophical double.[143]

This identification of the cultural subject with the productive powers of humanity provides us with the key insight into the social constitution of the modern concept of culture from which the analysis that follows will proceed: both culturalism and Marxism have proceeded from the standpoint of the laboring subject. Taking to heart Lukács's injunction that "it would be a mistake to think that these discussions [in classical philosophy] are no more than the problems of intellectuals and the squabbles of pedants," I shall argue in the chapters that follow that Bengali cultural discourse turned precisely on the rejection of the circulatory dimension of capitalist society from the standpoint of objectifying activity—even if it proved incapable of recognizing itself in these terms.[144] But this culturalist conflation of human autonomy with the productive dimension of capital (labor) produces only a partial critique of capitalist society. Lukács's turn to Marxism served primarily to clarify the idealist logic of cultural discourse by replicating it at the level of social analysis: elaborating a powerful critique of affirmative culture, but precisely in terms of its fragmentary and heteronomous constitution—which is as much as to say, from the standpoint of a more adequate conception of culture. A more thoroughgoing and radical critique than this culturalist critique of bourgeois culture would instead have to proceed from a deeper historicization of the concept of culture—not to simply negate the notion of autonomous subjectivity to which it aspires, but to interrogate the terms in which such freedom has been construed. This would require a reconstruction of Marxian theory of the kind Moishe Postone has called for in his major theoretical intervention, *Time, Labor, and Social Domination;* one that, rather than proceeding from a juxtaposition of reification (exchange, distribution, the market) and truth (the labor theory of value, the proletariat, productive humanity), instead conceives of both terms of this antinomy as practical dimensions of capitalist society.[145] Totality ceases to be the standpoint for the critique of the fragmentation of man in capitalist society, as it was for Lukács, and becomes instead the object of a critique of the domination of human social life by capital. This historicizing move does not primarily engage the philosophical question of whether human beings always make themselves through forms of practice. It leads rather to a more contained theoretical claim: there is something peculiarly modern about the notion that such self-constituting practice should lead to the autonomous human subjectivity that culture names. Through the narrative of Bengali intellectual history I offer in the subsequent chapters, I draw on the insight the Lukácsian tradition provides through its explicit conflation of productive activity with transcendental rationality, to account for the modernity of cultural conceptions of human autonomy.

The remarkably consistent tendency of the concept to global dissemination over the past two and one-half centuries seems in itself to militate against an account that depends solely on the specificity of contingent historical conjunctures. An emphasis on structural continuity over contingency and heterogeneity, and conceptual content over discursive effectivity, flies in the face of the conventional disaggregative wisdom of contemporary intellectual history, whether of the Foucauldian or Skinnerian varieties. Yet the approach I am suggesting here does not necessarily have to abandon the considerable insights of this literature in the dubious cause of flattening the historical process of the globalization of the concept into a homogeneous monocausality; it allows for the possibility that culture arrived in specific locations embedded in specific discursive frameworks, serving potentially quite different concrete functions in the hands of quite different historical agents intervening in quite different historical contexts and conceptualizing the appropriate agent of subjective autonomy in quite different ways. Nonetheless, I submit that there seems to be a deep coherence to the history of the culture concept, and recognizing this could form the starting point for further historical investigation into its global dissemination and circulation. Such an investigation could do worse than to broadly follow Williams in proceeding from a question quite different from the kind normally asked in the history of ideas: Under what circumstances has the problematic of subjective autonomy come to assume such global resonance in the modern age? If the culture concept has indeed consistently articulated a claim about the underdetermination of human subjectivity, its movement might well track the dissemination of a more fundamental problematic: the definitively "modern" problematic of subjective autonomy. It is the historical conditions for the global emergence of this problematic, rather than the history of ideas or of the transfer of discursive/institutional apparatus from metropole to periphery, which should form the basic material for a truly global history of the culture concept.

———— ✳ ————

CHAPTER THREE

Bengali Liberalism and British Empire

WHEN WE look at the first half-century of the Bengal Renaissance, we see a form of liberalism setting the agenda of public discourse rather than the culturalism with which Bengal is so deeply associated. Conservative voices in this era elaborated no philosophical standpoint beyond that of the authority of custom and maintenance of ritual purity—though they would establish many of the concrete themes that would later be transfigured by the adoption of the culture concept from the 1880s. Bengali culturalism emerged as an ideological formation, I shall contend, from a crisis in the plausibility and coherence of nineteenth-century classical liberalism. To understand its emergence, which marked a significant discontinuity in the conventional narrative of national awakening, will require two preparatory exercises: a historically situated analysis of the reformist ideological formation that developed in the first half of the nineteenth century, and an examination of the sociohistorical conditions and determinate form of its subsequent descent into crisis in the second half of the nineteenth century. Only thus can we arrive at an understanding of the ideological space from which the new culturalism would emerge.

We need to begin, however, by acknowledging that colonial India's so-called Age of Reform in the 1830s and 1840s has been through something of a tough time in recent historiography. The attempts of William Bentinck and Lord Thomas Macaulay to transform India through the enlightening touch of Western civilization have begun to look rather marginal to the overall political and social dynamics of the early nineteenth century. Looking at the subcontinent as a whole, the entire period from at least the late 1820s until the early 1850s would seem to represent a period of peasantization, the destruction of indigenous manufacturing industries, inland de-urbanization, and the reinforcement of neotraditional tendencies in social and religious institutions, driven by the combination of an extended period of economic stagnation and the choking grip of a military-fiscal Company state that was dominated by a senior cadre drawn overwhelmingly from the army, and whose extensive military campaigning led to enormous revenue demands. It was not until Lord James Dalhousie's governor-generalship in the latter half of the 1840s—when the old guard had mostly been replaced by a new generation of British-trained civil servants, new technologies had brought India into closer communicational and infrastructural proximity to Britain, and the economy began to recover as new investment flowed into production and new markets opened up for India's primary products—that Westernizing reformism was able to gain any real purchase. And even this brief window was soon slammed shut by the cataclysmic eruption of the Indian Mutiny that it was in part responsible for provoking.[1]

Although Bengal's Permanent Settlement cushioned it from the impact of some of the more extreme dimensions of the Company state's military fiscalism, it cannot on the whole be said that the Bengal Renaissance has fared much better historiographically than the Age of Reform. The conventional narrative of national awakening from mediaeval slumber, thanks to the individual courage of succeeding generations of brilliant men, has given way to a sense of the superficiality and fragility of an isolated elite movement uninterested in broad-based mobilization and continually backsliding away from its professed radicalism. The best-known American historian of the Renaissance was happy to admit that, "so long as the fundamental material aspects of modernization [referring to industrialization, democratization, and universal education] were arrested in their own country, the corresponding reformation of Hinduism was bound to be limited because only a comparative handful could be educated as moderns."[2] Meanwhile, in India, Barun De, Sumit Sarkar, and Asok Sen were developing a more radical and more rigorous formulation of much the same point: The "so-called Bengal Renaissance" was a story of failure—not because of character defects in its leaders, but because the great principles of modern political and social consciousness that its spokesmen had learned from the West had no ground in which to plant themselves in a colonial context of stunted development. The historical analogy behind the term *Renaissance* implied a transition to bourgeois capitalist modernity that never successfully occurred in India, where colonial exploitation had produced deindustrialization, a service class without any dynamic role in production, and the reinforcement of neofeudal hierarchies rather than a vibrant civil society and industrialization.[3]

If Bengal had failed to make the transition from feudalism to capitalism, what motivated the modernism of a Rammohun Roy? In other words, when Rammohun sat down to think about the world around him, what allowed him to find in individuality, freedom, equality, utility, and property appropriate categories with which to make ethical, political, economic, and, in a word, social meaning out of that context? What made a social critique of this peculiarly abstract and universalistic kind possible in this particular historical context? In the particular Marxist framework of De, Sarkar, and Sen, the question was in a sense forestalled by their shared ethical and political commitment to the transcendent validity of all but one of these categories. After all, their criticism was not the postcolonial objection that Bengalis had accepted the normative force of enlightenment, but rather the "enlightenment" objection that Bengalis had in reality failed to awaken from their slumber. But once the question of the foundations of Rammohun's modernism had been opened up, it was hardly surprising, in the absence of a Marxist theory that did not turn on the application of the transition narrative of Europe's passage from feudalism to capitalism as a normative model, that increasing weight would be put on the efficacy of colonial pedagogy, and symbolic violence more generally, to fill the interpretive gap. In other words, if the modular forms of modernity were the arbitrary artifacts of a peculiarly European history, then colonial modernism would correlatively have to be seen as the outcome of interpellative practices that imposed the curious particularities of Western civilizational history on a generation of privileged Bengalis.[4] As Anthony Pagden has so baldly epitomized this approach: "the modern heirs of Alexander tend to assume that a rule of law that respects individual rights and liberal democratic government (as practiced in the United States) is a universal, and not, as it most surely is, the creation of Greco-Roman Christendom."[5]

The irony here is that the critique of modernizing universalism is predicated on an ethical language of self-determination built into both the explicit agenda of postcolonial criticism and the concept of culture on which it so fundamentally turns. But even beyond this basic philosophical problem, there remains a historical one: leaving aside for a moment the most obvious objection that Rammohun's generation were the founders of colonial pedagogy rather than its beneficiaries, if we accept this resort to symbolic violence to explain colonial modernism, it becomes frankly rather difficult to understand the enthusiasm with which the subsequent generation of Young Bengal—those most often dismissed even in their own time as the dummies of a colonial ventriloquism, despite being educated at a school founded by prominent Bengalis (both modernist and conservative) and inspired most profoundly by a Eurasian teacher who proudly identified himself as "East Indian"[6]—outstripped the comfort zone not just of conservative society but also of many colonial Whigs with the radicalism of their free thinking.

Both Rammohun and the Young Bengal movement were indeed delving into and drawing from the literatures of modern Europe; but that tells us little about the nature of Bengali modernism. Surely, to begin with, we can be more specific as to the ideological formation of this first half-century of the Renaissance: it was not just European modernity from which they were drawing inspiration, but Western liberalism. Such a specification, which I hope will become clearer in the following section, in turn leads us to two further fundamental questions: Firstly, whence came the enthusiasm for this specific strand of European political ideology—a strand at best ambiguously articulated in the Company's (monopolistic) political-economic agenda, and far from being coextensive with the full spectrum of modern British (let alone Western) ideological imaginations? And secondly, how did they find an object for their discourse if their liberalism was so utterly disjunctive from their social environment?

This returns us to the older Marxist problematic with which we began. But De, Sarkar, and Sen posed the problem in terms of a distinctly totalistic national history: the question is *whether* India passed from feudalism to capitalism under colonial rule. Posed in these terms, the criteria for a transition to capitalism can only be modular: did India pass through the kind of transition that Western Europe passed through in its passage from feudalism to modernity? The answer, as their critique of the Renaissance analogue makes clear, is a resounding *no*—and it is surely hard to disagree with that. But what if, instead of asking *whether* or *when* India became a capitalist society, we reframe the question so as to ask *in what ways* the integration of India into global structures of capitalist social organization were directly or indirectly transforming Indian society? Without suggesting that that transformation was absolute, total, or immediate, it seems safe enough to suggest that both colonial Calcutta and parts of Lower Bengal were already undergoing significant social transformations under the impact firstly, in the later eighteenth century, of the commercialization of peasant agriculture under the impetus of indigenous capital; and secondly, in the eighteenth and early nineteenth centuries, of both the East India Company (in its multiple capacities as textile exporter, opium cultivator, revenue collector, and regional government) and a subsidiary commercial arena constituted by the local capital of independent European private traders, Company servants

[handwritten margin note: Bengal undergoing social transformation because of influence of capitalism (western)]

and Indian merchants investing most notably in land and indigo cultivation. As I have already argued in chapter 2, the default conception of a small elite of zamindars and traders skimming the surface of an intransigently particularistic indigenous social order is simply no longer tenable. There is too much evidence that commercialization and capital had reached deep into the fabric of eighteenth- and early nineteenth-century Bengali society, far into the up-country networks, subordinating and subsuming first Bengal's textile manufacturing sector and later its agricultural sector—and that the traditional peasant society that nineteenth-century India would become was, as D. A. Washbrook and C. A. Bayly argue, as much a consequence of deepening integration into Britain's global trading system as a residue of the precolonial, premodern past.

Hugh Urban's research into heterodox and esoteric religious traditions has thrown new light on the ways in which this commercial society impacted the life and thought of even those most socially distant from the British. The Kartabhajas, a Hindu religious sect that emerged at the turn of the nineteenth century from the impoverished underworld of Calcutta's Black Town, and the Sahebdhanis, a closely related offshoot in Nadia district (one of the centers of commercial indigo cultivation), elaborated an esoteric symbolism drawn from the world of commerce to express a Tantric socioreligious imaginary. The sects' songs announced the existence of a secret "marketplace of love" in which the just "merchants" (spiritual leaders), whose "new Company" (the Kartabhajas themselves) had arrived with fresh "merchandise" (spiritual truths), challenged the "old Company" (orthodox Gaudiya Vaishnavism) that had grown corrupt and had sunk into the more general "marketplace of material things."[7] Urban mainly sees in the extraordinary poems he has translated evidence of the vibrancy of indigenous religious tradition in the changing circumstances of colonial society; but these movements might be better understood as evidence of the degree to which the lower classes of both Calcutta and parts of its agrarian hinterland were being exposed to the effects of new commercial forces driven by the Company state, European private traders, and Indian mercantile and landed allies. Instead of showing how the Company, capital, market, commodities, and merchandise (used as metaphors variously for both worldly corruption and spiritual truth) rearticulated older Vaishnavite and Tantric doctrines, he arguably might have more productively explored how and why the doctrines of spiritual equality and universal humanity that the Kartabhajas and Sahebdhanis preached should have become susceptible to this very specific, and striking, reconceptualization through the language of commerce.

Certainly, the Kartabhajas and Sahebdhanis were not liberals in any meaningful sense. But the liberal Bengalis of the Calcutta elite in the 1820s, 1830s, and 1840s were nonetheless doing something strikingly analogous to these movements: using the logic of commercial society to articulate a political, social, religious, and ethical imagination. They were thereby participating in a much larger imperial formation that stretched westward all the way to the Americas—an ideological conception of the British Empire as the vehicle of a civilization whose liberality was closely tied to its commercial character.[8] Bengali liberals did not invoke commerce by means of esoteric analogies between spirituality and capital, or between a new dispensation and imported merchandise. Nevertheless, the deep connections between liberal ideology and commercial society expressed themselves just as strikingly, if more abstractly, in the practical referents of its foundational categories of civic equality, liberty under the law, reason and conscience, property and labor, individuality, and interest. Liberalism certainly did not have to await the emergence of a full-blown market society to find its voice. After all, liberal politics advocated as its central social, economic, and political program the extension of free exchange as a model of human interrelations at the expense of other dimensions of the existing forms of social organization; it did not merely celebrate an achieved universalization retrospectively. Nonetheless, the plausibility of liberal conceptions of individuality and society were historically predicated on the role of commodity exchange as the primary medium of social interdependence. In specifying the ideological impulse of this first phase of the Bengal Renaissance as liberal, I want to do more than merely indicate its progressive or reformist inclination; I mean rather to ground the logic of that thought in one specific dimension of capitalist society, the sphere of circulation. This was surely Marx's point when, with withering irony but also deep seriousness, he referred to the "sphere of circulation or commodity exchange"—the constitutive characteristic of "commercial" or "civil society"—as "a very Eden of the innate rights of man" and "the exclusive realm of Freedom, Equality, Property and Bentham." The buyer and the seller enter into exchange of their own choice (freedom) as commodity owners (property) seeking to exchange equivalent values (equality) to achieve their own private ends (self-interest) while inadvertently promoting the common weal (Adam Smith's universal opulence, Jeremy Bentham's greater good).[9] "Equality and freedom are thus not only respected in exchange based on exchange values, but, also, the exchange of exchange values is the productive, real basis of all *equality* and *freedom*."[10]

Steve Pincus has argued that a liberal ideology that "valued human choice, the human capacity to create wealth, and epochal change in human history," first emerged among radical Whigs in mid-seventeenth-century England as "a political economy and a conception of interest appropriate to a commercial society." The radical defenders of the English Commonwealth "borrowed many of the old tropes of classical republicanism—especially their devotion to the common good and their hatred of tyranny—and blended them with a newly appropriate vocabulary of interests and rights in defense of the common good. Their experience of the newly emerging commercial society as much as their reading determined their political outlook."[11] Bengali liberalism, I suggest, can be read in exactly the same manner, as an attempt to mediate between established textual themes and the social context of their reception. Unlike either the Kartabhajas or the defenders of the English Commonwealth, Bengali liberals did not have to invent a new political or religious idiom. But to be persuaded by the liberal ideological framework that they were very deliberately appropriating from metropolitan sources, Bengali liberals needed to be able to relate the textual abstractions and ideological concerns of wider imperial discourses to their own regional social and political context. From the perspective to be adopted in this chapter, recent polemics about the centrality and importance of indigenous philosophical frameworks or the complexity of discursive hybridization in Renaissance thought will prove largely beside the point.[12] The movement of the intellectual history I wish to narrate in this chapter is driven not by the logic of any particular discourse formation, but rather by transformations in the sociohistorical context within which these discourse formations were located. As such, that a figure like Rammohun Roy drew on the formal models and textual authorities of Vedantic philosophy as often as on Christian Unitarianism, liberal political theory or liberal political economy, or that he was able to find in the vast Sanskrit corpus themes that he could appropriate to his own ideological agenda, does not fundamentally compromise the characterization of his thought as liberal—so long as we locate the impulse of that liberalism not in textual authority but in the social transformations of his own era and social context—that is, in the referential domain. The issue would rather be to ask why it is that Rammohun felt the need in the early nineteenth century to reconceptualize Vedantism as an indigenous form of liberal religion—something that Sankaracharya, the authority on whom he most heavily relied, surely never imagined back in the eighth century.

It is not particularly controversial to observe that Calcutta was home to a vibrant, if unstable, commercial society in the early nineteenth century; that that commercial society was a local eddy in the vast structure of

Britain's global empire; and that the city's Bengali social leadership, both liberal and conservative, was largely composed of the beneficiaries of the mercantile, revenue, credit, and land revolutions of the eighteenth century.[13] It is true, as Marxist scholars like De, Sarkar, and Sen have pointed out, that this early colonial commercial society was not rooted in any significant transformation toward the formation of an industrial society on a larger subcontinental scale—despite the efforts by both colonial administrators and local capital to promote just such an outcome. But it is surely a classic case of what Manu Goswami has called *methodological nationalism* to take the spatial framework of the national economy as the naturally given unit of analysis.[14] Calcutta had from around the 1780s developed into the center both of a regional administration and of a commercial culture, an important local nexus in the imperial structure of commodity and capital, information, and personnel flows generated by the East India Company's transoceanic trading networks—an implication in global capitalist structures already deep enough to render the regional economy of Bengal susceptible to metropolitan economic fluctuations in the late 1820s, early 1830s, and late 1840s. Since the middle of the eighteenth century, furthermore, initially subsidiary but increasingly assertive regional commercial and financial interests, whose assets were drawn from the savings of Company servants, and from the capital of European private traders and Calcutta's native merchants and landlords, were developing aspirations to usurp the Company's trading system under the ideological banner of free trade.[15] "Bengal and the dominions dependent thereon are entirely commercial countries, which can only flourish while trade is prosperous," declared William Bolts in a blistering 1772 critique of Company despotism, "the principles of which are invariably the same in all climates."[16] Dwarkanath Tagore's rise in stature as a landlord, merchant, and indigo investor in the 1820s; his remarkable assumption of commercial preeminence for more than a decade in the wake of the financial crises of the early 1830s; and his aspirations, in the wake of the substantial reduction of Company trading privileges after the Charter renewal of 1833, for a new era of bourgeois prosperity and interracial business cooperation centered on the development of indigo production in Lower Bengal, can be seen from different perspectives either as an anomalous and ephemeral last gasp of native capital in a larger story of its marginalization from the higher echelons of trade, or, and perhaps more relevantly here, as the culminating efflorescence of a half-century of native participation in British commercial activities and investment in land and business.[17]

Calcutta's civil society would be enviously extolled in the *Bombay Gazette* of 1839: "We are one good century behind Calcutta in matters of improvement, speculation, and so forth. We have here no public scheming and projecting, no active open system of public spiritedness, no companies forming, no societies emerging.... In Calcutta ... we do recognize something like community of feeling and a combined idiosyncrasy; societies, meetings, projections follow in quick succession, and a current of healthy sympathy and sentiment seems to pervade the monied mass. Instead of maintaining the lonely icicled state of magnificence in which we exist [in Bombay], the thaw of social harmony has produced a permeative process of coalescence, which is spreading in every direction, and resolving into one community both Europeans and Natives."[18] We might well balk at the teleological imagination implicit in such (highly conventional) claims about Bengal as India's future—though we might do better to wonder about their apparently widespread plausibility in the nineteenth century rather than merely to dismiss them as wrongheaded in light of developments in the twentieth. But that aside, claims like this do suggest that Calcutta's location as a key site in an imperially constituted "commercial society" is surely as good a place as any to start making sense of Bengali liberalism. After all, as we shall see, Bengali liberals of the first half of the nineteenth century were self-consciously locating their politics at the interface of an imperial scale of polity and a (territorially composite[19]) native society whose interests they claimed to represent within that larger polity.

In the first two sections of this chapter, I set out to specify what it means to see the Bengali reformism inaugurated by Rammohun Roy's religious, social, and political activities in the early nineteenth century as a form of classical liberalism—rather than, say, as protonationalism, anglophilia, or some other more generally modernizing agenda. If, as I go on to argue in the subsequent two sections, Bengali liberalism went into retreat as a paradigm of political-economic discourse starting in the middle of the nineteenth century, it was surely not because Bengali liberalism had all along lacked roots in local social realities, but rather because Bengalis could no longer relate liberal categories to their social and political context in the same way as they had earlier, for specific reasons relating to transformations in the structure of social organization in colonial eastern India, in the subcontinent as a whole, and in the structure of Britain's imperial economy. I conclude by showing how liberalism's gradual drift into a crisis of relevance produced the conditions of possibility for the emergence in the 1880s of an alternative ideological paradigm centered on the concept of culture.

RAJA RAMMOHUN ROY

"The Indian reformer Raja Ram Mohun Roy," Chris Bayly has recently stressed, "made in two decades an astonishing leap from the intellectual status of a late-Mughal state intellectual to that of the first Indian liberal."[20] Even when criticized for his compromises and limitations, Rammohun Roy (1772–1833) remains nevertheless the undisputed founding figure of Bengali colonial modernity.[21] This was certainly not because of any mass following that he managed to draw behind any of his reform agendas, whether social, religious, economic, or political. On the contrary, supporters of the conservative cause always vastly outnumbered the small progressive faction concentrated in Rammohun's Atmiya Sabha (Friendly Society) and Brahma Sabha (Assembly of God), no matter how socially elevated the latter might be; for instance, the signatories of a petition supporting European colonization numbered three hundred, while those willing to back a petition rejecting it numbered in the thousands.[22] One might well in part attribute his stature to the exceptionality of his views—it was precisely his ability to provoke "the hatred of nearly all his countrymen for several years" (*EW* 548-49) that made him Bengal's first "modern." To that we might add the crucial boost in credibility that resulted from the moral and social reinforcement he received from certain individuals, newspapers, and political factions among the colonizing British.[23] And we must keep firmly in mind the long tradition of finding in Rammohun whatever one happens to be looking for, be it cosmopolitanism, anglophilia, or protonationalism; neo-Hinduism, ecumenicism, or protosecularism; democratic virtue, class ideology, or native corruption.

But setting all this aside, there remains one final factor that was crucial in securing for Rammohun both his iconic status in Bengali intellectual life and his status in the society of his time. It certainly might be difficult to argue that Rammohun inaugurated a vibrantly liberal age in the Bengali intellectual world. Nevertheless, his interventions did inaugurate a period in which it was the vibrancy of liberal ideas that set the agenda of Bengali public debate across a quite remarkable range of issues. I therefore begin my analysis of Bengali liberalism by reconstructing the ideological structure that underlay Rammohun's thought. My aim is not to deny that Rammohun's liberalism was rather moderate in its actual political application, but simply to show that the standpoint of his political and social imagination was grounded in a consistently liberal structure of argument. Rather than proceeding from the practicalities of politics and policy then, I begin with the most abstract of Rammohun's theoretical speculations. This is not because I think that his procedure of working through practical issues of policy and politics was so systematic or methodical, nor because I am under the delusion that he was incapable, thanks to an impossible high-mindedness, of thinking through issues at the practical level of interests. Rather, I seek to isolate and clarify the conceptual logic through which he construed the nature of his practical interests.

Rammohun was a rationalist religious reformer who advocated an uncompromising monotheism in the face of both Pauranik Hindu polytheism and Christian Trinitarianism. As early as 1803 or 1804, Rammohun had argued that a natural human propensity for monotheism was the universal foundation of all religions, regardless of every faith's subsequent corruption (*EW* 941–58). He would later elaborate this argument, identifying the nondualist (Advaita) reading of the Vedanta as the "real Hindooism, as that religion was practiced by our ancestors," holding that "God has no second that may be possessed of eternal existence, either of the same nature with himself or of a different nature from him, nor any second of that nature that might be called either his part or his *quality*," and that the universe has no existence separate from or independent of a unitary godhead (Brahma) (*EW* 90, 96, 152, 154, 562). "I do no more than assert," he would go on to explain, "that if correct reasoning and the dictates of common sense induce the belief of a wise, uncreated Being, who is the Supporter and Ruler of the boundless universe, we should also consider him the most powerful and supreme Existence,—far surpassing our powers of comprehension or description" (*EW* 4). It is consequently "absurd" to direct the "rational worship of the God of Nature" toward any representation modeled on man or any visible or tangible material object (*EW* 4, 21, 36, 67–68, 94, 112–13). Rammohun understood the godhead as both the "efficient" and "material cause" of the universe—god created the world, whose continuation and transformation are due solely to his volition and have no existence separate from him (*EW* 12, 69, 96–97, 151–58). It follows that the individual human soul is also of one and the same substance with the indivisible unity of the godhead; for just as "the reflections of the sun are seen on water placed in various vessels," and "these reflections of the sun seem to be moved by the motion of the water of these vessels without effecting any motion in the sun, so souls, being, as it were, the reflections of the Supreme Soul on matter, seem to be affected by the circumstances that influence matter, without God being affected by such circumstances" (*EW* 154). And just as "the reflections of the sun, though without light proper to themselves, appear splendid from their

[margin handwritten note: Rammohun advocated uncompromise monotheism]

connection with the illuminating sun, so the soul, though not true intellect, seems intellectual and acts as if it were real spirit from its actual relation to the Universal Intellect" (*EW* 155).

We might begin to unravel what was at stake in this trenchant monotheism by looking at the targets of Rammohun's critique. Rammohun's attack on polytheism began with a critique of idolatry and empty formalism. Many of "the ceremonies that have been instituted" by modern Hinduism "are of a tendency utterly subversive of every moral principle," and "not only deprive Hindoos in general of the common comforts of society, but also lead them frequently to self-destruction, or to sacrifice of the lives of their friends and relations" (*EW* 35, 63, 68). Idolaters worship their "supposed deities," who are mere "inventions" insofar as they "bear figure and appellation," through contemplation of the "wicked conduct" that so often features in their immoral adventures, through indecent gestures and other even grosser forms of debauchery, and even through murder and human sacrifice (*EW* 63, 98–99, 124–26). Ascribing to his images "at once the opposite natures of human and superhuman beings," the idolater conflates the particular attributes of their god with the universality of the incomprehensible and indescribable Creator, and thus remains irrationally bound by "puerile" superstitions and harmful prescriptions that contradict the universal dictates of "common sense" (*EW* 35, 45, 68). "My constant reflection on the inconvenient, or rather injurious rites introduced by the peculiar practice of Hindoo idolatry," which, "more than any other pagan worship," "destroys, to the utmost degree, *the natural texture of society*," and "prescribes crimes of the most heinous nature, which even the most savage nations would blush to commit," had impelled Rammohun to "awaken" his countrymen "from their dream of error" by promoting a form of "religious conduct . . . becoming the dignity of human beings" (*EW* 5, 45, emphasis added). Such a religion was one that recognized the immediate presence of the godhead to, and indeed in, every individual.

But why could Hindus not liberate themselves from the burden of "superstition," "custom and fashion," "the fruit of vulgar caprice," and "popular whim" (*EW* 70–71)? The answer was that classic trope of the British liberal tradition: priestly cunning. Hindus had been led to embrace the "superstitious puerilities" of modern Hindu worship by "their self-interested guides," the Brahmans, "who, in defiance of the law as well as common sense, have succeeded but too well in conducting them to the temple of idolatry" where they "find the source of their comforts and fortune" (*EW* 66, 73). Brahmans substituted for the "true substance of morality . . . a weak attachment for its mere shadow," their empty ritual prescriptions comparing poorly with Christ's message to mankind that "forms and ceremonies were useless tokens of respect for God, compared with the essential proof of obedience and love towards him evinced by the practice of beneficence towards their fellow creatures" (*EW* 73–74, 551). In contrast to Rammohun's self-declaredly sincere and disinterested effort to restore Hindus to their ancient faith by laying before them their own scriptures, the Brahmanical defenders of idolatry bade the people: "Believe whatever we may say—don't examine or even touch your scriptures, neglect entirely your reasoning faculties—do not only consider us, whatever may be our principles, as gods on earth, but humbly adore and propitiate us by sacrificing to us the greater part (if not the whole) of your property" (*EW* 71). In fact, his own decision to choose "the path which conscience and sincerity direct" over his own Brahmanical heritage had exposed him to "the complainings and reproaches even of some of my relations, whose prejudices are strong, and whose temporal advantage depends upon the present system" (*EW* 5).

Finally, Rammohun went to significant lengths to suggest that the rather austere monotheism he preached was best calculated to lead individuals "to both temporal and eternal happiness" (*EW* 71). Key to his mission was a fundamental departure from the authority he claimed to be most directly relying upon, Sankaracharya, who had argued that the direct contemplation of the Supreme Soul was a path of spiritual practice (*sadhana*) available only to the Brahman renouncer (*sannyasi*). In contrast, Rammohun's translation of the *Isopanishad* rejected this key element of Sankaracharya's doctrine, presenting instead the contemplation of the Supreme Soul as a universal path of salvation, and condemning those who devoted themselves to the observation of religious rituals and the adoration of celestial gods to damnation (*EW* 65, 75–77). "A pious householder is entitled to the adoration of God equally with an Yati [renunciant]," he had earlier declared in his *Abridgement of the Vedanta;* and had again insisted on the householder's qualification for "the worship of Brahma" in his translation of the *Mundakopanishad* (*EW* 15, 25). Rammohun thus elevated the "godly householder" (*brahmanishtha grihastha*) to spiritual preeminence, because it was (in Brian Hatcher's words) "only in the householder stage that all the duties of life could be fulfilled"—including not only worldly and moral responsibilities, but also the pursuit of absolute spiritual knowledge.[24] It was in the end this, rather than any substantial disagreements about the ontological doctrines of Vedantism, that most fundamentally divided Rammohun from his most eminent critic, Mrityunjay Vidyalankar. Rammohun insisted that those who were incapable of rising to the highest form of spiritual striving, and hence were explicitly permitted the use of idols according to Upanishadic authorities, were a subnormal exception to common humanity (*EW* 109). Mrityunjay, in contrast, insisted on Sankaracharya's position that it was only an elite that was adequate to the rigors of worshipping the formless godhead.[25]

The "true system of religion ... leads its observers to a knowledge and love of God, and to a friendly inclination towards their fellow-creatures, impressing their hearts at the same time with humility and charity, accompanied by independence of mind and pure sincerity" (*EW* 46). In the restoration of the "natural texture of society," where "social rules" backed by divine sanction "separate the property of one from that of another, and provide for the removal of pain which one gives another," Rammohun envisages worldly householders directly pursuing a rational knowledge of the universal godhead through a practice of devotion that combines meditation (unmediated by rite or priesthood) with the cultivation of natural reason and practical morality through the detachment of the mind from ephemeral sensuous pleasures (*EW* 947).[26] This religion could only be commonsensical to any rational being capable of laying aside that "obstinate adherence" to prejudice and custom, under whose influence "reason is seldom allowed its natural scope," in favor of "the proper and moderate use of reason" and the "rational performance of your duty to your sole Creator" (*EW* 71, 74, 666).

We should be clear here on what is truly radical in Rammohun's agenda. In his earliest work, he was remorseless in his critique of all mediations between man and god, rejecting prophetic revelation as redundant in the face of the immediate legibility of natural revelation, and asserting that "the intellectual powers and faculties" with which god had endowed man demanded that he "not, like other animals, follow the examples of his fellows, but should exercise his own intellectual power with the help of acquired knowledge, to discern good from bad" (*EW* 953, 957). It is quite true, as his Derozian critics would observe, that Rammohun would later retreat from the radical emancipation of human reason, which, untempered by revelation, "only serves to generate a universal doubt, incompatible with principles on which our comfort and happiness mainly depend" (*EW* 37).[27] But even so, he continued to insist that "the writings supposed sacred are only, when consistent with sound reasoning" (*EW* 396). Furthermore, he continued to systematically advocate the emancipation of the householder from religious institutions that mediated his individual relationship to universal truth. While Rammohun's attacks on ritual formalism, idolatry, and priest craft could all be read as continuous with any number of Indian and Islamic textual traditions, seen in the wider context of his larger political and social agenda it seems clear that they were fundamentally indistinguishable in ideological function from British liberalism's use of anticlericalism and anti-Catholicism to assert freedom of conscience and the individual right to pursue rational self-interest. The individual householder was to be freed from institutional forms that used illegitimate authority to check "independence of mind." His intervention rendered the householder's worldliness commensurate with—indeed, a crucial part of—a rational spiritual practice, and established utility as a key measure of spiritual truth, limiting the abstract operation of reason in the pragmatic cause of "comfort and happiness," and sanctioning such fundamental doctrines as belief in the soul and the existence of the next world on the instrumental basis of "the welfare of society" while rejecting further doctrinal appendages as "detrimental to social life" (EW 37, 947). As Bruce Robertson has recognized, Advaita Vedanta became, in Rammohun's hands, a doctrine of liberal egalitarianism.[28]

The householder religion that Rammohun outlined was thus centrally concerned with problematics of moral, spiritual, and intellectual independence. We can now approach his political and social polemics to examine how they served to elaborate these rather abstract conceptions of independence and reason as the warp and weft of the "natural texture of society." In his famous writings against sati, Rammohun's argument proceeded simultaneously on the plane of scriptural authority (inevitably the more cumbersome element of his discussion) and of rational ethical judgment. In the case of the latter, his position proceeded from a radical assertion of abstract human equality against arguments that asserted the natural inequality of the sexes. Contesting his opponents' characterization of women ("even of respectable classes") as peculiarly "prone to pleasure" and "subject to their passions," he argued that "all mankind, whether male or female, are endowed with a mixture of passions" that, "by study of the Shastras, and frequenting the society of respectable persons . . . may be gradually subdued" to ultimately achieve an "exalted state." It is largely because women are "in general inferior to men in bodily strength and energy" that men have been able to deny "to them those excellent merits that they are entitled to by nature," as if they were "naturally incapable of acquiring those merits." Lacking "understanding" for want of education, while perhaps exceeding men in resolve, fidelity, continence, and virtue, women stand in the same, fundamentally human relation to spiritual self-discipline as men: "We ought, therefore, to endeavour to withdraw both men and women from debased sensual pleasures" so as to "procure for them final beatitude" (EW 350–51, 360–63).

If women were victims of violence, Rammohun argues, it was not merely in the narrow sense of their being physically thrust onto the funeral pyres of their husbands. "What I lament," he declared, "is that, seeing the women *thus dependent* and exposed to every misery, you feel for them no compassion, that might exempt them from being tied down and burnt to death" (*EW* 363, emphasis added). Dependence was the key to this abuse. When widows willingly allowed themselves to be cast into the flames, it could not be "from religious prejudices and early impressions only," but necessarily stemmed "also from their witnessing the distress in which widows of the same rank in life are involved, and the insults and slights to which they are daily subject." Widows who declined to burn with their husband—and as a result of the polygamy practiced by the highest (*kulin*) subcastes, there were often more than one at any given death—were constrained either to "live a miserable life as mere slaves to others," or to "walk in the paths of unrighteousness for their maintenance and independence" (*EW* 379). At the root of the problem of sati was the denial of female inheritance rights. Because women were not entitled to any share in their father's property, they had to choose between abject dependence and prostitution. Furthermore, their fathers and brothers "generally bestow them in marriage on those who can pay most" in what blatantly constituted "an actual sale of females." Deprived of the right to property through the combined force of law and social pressure, women sank instead to the status of property, condemned to "a miserable state of dependence" (*EW* 381–83).

If female inheritance was the key to understanding sati, at the root of the problem of female inheritance was an implicit understanding of what constituted the practical foundation of individual independence—namely, property. Rammohun considered security of property to be the lynchpin that linked the individual pursuit of independence and happiness with generalized prosperity. He went to great lengths (in part motivated by very personal concerns with the status of his own inheritance) to demonstrate that, according to Hindu law, "the father is the sole and independent owner of the property in his possession, whether self-acquired or ancestral" (*EW* 402). His affirmation of the right of women to inherit property should in no way be taken to imply that he endorsed a collective form of ownership by the lineage. On the contrary, property had to be understood as strictly individual if it was to guarantee the security and independence of individuals. The recognition of a father's right to freely alienate even ancestral property in land, without requiring the consent of his sons, was fundamental to the continued prosperity of the country—not just because a reversal of this prin-

ciple would render the entire history of real estate transactions since the Permanent Settlement open to challenge, but also because an individual's capacity to "procure easily . . . loans of money to lay out on the improvement of his estate, in trade or in manufactures," generally depended on his ability to offer landed property as collateral (*EW* 393–96). Any change in the basic principle of absolute individual ownership would be "arbitrary" and utterly irreconcilable "with the principles of justice, with reason, or with regard for the future prosperity of the country" (*EW* 394).

Rammohun was certainly capable of being critical of the Permanent Settlement—but not because of the security of property it founded. He acknowledged that, for a decade or so after the Settlement, many old zamindar families lost their lands. This, however, had only led to the emergence of a more entrepreneurial class of landlords who, "by their active exertions and outlay of capital, improved many of their estates, and increased their own fortune" (though their heirs had often in turn proven more susceptible to the lures of extravagance and indolence) (*EW* 281). Rammohun voiced a classical Whiggism when he declared: "None will, I think, hesitate to rejoice in the augmentation of incomes of proprietors [of land] derived from the extension of cultivation, as every man is entitled by law and reason to enjoy the fruits of his honest labour and good management" (*EW* 289). Challenging the contention of one critic that, "All subjects are dependent, the king alone is free," he would respond in a tone of outraged good sense: "I trust your learned correspondent does not mean . . . to establish that all subjects have a dependent right in their lawful possessions, and that the king is privileged to take or give them away at his pleasure" (*EW* 426–27). It is hardly surprising, in the light of his embrace of this discourse of private property, that Rammohun was also a free trader in principle; although he thought that the move to liberalize trade should be gradual and cautious in its implementation, he certainly accepted the fundamental argument that the "opening of the trade in 1814" had increased the value of land and its product (consequently benefiting "landlords and dealers in commodities"), and allied himself publicly with British and Indian merchants in their quest to have the remaining trading privileges of the Company abolished (*EW* 288).[29]

Rammohun and his allies celebrated the role of indigo production, notwithstanding their limited admission of the existence of abuses that in the 1850s and 1860s would rise to central prominence in urban middle-class consciousness as a key symbol of colonial racial violence and exploitation. Indigo increased the value of land, and equally importantly, it had allowed peasants, who previously had been "forced by their zumendars [*sic*] to labour for them without any remuneration or for the gift of a small quantity of rice," to claim instead the status of independent individuals, "enjoying some freedom and comfort under the protection of Indigo Planters," not as servile clients, but rather as wage earners, "better clothed and better conditioned" than others, and "each receiving for his labour, a salary of about four rupees per month."[30] This was certainly a rosy view of the indigo industry (although, as Sugata Bose has suggested, it may have represented a carryover from an earlier period when indigo was possibly more remunerative for the grower[31]); but it expressed with admirable clarity his sense that the potential for individual emancipation was grounded in the commercialization of social relations already transforming the Bengali countryside. He further advocated the abolition of limitations on the capacity of Europeans to own land outside Calcutta as a means of more deeply injecting modern commercial civilization into rural relations—an agenda announced by a 1929 Minute by Lord Bentinck, "entirely in accordance with the feeling of the free merchants in India and the advocates for annihilating the Company," and greeted with horror by British manufacturing interests who "saw in colonization the spectre of another Lancashire on the bank of the Ganges."[32] He argued that further colonization of the countryside by respectable Europeans would introduce improvements in techniques and technologies of cultivation and commerce, an emancipating intellectual and social influence on a people "subjected . . . to social and domestic inconvenience" by "superstitions and prejudices," a more stringent defense of "the rights belonging to the subjects of a liberal Government" by the Whiggish European traders, a more informed and interconnected imperial public, and finally, a more loyal populace deeply invested in the continuity and security of an "enlightened" and "liberal" British connection.[33]

As such, if the Permanent Settlement could be faulted, it was certainly not because it had ascribed proprietary rights to landlords. This had been its great virtue, the very founding moment of Bengal's aspirations to a new prosperity and freedom. Rather, the Settlement had been imperfect because it had affirmed the rights of property too narrowly: "I am at a loss to conceive why this indulgence" of a "perpetual settlement" of the revenue demands made of zamindars "was not extended to their tenants" (*EW* 290). This erasure of the claims of cultivating tenants through the exclusive affirmation of the zamindar's claim to proprietorship effectively excluded tenants entirely from participation in the new commercial prosperity of the province and the individuated independence it inaugurated. "In former times *Khud-Kasht Ryots* (cultivators of the lands of their own villages) were considered as having an absolute right to continue the possession of their lands in perpetuity on payment of a certain fixed rent. . . . From a reference to the laws and the histories of the country, I believe that lands in India were individual property in ancient times." But the Muslim conquerors' practical violations of the right of property were subsequently compounded by its legal entrenchment under their British successors (*EW* 272–73). While previously under Muslim rule improvements to zamindari estates had been discouraged by the capacity of the ruling power to arbitrarily "augment or reduce the rates of revenue demandable" from landlords, the terms of the Settlement, even while guaranteeing the landlord's security of property, reproduced that "despotic power" in the relations between landlord and tenant (*EW* 289–90). The result was that, while the zamindars had benefited handsomely from the Permanent Settlement, raising their incomes by improving their estates and reclaiming wastelands without the threat of increased revenue demands, cultivators had no means of accumulating capital and "very few, if any (besides proprietors of lands) . . . have the least pretension to wealth or independence, or even the common comforts of life" (*EW* 282, 288).

"In politics, Rammohun Roy was a republican," declared his *Times* obituary in 1833, referring no doubt to his well-known enthusiasm for the 1830 revolution in France. "Among Europeans he associated chiefly with the ultra-liberal party."[34] The *Times* was no doubt thinking of his friendship with James Silk Buckingham, the coproprietor with Rammohun of the *Calcutta Journal* and a radical advocate of parliamentary reform and enemy of slavery and Company despotism.[35] Indeed, in England in 1832, Rammohun would remark that he had publicly avowed to renounce his connection with Britain had the Reform Bill—an act he identified with "the salvation of the nation, nay, of the whole world"—been defeated.[36] It would be simplistic to understand Rammohun's often-attested loyalty to British rule too naively. As he could make perfectly clear in the very texts where he most loudly proclaimed it, that loyalty, having been "produced by the wisdom and liberality displayed by the British Government in the means adopted for the gradual improvement of their social and domestic condition" and further consolidated by Bengali investment in Britain's public debt, was nonetheless conditional—"in proportion as they [the natives] experience from it the blessings of just and liberal treatment" (*EW* 439–40). The performative function of his polemics, calling upon liberal Britons to live up to their avowed principles by removing the inequities of racial discrimination in appointments to the revenue and judicial services, press censorship, and Company monopoly, cannot be ignored.[37] But that should in no way compromise our recognition of the deep sincerity of the loyalty built into Rammohun's rhetoric of conditionality, wherein the threat of lost native loyalty must presumably have implied a regression to superstitious and despotic barbarism rather than a restored national independence. To be at all desirable, India's independence would necessarily have to lie on the thither side of British rule. How else could it hope to "succeed sooner or later in enlightening and civilizing the surrounding nations of Asia" as the agent of emancipation in its turn (*EW* 317)?

The security of property, the rule of law, and the freedom of public communication that the British had established in Bengal represented for Rammohun a moment of transformative possibility—the possibility of restoring Bengal to that universal "natural texture of society" in which, regardless of location or nationality, independent individuals promoted general prosperity through the rational and regular pursuit of their own private interests.[38] As Chris Bayly has recently stressed, Rammohun's argument rested in large part on a conception of India's "ancient constitution."[39] And as his willingness to act as ambassador of the Moghul emperor during his trip to Britain in 1830 made clear, he sought to establish India's position within the British imperial ecumene by emphasizing not only the indigenous roots of a liberal constitutional order but also an existing sovereignty whose eventual supersession was to guarantee a position of national equality in subjection to the British Crown (on the model of the several nations of the United Kingdom). But what Rammohun sought to establish through such appeals to these Burkean tropes was the applicability of a natural law of liberty to India. In this sense, as leader of the loyal opposition, Rammohun was a sincere liberal imperialist; while he clearly understood himself to be part of a cosmopolitan liberal moment, there is little reason to doubt that he considered the British Empire (as his profound investment in the Reform Bill issue makes especially clear) to be the preeminent institutional vehicle of a cosmopolitan liberal polity that could be upheld in turn by a universal religious sensibility "destructive of differences and dislike between man and man, and conducive to the peace and Union of mankind" (*EW* 564).[40]

The peasantry were, Rammohun argued, "quite ignorant of, and indifferent about either the former or the present government," being aware only of "the conduct of the public officers immediately presiding over them." Men of the old aristocracy were disaffected with the British regime, having lost so much from its accession. "Many of those, however, who engage prosperously in commerce, and of those who are secured in the peaceful possession of their estates by the permanent settlement, and such as have sufficient intelligence to foresee the probability of future improvement which presents itself under the British rulers, are not only reconciled to it, but really view it as a blessing to the country" (*EW* 300). Rammohun, whose family's prosperity and status had been established essentially in the post-Plassey era, was himself one of these last. His social respectability had been built upon his family's involvement in Mughal administration, and subsequently in their participation in the revenue apparatus of their British successors. His advocacy of individual property against its collective form was more than just an abstract ideological commitment. Rammohun's father, Ramkanta Roy, had already been divided from his brothers "in food Estate and interest" in the generation before, and in turn partitioned most of his real property among his three sons some years before his death, after which "their property always continued distinct" even when sharing household expenses, and they never "form[ed] an undivided Hindoo family."[41] At the same time, the fragility of Rammohun's social respectability also stemmed from this commitment to the worldliness of commercial and administrative pursuits under the new regime—a worldliness already intimated by his family's tradition of Mughal service, reinforced by his activities as a financial and property speculator, moneylender, and government servant, and outwardly symbolized by his Persianized manners and functionary surname.[42] His assault on idolatry and ceremony were inseparable from his advocacy of individual property and independence. If his conservative critics recognized in him a prioritization of worldly pursuits (*bishaykarma*) over ritual duties to gods (*daibakarma*) and ancestors (*pitrikarma*), we might correlatively argue that his advocacy of religious rationalism was a theological attempt to imbue worldly activity with spiritual virtue.[43] The point here is not that Rammohun's liberalism was a function of his class position—the roots of his wealth were largely indistinguishable from those of Radhakanta Deb, his chief conservative rival. Rather, it is to suggest that Rammohun was peculiarly well positioned to appreciate the social and political possibilities of the social transformations that were already taking place—namely, the practice of commodity exchange built into commercialization. In the process, Rammohun was opening up an entirely new discursive universe in a new Bengali public sphere, asserting the crucial importance of the active exercise of a form of individual independence, grounded in security of property and free exchange in civil society, simultaneously for the advancement of the common weal and the achievement of personal prosperity, moral exemplarity, and spiritual salvation. He was thereby pitching the critical potential of a colonial civil society, which had made his wealth and station possible even as it instituted violent forms of exclusion and exploitation, against the institutional hierarchies of both indigenous and European society and the practical constraints of Company monopoly.[44]

"In speaking of British subjects," William Bolts explained in the preface to his radical Whig tract of 1772, "we would be understood to mean his Majesty's newly acquired Asiatic subjects, as well as the British emigrants residing and established in India."[45] But as one Madras civil servant by the name of Everett would much later complain in 1853, "India has never yet been regarded as part of the empire. It goes by the unhappy name of colony, a place ... made expressly to be plundered by the Mother-country."[46] Yet in the 1820s and 1830s, men on both sides of the colonial divide were imagining the possibility of just such a vision of liberal empire. What was this conception of *empire* that aspired to negate the exploitative grubbiness of the term *colony?* When Lord Bentinck ended his tenure as governor-general of British India, educated Bengalis eulogized him as the man who "first taught us to forget the distinction between conquerors and conquered, and to become, in heart and mind, in hopes and aspiration, one with Englishmen."[47] And speaking at Bengal's recently formed Zamindary Association in 1839, T. E. M. Turton, a business ally of Dwarkanath Tagore, gave equally lucid expression to the vision that underpinned the liberal-imperial imagination: "It was not as a conquered nation that he desired to retain the inhabitants of India as British subjects, but as brethren in every respect; as constituting a part of the Kingdom of Britain, as fellow subjects—with the same feelings, the same interests and objects, and the same rights as the British-born inhabitants of England. He admired the principle adopted of old by the Romans, of incorporating their conquests with Rome, and granting to the conquered the privileges of Roman citizens."[48] This dissident conception of empire was the inclusively cosmopolitan liberal polity that Rammohun was also imagining as the moral basis of his demands for opening more senior government positions to Indians, expanding structures of Indian representation (especially through juries[49]), allowing (respectable) European colonization of the *mofussil* (the rural hinterland), respecting the freedom of the native press—in short, building a free civil society in India from the ground up.

THE 1830S AND 1840S

The political dimensions of Rammohun's liberalism did not disappear with his departure to England in 1830 or his death in Bristol in 1833. The mantle of leadership of the small liberal faction he had led passed to Dwarkanath

Tagore, a Bengali businessman who dazzled both European and native Calcutta with his hospitality and largesse through the 1830s and 1840s. Although he had been a member of the Brahmo Sabha, Dwarkanath was far too practical by disposition to be deeply enthused by Rammohun's theological zeal, and left the society to languish for a decade. At least part of the reason that Dwarkanath was indifferent toward Rammohun's religious mission was, arguably, his enduring attachment to Vaishnavite spiritual practices.[50] If Rammohun was attempting to reconceive Hindu religiosity as consistent in its fundamental conceptual schema with his social and political philosophy, Dwarkanath was actually much closer in spiritual temperament to Rammohun's conservative critics, maintaining a sharp practical distinction between worldly affairs and ritual duty. That he fell into Rammohun's camp nevertheless surely had more to do with his fundamental prioritization of worldly interests over ritual purity, something the conservatives could never accept. And it was Rammohun's social, political, and economic agenda that Dwarkanath would pursue in the subsequent decade and a half.

The age of Dwarkanath Tagore seemed to hold out, for a brief period during the "age of reform" in the 1830s and 1840s, the practical possibility of realizing Rammohun's vision of cosmopolitan empire—for a small elite of Calcutta's rich and powerful at least. Nothing symbolized the sense of possibility of this moment (as too the underlying instability that would ultimately destroy it) more than Calcutta's largest business enterprise in the period between the financial crises of the early 1830s and the late 1840s, the Union Bank, a joint stock company under both European and Indian management and with both European and Indian shareholders (as of 1835, of the 202 proprietors, seventy-five were Indian, as were four of its board of directors) whose policy was essentially controlled by Dwarkanath until 1844.[51] Like Rammohun, Dwarkanath's stature rested on his secular pursuits as a zamindar, businessman, and social leader, rather than on his lineage's ritual status (which, since he was from a degraded [pirali] Brahman sub-caste, was far from elevated).[52] And like Rammohun, he was sincerely committed to liberal political economy and a vision of cosmopolitan empire in which Indians could participate politically and economically as full subjects of the British Crown, even taking seats in the British Parliament.[53] He would advocate for free trade and the abolition of Company monopoly; promote the advancement of government employment for Indians; understand his status as zamindar not in paternalistic, but rather in strictly contractual and ruthlessly capitalistic terms; contest the prioritization of metropolitan interests over Indian interests in government policy; build important business partnerships with European capital; defend the interests of indigo planters as crucial instruments of capitalizing agriculture and thereby improving the value of both land and product; attribute to Calcutta's private traders (the very private traders who had invoked the ideology of Whig radicalism against Company monopoly in the late seventeenth and eighteenth centuries[54]) the responsibility for raising Calcutta's native merchants out of slavery to the Company; envision the development of a manufacturing economy on the banks of the Hooghly; and donate to international and European charitable causes as a means of establishing his moral equivalency with Europeans as a cosmopolitan subject.[55] Indeed, in Dwarkanath we see the clearest convergence of interest and ideology (by which I mean the naturalization of historically determinate social forms): Dwarkanath would ruthlessly pursue his interests as a capitalist landlord and also act as a fierce advocate of indigo interests—an advocacy that surely had less to do with his direct investments in indigo factories than it did on the ultimate reliance on indigo production in Lower Bengal of the entire edifice of Calcutta's financial world, at the head of which stood the Union Bank. It was in Dwarkanath that the realities of capitalist production would most impolitely intrude into the ideals of circulation—as in his unseemly deal, in an era of cooperation between zamindars and indigo planters, to support his European business allies in defeating Macaulay's 1836 so-called Black Act, which sought to end the European exemption from the civil jurisdiction of Company courts in the mofussil, a move seen by indigo planters as not only subjecting them to a subordinate race but more importantly as undermining their ability to guarantee returns on their advances.[56]

Nevertheless, Dwarkanath certainly understood himself to be a liberal in the tradition of Rammohun. While visiting Britain in 1841–42, Dwarkanath established important contacts with the Whig parliamentarian, Lord Brougham, to whom he had been introduced by a mutual friend as Rammohun's successor and "the head of everything liberal in India." He also succeeded, on behalf of the Landholders Society, in persuading George Thompson, despite his initial hesitancy, to accompany him back to Calcutta.[57] Thompson had, along with Lord Brougham and William Adam, been a cofounder of London's British India Society, an institution with which the Landholders Society had officially committed itself to cooperate since 1839 and which had itself been established to promote "the improvement of the condition of the native population."[58] His real fame, however, had emerged from his firebrand oratory as an antislavery abolitionist, as well as a free-trader ally of Joseph Hume and an Anti-Corn Law activist. He was, in other

words, a celebrity from the very core of British radicalism. The surprise
that one journalist expressed "that there should be any sympathy" between
a middle-class radical and a princely magnate with Persianized manners
was, however, arguably soon born out.[59] While Thompson's presence briefly
galvanized the Landholders Society, he also engaged in wider activities that
far exceeded the narrower class concerns of that organization, successfully
promoting the formation of the Bengal British India Society "for bettering
the condition of the people and disseminating correct information respecting the Institutions, Law and Government of the country, with a view to
the expansion of the just rights, and the protection of the interests of all
classes of Her Majesty's subjects on these shores."[60] Its ranks were primarily drawn from graduates of the Hindu College; and especially prominent
among them were those who had fallen under the charismatic influence
of the radical freethinker, Henry Louis Vivian Derozio, and who had later
gone on to form the Society for the Acquisition of General Knowledge
(SAGK) where Thompson spoke early in 1843.[61] To no one's real surprise,
Dwarkanath, though Thompson's sponsor, did not join this new, more radical organization.[62]

Young Bengal, as this younger generation of radicals were known, had
from the beginning assumed a more uncompromising stance in their criticism of Rammohun's camp as half-liberals who were too moderate, too
equivocating, and too interested in the pursuit of wealth and high station—
though, lest we draw the contrast too sharply, Tarachand Chakrabarty, the
president of the SAGK after whom the "Chuckerbuttee faction" (as they
came to be known in the press) was named, had been closely associated
with Rammohun as the first secretary of the Brahmo Sabha, and had been
the first person to float the idea of collecting his complete writings for publication.[63] More uncompromisingly provocative they might have been in their
free-thinking repudiation of Hindu superstition and native barbarism and
in their willingness to pursue liberal premises to their (still rather moderate)
political conclusions, but in the broad logic of their liberal ideological paradigm, which assumed the standpoint of the rational individual to critique
institutional limitations on independence and civic equality, there was little
that fundamentally distinguished them from Rammohun.

> In matters of politics, they are all radicals, and are followers of Benthamite
> principles. The very word Tory is a sort of ignominy among them. . . . They think
> that toleration ought to be practiced by every government, and the best and
> surest way of making the people abandon their barbarous customs and rites

is by diffusing education among them. With respect to the questions relating to Political Economy, they all belong to the school of Adam Smith. They are clearly of opinion that the system of monopoly, the restraints upon trade, and the international laws of many countries, do nothing but paralyse the efforts of industry, impede the progress of agriculture and manufacture, and prevent commerce from flowing in its natural course.[64]

"Hindu by birth, yet European by education and its concomitants," Young Bengal assumed the position of a loyal opposition too sharp in its criticism for the comfort even of many self-declared Whigs—insisting that they were not attacking British rule as such, but assertively demanding nevertheless more representational government; more native appointments in the government services; a more equitable, more efficient ,and less corrupt administration of justice; an end to the conflation of governmental and commercial functions in Company rule; the promotion of education throughout Hindu society (including among its women); and the universal protection of rights and promotion of general social utility.[65]

"Whatever diversity of opinion there may be on the origin of Government—whether it was traceable to contract, heavenly ordination, or the natural course of events, there can be no question as to political institutions having been subsequent to the existence of private property," explained Peary Chand Mitra, one of the secretaries of the SAGK who would also go on to be a founding member of the Bengal British India Society, in an 1846 article on agrarian relations that could be read as a manifesto of the Society's political agenda.[66] "The idea of property, as being the product of labor, is *natural* with man. Land unreclaimed from sterility is common property. It is the first tillage and cultivation which constitute private property. In proportion as agricultural pursuits are thus carried on," he would conclude in what essentially amounted to an implicit vindication of the very Lockean contract theory about which he had moments before disingenuously avowed agnosticism, "the curtailment of the natural liberty and the want of mutual protection are felt; and it is private property which gives rise to Government, and not Government to private property."[67] On this basis, he would go on to pursue Rammohun's call for the protection of ryot rights from an even more radical standpoint, challenging both the argument of Sir John Shore and others (notably James Mill) that it was the government, rather than the zamindars, that possessed the proprietary right in the land, and, in a move that far exceeded Rammohun's agenda, the "radically wrong basis of the permanent settlement" in its mistaken attribution of property rights to the Mughal revenue-collecting gentry, or zamindars.[68] As even the Laws of Manu had recognized, "the right in the cultivated land" lay with him *"who cut away the wood, or who cleared and tilled it"*—the ryot himself.[69] As such, the Permanent Settlement should have fixed the property rights of ryots, encouraging them to accumulate capital rather than condemning them to an at best bare subsistence. The Permanent Settlement "abstractedly considered" had certainly been right to try to encourage improvement to estates by fixing revenue rates, for "the absence of fear in the enjoyment of the fruits of labor operates as a powerful stimulus to exertion, and the increased employment of capital." In practice, however, it had led to nothing but a class of exploitative absentee landlords who were "aliens to the internal economy of their Zemindaries" and compounded exorbitant rents with illegal cess taxes, complemented by a class of moneylenders preying on the hand-to-mouth existence of the cultivators.[70] "The unsettlement of the rent paid by the Ryot . . . materially detracts from his security in the enjoyment of property, and necessarily prevents that undivided and hearty application to the improvement of the land which would otherwise be given."[71] As such, the government must settle the rents, at a rate fairly determined on the basis of calculations grounded in the Ricardian differential theory of rent, to create proper incentive to labor, allow ryots to accumulate capital to improve their lands and free themselves from the moneylenders, convert "many a jungle now teeming with ferocious beasts . . . into a scene of smiling plenty," and ultimately rescue a degraded peasantry sunk in ignorance as a direct result of their poverty so that they might know "how to direct their labours most advantageously" and "understand their rights, obligations and responsibilities as men."[72]

The Young Bengal group's Benthamite commitment to "the grand deontological maxim . . . [that] what it is a man's duty to do, cannot but be also his interest," was hitched to an arguably even more fundamental commitment to a liberal conception of natural rights and the individual pursuit of interests. When in 1832 there arrived in Calcutta about a hundred copies of Thomas Paine's *Age of Reason* (a text that shared so much in common with Rammohun's rationalistic creed) they were initially sold at a rupee a copy—but were soon driven up to five rupees each in the face of an insatiable demand that, even at that exorbitant price, still saw the entire stock gone within a few days.[73] Dakshinaranjan Mukherjee, one of Thompson's key allies in forming the Bengal British India Society, laid out with admirable clarity a classic liberal argument whose invocation of a discourse of natural rights would have surely struck Bentham as absurdly metaphysical: God had "created all men alike equal to one another, in their birth-rights," an original perfect equality and freedom that, with the initial steps out of barbarism, called into existence government and law to institute the "security and protection of admitted rights between man and man" and to pursue the "general advantage." If in India this equality had been so deeply subverted, it was a direct consequence of its "ambitious and domineering priesthood, and subsequently upheld and sanctified by ignorance and error, tending to stultify human reason, lest it should remind men of their right to think for themselves."[74]

THE CRISIS OF LIBERALISM

If there is one year from which we can date the beginning of Bengali liberalism's crisis, it is 1848. Certainly, long before that date liberals had been led by the practical constraints of interest and circumstance to compromise their abstract principles and to form coalitions with conservatives. Rammohun himself had always sought to pitch his polemics from within the bounds of Brahman respectability.[75] And even in his heyday in the 1830s and early 1840s, the ever-pragmatic Dwarkanath had been even more inclined to compromise than Rammohun, and was increasingly drawn by the pursuit of class interests into political and institutional alliances with the conservative leaders who had been his most vocal opponents. The Zamindary Association that Turton addressed in 1839, known better to historians as the Landholders Society, was not only the first political association in Bengal but also one of the most significant instances of such compromise. While Dwarkanath was its prime mover, Radhakanta Deb, the pro-sati lobbyist who had been Rammohun's archrival, was selected to be its first president, and membership was available to anyone who possessed an interest in the soil, whether European or Indian, conservative or liberal.[76] But it was in 1847-48, in the wake of a global financial crisis that spread from Britain to India, destroying the financial structure of the indigo business through a fatal combination of low prices and a shortage of credit, that the great Union Bank died an irreversible death, signaling the final failure of the Calcutta mercantile world's viability as an independent center of capital accumulation and investment.

Where the crisis of the 1830s had served partly to spur on what Blair Kling called the "age of enterprise" in Bengal, the crisis of 1847-48 played out quite differently. First of all, there was a generalized sense among Indian businessmen in Calcutta that they were being unfairly burdened with the consequences of European bad management (and, it must be said, not without reason); so much so that the *Bengal Hurkaru* warned that as to the natives, who it is so desirable to see becoming members of Joint Stock Companies, the Union Bank affair has given a death blow to their confidence in any such associations. We have heard several highly respectable natives declare that nothing would induce them to take shares in any of them and that such was the general feeling among their countrymen. Who can be surprised at such a result? No power of logic will ever persuade a native that there is any justice in a law, which, as if the loss of the capital vested by him in the Bank were not sufficient, makes him liable also for an enormous amount of debts contracted without his knowledge and in violation of every principle and role of the association.[77]

Bengali capital did indeed flee back to the relative safety and stability of investment in land. If it stayed there for so long after the commercial crisis of the 1840s had passed, however, it was because it was increasingly locked out of any other significant avenues of investment in the subsequent decades. The failure of local capital in Calcutta expressed so cataclysmically in the failure of the Union Bank, coupled with improved transportation and communication infrastructures, opened the door for an influx of metropolitan capital whose European-based management was far more insulated from local influence and native collaboration, and that would seize a degree of control over eastern India's economy unparalleled elsewhere in the subcontinent to constitute the political-economic formation that has come to be seen as the classic form of imperialism—with India increasingly locked into its dual role as a captive market for British manufactured imports and as a producer of primary products for export.

State consolidation and the dramatic extension of financial, communications, and transportation infrastructures in the post-Mutiny era in turn constituted what Manu Goswami has referred to as new sociospatial practices that, by at once enclosing and internally interconnecting subcontinental political, economic, and social networks, underpinned specifically national and nationalist conceptions of economy and territoriality, even as they served to lock India more deeply into an increasingly globally integrated imperial economy. The much more financially stable banks and businesses that functioned within this imperial economy had none of the Union Bank's regional commitment to interracial cooperation and would remain until the final decades of colonial rule overwhelmingly hostile to the participation of native capital and to the employment even of British-trained Indians. The result was a transformed Calcutta, in which institutions and individuals who could bridge the sharpening lines of racial demarcation were thinner and thinner on the ground, in which Bengali capital was locked into zamindaris and intermediate tenures, and in which employment for the educated middle-class Bengalis who were coming out of the schools the previous generation had established was limited to low-level clerical and functionary positions in government service and the offices of private companies.[78] Increasingly locked out of commerce (*byabsa*) and consigned to salaried employment (*cakri*), Bengalis would respond to their new situation with a composite class language that, as Tithi Bhattacharya has shown, grounded respectability (*bhadrata*) primarily neither in the conservative discourse of ritual purity nor in the increasingly depreciated display of prosperity, but rather in education (*shiksha*) and knowledge (*vidya*).[79]

"Britain's new industrial power forced Bengal—economically the core of the British empire in India—into the mould of a dual economy characterized by the domination of the peasant subsistence economy and by an urban import-export sector based on Calcutta."[80] It is from the middle of the nineteenth century that one can date the sharp internal bifurcation of eastern India's colonial economy. The Calcutta-centered commercial world would be marked as constitutively white and Western by the marked exclusivity of European control and management of capital-based enterprise—in the sense of the profound subordination of the regional economy to the metropolitan capital market and in the sense of the racial exclusivity of locally based business interests that were no longer dependent on native investment. In stark contrast stood an agrarian social order that defined the quintessence of nativeness, with its production processes grounded in a reconstructed landed gentry on the one hand and a smallholding agriculture organized not on the basis of the familiar separation of household and workplace, but rather (as discussed in chapter 2) through transformed structures of household, kinship, and community on the other.

Goaded by the cataclysm of the 1857 Mutiny, the political instability of Bengal's Blue Mutiny in 1859–60 (in which peasant labor mounted a series of boycotts and jacqueries against the coercive indigo system), and the failure to achieve anything remotely like stable economic vitality in the region, British administrators began to turn to strategies of managing and manipulating traditional social forms and fundamentally reevaluating the applicability of the universalistic political-economic doctrines that had underpinned both the Permanent Settlement and the alternative utilitarian approaches that had been adopted in other regions. By the 1860s and 1870s, influential figures as diverse as John Stuart Mill, Sir Henry Maine, Sir Charles Wood, and Sir George Campbell were identifying *custom*, the peculiar logic of native society, as the new watchword of British policy.[81] In fact, with the collapse of the indigo system in Bengal and the development of better transportation infrastructures, the 1860s and 1870s were actually a period of deepening commercialization of smallholding agriculture in rural Bengal, most notably in the form of jute cultivation; but the commercialization of capital and product markets, both increasingly subordinated to metropolitan capital, went hand in hand with the reshaping and reinforcement of ostensibly native and customary structures of land and labor hierarchies.[82] Commercial society was increasingly understood as a superficial colonial imposition sitting atop forms of social institution that were fundamentally different in their organizing logic. A move to consolidate the legal rights of ryots (envisioned as the new vehicles of agricultural improvement and capital accumulation) evident in the agrarian policy of the Bengal Presidency in the post-Mutiny period was consistently articulated in terms of the limited applicability of classical political-economic postulates to the Indian context: "The principles of political economy apply only to rents settled by free competition," explained an anonymous author in 1865. "In the Mofussil there is no such thing known; and the principle, if introduced among a population almost purely agricultural, would result in a cottier system of pauperism and misery. The custom, or theory, of rent here, has always implied a limitation of the landlord's demand long before it reached the point assigned by Ricardo as the limit on his system."[83] In other words, native society was organized on principles quite different from those characteristic of the kind of commercial society found in the West; and as such, the rationality of political economy was not universal and could not be deemed to pertain to the Indian context. The old arguments of Rammohun Roy and Peary Chand Mitra in favor of tenancy reform would now be revived and even, in 1859 and 1885, legislated; but they would increasingly be grounded in the quite distinct and radically allochronizing logic of a customary right rather than in the universalistic logic of labor, property, and rational interest. A new "science of political economy" would no longer be grounded in the universalist assumptions that Roy and Mitra were advocating, but instead "takes its date and forms its inferences from the state of society we find here."[84] The collapse of regional capitalist enterprise in Calcutta would increasingly give commercial or civil society—the practical foundation of an earlier Bengali liberalism's ideological agenda—the appearance of an alien imposition over an underlying traditional society that modern capitalism had never succeeded in penetrating. By the 1870s, a nascent comparative sociology had come to grips with the implications of this bifurcation in the high-colonial social formation of eastern India by positing the difference between India and the West as that between custom and political economy. In so doing, it implicitly posited that Indian society did not partake of the logic of civil or commercial society, and correlatively that the liberal categories that were tied to the sphere of circulation were distinctively and peculiarly Western in nature.[85]

We should not oversimplify the dynamics of this transformation. It was in the immediate aftermath of these events, during the controversy surrounding the 1849 Black Act that had sought to end European exemption from the criminal jurisdiction of local courts in the mofussil, that we see the first serious attempt to organize and voice the political demand for racial equality before the law—a political mobilization that led directly to the merger of the Landholders Society and the Bengal British India Society into the British Indian Association in 1851.[86] But whereas, in 1836, Dwarkanath had been led by his active alliances with local European trading interests to adopt an unsavory public opposition to Macaulay's earlier Black Act, the emergence in 1851 of what was arguably the first effective Indian political organization saw the exclusion of the many Europeans in Calcutta who had been active members of the two preceding organizations out of which it was formed.[87] Liberalism did not simply die in 1848: the categories of liberal thought would go on to enjoy a long and eminent ideological career in the second half of the nineteenth century, in the Indian Association and the Congress. But just as the economic and social organization of (especially eastern) India was becoming profoundly bifurcated along a racial divide—a racism that was certainly not in itself entirely new to the midcentury, but which was undergoing a profound reconstitution and intensification under the impact of the transformation of eastern India's social organization (and, in the context of contemporary transformations in racial discourses in Jamaica, we might also say the global reorganization of empire[88])—so too was its politics.

In earlier decades, the spokesmen for capitalist development in Calcutta had largely been arguing for a more rigorous application of free-trade principles through the dismantling of inequitable duties protecting British industrial interests. In the 1860s we find the first concerted articulation of the Bengali critique of laissez-faire; but still, this critique would take the form of an attempt to recuperate liberal categories for a transformed context. In 1864, Sunjeeb Chatterjee (Bankim's brother) was defending the 1859 legislated intervention into rural property relations through a seamless combination of an appeal to John Stuart Mill's invocation of the category of custom in India, and a strictly economic justification for the accrual of a right of occupancy to the cultivator who, having "increased the productive powers of his land," was entitled to "enjoy the remainder of the fruits of his labour" by retaining "the land he cultivates, longer than the caprice or love of gain of his landlord may allow."[89] Like Peary Chand Mitra, an intervention in the operation of free exchange in rural society was intended to extend the benefits of security of property to a wider sector of the population, to allow the great body of Bengali ryots to participate more fully in the sphere of circulation. In 1869, Chandranath Bose went a step further, calling upon the government to give systematic encouragement to the development of a manufacturing industry in India. Bose's aim was not however to mount a critique of imperialism in the name of an independent nation, but rather to transform the unequal relationship between metropole and colony.

> [India] is yet only a hewer of wood and drawer of water for English civiliza-
> tion in the East. But once let manufactures be established in Bengal, let Bengal
> once know that the cloth which she wears, the paper on which she writes, and
> knife with which she cuts will be no longer prepared for her by England, and
> she will perceive the necessity of looking beyond the resources of her own
> art and science, to consult the whole of Europe on the methods of manufac-
> turing industry, to examine Nature with a minute and scrutinizing eye. When
> Bengal becomes a country of manufactures, she will begin to think and act;
> then will she rise in the esteem of civilized Europe; then, for the first time in
> her history, will she acquire a position of dignity and importance in the great
> commonwealth of nations. Then chiefly, will Bengal find it necessary to culti-
> vate the acquaintance she has formed with England—the great mistress of the
> commercial world. Then will England herself form with her a friendship more
> close, more intellectual than subsists at present, and then will that friendship be
> placed on that basis of mutual esteem and respect, without which friendship is
> a serious misnomer.[90]

Bose was calling for government intervention in the freedom of exchange not to overcome the logic of the sphere of circulation, but to strengthen it; and not to undo the cosmopolitan imperial framework that Rammohun had imagined, but to revivify it in the face of economic and political bifurcation.

Just a few years later, Bholanath Chandra would publish a series of articles in *Mookerjee's Magazine* that introduced the "drain of wealth" theory that, as Manu Goswami has discussed, would become in the subsequent decades so central to the great Indian political economists' critiques of imperialism from the standpoint of a national economic space.[91] The shift to a properly nationalist political economy that we see in Bholanath Chandra, however, also remained continuous with Bose's argument in crucial ways. The critique of a cosmopolitan liberal political economy was driven by a desire to restore the vibrancy of commercial society in Bengal and thereby rescue native society from its post-1848 lethargy. Railing against the "enormous and unceasing drain upon the profits of Indian labour" by exploitative foreign capital, Chandra denounced laissez-faire doctrine in the name of the government's duty "to govern India upon the principle of European equity and equality."[92] The national developmentalism of the Congress political economists, as Goswami has pointed out, criticized the contradictions of global capitalism and British imperial domination of the global economy by advocating the concentration of capital within a national economic space.[93] But I think we can specify the nature of this critique even further: in the 1860s and 1870s, what we see emerging is a specifically liberal national political economy that sought to rescue the saliency of liberal categories from the effects of the transformations in colonial society and economy in the post-1848 period by promoting a vibrant commercial society through deliberate political intervention. Liberalism had to start making sacrifices for the feasibility of its own social logic—and it had to begin with the inviolability of free circulation. But the aim of protectionism was, after all, a more vibrant and sustainable national civil society. From this perspective, we can begin to distinguish the liberal national political economy of the Moderate Congress, whose highpoint in Bengal would be Romesh Chandra Dutt's two-volume *Economic History of India* published in the first years of the twentieth century, from the culturalist national political economy of the Bengali Extremists, to which we will return in chapter 5.

SATIRIZING THE BABU

In October of 1831, the editor of the *India Gazette* commented on the "conflict going on between light and darkness, truth and error" among the "more intelligent and educated classes of the Native population of Calcutta." "The labours of Rammohun Roy and the establishment of the Hindoo College" together had given a "shock to the popular system of idolatry in Calcutta" and produced in turn a new generation of young men who "have embraced liberal sentiments." It was the "Ultra or Radical party" among these latter that enjoyed "the warmest wishes" of the editor—albeit not without some crucial reservations about their grasp of "the nature of the means most likely to promote" their crucial mission. For these young men, whom we have already encountered in later life as Young Bengal, were making a crucial error of judgment when they "unnecessarily run counter to the customs and institutions of native society" by confrontationally asserting their "right of exercising their own judgment on moral and religious truth" even with respect to issues that "need not trouble any man's conscience." Notable here was their "radical intolerance which is utterly opposed to that philosophy and love of freedom and truth and virtue of which such ample profession is made," and also their "indiscriminate eating and drinking, i.e. eating and drinking not in conformity with the rules of caste," which precluded them from the respectability necessary for their acting as a "salutary influence over those who compose that society." "When it is considered that the writers are young and inexperienced, imperfectly acquainted with the language in which they write, superficially informed on the religions of their forefathers which they have forsaken, and not even professing to have any system of their own to substitute for it, we may conclude with what feelings the assumption of this tone is regarded by their countrymen."[94]

The dismissal of Derozio from his position at the Hindu College on the charge of promoting immorality and atheism a few months earlier had already amply demonstrated the feelings with which Young Bengal's provocations had been regarded.[95] But while the 1830s and 1840s saw the strengthening of the political position and influence of liberal voices in Calcutta—symbolized by Radhakanta Deb's acceptance of Debendranath Tagore's leadership during the antimissionary mobilization of the 1840s[96]—the basic thrust of the *Gazette*'s critique of the Derozians' subordination of the substance of social reform to the public self-presentation of radicalism would live on.

In the 1820s, Bhabanicharan Bandyopadhyay had voiced an implicit critique of the luxurious indulgences of the Persianized business elite of which both Rammohun and Dwarkanath were such prominent examples. The standpoint of this criticism of the excessive absorption of the new babus in the worldliness of salaried labor and the pleasures of consumption was a pragmatic compromise in which true caste Hindus subordinated the practical exigencies of worldly affairs to the duties to gods and lineage through which they maintained ritual purity.[97] But in a classic satire of 1859, alongside a conventional representation of the Briton as arrogant, ignorant, and both verbally and physically abusive, Michael Madhusudan Dutt depicted the liberals of Young Bengal frequenting a "River of Knowledge Society" (*jnanatarangini sabha*), where they threw about clichés of social reform and individual emancipation, flaunted their English skills, and advocated the forbidden pleasures of alcohol, meat, and dancing girls as the core values of the new civilization.[98] Here the object of the critique was no longer the excesses of the new civilization, but rather the inadequacy of Young Bengal's instantiation of the new civilization. It was not because Young Bengal espoused the language of emancipation that they were objects of ridicule, but because the petty Anglicisms they mistook for emancipation were a travesty of emancipation. The standpoint of the satire had shifted from that of a ritual purity beyond the limits of the new civilization to that civilization's own essential and universal values. For while respectable Bengalis of the second half of the nineteenth century might have been growing increasingly censorious about the corrupting influence of sensuous pleasures and conspicuous consumption, "wealth" nevertheless remained, as a minor moralist explained in 1864, what "makes exchange possible." It was as such "a fundamental necessity of human beings," in the absence of which the "illiterate and poor" were doomed to an unorganized, dirty, and slovenly existence devoid of the elevating touch of learning (*vidya*).[99]

Dutt's identification with the values of *true* civilization would remain the dominant hallmark of the new babu satire that would flourish in the second half of the nineteenth century.[100] The most famous of all babu satirists, Bankimchandra Chatterjee, remained consistent with the general thrust of this tradition through the 1870s.[101] "Baboo," explained the *Hobson-Jobson*, a dictionary of Anglo-Indian patois, was "properly a term of respect attached to a name, like Master or *Mr.*," but "is often used with a slight savour of disparagement, as characterizing a superficially cultivated, but too often effeminate, Bengali."[102] The effeminacy of the Bengali had been contrasted to the manly physicality of the Briton since the eighteenth century. But the babu femininity that Bankim was invoking was more specific than this older stereotype. Nor did the effeminacy of Bankim's babu refer to the femininity of what he called Bengal's "old-style woman," a formidably earthy figure that no one in his or her right mind would want to mess with. He was invoking the femininity of the "new woman," herself an "appalling babu" whose taste and sophistication were achieved at the cost of her laziness, vanity, and selfishness.[103] This trope of femininity served to hitch indulgence in sensual pleasure to the weakness of submission to another's will—an association indexed by the babu's stereotypical uxoriousness. "The English master leads you by the nose and sets you to circling the grindstone, and around you go because you have no strength," scoffs an imaginary female respondent to Bankim's attack on the new woman. "And we [women] also lead you in circles by the nose, and around you go because you have no intelligence" (*BR* 254). As a nonproductive consumer, it is the babu's wife who not only represents babuism in its most exacerbated form but also the system of worldly attachments that drives the babu to absorption in worldly affairs: "We can see that having learnt English you have learnt clerkship," the same respondent mocks. "But humanity?" (*BR* 254). Thus the trope of femininity in turn denotes the humiliation inherent in the babu's degrading and tedious existence as a low-level salaried office employee. "In Bengal, humanity is measured in terms of one's salary—one must measure precisely the tail of someone who is so great a monkey. No other country has ever suffered such degradation. The prisoner displays and boasts about the length of his leg-irons" (*BR* 116). Such an existence does not admit of the realization of independence in the commercial exchange of labor power for salary, but only the curse of subordination. It is thus precisely as a participant in commercial society that the babu becomes a trope of heteronomy.

The other conventional theme of *babuyana* (babuism) that Bankim invoked with regularity in his satires was the inauthenticity of the babu's pretensions to civilization. "We have cast away caste," declares Bankim's imaginary spokesman for Young Bengal. "We have outlived the absurdity of a social classification based upon the accident of birth. But we are not such ultra-radicals as to adopt for our catchword the impracticable formula of 'Equality and Fraternity.'"[104] The babu's embrace of Western learning and reformism was not the result of any genuine engagement with the substantial content of those ideals, but rather from the desperate desire for social or professional advancement and for the approval of the colonial Master. Whereas Bankim could on the one hand invoke the Western-educated babu as the vehicle of emancipation from the ancient bonds of superstition and ignorance (*BR* 288), he could on the other hand deride the pretensions of the babu mercilessly: "Oh you who can read our minds! Whatever I do is to entice you. So that you might call me a philanthropist, I donate to the public welfare. So you might call me erudite, I study. So, oh Englishman! Smile upon me. I lie at your feet in obeisance" (*BR* 10). The babu never genuinely appropriated the universal truths of Western civilization for himself or his people, but rather sought to distance himself from the taint of nativeness through "a scrupulously exact English costume, with its collateral incidents of occasional invitations to dinner from Englishmen and occasional salaams from Railway porters and cabmen, and secondly, a habitual manifestation, by word, look and gesture, of a thorough contempt for 'niggers.'" But while "the transmigration from black to white defies the existing resources of chemistry and cosmetics," he would never quite be able to raise himself to the status of an Englishman, and could only reduce himself to a pathetic caricature of that notional model of enlightened, virile independence.[105] The result of this impasse was the babu's propensity to dissolve all practical matters into a haze of empty verbiage: "He whose words are one in his mind, ten in his speech, a hundred in writing and a thousand in dispute, he is a babu. He whose strength is onefold in his hands, tenfold in his speech, a hundredfold on his back and invisible at work-time, he is a babu" (*BR* 12). The babu was the ultimate travesty of the promise of worldly emancipation: "Those who will accumulate without purpose, earn in order to accumulate, study in order to earn, and steal the questions in order to study, they are babus" (*BR* 10).

Little here suggests, however, that Bankim's satire was intended to take aim at the actual ideals of emancipation and independence that the babu was claiming or aspiring to represent. Even as he decried an anglicized culture in which a respectability defined by "the balance at the banker's" had toppled "the cumulative humanities of a hundred generations," he continued to identify explicitly with the project of enlightenment, questioning only whether that enlightenment was best served by English or Indian sources of inspiration.[106] In keeping with the uneasy spirit of what we might call a liberal mode of satire, when the babu was ridiculous, it was because he had failed to live up to the ideals of humanity that he so volubly, yet crassly, articulated. This standpoint is quite consistent with other registers of Bankim's contemporary writings, for in the 1870s, when he was composing these satires, he stood out as one of the most trenchant and rigorous exponents of the Bengali liberal tradition. In his long essay on *Equality*, first published serially from 1873 to 1875 and subsequently collected into a short book in 1879, Bankim would return directly to the themes of Peary Chand Mitra's essay on landlord-tenant relations, and reiterate many of the same arguments about the immiserating burdens of rent, debt, corruption, and coercion (*BR* 389–99). Natural inequalities, Bankim argued, might legitimately be recognized in society through, for example, a meritocratic division of labor. But such inequalities could nonetheless never be used to abrogate the universality of equal rights and justify unnatural inequalities instituted in human society, including discrimination on the basis of caste, gender, race, and class (*BR* 388–89). It was a key feature of "advanced societies" that "the members of those societies have through friction with one another eliminated [unnatural] inequality. Prosperity has arisen in all those realms." But it had been India's peculiar curse to develop unparalleled degrees of unnatural inequality. "Of all the reasons for the obstruction of progress and degradation, an excess of inequality is foremost among them. The specific reason that India has for so long been in such misery is this same excess of social inequality" (*BR* 382). *Equality* was a self-conscious attempt to connect the ethical values of liberalism with the social benefits of prosperity through the practice of free exchange in civil society.

Civilizational development, Bankim argued, stemmed from two primal sources. The first was the desire for knowledge, the second the desire for wealth. But while the first of these was certainly more palatable, in reality the notoriously selfish and base desire for wealth, as the more universally prevalent and the less easily sated, was undeniably the more fundamental engine of improvement. The independent pursuit of individual interests was the ultimate font of material prosperity and intellectual progress, Bankim argued. The spiritual contentment characteristic of Hindu otherworldliness was in reality "a deadly poison for social life" leading to that "habitual laziness and want of energy" so characteristic of the inhabitants of fertile tropical lands (*BR* 392–99). Bankim's linkage of free exchange, prosperity, and the liberal values of equality and freedom was even rigorous enough for him to stand forth as the last prominent Bengali intellectual to offer, in his 1873 essay on "Bengal's Peasants," a trenchant defense of British free-trade policies against the rising tide of Bengali protectionism. Invoking classical political economy, he argued that rather than being poorer than it had been before colonization, India had actually been made more prosperous by foreign trade; that, as a form of equal exchange, foreign trade did not drain wealth from the country; and that the destruction of India's handicraft industries simply led to a reallocation of labor to other, more buoyant sectors of the economy (*BR* 310–13). His vindication of free exchange as the natural engine of prosperity and improvement extended right down to his critique of the confinement of women to the zenana as the most "merciless, abominable and unethical inequality" from the standpoint of a fundamental naturalization of unconstrained mobility (*BR* 402). "If nobody was excessively rich and powerful, and if the common people enjoyed freedom of choice, every person could become authentically human. There would be no limit to the country's progress" (*BR* 314). And once again, the institutional lynchpin of this liberal imagination was the British Empire: "On behalf of those sixty million destitute and deprived Bengali cultivators, I weep with hands clasped—Let them be prosperous!—May British rule never end!—Let the English cast their glance upon the helpless cultivators!" (*BR* 307).

But the standpoint of Bankim's satires will not be quite so neatly contained as his trenchant liberalism would suggest. The figure of the old-style woman, representing the simple strength of native authenticity against the hollowness of cosmopolitan sophistication and colonial mimicry, introduced a new alignment of independence *with* popular tradition and *against* commercial society.[107] Correlatively, the critique of colonial society showed a tendency to balloon: "English civilization has pulled down the three hundred and thirty million deities of Hinduism, and set up, in the total space once occupied by them, its own tutelary deities, Comfort and his brother, Respectability."[108] He ridiculed the utilitarian philosophy that had so inspired nineteenth-century Bengali liberals—including not least among them Bankim himself—as mere "belly-philosophy" (BR 54–56). Ultimately, the entire world of social interactions would be transfigured in his imagination into a phantasmagoria of venality: "this entire universe of attachments [vishvasangsar] is an enormous marketplace. Everyone there fits out their own shop. Everyone's aim is to get their price. . . . The ceaseless effort to buy cheap is called human life" (BR 76).[109] The worshipful pursuit of material wealth, along with the recitation of "mantras from Adam Smith's puranas and Mill's tantras," leads the babu to damnation (BR 61). And where "worldliness" had seemed to promise "independence," it delivered in its stead only "a habit of heartless isolation."[110] In satirizing the babu, Bankim was satirizing not just the inadequacies of the Bengali's absorption into the logic of commercial society and of his hollow appropriations of Western civilization, but also inevitably Western civilization itself insofar as it was understood to be constituted in its essence by the values of commercial society. By 1880, when he published his last satire, we see the direction of a new, harsher anger at the babu—an anger that negates the earlier self-reflexivity of his ridicule and bespeaks instead a deepening dis-identification from the object of ridicule.[111] This is the first strong indication that Bankim was about to abandon the liberal critique of false civilization, projecting instead an external standpoint for the critique of babuism, and with it commercial society. It is at the moment of such a transition that we see emerging the now familiar dismissal of Bengali liberalism as the imitative shadow of an *alien* (commercial) civilization.

The stridency of Bankim's liberal political rhetoric in the 1870s should not distract us from the tensions contemporaneously emerging in his satirical literature. The increasing rupture separating Bengali society from commercial society at the practical and the conceptual levels, coupled with the deepening sense of marginalization, subordination, dehumanization, and degradation that characterized the babu's sense of his participation in commercial society as a salaried employee, were together already in the 1860s and 1870s working to produce a sense of fragility at the heart of Bengali liberalism—a fragility expressed in the political-economic language of protectionism and in the satirical language of *babuyana*. This fragility was not in itself sufficient to undo liberalism; after all, salaried labor is by its nature participation in commercial society regardless of whether it is demeaning or not. Indeed, it was precisely the demands for greater opportunities for advancement and greater participation in government—demands for racial equality that fundamentally express the logic of circulation—that would fuel the political agenda of the British Indian Association from the 1850s, the Indian Association from the mid-1870s, and the Indian National Congress from the mid-1880s.[112] And, after all, it is not hard to see that it is precisely in the face of substantive limits to the full realization of formal freedom and equality that the liberal imagination has sought to establish the full rights of commodity ownership, and hence transform a liberal philosophy into a liberal politics.

But having moved to Chinsura in 1879 and there made the acquaintance of a new circle of intellectuals including the Comtean, Jogendra Chandra Ghosh, and the conservative educationist, Bhudeb Mukhopadhyay, Bankim was increasingly inclined to take a different path.[113] His satirical portrayal of the inadequacies of the babu's instantiation of liberal subjectivity led him in turn to a characterization of liberal subjectivity as itself a quintessentially Western norm incongruous with being native. In the face of this distancing of commercial society as a Western domain, there emerged for him an alternative approach to the predicament of colonial subjectivity. Where the practices of (Western) commercial society presented only a travesty of independence, indigeneity might provide an alternative path of authentic self-realization. In the space that the older conservatives had carved out for the defense of the integrity of caste and lineage, Bankim would set out to erect something much more ambitious: a dynamic ethical and social philosophy grounded in the concept of culture. And so in the 1880s, he would repudiate *Equality* unequivocally: "Bankim babu said: 'At one time [J. S.] Mill had a powerful influence over me, now all that is over.' When the subject of his own essay came up, he said, '*Equality* is completely erroneous. It is a very good seller, but I shall not reprint it.'"[114] Republishing "Bengal's Peasants" in 1892, he introduced the essay as a historical curiosity, and repudiated the economic arguments in it. "When it comes to economics, it is impossible to determine which claims are wrong and which are definitely true," he would note, thus recalling the permanent closure of his interest in political economy, and with it liberal social critique (*BR* 287). Henceforth, Bankim would shine forth as the prophet of a new ethical and social imagination—one that turned on a language of sacrifice rather than happiness, worldly renunciation rather than the pursuit of self-interest, and India's cultural rather than Europe's material civilization.

CHAPTER FOUR

———— ✳ ————

Hinduism as Culture

The successive waves of revival and transfiguration of the old regime *in Europe will prepare us for a study of the parallel movement in Bengal known as neo-Hinduism, or the Hindu revival. . . . Said Chateaubriand . . . "I am a Bourbonist in honour, a monarchist by conviction, and a republican by temperament and disposition"; and in this country, in need of an equally comprehensive plea, stands no doubt, the thinker who contributed to its literature of Illumination an article entitled "Mill, Darwin and the Hindu Religion," another headed "Miranda, Desdemona and Sakuntala," an exposition of the* Samkhya *philosophy, and a pamphlet on* Samya (Égalité), *once leader of the vanguard of emancipation and deliverance, now the Balaam of the children of Moab and, we may say too Philistia!*

BRAJENDRANATH SEAL,
"THE NEO-ROMANTIC MOVEMENT IN LITERATURE"[1]

SOMETIME around 1880, when he began composing his most (in)famous novel, *Anandamath* (*The Abbey of Bliss*), Bankimchandra Chatterjee underwent a major intellectual reorientation. The philosopher, Brajendranath Seal, writing in the closing years of the nineteenth century, seemed to characterize this shift as a retreat from the rigors of enlightenment into the atavistic consolations of national sentiment. From this perspective, Bankim's revivalist turn must pose a fundamental problem: how can it be that an intellect critical enough to play the role of "leader of the vanguard of emancipation and deliverance" could have been seduced by so intellectually vacuous a project as neo-Hinduism?

The story of the continuous retreats that the so-called Bengal Renaissance beat over the course of the nineteenth century has, as we have already seen, constituted one of the key narratives of the historiography on modern Bengal. But Bankim and his generation inaugurated, Seal argued, a new phase in Bengali intellectual life that went beyond merely reactionary resistance to the social and intellectual transformations brought about most immediately by British rule. Bankim, howsoever inadequately, introduced a "neo-romantic element of reconstructive transfiguration which is the child of illumination."[2] According to Seal, the "vital characteristic of modern life and culture" is "a sense of discordance or disturbance, of a want of proportion between the ideal and norm of consciousness on the one hand, and the embodiment and constitution of nature and society on the other."[3] Faced with the "general wreck of an old-order world," it was the distinctive contribution of the neo-Romantic impulse to synthesize a new and more adequate form of life and consciousness by embodying modern ideals in living institutions that were grounded in "the sympathies and affinities, the historic associations and imaginative interests of the race," thereby enlisting "the conservative instincts of order, obedience and reverence in their behalf."[4] Bankim's transformation into the false idol of neo-Hindu revivalism would seem to represent for Seal a (deeply flawed) instantiation of this neo-Romantic impulse toward the positive reconstruction of society as an expression of modern subjectivity. For what the tunnel-visioned children of Moab and Philistia failed to recognize was that Bankim's neo-Hindu impulse stemmed from the dilemmas of a distinctly modern form of subjectivity posited by the nihilistic critical energies of Enlightenment reason, and not from the particularities of Indian tradition. Neo-Romanticism revived "the antique in masquerade," the "double" or "reflex" of a premodern symbolic consciousness raised by negative criticism "into self-consciousness and subjectivity."[5] As such, it sought not to return the fractured present to the past, but rather to use the forms of the past as the vehicles that would carry it to a new future.

[It was the Bankim of the later, "revivalist" phase who would elaborate a new humanism founded on the concept of *anushilan,* a Sanskritic-Bengali word denoting repetitive practice or training that he adopted as his standing equivalent for the English words *cultivation* and *culture.*] In doing so, Bankim made few converts to the specific tenets of his new theology and philosophy—though it would be hasty to underestimate the Swadeshi generation's enthusiasm for the general tenor of his later writings, or the importance of his inauguration of the *Bhagavad Gita*'s new theological preeminence in Bengal and elsewhere. (It preempted many of the philosophical themes that would be central to Bal Gangadhar Tilak's more famous 1911 commentary, for example.) What Bankim did arguably do, however, was to raise *culture* to the status of an explicitly formulated concept for the first time in Bengali. It is true, as Tithi Bhattacharya has recently argued, that from around the 1850s the Bengali bhadralok had been increasingly turning to notions of education and knowledge as a language of social distinction.[6] Bankim, however, first sought to systematize culturalism into a relatively coherent, and distinctly nonliberal, ideology. This was a move that made a lasting impact on his contemporaries and successors—not because Bankim was the originary font of a persisting intellectual influence, but rather because he was among the first, and certainly among the most prominent, to elaborate the outlines of a compelling conceptual framework for articulating a response to a historically generated problematic.

The discussion that follows will take very seriously Seal's argument that the neo-Hindu project of Bankim's later period was grounded in the predicament of a distinctly modern subjectivity. At the same time though, it will seek to eschew his easier narrative of the dialectical movement of ideas. What, I ask, would Bankim's subjective dilemmas and neo-Romantic syntheses look like if they were grounded in historically generated structures of social practice, rather than in Seal's implied and rather conventional narrative of colonial pedagogy (Enlightenment)? This new project would have to abandon the more conventional hypotheses of a retreat from the rigors of enlightenment into the consolations of sentiment, of a failure of the forces of modernization to overcome the resistance of a residual precapitalist feudalism, or of a straightforward recognition of the cultural particularity of European Reason (and its consequent inadequacy for authentically articulating the logic of Bengali social forms). We must see the logic of the emergence of the culture concept as internal to the subcontinental history of capitalism.

SUBJECTIVE FREEDOM AND WORLDLY AGENCY

In his 1877 essay "Manushyatva ki?" ("What Is Humanity?") Bankimchandra Chatterjee set out from a stark, but utterly conventional, dichotomy between two different views of the purpose of life. On the one hand, there were those who would derive man's nature from that of the microscopic life-forms that inhabited the oceans long ago. On this view, man does not choose his life on the basis of any process of decision-making, but rather seeks to fill his belly, to satisfy his external senses, and ultimately to achieve preeminence over others through wealth, position, and reputation. On the other hand, there have been spiritual teachers, both in India and in Europe, who have taught instead the necessity of renouncing the riches of this world in the quest for salvation in the next. In the first instance, man's life is reduced to a meaningless hunger for ephemeral pleasures at the expense of the common good of society. In the latter instance, we search for salvation without any way of choosing between the prescriptions of different faiths, or even of knowing whether there is a future life at all. In the former instance, we have worldly agency without the higher purpose of the moral or social good. In the latter instance, we have a subject who privileges a higher purpose at the expense of worldly agency. In the first instance, we have an agency that is achieved through the dissolution of the subject into nature. In the latter instance, we have a subject who is preserved through a complete renunciation of worldly agency (BR 374–75). By his own account, Bankim was sketching a problematic fundamental to the long durée of human history, an old conflict between materialism and spiritualism that had begun with the teachings of the Buddha. But there is good reason to see this dichotomization as diagnostic of a more historically specific condition—a deepening experiential conflict between the realm of objective necessity and the realm of subjective freedom that made itself increasingly apparent in the trajectories of the post-Rammohun Brahmo movement in the 1840s and 1850s, trajectories with which Bankim was thoroughly acquainted through the pages of its prestigious magazine, the *Tattvabodhini Patrika*.

Rammohun's theological position had been self-consciously grounded in the tradition of nondualistic (Advaita) Vedanta, which, following the eighth-century theologian Sankaracharya, argued that the experience of phenomenal diversity belied an underlying divine reality that negated all distinction, change, or description. His position explicitly held that, as both the efficient and material cause of the universe, God was unitary and eternal and admitted of no second. In framing his theology in these terms, Rammohun would explicitly argue for the essential unity of the individual soul with the Supreme Soul. In fact, since God was the material cause of the world, although He could not be considered to be identical with the material universe in a pantheistic sense, nonetheless matter was in some sense an expression of a transcendent subjectivity rather than merely the negation of subjective agency. We could then arguably see Rammohun as trying to elaborate a theological doctrine that *mediated* subjectivity and objectivity through the transcendent category of the Supreme Soul, Brahma, who was distinct from the ephemera of mundane experience, yet nonetheless irreducibly constitutive of mundane experience in both its subjective and objective dimensions. By maintaining this implicit mediation, Rammohun was able to retain his sense that the negative conception of emancipation that he espoused in his religious reform (freedom from illegitimate mediations like priest craft and idolatry) would logically correlate with a positive freedom of autonomous subjectivity.

Yet for all this, Rammohun was not devoid of serious equivocations on this issue of the nondualistic nature of existence. Responding to the critiques of Christian polemicists, we find Rammohun rejecting the charge of pantheism through an insistence on the nonidentity of the material world with God, insisting that the claim that the Supreme Soul is "one without a second" means only without a second of an eternal nature. He in turn set up a dualism of matter and spirit (object and subject) that is alien to Advaita Vedanta (*EW* 69, 152–55).[7] We might well accept that these kinds of compromises and equivocations were driven primarily by the contingencies of polemical exchanges with Protestant missionaries and the influence of friendly interaction with Unitarian collaborators—even perhaps by his Vaishnavite background. But there is also reason to think that the difficulty of maintaining a nondualist position was being posed at a more profound level of ideology. Rammohun's theology was centered on the emancipation of individual spirituality from illegitimate concrete intermediaries; but when we look at that emancipation through the lens of his social and political philosophy, we soon recognize that the independence it promised could only in the end exacerbate the experiential tensions between the categories of subjective inclination and objective circumstance. The free, equal, and property-bearing individual who emerges from the practices of the sphere of circulation, and who constitutes the standpoint of Rammohun's liberal reformism, confronts the world of objects and, through them, of social relations as "a mere means towards his private purposes, as external necessity."[8]

This internal tension would be first brought to fruition in the theological thought of Dwarkanath Tagore's son, Debendranath. While the Brahma Sabha had languished throughout the 1830s, Debendranath had nonetheless come under the spiritual influence of its presiding minister, Ramchandra Vidyabagish, much to his father's annoyance: "I always thought Vidyavagish was a good fellow," Dwarkanath reportedly declared, "but now I find that he is spoiling Devendra with his preaching of *Brahma-mantras*. As it is he has very little head for business; now he neglects business altogether; it is nothing but Brahma, Brahma the whole day."[9] Where Dwarkanath had pursued some of the social and political dimensions of Rammohun's liberalism, it was left to his son to revive his theological reformism. Like Rammohun,

Debendranath would come to be uncompromisingly critical of idolatry in any form, upholding the independent relationship with God as a core supposition of true spirituality.[10] Like Rammohun, he would be unremitting in his defense of the underlying rationality of Hinduism from its Christian detractors, leading even Rammohun's old foes like Radhakanta Deb into the formation of a society for the defense of Hinduism against missionary efforts.[11] And like Rammohun, he would accept the householder as the only proper subject of true religiosity.[12] It is not surprising that Debendranath would set out to revive the moribund energies of Rammohun's religious reform. In 1839, he founded, with Vidyabagish as its preceptor, the Tattvabodhini Sabha, or the Society for the Diffusion of Essential Truth, a forum for the discussion and promotion of Upanishadic learning that succeeded in attracting a remarkable array of the most brilliant literary and scholarly figures of the day.[13] Riding this success, he would in 1843 go on to establish a monthly journal, the *Tattvabodhini Patrika*, to act as the society's public organ.[14] And in 1842, he and his most devoted followers had begun the revival of a new Brahmo Samaj from its predecessor's practical extinction.

Debendranath was a self-conscious follower of Rammohun, but that did not stop him from engaging in a life-long polemic against the philosophical system upon whose authority Rammohun had sought to establish the rationality of Upanishadic Hinduism. "We had no faith in the Vedanta philosophy," Debendranath recalled of the new Brahmo Samaj he had come to lead in the 1840s and 1850s, "because Sankaracharya seeks to prove therein that Brahma and all created beings are one and the same. . . . We were opposed to Monism just in the same way as we were opposed to idolatry."[15] Elaborating the systematic outlines of an emphatically dualistic theology in a series of lectures in 1850–51, he established categorical distinctions between sensible matter (*jar*) and the knowing *I* or individual soul (*jibatma*), and between the individual soul and the Supreme Soul (*paramatma*).[16] "The individual soul is superior to matter and the Supreme Soul is superior to everything. Matter and soul are as different as darkness and light. These two things share no common properties. . . . Moreover, as different as the individual soul is from matter, still more different in His infinitude is the Supreme Soul from the individual soul."[17] The Supreme Soul is omnipresent both within us and in nature, but He is in no way to be construed as consubstantial with either. For Brahma is absolutely not, as in Rammohun's Advaita doctrine, the "material cause of the universe," but merely manifests His will in the purposive design of the universe. To suggest that the universe and the living souls who inhabit it were in any sense the manifestation or embodiment of the Supreme

Soul was to argue the impossible: the eternal and immutable had become mutable, a transcendent being could experience the joys and sufferings of worldly attachment, and that which admits of no divisibility is composed of the many distinct souls that inhabit the universe. "All these living creatures and inert materials are never part of Him, nor do they ever share the same substance with Him; He has not negated himself by manifesting himself as inert matter, nor has He bound himself to grief, ignorance, sin or sorrow by transforming himself into living creatures; He has created this inconceivable universe while dwelling in His own eternal nature."[18]

Rammohun's nondualistic emphasis on the Supreme Soul as a category of subject/object mediation was arguably fundamental to his ability to formulate a theology that held at bay the opposition between religion and worldliness; by identifying the essence of the individual subject with the Supreme Soul as both efficient and material cause of the universe, the negative freedom of emancipation (from sensuous attachments, historical accretions, and illegitimate coercion) could at least implicitly be linked to the positive freedom of worldly agency. Debendranath followed Rammohun in looking to a practice of self-discipline as the means of aligning the individual soul with the wishes of the Supreme Soul: "I began to train myself to listen for His command, to understand the difference between my own inclination and His will. What seemed to me to be the insidious promptings of my own desires I was careful to avoid, and what appeared to my conscience to be His command, that I tried to follow."[19] He also put the negative freedom of emancipation at the center of his conceptual schema. But if that emancipation took as its core problematic the fact that the "individual soul is locked from birth in the cage of the body," the independence that Debendranath envisaged for the pious householder could only be the negation of worldly attachments through the immersion in otherworldly worship of the Supreme Soul, Brahma.[20] When his father's company, Carr, Tagore and Company, collapsed in 1847, Debendranath would inwardly celebrate: "Things turned out just as I wanted,—all our property went out of my hands. As in my mind there was no desire for the things of this world, so also no worldly goods were mine."[21] In fact, the more his "antipathy and indifference to the world" increased, the more eager did he become "to descend into the deeper recesses of my soul in search of the Supreme Soul."[22] So Debendranath would wryly advise his more worldly associates (much to their amusement) to avoid religious enquiry: "Reading the Tatwabodhini [Patrika] brings one to such a plight as mine."[23] Unlike Rammohun, Debendranath fundamentally de-linked the negative freedom of individual independence from the positive freedom of worldly agency.

Worldly agency could only be object-bondage. The individual soul could only confront the world now as an alien arena of heteronomy to be overcome by the contemplation of a transcendent deity entirely separate from it.

Where Debendranath rescued the freedom of the subject at the expense of worldly agency, his main rival for control of the Tattvabodhini Sabha and Brahmo Samaj, Akshay Kumar Dutt, developed a radically different resolution from the same dualistic premises. Dutt first emerged to prominence when he was selected by Debendranath to edit the *Tattvabodhini Patrika* in 1843, but it soon became apparent that the two men differed in their philosophical inclinations. As Debendranath famously put it: "I used to pen through such portions of his writings as went contrary to my opinions, and try to bring him round to my point of view. But this was not an easy matter for me, we were poles asunder. I was seeking to know my relations with God, he was seeking to know the relations of man with the outer world. The difference was as between heaven and earth."[24] Debendranath was making an undisguised reference here to one of Dutt's most-read works, *Bahya bastur sahit manab prakritir sambandha bicar* (*A Consideration of the Relationship between Human Nature and External Matter*, 1851–53), wherein he had formulated the general proposition that, as the natural laws of the universe were an expression of divine intention, so it followed that happiness resulted from compliance with those laws, and suffering from their transgression.[25] Self-interest, informed by a proper understanding of natural laws acquired through scientific observation, thus became indistinguishable from morality—in the end both conform to instrumental reasoning that takes utility as its aim. Obeying the dictates of externally imposed constraint becomes the essence of dharma, which for now we might gloss as ethical duty. Dutt sought to fulfill the promise of prosperity and happiness that Rammohun's liberalism had held out as the consequence of emancipation—but, in contrast to Debendranath, he could only do so by making the subject conform to the lawlike regularities posited in the natural world. In other words, it was by dissolving the subject into the object world that Dutt sought to recuperate liberalism's promise. Where Debendranath had sacrificed any vision of a worldly agency that could deliver the utility that emancipation had promised in his quest to salvage human subjectivity, Dutt instead sacrificed human subjectivity to salvage a worldly agency that could deliver utility.

The Bankim of "What Is Humanity?" could not accept the negation of worldliness as the condition of Debendranath's subjective emancipation. Like Dutt, Bankim rejected any view of human life as a mere testing ground for the afterlife: if an action was deemed virtuous by the measure of the next world (whose existence did not even admit of demonstration), there was no reason why it should not also be virtuous by the measure of its effects in this world. But Bankim was also clearly hesitant to accept Dutt's dissolution of human subjectivity into the lawlike regularities of the object world. Bankim wanted a theory that overcame the dichotomy between spirituality and worldliness, subjectivity and agency, that had developed such experiential urgency with the hollowing out of the Bengali liberal subject in the second half of the nineteenth century. "In reality, the purpose of human life," he concluded, "is the holistic cultivation [anushilan], the complete unfolding and appropriate development and perfection of all the various mental faculties," including both the "practical faculties" whose purpose was action and the "cognitive faculties" whose purpose was knowledge (BR 375). Acceding neither to the conception of a nonagential subject nor that of an agential nonsubject, Bankim instead sought to elaborate a doctrine of agential subjectivity grounded in the concept of culture. Unprepared in 1877 to renounce his attachment to liberalism, Bankim would conclude by holding up John Stuart Mill and Goethe as the two great modern exemplars of this model of personhood—figures whom he clearly thought to have infused liberal ideology with an emphatic doctrine of cultivation (BR 376). When in the 1880s he finally broke more radically from his earlier liberalism, he would replace Mill and Goethe with figures drawn from the Hindu tradition. He would spend the entire decade of the 1880s elaborating this turn to culture.

A NEW UNIVERSALISM

Responding to an intemperate assault on Hindu idolatry by a Scottish missionary in 1882, Bankim asserted the privilege of native understanding to fundamentally question the capacity of any European to grasp the essential core of Hinduism.[26] Translations might be competently executed by European scholars, but

> no translation from the Sanskrit into a European language can truly or even approximately represent the original. . . . You can translate a word by a word, but behind the word there is an idea, the thing which the word denotes, and this idea you cannot translate, if it does not exist among the people in whose language you are translating. . . . If Mr. Hastie thinks he can comprehend the vast complicated labyrinth of Hindu religious belief without studying it in the original sources of knowledge . . . he will fail in arriving at a correct comprehension of Hinduism, as—I say it most emphatically—*as every other European who has made the attempt has failed.*[27]

Pitfalls of translation onto the loss of ideas

Role of language

It was indeed Europeans who had revived the study of Vedic literature, but the Vedas "do not represent the living religion of India."[28] Both as foreigners with at best limited access to Hinduism's living, often oral tradition, and as nonbelievers who could only view religious doctrines as "mere dead formulae, the lifeless carcass which may yet yield a lesson to the anatomist, but which is useless to the student of human nature," Europeans had only ever gnawed on the "husk" of the coconut of Sanskrit learning, without ever reaching its "kernel."[29] In the end, "Hinduism does not consider itself placed on the defense. In the language of lawyers, there is not yet a properly framed charge against it."[30]

Bankim was trying out a strikingly relativistic strategy in order to carve out a space of autonomy for his new project of developing a philosophical foundation from within the bounds of a Hinduism never yet grasped by its European, Orientalist critics. Yet what is most striking is that he would never again invoke this kind of relativistic argument. Through the 1880s, Bankim composed a series of treatises and novels that sought to elaborate his vision of a revivified Hindu order—most notably in *Dharmmatattva: Anushilan* (*The Essence of Religion: Culture*[31]) and *Krishnacarittra* (*The Life of Krishna*, 1886[32]), two works conceived and composed together as a complementary pair representing, respectively, principle and example, ideal and embodiment.[33] But much in these works must be puzzling for those who would see Bankim's rejection of the liberal values of the sphere of circulation as an atavistic (or emancipatory) retreat from modern categories of universalistic reason into the consolations of traditional authority. The new subjectivity he envisioned in these works would indeed be constituted within the indigenous realm of Hindu thought and practice rather than the alien realm of civil society that had grounded the inauthentic existence of the babu. But Bankim consistently avoided resorting to arguments about the incommensurability of India and the West as two irreducibly particularistic traditions, instead judging each by the standards of an uncompromisingly universalistic critical standpoint that was fully capable of discriminating among specific Hindu traditions and of incorporating elements from outside those traditions. This clearly implies, as all analyses of Bankim have explicitly or implicitly recognized, a standpoint that cannot be adequately explained in terms of the internal conceptual logic of indigenous traditions.

Bankim's indigenist turn was not a revocation of universalism as such, but rather the revocation of a more specific mode of universalistic rationality grounded in the emancipatory potentialities of the sphere of circulation. Having become increasingly critical of the emancipatory aspects of civil society, Bankim instead adopted the category of culture to explicate a form of rationality grounded in practical activity (at the individual level of objectifying activity and at the sociological level of functional coordination) that was supposedly immanent to the logic of Hindu thought. He was thereby able to transform the defensive posture of conservative attempts to demarcate the boundaries of colonial authority and worldly necessity into a dynamic social and ethical philosophy.

The essence of dharma, explains a guru to his disciple in *Dharmmatattva*, is neither ritual nor worship, but rather the proper cultivation of one's innate capacities. Such self-cultivation should be holistic, encompassing all the mental and physical faculties possessed by mankind. The result of this is the cultivation of that harmonious totality, "humanity" (*BR* 584–96). The practice of an adequate system of cultivation—the Bengali word used is *anushilan*, which in standard usage in fact means *practice*, but which early on in the text is explicitly identified by Bankim as a Bengali synonym for the English word *culture*—leads to the only true happiness: the happiness that comes from exercising a properly cultivated faculty. The guru explains this with an example. Why, he asks, does eating Bengali sweets cause his disciple happiness? After all, on the one hand one would scarcely be able to coax an Englishman newly arrived in Calcutta to swallow a Bengali sweet—while on the other hand, it would bring no happiness to the disciple to gnaw on a piece of roast beef. As such, the happiness that results could not come directly from the sweetness itself. The disciple replies that it is "habit." The guru corrects him: "Call this culture (anushilan) instead." Culture (anushilan) and habit (*abhyas*) are crucially different. The cultivation of taste is the education of the senses through repetitive practice (anushilan), and as such represents the expansion and development of one's innate, potential capacities. The dulling force of habit is, in contrast, something that diminishes and inhibits the expansive tendencies of human agency. It is by cultivating one's faculty of taste through exercising that faculty that one experiences happiness, and it is the harmonious cultivation of all the faculties that leads to true happiness (*BR* 587). The excessive cultivation of any one faculty at the expense of the harmony of the whole person leads only to ephemeral pleasure at the expense of lasting happiness. To cultivate a taste for sweets is good; to become addicted to them is gluttony.

Harmonious cultivation leads to a human being who achieves release (*mukti*) from the sorrows of this world, for it is in the exercise of the faculties for their own sake, rather than in the rewards of the action's outcome, that happiness is achieved (*BR* 585–86). Such a practitioner of *nishkam karma*—

[handwritten margin note at top: Freedom is no longer conceptn of rational self-intes from social determination]

the "desireless action" preached by Krishna in the *Bhagavad Gita*—has cultivated his innate capacities in such a way that he can, practically speaking, better overcome difficulties in the world. Making right action its own end, he has moreover released himself from bondage to the fruits of his actions and thereby achieved autonomy from the object world without sacrificing worldly agency (*BR* 589, 631-33). Freedom is no longer to be grounded in the emancipation of rational self-interest from the social determinations of willful authority (whether of priests or kings). The renunciation of desire was to be the basis of a freedom that located real happiness in the self-constituting quality of objectifying practice—not in the negation of external authority in the act of free exchange, but in the realization of one's own power in nature-commanding activity.

[handwritten margin note: Renunciation of desire is the basis of freedom]

But where could one find a model, an ideal for emulation, of such fully realized "humanity"? It will be no surprise that after 1880, Bankim emphatically refused to look westward for his answer. "This is the Western [*bilati*] *Doctrine of Culture!*" exclaims the disciple after hearing the guru's exposition. But the guru replies that "*Culture* is not a European thing. It is the essence of Hindu dharma" (*BR* 585, italicized words in English in original). If Western philosophers have elaborated this theory of culture most explicitly in modern times, this does not make culture Western. Rather, if anything, it makes such philosophers Hindu. "The fact that Europe has been able to grasp after much groping even half of the broad substance of Hinduism, is not trifling evidence of Hinduism's excellence" (*BR* 596). Correlatively, the model for emulation was no longer Mill and Goethe. Rather, it was God—and more specifically, a *personal* God, who has been incarnate on earth—who embodied the fullest all-round development of the human faculties.

Since such a God was not immediately present before us, humans would have to meditate upon him with devotion (*bhakti*). The state of true devotion, "*when all of man's faculties are directed to God or follow God,*" thereby became a means to shape man's own nature according to the ideal represented by the divine (*BR* 620, emphasis in original). "Liberation is nothing other than the attainment of a nature in imitation of God through the guidance of a divine model" (*BR* 593). Devotion was hence the foremost means of culture, and the highest human faculty. The harmony of all the other faculties was best guaranteed through the cultivation of this one faculty, since by its very nature it directed all faculties toward the emulation of the highest ideal of harmonious self-realization. Through devotion we develop our faculties on the model of the divine ideal, and hence approach a union with god that at the same time involves the expansion of human powers in *this* world. If the divine ideal should prove too lofty to approach directly, the devotee can begin by focusing on "religious history," wherein are recounted the character and deeds of men who most closely approximate that divine ideal and as such can be considered parts of god (*BR* 593). Thus one passes from the various royal, Brahman, and divine sages of the Hindu scriptures to the very highest model of humanity available to mankind—a model superior to any other figure in the Hindu pantheon, as well as to the Buddha, Muhammad, and, most importantly, Jesus Christ. This was Krishna (*BR* 592–94).

It is crucial to recognize, before proceeding any further, that the identification of "Krishna" as the supreme embodiment of the divine was not a straightforward reaffirmation of the indigenous Bengali (Gaudiya) tradition of Vaishnavism. It was emphatically *not* the licentious Krishna sporting with Radha and the Gopis in Vrindavana—the Krishna of Caitanya, the Puranas, and folk legend—that Bankim was endorsing. In *Krishnacarittra,* he set out to systematically critique the scriptural primacy that Bengali Vaishnavites had traditionally accorded the *Bhagavata purana,* where the exploits of this other Krishna are narrated. Bankim was thereby mounting a sustained assault on the entire received tradition of Bengali Vaishnavism as elaborated by the six Gosvamins, Krishnadas Kaviraj, and other major late-mediaeval Caitanyaites.[34] In its place, Bankim sought to establish the supremacy of the *Bhagavad Gita* as *the* authentic source of Vaishnavite theology—and with it a more severe model of bhakti principled on hierarchical emulation and desireless action, not emotive practices (such as singing and dancing) grounded in the erotic metaphor of Krishna's frolic with Radha. While the playful Krishna of the *Bhagavata* had always been notionally identified with the profoundly solemn Krishna of the *Gita,* it is difficult to overstate just how radical a move it was for Bankim to raise the latter to theological primacy through his critical excavation of an authentically historical divine figure from (what was now consigned to the status of) the mythical accretions and dubious interpolations of the Hindu textual tradition.[35]

The Vaishnavite-Hindu tradition that centered on the *Bhagavad Gita* represented the highest form of religion, not because a self-proclaimed revelation from god made it so, but because it accorded in its most essential principles with propensities inscribed in man's universal nature—his propensity for the self-constituting activity of cultivation or culture (*BR* 791–92). Hinduism was a system grounded in the universal principles of *natural religion,* whereas Christianity, Islam, and Buddhism were all particularistic deviations, to varying degrees, from that standard. In fact, Hinduism's principles were so deeply grounded in natural laws that it was not even necessary to believe in an afterlife in order to recognize the legitimacy of its claims (*BR* 602-5). Even the atheistic class of Western-educated Bengalis could be persuaded of the power and validity of Hinduism because the "happiness" and "emancipation" that his religion promised were to be achieved simultaneously for this life and for the next (*BR* 602). By attempting to emulate the perfection of a personal god, the devotee enhanced and elevated his capacities for action, thus redeeming his existence from its animalistic baseness in this world, at the same time that he unknowingly approached a salvational union with the divine (*BR* 593).

THE NATION AS ETHICAL FORM

In fact, culture already reached deep into the practices of everyday life for Bankim.[36] His list of examples of how the "principle of culture" (*anushilana-tattva*) pervades existing Hindu social forms ends up being extensive. In the series of life stages prescribed for the higher castes, the worship of husbands as gods by their wives, the austerities of widows, the practice of vow taking, and Tantric and yogic exercises, we see a system of culture more pervasive and comprehensive, the guru claims, than anything a Western "cultural-ist" (*anushilanabadi*) like Matthew Arnold could even begin to conceive (*BR* 585).[37] The entire system of hierarchies within Hindu society is recoverable, in Bankim's view, to the principle of culture: "Whoever is superior to us, and from whose superiority we are benefited, is a worthy object of devotion" (*BR* 615). Hence it is appropriate that society be organized on the basis of the hierarchical subordination of wives to husbands, children to parents, and of the people to their king and to the educators of society, who in ancient India were called the Brahmans (*BR* 616-19). Caste forms like Brahmanism, the guru concedes, had widely degenerated in modern times into charlatan-ism, exclusivity, and indefensible privileges that were no longer grounded in the performance of proper social functions. However, caste, too, the guru argued, was in principle nothing other than a coordinated form of the division of labor, with the special activity of each caste correlating to the different classes of action that mankind undertook in society: the Brahmans pursued knowledge, the Kshatriyas preserved and protected, the Vaishyas collected and distributed, and the Shudras produced (*BR* 617-19, 678-79). This division of labor in turn encoded structures of hierarchy that embodied cultural principles in everyday life.

Bankim had no difficulty recognizing the conceptual kinship that linked Edward Tylor's anthropological culture concept with the humanistic culture concept upon which he himself was most directly drawing. Bankim's distinction of *habit* and *culture* directly echoed Tylor's contrast between *custom*, representing regressive holdovers of the past, and *culture*, referring more specifically to the genuine, progressive development of human moral and intellectual capacities in society.[38] The Bengali's enjoyment of sweets and the Englishman's love of roast beef are each forms of culture because they are formed by social practices and develop human capacities beyond their uncultivated state.

> In an uncivilized state, man is like an animal. . . . So long as men exist without society, they have no dharma other than the dharma of their bodies. Society is necessary for the practice of dharma. Without society there is no progress of knowledge; without the progress of knowledge there can be no knowledge of right and wrong (*dharmmadharmma*). Without knowledge of dharma there can be no devotion to god; and where there is no relationship with other men, even the dharma of love for other men, and so on, is not possible. (*BR* 658)

Culture is now seen to distance man from beast through the intervention of society, in a hierarchy that stretches from the primitive to Krishna: "Just as grass has the quality of plantness, so too does a Hottentot or Chippewa have the quality of humanity. But just as grass does not have that quality of plantness that we call treeness, so too does a Hottentot or Chippewa lack that humanity which we call the human essence [*manushyadharmma*]" (*BR* 590). Hindu social practices represented culture precisely to the extent that India's history inscribed the process of the collective cultivation of human powers and instituted social forms that enhanced individual capacity for such cultivation. Bankim was able to assimilate Tylor's anthropological narrative of the history of the progressive development of culture in human society into his own conception of the cultivation of the faculties.

Of course, if Hindu society were already thoroughly pervaded with the highest principles of culture, then it could not have been in the disoriented, decadent, and subjected state in which it now found itself. Just as society's educators could redeem the country, so too had they betrayed it in the past through corruption, exclusivism, and otherworldliness—by transforming culture into mere custom or habit. And Western education had only led Hindus further from the source of true religion. But there was a more fundamental reason for Hindu India's benighted condition. It was the *superiority* of Hinduism's ethical universalism, curiously enough, that was most responsible for its downfall. The highest achievement of Hinduism's doctrine of devotion to god was a sentiment of love for the whole of creation pervaded by his presence (*BR* 649-50).[39] In contrast, Europeans relied on the principle of natural love which as it is cultivated radiates in concentric circles from oneself, to one's family, to one's clan or tribe, to one's nation. This natural and exclusive love was particularly highly developed among Europeans, because the higher ethical idealism of Christianity had been easily overwhelmed by the stronger hold that the inferior classical and Hebraic traditions (neither of which rose above this exclusivist sentiment) held over its peoples. This fierce love for their own people, coupled with their utter disdain for anyone else, was what underpinned the European nations' extraordinary capacity for progress and their aggressive attitude toward the rest of the world (*BR* 648-49).

Given that Bankim is best remembered for the intensely nationalistic imagery of the nation as an object of devotion in his late novels, this might seem a strange criticism for him to make. In *Anandamath* (1882), a group of eighteenth-century ascetics have sworn themselves to the single-minded struggle to free Bengal of foreign domination, both Muslim and British. Having argued many years earlier that the political downfall of India had resulted in large part from its disunity, in his later fiction he would develop a powerful rhetoric of both denunciation and bloodshed in envisioning the historic struggle between an organic Hindu nation and its virile but impure Muslim conquerors (*BR* 234-41).[40] The ascetics of *Anandamath* describe themselves as children of the Mother—the goddess who is also the incarnation of the primal power or substance (*adya shakti*) that constitutes and moves the phenomenal world.[41] This conception of the nation-as-mother was grounded, as Dipesh Chakrabarty has argued, in a Bengali kinship practice that privileged the integrity of the patrilineage (*kul*) over the pursuit of interests in civil society. In the context of this devaluation of civil society, the fraternity that was to underpin the new nationalism of the second half of the nineteenth century could not be imagined on a Lockean model, as constituted by the coming together in civil society of brothers whose equality was guaranteed by the destruction of paternal authority. Rather, the common, loving submission of all the sons to the parental authority of the Mother, whose kindly nature maintained harmony within the family, guaranteed the internal unity and integrity of the nation as a superfamilial entity.[42] An ethical collective life was thus imagined in terms of the extension of the internal structures regulating the ethical orders of the household and kinship to social relations as a whole, thereby negating the intermediate space of civil society.

Subordinated to the principle of culture, however, this devotion to the motherland as a replication of the ethics of the patrilineage cannot be understood as a withdrawal from the universal into a narrowly inward-looking posture. On the contrary, Bankim's vision of nationalism sought to redeem the indigenous by rendering it a function of a universalistic ethics. The new Hindu nationalism through which Bengal/India[43] was to raise itself from decadence and subjection, without forsaking the high principles of its ancient religion, was not to be the "terrible, ghoulish sin" of "European patriotism," a form of self-love that celebrated the plunder and ruination of other societies in the pursuit of their own national wealth and glory (*BR* 661, italicized in English in original). Hindu nationalism would trump European patriotism because it would be grounded in the performance of ethical duty as a practice of desireless action (*BR* 651). Action based on forms of self-love could thereby be harmonized with universal love. Citing Herbert Spencer to the effect that a "creature must live before it can act," the guru argues that self-preservation is a duty fundamental to the preservation of god's creation. Insofar as self-preservation is undertaken from this higher perspective, and not from an unmediated self-love, it is therefore legitimate (*BR* 651-52). But sometimes one must sacrifice one's own life if a greater good can thereby be accomplished. So, for example, the love of one's children and one's family can take precedence over immediate self-preservation, for only thus is god's desire that the generations should reproduce themselves guaranteed. Following this same logic, preservation of society overrides all other considerations, for man is reduced to bestiality in the absence of society, and therefore entirely lacks dharma and, hence, culture (*BR* 652, 655-60). The love of one's country is in the end the very highest form of self-love when it is practiced on the basis of this elevated ethical conception, for through the cultivation of this love one acts in defense of the total integrity of the *social organism* (again, Spencer's term), without which there can be neither dharma nor progress (*BR* 660-61).

Bankim's elaboration of the duty to love one's country (out of the category of self-preservation and via the natural love of the family as the core element of society) was grounded in the ethics and practices of the patrilineage rather than the principles of civil society. In fact, for Bankim, it was the immanence of the principle of culture in Hindu social forms that made it possible to recuperate such practices and rearticulate them as constitutive elements of a modern nationalist politics. In an imperfect world of exploitation and domination, this higher form of nationalism emerged as a necessity and a duty. "When devotion to god and love for the whole of mankind are one, then can it be said that, except for devotion to god, the love of one's country is the most compelling dharma of all" (*BR* 661). Such a nationalism is no retreat into parochial ties; it is rather an attack on the role of civil society as a medium of social integration, in the name of indigenous practices that are seen to combine an overtly ethical form (as against the amoral and anomic qualities of economic exchange) with an immanent, if not obvious, rational functionality that guarantees both individual cultivation and social preservation. As we shall see, Bankim proposed "desireless action" as a model of political subjectivity adequate to an organicist conception of the nation.

THE NATIONAL CHURCH

"I have not the slightest doubt," declares the disciple in response to the guru's elaboration of the ethical foundation of nationalism, "that if India can grasp the doctrine of culture that you have elaborated and realizes it in action, then it will ascend to the throne of highest excellence among the nations of the world" (*BR* 661). Bankim's nomination of Hindu dharma as the most perfect realization of the principle of culture renders Hinduism not just legitimate in itself—it endows it with a universal mission to cure the failings of Western society and bring about a global ethico-social renewal. This ready ability to identify a global mission for the Hindu doctrine of culture was an implicit recognition on Bankim's part that his intervention in the discourse of culture represented the adoption of a set of problematics concerning the role of religion in society receiving lively attention in the West, too, at the time of his writing.

In *Church and State* (1829), Samuel Coleridge had recognized in the Church of England one of the foundations of the British social and political order: a "clerisy," trained in the universities and sent throughout the land to consolidate English national community, preserving the best of past civilization, further elaborating and perfecting this national patrimony, diffusing through the whole community the knowledge necessary for the recognition and performance of each man's rights and duties, and thereby guaranteeing a degree of civilizational excellence "without which the nation could be neither permanent nor progressive." The importance of this clerisy can only be fully understood when we recognize that the "science of theology" actually represented "all the main aids, instruments, and materials of national education, the *nisus formativus* [formative impulse] of the body politic, the shaping and informing spirit, which *educing, i.e.* eliciting, the latent *man* in all the natives of the soil, *trains them up* to citizens of the country, free subjects of the realm."[44] Theology allowed man to be understood and valued as a *spiritual* being and thus an end in himself, and theology thereby acted as a

necessary check to the extension of the dangerously dehumanizing materialism symbolized by Lockean sensationalism, and enacted in commercial society's performative reduction of human beings to the status of instruments
or things.[45] Coleridge's call for the renewal of England's National Church
tradition represented an attempt to identify an existing institution within
society that could counterbalance the materialistic tendencies of commercial society (civilization) through the cultivation of the spiritual qualities of
man. Seen from this perspective, the National or Broad Church movement
in nineteenth-century Britain had much in common with the neo-Catholic
Tractarians led by John Henry Newman, despite their polemical polarity.
Both involved an emphatic rejection of the individualistic, inward-looking
austerity of the Dissenting traditions to reassert the integrative social role
of the Visible Church as the embodiment of human community and the
antithesis of atomistic individualism.

Sir John Seeley, the professor of modern history at Cambridge upon
whose thought Bankim drew heavily in his elaboration of his "doctrine
of culture," is best known today as the political historian who wrote *The
Expansion of England* (1883). In the later nineteenth century, however, he was
equally well known as an exponent of the National Church ideal. In 1865 he
had published the controversial *Ecce Homo,* in which he portrayed Christ as
the founder of a new kind of ethical polity grounded in the example of his
own moral perfection rather than in the merely intellectual demonstrations
of philosophy—a clear source of inspiration for Bankim's reconception of
theism.[46] Seeley's insight into the affective quality of religion would be much
elaborated in his later work, *Natural Religion* (1882). Faced with the challenge
of a scientific vision of the world that seemed to preclude religiosity, Seeley
sought to elaborate a conception of religion not in opposition to science,
but rather as science's underlying higher principle. What Seeley described
as "natural religion" was grounded in the sentiment of awe and admiration that occurred when man confronted creation in all its enormity, beauty,
and complexity. Seen in this light, science ceased to be inimical to religion
and instead became a practice ultimately rooted in a religious orientation
to the world.[47] On the defensive from the secularist assault, however, this
most basic conception of religion had been forced to elaborate itself, Seeley
claimed, under the alias of "culture." "It is in the growth of the doctrine and
theory of culture in the modern world rather than in any mere signs of reviving activity in religious bodies that we see the true revival of religion and
the true antidote of secularity."[48] It was this tradition that best understood
the nature of religion as *worship,* that is, "habitual and regulated admira-

[margin annotation: Religion as the underlying principle of science]

tion." Thus the "worship of visible things which leads to art" was opposed to secular materialism's paralysis of man's aesthetic capacities. The "worship of humanity which leads to all moral disciplines" (especially through the admiration of "saintly humanity" headed by Christ himself) was opposed to man's reduction to animality. Finally, "that worship of God which is the soul of all philosophy and science" was opposed to the mechanistic "substitution of automatic custom for living will and intelligence."[49] This religion of culture would provide the basis for a renewal of collective human agency through the subordination of scientific instrumentality to the conscious and cultivated will of a national subject embodied in the complementary institutions of church and state.[50]

Singling out Seeley as "one of the greatest of the modern commentators on religion," Bankim was not challenging Western universalism from a colonial outside of native particularity (BR 675). He was attempting to participate in a metropolitan rethinking of specific liberal modes of universalism that no longer seemed adequate to a changing historical situation. The specificity of Bankim's contribution was to challenge the adequacy of Christianity, and its ascetic, otherworldly Christ, to the category of natural religion, and instead to identify a particular model of Hinduism with that ideal (BR 515-17). The immediate identity of Western particularity (Christianity) and the universal, Seeley's *Natural Religion* suggests, had been broken by the challenge of scientific disenchantment. This is what opened up the space for Bankim's project of disrupting the colonial identification of civilization and Christianity. Bankim's critique of the West is quite separate from his critique of Christianity. The moral failings of the West stem not from its being Christian, but from its not being Christian enough (BR 648-49). The implication of Christianity in this indictment extended only to the fact that it was Christianity's innate otherworldliness (expressed in Christ's ascetic character) that had prevented it from more effectively shaping Europe's moral sensibility. Bankim was making Hinduism the basis of a new nationalism on the model of the tradition of the Western philosophers of culture and national religion; he was vindicating Hinduism as the historical form most adequate to the universal; and he was positioning the Hindu social order as an *external* standpoint for the critique of Western (commercial) society. If this strategy constituted an accommodation of Hinduism to Christian categories of religion, it is in the end perhaps less important that it was a qualified accommodation, than that the "Christianity" to which Bankim appeared to be accommodating Hinduism was not an enduring "tradition" of "Western civilization," but was a rearticulation specifically developed in response to historical problematics posed in the course of the nineteenth century.

Bankim's
charque
of the
West
and
Christianity

This is not to repudiate the argument that Bankim's turn to indigenism was grounded in the specificity of a particular historical conjuncture in later nineteenth-century eastern India. Rather, it is to suggest that the mutual articulation, in a common conceptual idiom, of the specific historically generated problematics with which Bankim and Seeley were respectively grappling was rendered possible and meaningful by the geographical non-specificity of the global structures of capital to which both were responding more or less contemporaneously. The historical conjunctures in which the intellectuals of different locations variously elaborated discourses of culture were obviously each specific in very important ways. But what was increasingly common from the end of the nineteenth century on a global scale was the use of discourses of culture as the conceptual standpoint for articulating a critique of the universalistic liberal values of the sphere of circulation, in the name of an organic moral, political, and social order that was the necessary agent of the rational command of natural and human resources, and for the full development of the inner spiritual nature of man.

THE PRODUCTIVE ORGANISM

We should, I would contend, understand Bankim's passion for the writings of the French philosopher, Auguste Comte, in the same light. Comte's positivism enjoyed a prominent following in Britain and Bengal in the second half of the nineteenth century.[51] In its uncompromisingly anti-idealist epistemology it was fundamentally opposed to the National Church tradition—but this desire to apply positive epistemology to the spiritual life of man was precisely the atheistic quality of Comte's thought to which Bankim was least sympathetic. Yet the Bankim of the 1880s clearly held Comte higher in his estimation than any other Western thinker. As early as 1873, he had explicitly identified Comte's prioritization of social interests as a compelling counterpoint to the individualism of the liberal-utilitarian precepts to which he remained basically committed. It would not be until the 1880s, however, that he would allow Comte's *sociology* (like *positivism*, a word of Comte's own coinage) to more fundamentally reshape his orientation.[52]

In the 1870s, British Positivists had split into two distinct camps, one primarily concerned with social and political reform, and the other, headed by Richard Congreve, organized as a Comtean Church of Humanity. This latter strain of Positivism found an enthusiastic audience in Bankim and his friends.[53] Comte shared with the National Church thinkers some of their most basic precepts: a critique of individualism in the name of the social whole; a fear of the social and political anarchy that democratizing forces and the anomic tendencies of specialization were producing in that whole; an emphasis on the key role of a Visible Church in underpinning the moral, intellectual, and functional unity of the social organism; the desire to reconceptualize religion as consistent with the principles of science; and the necessity of cultivating a new clerisy to provide the spiritual and intellectual guidance for founding a stable yet progressive society out of the chaotic elements of the existing one.[54] John Stuart Mill, responsible more than anyone for popularizing Comte's thought in England, first introduced the commonplace division of Comte into the good-epistemological identity of his earlier writings (positivism as it is understood today) and the bad-sociocratic identity of his later writings (the side that was especially appealing to Bengali intellectuals of the later nineteenth century[55]). Yet Comte's positive epistemology was from the very beginning conceived as a means of extending society's capacity to command the resources of nature, of rising above the demands of conflicting particular interests, and of grounding a vision of progress in existent society to counter the revolutionary appeal to abstract principle.[56] It played, in other words, a conceptual role surprisingly complementary to the National Church appropriation of idealism in Britain.

British critics for the most part wanted to compensate for the social instabilities of commercial society with a system of moral, aesthetic, and intellectual culture that was the negation of calculation, industry, and the cash nexus. Comte, in contrast, envisioned a far more fundamental reordering of society on the basis of what he saw as its already demonstrated tendency to functional integration and command over nature—and it was no doubt this rigor that accounts for the greater primacy Bankim accords his thought. Comte understood himself to be living through a "season of anarchy" driven by ideologies of individual liberty, primal social contract, and, of course, political economy, with its celebration of the "metaphysical" conception of a self-regulating market that governments could not and should not direct.[57] Society was an organism made up of homogeneous individual units (the underlying, core truth of the dangerous liberal dogma of equality) functioning in established structures of authority—rather like the industrial productive unit that Comte identified as the practical harbinger of the positive age. The "philosophical character" of modern industry, after all, was nothing other than "the systematic action of Man upon the external world, guided by the knowledge of natural laws."[58] While the negativity of "restless spirits" sought to reform society by tearing down established hierarchical institutions, Comte sought their transfiguration into properly functional and rationally coordinated elements of the social organism. For example, the division of mental and material labor had in the past been a means of dividing humanity into qualitatively separate castes and interests. In the positive polity, however, this division of labor would not be simply abolished, but rather converted into a fully rational mode of social "coordination" that would maximize the collective capacity of human beings to command nature's resources.[59]

To effect such coordination, social practices needed to be subordinated to the rational intellect (just as manual labor had to be subordinated to intellectual labor in modern production), and this could only be accomplished on a broad social basis by utilizing the medium of affect—a model strikingly similar to Seeley's distinction in *Ecce Homo* between a rational moral philosophy that tells us what is right and an emotive religion that inspires us *to do* what is right.[60] In his later writings, Comte further emphasized the importance of affect in underpinning social solidarity, and it was to the end of shaping and bolstering collective and integrative sentiments that he had elaborated his secular Religion of Humanity.[61] The deliberate and rational will that was to result from this integration would triumph over particular interests through simple force of argument, through the directive action of the state, and through the educational efforts of the new clerisy.[62] In so doing it would banish the moral, intellectual, political, and economic anarchy of Comte's own day by harnessing the forces of progress while preserving the forces of order. Humanity would finally achieve its highest capacity for self-determination by fully integrating its various constituent individuals and institutions into a unified organism pursuing a common social good through rational means.

It was the atheist Comte, according to Bankim's guru, who had formulated the finest and most succinct definition of religion:

> "Religion, in itself expresses the state, of perfect *unity* which is the distinctive mark of man's existence both as an individual and in society, when all the constituent parts of his nature, moral and physical, are made habitually to converge towards one common purpose." That is to say, "Religion consists in regulating one's individual nature, and forms the rallying-point for all the separate individuals." Of all the explanations I have presented, this seems to be the best. (*BR* 676)

Religion, following this formulation, was the institution and practice of moral integration that guaranteed the felt participation of each individual in the organic life of the collective social subject. It represented the subordination of social functions to a deliberate moral and intellectual consciousness

Comtes view of religion

through the practical force of the affective life. When the guru typologizes knowledge, he cedes superiority to the West when it comes to knowledge of the world (mathematics, astronomy, physics, and chemistry) and knowledge of the self (biology and sociology). He reserves only the knowledge of God as the special preserve of Hindu scripture (BR 630). But this should not be taken as a merely quasi-Orientalist circumscription of the authority of indigenous tradition to the realm of the spiritual. On the contrary, in keeping with the Coleridgean tradition, it is the knowledge of God that underpins Bankim's entire system of culture; that allows the individual will to be coordinated with the social whole; and that guarantees that such coordination represents the practical realization, rather than dissolution, of human subjectivity.

Bankim's Krishna embodies, in his divine personhood, the ultimate apex of human development—the universal expansion of all human powers in harmonious unity. He does not, in other words, represent any particular form of practical capacity—as king or priest or merchant or cultivator—but rather the harmonized fruition of all the faculties that go into the reproduction of society (which is the highest object of devotion, remember, short of God himself). The culture for which Krishna provides the preeminent model is not merely the cultivation of rarified tastes, nor a social prophylaxis against the sullying stain of manual labor. Krishna's existence asserts the fundamental equivalence of all forms of human activity as the expression of universal human faculties cultivated through practice. To labor in a field or wield a sword is not the exclusive and natural characteristic of a particular class of human beings, but rather is merely a specific instance of universal human capacities as such. The standpoint for the critique of fragmentation and one-sided human development is a figure who concretely embodies the abstract equivalence of all specific forms of activity: the many-sided development of the individual can be an ideal only insofar as every human being is deemed (at least in principle, and with whatever talent) capable of every form of human activity.

The human being who devotes himself to Krishna seeks to reproduce within his own person the harmonious coexistence of all forms of social practice. This is the form of political subjectivity adequate to a certain conception of the social organism—an organism that is constantly appropriating nature to the ends of its own free collective subjectivity. Bankim's humanism of culture consistently juxtaposed the harmonious unity of the cultivated individual to his one-sidedness in the division of labor, his fragmentation in the different spheres of life (for example, religious and secular), and his dissolving absorption in material interests. But he never objected to the cultivation of specialized knowledge as such. He demanded only that specialized knowledge not be pursued at the expense of an all-round development of every individual—the cultivation that is the prerequisite for any real unity in the social organism (*BR* 678–79). In this he made clear his profound affiliation with Comte, who explicitly thematized the relationship between particular forms of laboring activity and the social totality. The point of harmonious, all-round cultivation is not just to compensate for the narrow one-sidedness of particular activities within the division of labor. Through a holistic culture, the individual who performs some specific activity in the social division of labor experiences his particular activity as just a specific instance of social labor in general. In other words, this was to accept, as had Comte, that labor mediates the individual's relationship with society as a whole, and it was furthermore, again like Comte, to search for a way to make this relationship palpable through religious practice. Thus the division of labor was redeemed, as each individual could feel himself, not cut off from society in the specificity of his narrow existence within it, but rather organi-cally unified with society precisely through the performance of his particular form of specialized labor. Hinduism's perfected understanding of culture as the essence of natural religion is thus the key to the subordination of special knowledge to human ends.

Society was to become, not a site of exchange among primordially free individuals pursuing their own interests, but rather a cooperative endeavor to subordinate the activities of its homogeneous individual units, as instances of social labor in general, to the higher purpose of the common good. Such coordination could not be a function of the impersonal forces of civil society, in which outcomes were arbitrary and personal interests could stand in opposition to the common interest. Rather, the transcendence of private and personal interests (and hence of civil society) through the practice of culture would make possible the transfiguration of society, on the basis of its own immanent and indigenous order, into a productive organism whose ratio-nality was founded simultaneously on a laboring subject who constitutes their own autonomy through pure practice (articulated through the Hindu category of *nishkam karma,* desireless action), and on the principles of func-tional subordination and collective agency characteristic of the sphere of production. On the one hand, this is clearly why the guru goes out of his way to insist specifically that the Hindu forms of devotion to men would need to be supplemented by a new practice of devotion for which, he confessed, there had never been any word, or concept, or tradition of practice in India: namely, a sense of "Official Subordination," a respect for the hierarchy of the workplace (*BR* 619). On the other hand, this new practice of devotion would supplement household, kinship, and communal institutions that already provided the fundamental social structures that organized not only "Hindu society" but also the actual practices of agrarian production through the kinds of (what have problematically come to be called) precapitalist relations already discussed in chapter 2.

It was no longer the critical weapons of liberal emancipation that Bankim wanted to import from the West, but rather the instrumental rationality of science and technology that could help transform an immiserated and oppressed Bengal into a dynamic and autonomous national subject. That subject could only be constituted through the practice of Hindu dharma. Culture, by definition conducive to human capacities (*anushilan shaktir anukul* [*BR* 587]), binds men to other men and to ethical conduct regardless of self-interest. One was no longer stuck in the dilemma of the mid-nineteenth century between objective necessity and subjective freedom, between Akshay Dutt's dissolution of subjectivity into the natural order and Debendranath Tagore's assertion of a spiritual subjectivity outside the material world.

Bankim's adoption of Comte's productionist logic by no means meant, however, that he envisioned an India transformed, on the British model, by modern industry per se. Britain's experience, as filtered through the writings of Victorian cultural critics, combined with the anti-industrial gentility of southern England's elites (for whom Manchester was the ultimate symbol of the grubby pettiness of middle-class interests), had instilled in Bankim a profound sense that industry was the primary instrument of the separation of economic life from ethical order, and the subsequent dissolution of that ethical order into a field of selfish interests (commercial society).[63] Victorian cultural critique consistently identified the industrialism of mills and factories as an aggravated form of commercial society, focusing on its reduction of workers to dehumanized instruments (rather than self-constituting subjects of productive activity), and on the socially corrosive effects of the narrow-minded selfishness of mill owners and the cash-nexus economy. Bankim was spared the dilemmas of trying to unravel this knot by the ethico-philosophical nature of his enterprise, remaining comfortably critical of the "demoness" at the wheel of the industrial engines whose materialistic energies were at the heart of modern social anomie. The widespread turn against laissez-faire and toward protectionism so evident in the Bengali press of the 1870s could have held little appeal for him. The centrality of the protection of the Bombay cotton mills to this discourse could only have underlined the fact that, rather than challenging the expansion of commercial society in India, the protectionist economics to which liberals were turning would primarily serve to further it.[64] In the end, for Bankim, turning to culture meant necessarily turning away from political economy. It would take another generation to forge the conceptual link between culture and the new Listian political economy—as we shall see in the next chapter.

Bankim's turn to religion in the 1880s represented an attempt to establish within Hinduism what Comte described as the "philosophical contemplation and labour" that would form "a basis" for a sustainable mode of worldly agency—to derive from indigenous practices, concepts, and traditions institutions and forms of subjectivity adequate to underpin the moral and functional existence of a collective social subject. The payoff was twofold. First, by identifying their particular labor with social labor in general, individuals were to be liberated from the narrowness of their laboring lives, feel themselves a constitutive part of their society, have the value of their subjective agency reaffirmed, and experience wholeness by mirroring the social whole within themselves. Second, having coordinated their labors into a functional unity, they would form a social organism powerful enough to abolish its subordination to the alien principles of civil society, and thus the heteronomy that structured the babu condition. Transfigured by the dynamic logic of culture, the social hierarchies and moral economies of native custom could be revitalized to become the foundation for a dynamic social organism that would negate the principle and practice of free exchange in the sphere of circulation. *Custom* transfigured into *culture* became the site of an indigenous collective will that negated the heteronomy experienced in the sphere of circulation. The old conservative argument that had sought to draw a religious limit to the authority of the colonial state and a ritual limit to the exigencies of worldly pursuits was inverted into an argument for an aggressive form of social rationalization that would lay the foundations for a reunion at last of subjectivity and worldly agency.

———— ✳ ————

CHAPTER FIVE

The Conceptual Structure of
an Indigenist Nationalism

(margin handwritten note: Dharma was the only sure foundation for national progress)

THE 1880s were, as the editor of the journal *Alocana* declared in its inaugural issue, a good time to be starting a periodical concerned with issues of "dharma, society and morality." Educated Bengalis, who had for so long disdained their religion, had finally come to understand that "dharma" was the only sure foundation for national progress. Without it, "man cannot become man, and society cannot function."[1] Although human societies may have progressed under the impetus of the pursuit of self-interest through social contract, another contributor explained, the history of mankind demonstrated that a higher union, grounded in religion and expressive of unselfish love, was destined to supersede this lower form of association.[2] Hindu dharma was well positioned, *Alocana* sought to argue, to take the spiritual and intellectual lead in this imminent new era. Writing fifteen years later, Lord Curzon, governor-general of British India, contemptuously intimated that the new ideological impulse that *Alocana* was sensing in 1884 was indeed gaining strength as the nineteenth century closed: "There is no doubt that a sort of quasi-metaphysical ferment is going on in India; strongly conservative and even reactionary in its general tendency. . . . What is to come out of this strange amalgam of superstition, transcendentalism, mental exaltation, and intellectual obscurity—with European ideas thrown as an outside ingredient into the crucible—who can say?"[3] The new cultural paradigm that had been announced in Bankim's later work was mounting a serious challenge to the primacy of liberal ideological forms in Bengali political discourse.

It was in fact Curzon's administration that would provoke this new voice into a more directly political confrontation with the British government.

In 1905, the Bengal Presidency of British India was partitioned into two separate provinces in the name of administrative convenience. Bengal, the government argued, had become too cumbersome to govern effectively as a single unit. But if administration alone was at stake, Bengali critics of the scheme were quick to reply, there was no reason why new provinces could not have been carved out of the large, non-Bengali-speaking populations of Orissa and Bihar rather than by dividing Bengal proper. The real motives underlying the government's plan were not difficult to see: firstly, to divide the troublesome Bengalis of Calcutta from the troublesome Bengalis of the eastern districts; and secondly, to promote the interests, and thereby court the favor, of the large Muslim population of eastern Bengal as a communal counterweight to the overwhelmingly Hindu "educated middle class" that dominated the lively politics of the region.[4] The Bengali response to the partition has entered the historiography of South Asia as the first major attempt in the history of Indian nationalism at popular mobilization under the leadership of the new middle class that had developed under British rule. Led by a new generation of leaders such as Aurobindo Ghose, Bipin Chandra Pal, and Brahmabandhab Upadhyay, Swadeshi nationalists called for a boycott of British manufactures and the promotion of the nation's economic, social, and spiritual autonomy, quickly shifting the focus of their rhetoric from the issue of partition to a direct struggle against British rule.

In chapter 3 we saw the bifurcation of Westernness and Indianness assuming the specific form of a juxtaposition between commercial and customary society. In chapter 4 we saw that distinction further elaborated as a juxtaposition of commercial society and culture. In this chapter we shall see more clearly how this binary in turn expressed a deeper opposition of exchange and production. These fundamental organizing categories of Swadeshi ideology attempted to elaborate the logic of Indian society as (in its primordial Hindu essence if not in all its corrupt concrete realities) grounded in forms of productive activity that were intrinsically ethical rather than commercial in nature. Unlike readings that emphasize intellectual provenance or institutional authority then, I shall argue that the plausibility of this conceptual logic lay in the practical structure of the colonial society it sought to grasp—a society in which the educated middle class experienced civil society as a domain of heteronomy, and, as we have seen in chapter 2, the small-holding agriculture that predominated more generally beyond the limits of the respectable classes was organized on the double axis of an exchange relation in its external relation and a kinship relation in its internal organization. Swadeshi discourse sought to subordinate the ethico-political implications of the first of these two axes, understood as an externally imposed form of Western individualism, to the ethico-political potential of the second of these two axes, understood as the indigenous principle that actually structured the productive process and was capable of genuinely dynamic agency. This reading will in turn imply a further claim: that the categories of Swadeshi ideology did have real theoretical purchase on the colonial society with which it grappled, even if they grasped its structure only in terms of its forms of appearance (racial or civilizational difference) rather than in terms of its essential determinations (the logic of capitalist society).

Some very major figures in the Swadeshi years, such as Surendranath Banerjea, will be bypassed in the discussion that follows. This is not because I underestimate their political significance, but rather because their Swadeshism belonged to the school of liberal compromise that I have discussed in chapter 3. In the analysis that follows, I focus on figures who articulated with greater consistency what I consider, despite its many shared elements, to be a qualitatively different kind of argument. I shall thereby attempt to reconstruct, as relatively coherent in its basic structure, the specifically ideological dimension of the Swadeshi movement, moving from the most abstract conceptual determinations of the logic of Swadeshi discourse to its more programmatic dimensions. In contrast to the established historiography, I do not seek to make sense of Swadeshism primarily in terms of its need to mobilize specific class constituencies; I try to show how a politics of popular mobilization was elaborated out of the conceptual logic of Swadeshi ideology. An overarching conceptual logic regulated all the different registers of Swadeshi discourse, whether theological, philosophical, political, economic, social, educational, or ethical. This regularity presents, furthermore, a fundamental challenge to explanations that turn on either the indigeneity or the derivativeness of elements of colonial discourse. Although undeniably a hybrid formation composed of elements of indigenous and foreign cultural norms and forms, the very regularity of this conceptual structure militates against the possibility of such eclecticism constituting the principles of its selectivity. As such, since the conceptual structure of this indigenist nationalism self-consciously served to organize the relations between categories of Indianness and Westernness, it must be accounted for in terms that exceed both. Instead, by arguing that the historical plausibility of Swadeshi discourse was underpinned by its misrecognition of the practical structure of capitalist society, I set out to explain why the Hindu nationalism that emerged at the end of the nineteenth century in Bengal linked an indigenist cultural politics with a productionist vision that grounded rationality in the historical constitution of subjective freedom through labor—a vision that was in turn the standpoint of an idealist critique of materialism, a historicist critique of abstraction, an ethical critique of commercial and civil society, and a political-economic critique of British rule. Whereas in chapter 3 we saw liberal thought increasingly turning to a discourse of national political economy to salvage the salience of its categories, in the present chapter we shall see the culturalist ideology inaugurated by Bankimchandra Chatterjee's later writings extended to incorporate national political economy as the logical negation of liberal conceptions of self, polity, and society.

THE CRITIQUE OF MENDICANCY

Where Bankim had largely avoided an explicit discussion of contemporary politics in his ethico-theological writings of the 1880s, by the early 1890s Aurobindo Ghose, a young Bengali freshly returned from schooling in England to a bureaucratic position in the princely state of Baroda (in western India), was confronting British rule and Indian liberalism head on. In New Lamps for Old, a series of controversial articles published in 1893–94 in Bombay's *Indu Prakash*, Aurobindo characterized the entire liberal project of the Moderate Congress as "a grand suit-at-law, best described as the case of India *vs.* Anglo-India, in which the ultimate tribunal is the British sense of justice." While its great leaders, bound to this loyally servile conception of their role, had nominated themselves as the nation's "counsel for the complainant," the Congress had utterly failed to develop any kind of popular character and thus represent the nation as a whole.[5] These Congressites had been quite explicit in their claim that the duty and function of representing the masses, who were "still unable to articulate definite political demands," devolved upon those of their "educated and enlightened compatriots" who had "learnt to think."[6] From strictly within the confines of its own class, and without "any direct support from the proletariate [*sic*]," the Congress drew "its origin, its support and its most enthusiastic votaries"—that is to say, from among "those of us who have got some little idea of the machinery of English politics and are eager to import it along with cheap Liverpool cloths, shoddy Brummagem wares, and other useful and necessary things which have killed the fine and genuine textures." This class, which had developed "with prurient rapidity under the aegis of the British rule," he identified as the "new middle class"—"for, when we are so proud of our imported English goods, it would be absurd, when we want labels for them, not to import their English names as well."[7] Neither "popular" nor "honestly desirous of a popular character," the "un-National Congress" had developed into "a middle-class organ selfish and disingenuous in its public action and hollow in its professions of a large and disinterested patriotism."[8]

In keeping with its borrowed identity, the middle class also borrowed from English history the justification of its providential role to plead for "just and remedial legislation on behalf of a patient and suffering people."[9] Aurobindo accepted the argument that "the experience of European races is all that we, a people new to modern problems, can find to warn or counsel us."[10] With what example, he asked, did England present India? Certainly it possessed the greatest system of political representation the world had ever seen. But alongside its great historical obsession with the external machinery of legislation and commerce, it also evinced a remarkable lack of interest in the improvement of the *inner* life of the people. The "morbid outcome" of this one-sidedness had been a process of unchecked social degeneration resulting in "an aristocracy materialised, a middle-class vulgarised and a lower class brutalised"—a general failure of social sentiment above all symbolized by the "strong antipathetic feelings of Labour towards Capital" that prevailed there.[11] England's progress represented the great instance of advance through political-cum-institutional methods, and its political philosophy was based on a deep faith in the efficacy of institutional machinery. But this philosophy took no account of the materials that pass through that machinery—whether of "high or low quality . . . of variant circumstances, of incompatibilities arising from national temperament, and other forces which no philosophical observer will omit from his calculation."[12] Having failed to recognize the necessity of balancing external forms of progress with the cultivation of the higher virtues in its citizenry, the English ended up coupling this utilitarian institutionalism with the "fierce, sharp air of English individualism" in which each person, endowed with a "narrow heart and commercial habit of mind," could only crassly view the world as an instrument to his own ends.[13]

Instead, Aurobindo gestured toward an alternative historical example on the other side of the Channel. In France, he explained, the framework of political institutions was an eclectic and unstable import from England and America. Yet despite the undue importance the French had admittedly conceded to institutional politics in their emulation of English models, the "best blood, the highest thought, the real grandeur of the nation" resided not in those institutions, but in "the artistic and municipal forces of Parisian life, in the firm settled executive, in the great vehement heart of the French populace—and that has ever beaten most highly in unison with the grand ideas of Equality and Fraternity since they were first enounced on the banner of the great and terrible Republic." The principle upon which French progress rested was the cultivation of a "sound and durable national character." The French recognized that "not by the mechanic working of institutions, but by the delicate and almost unseen moulding of a fine, lucid and invigorating atmosphere, could a robust and highly-wrought social temper be developed." Hence they relied more on a "fine development of social character and a wide diffusion of happiness," than on "the mechanic development of a sound political machinery."[14] Where the Englishman and American "direct their whole active powers into the grosser sphere of commerce and politics," the Frenchman "prefers to conserve the high calibre of his national character by the infusion of light, gaiety and happiness into the common life of the people."[15]

Aurobindo was in no doubt that Indians had more in common temperamentally with these Gallic Arnoldians than with the Anglo-American Benthamites. All the more important then that Indian leaders recognize the immediate necessity of turning their efforts away from "silly squabbles about offices and salaried positions" grounded in "narrow class interests," and from feeble appeals to British justice to solve the country's problems through political instruments, and instead to turn their attention toward the "first and holiest duty, the elevation and enlightenment of the proletariate [sic]," that is to say, the dissemination of intellect, lucidity, and happiness throughout society.[16] Although "torpid" and "immobile," the proletariat (by which he clearly meant everyone beyond the pale of *bhadrata*, or respectability) was the real key to political power: whoever succeeded in understanding this "very great potential force . . . becomes by the very fact master of the future." The only hope for real success that the "burgess," represented by the Congress, had ever had was "to base his cause upon an adroit management of the proletariate [sic]. He must awaken and organise the entire power of the country and thus multiply infinitely his volume and significance, the better to attain supremacy as much social as political. Thus and thus only will he attain to his legitimate station, not an egoist class living for itself and in itself, but the crown of the nation and its head."[17] Where "poverty of organic conception" had characterized the old leadership, the new leadership should instead use its educational advantages to lead the entire people forward as a national unity.[18]

The vague talk of democracy, the French Revolution, and the importance of the proletariat should not distract us from the fundamentally Arnoldian tenor of these essays.[19] In New Lamps for Old, Aurobindo was calling for a

mode of civic activism that would be more authentically popular in character. ~~Liberal polities, he argued, sought to borrow~~ both the agenda and
~~the agency for its reformist program from the colonial state and colonial
culture.~~ Aurobindo was instead invoking a different conceptual framework
to ground his new civic project, one drawn from the (by then commonplace)
Arnoldian conception of universal culture. The French nation embodied for
him a society with a powerful sense of organic unity, a "homogeneity of
sentiment" pervading an educated populace whose civic commitment represented not a utilitarian subordination to external, institutional forms, but
a real and substantial understanding of the primary importance of national
solidarity and ethical life.[20]

The agency underlying and driving the new politics of liberty and equality could no longer be the colonial state as the juridical mediator of a universalistic discourse of rights. Rather, it would be "the people" itself, rescued from their torpid inertia and drawn into the cause of national progress
through a consciousness renewed by the pedagogical activities of a new
"new middle class." Young Aurobindo's project set out to de-link liberty and
equality from their dependence on the colonial state as juridical mediator,
and to build them instead on a broad-based national foundation. To do so
inevitably required reframing the national project as a renewal grounded
in the life and thought of the people. In doing so, he would be increasingly
drawn into an attempt to overcome the alleged shallowness of colonial political categories—the liberal categories of exchange—in the name of a new
culturalist politics rooted in the practical life of the people. In the process
of working out this agenda, he and his allies on the more radical edge of
Swadeshi thought would fundamentally transform the meaning of liberal
conceptions of emancipation into categories of an ideology that linked the
culturalist conception of humanity to the indigenous tradition of Hinduism.
And indeed, it was in the language of Hindu theology that this new sociopolitical imagination would find its most rigorous abstract formulation.

IMMANENTIST MONISM

By the beginning of the twentieth century, Bengali intellectuals had a highly
developed conceptual apparatus for grasping the distinction between the
liberal politics of the old Moderates and the new politics grounded in the
life of the people. The "radical reformer" and "abstract cosmopolitan," Bipin
Pal explained in 1904, "believes that man is man, and there exists nothing
on earth of any vital value, except the individual here below and God above."

He therefore must necessarily regard "all racial differences and national peculiarities as superstitions and shortcomings, which, in the highest stages of ethical and spiritual life, are absolutely overcome and obliterated."[21] Pal was thinking above all of the Brahmo tradition that stemmed from Rammohun Roy—a tradition with which he had himself earlier in life identified. Rammohun's egalitarian reformism aimed to release individuals from the corrupt mediations of idolatry and priest craft, restoring their capacity to seek direct knowledge of the Absolute—while at the same time coming to enjoy worldly prosperity as a result of their newfound emancipation into civil society. Pal was not wrong in seeing a social correlate to this kind of theological argument. "The prevailing and popular social philosophy of the Brahmo Samaj has so far been more pronounced on the cosmopolitan than on the national side. As in Brahmo theology nothing mediates between the individual and the Universal, so in Brahmo sociology nothing stands, as a medium of relation or realisation, between individual man and universal humanity."[22]

For Bipin Pal, this cosmopolitan religious reformer was closely related to the subject of civil or commercial society—a figure who could only confront social structures of institutional authority from a primordially external standpoint of atomistic individual autonomy, and from there evaluate them in terms either of despotic imposition (the despotism of custom and priest craft) or of utility to private or collective interests. Confronted with the hierarchies and practices of a native society defined, as we saw in chapter 3, as the negation of civil society, such a reformer could only love an abstract conception of India, grounded in the "supreme ambition ... to reproduce Europe in India. ... In the name of India we loved Europe, and therefore, we fed our fancy not upon Indian but upon European ideals, European arts, European thought, European culture. We loved the abstraction we called India, but, yes, we hated the thing that it actually was."[23] To be an emancipated and reformist subject on the model of "the educated classes thirty or forty years back" was inseparable from a profound feeling of self-hatred, and of contempt for the concrete realities of their own society.[24]

While the logic of emancipation and Westernization tended to reduce society to relationships of utility, "standing in a [social] vacuum" did not come naturally to Indians, whose national genius, argued Rabindranath Tagore in the same year, was rather to establish "a relationship of kinship between man and man" and thus "use relationships of necessity only after we have sanctified them with relationships of the heart."[25] As a result of their English education, complained Bipin Pal, many young Bengalis had gotten caught up in "the contagion of European rationalism of the last century, and thus set up [their] individual conscience as the ultimate arbiter of both what is true and what is good." But this "individualistic rationalism," epitomized in Pal's view by the Brahmo Samaj, "ignored the fact that neither our individual reason nor our individual conscience works by itself but is practically dependent for its conclusions upon what may be called the social reason and the social conscience."[26] Against this illusion of isolated individuality, Pal posited the idea of the organic constitution of society: "A nation is not a mere collection of individuals. A nation is an organism; it has organic life; and like all organisms a nation has an end unto itself, which is different from the ends that regulate the activities of other similar organisms, other similar nations. The nationality that constitutes a nation is the individuality of a nation."[27] A nation is not just one more form of "association," of the kind one sees in civil society, wherein individuals "stand by themselves" even when "moved by a common impulse."

> In a nation, the individuals composing it stand in an organic relation to one another and to the whole of which they are limbs and organs. . . . Organs find the fulfillment of their ends, not in themselves but in the collective life of the organism to which they belong. Kill the organism—the organs cease to be and to act. . . . An organism is logically prior to the organs. Organs evolve, organs change, but the organism remains itself all the same. Individuals are born, individuals die,—but the Nation liveth for ever.[28]

That all members of society are of a single organic substance beneath their phenomenal variety was an insight grounded in what Pal identified as the most fundamental principle of Hindu thought: the underlying nonduality of self and not-self. India's awareness of the immanence of the divine spirit in all creation allowed it to pursue its national interest as a means toward realizing the universal rather than particularistically negating it.[29] It is, perhaps unexpectedly, in theology that we find a crucial idiom for the articulation of a new sociological imagination, one that sought to grasp the relationship between the concrete and the abstract in a radically new and postliberal way.

The later nineteenth century saw the emergence to prominence in Bengal of a new brand of traditional gurus, whose prestige rested in large part on the romantic appeal of their rural folk idiom and lack of formal Western-style education—starting most famously with Ramakrishna Paramhansa.[30] Aside from their halo of indigenous authenticity, one other feature that stood out in these new gurus was their role in promoting specifically Tantric theological ideas.[31]

The monistic doctrine had been most famously postulated in Sankara-charya's Advaita (nondualistic) Vedanta, which argued that the phenomenal world was a mere illusion (*maya*) cloaking a transcendental, unchanging, and undifferentiated divine reality. We have already seen this form of Vedanta philosophy adopted as the theological underpinning for Rammohun's critique of the concrete mediations that stood between the individual consciousness and the pure consciousness of the abstract godhead. But the Tantrics of the Shakta branch of Bengali Hinduism deployed a somewhat different understanding of nonduality to underpin their metaphysics of *adya shakti*, or primordial power.[32] The *mataram*, or Mother, in the ubiquitous Swadeshi war cry, *bande mataram* ("Hail to the Mother," the song and rallying cry used by the warrior monks in Bankim's novel *Anandamath*) was the *adya shakti bhagabati*, or goddess of primordial power, whom Shaktas understood to embody the underlying spiritual substance that constitutes, shapes, and moves the world. While Shiva, the male aspect of the divine, was a figurative representation of the godhead's transcendent and eternally unchanging aspect (nonduality), his female consort (manifesting herself variously as Durga, Kali, Chandi, Bhawani, Lakshmi, and so forth) represented the self-differentiating, active quality of the godhead's powers (*shakti*). Shakti is that aspect of the eternal and divine noumenal substance whose nature it is to present itself in the form of particular phenomena. So whereas Sankaracharya's disciples are conventionally understood to argue that the multiplicity of the phenomenal world—including individual selfhood—is a false overlay to the indivisible, indescribable, and undifferentiated substance of the pure consciousness of the godhead, the Tantric tradition of shakti worship, which dominated the religious life of Bengal's upper castes, instead posited the necessity of approaching the godhead's unity from within the world of phenomena in which that transcendent truth presented itself to human consciousness.

Siva Chandra Vidyarnava Bhattacharya, the great late nineteenth-century defender of Shakta Tantrism, undertook a critique of both abstract monism (phenomena are illusory and reality is transcendent) and dualist theism (god and his creation are distinct) from the standpoint of what we might call an *immanentist monism* (phenomena are the form of appearance of a transcendent reality). Rather than approaching the divine truth from the standpoint of an abstract knowledge of divine unity (*jnan-yog*, the path to emancipation from worldly attachments through gnosis), the Tantric devotee instead sought to approach divine truth from within the flux of phenomenal experience. So "despite the essential truth of the monistic principle," the Tantric devotee does not "at the outset ignore this visible, palpable dualistic world. . . . In order to realize monistic truth, one must progress slowly through the dualistic world." For the diversity of the phenomenal world was nothing but the expression of the fluctuating form of appearance of the godhead. From this standpoint, the phenomenal world is itself the expression of divine unity, and the "Divine Mother . . . is in every molecule, in every atom, in all things which constitute the world." The illusory quality of phenomenal existence lies solely in the fact that its dualistic appearance serves to obscure its deeper monistic substance. The Tantric devotee does not renounce worldly attachments (remaining, for example, a householder), but rather embraces "both dualism and monism" and "realizes the sweetness of the [divine] play" (of phenomenal flux) by "plung[ing] into the non-dualistic Truth after having churned the dualist world."[33] The proper embrace of dualism took the form not of contemplation but of a method of "spiritual self-culture," the scripturally prescribed practice of *sadhana*. If the intellect is incapable of judgment in matters about which it had not yet been instructed, then it is by practice (*karma-yog*) that spiritual self-realization must be acquired.[34]

Not only was such a monism compatible with devotion to embodied deities, as a practice mediating the approach to the absolute, but it was specifically the female representations of the godhead that were the primary object of worship. "Special preparations are in progress," declared the *Sandhya*, the incendiary newspaper edited by Brahmabandhab Upadhyay, "for what the Mother *Mahashakti* will become when she will sit on the throne of Anandamath (the abbey of bliss)."[35] Nationalists embraced the precolonial figure of the Mother to represent and embody the collective power of the Indian nation, not as an assemblage of individuals in civil society, but as an organism logically prior to that assemblage.[36]

> Durga is the Goddess of Strength, the symbol of Prowess. . . . As long as we were weighted down with a paralyzing sense of our own impotence, Omnipotence had no message for us, except that of a crushing and mysterious Fatality. But the Bengali Hindu has suddenly risen into some consciousness of power within himself, and the worship of the Goddess of Power has, therefore, a note of reality to it now, which hardly it had before. Durga stands today to immense numbers of the Bengali people, not merely as a Pauranic Deity or as a mythological figure, but as the visible representation of the Eternal Spirit of their Race. On her right, stands the Power of Wealth, protected by the invincible Power of Arms; on her left, stands the Power of Culture guided by the Power of Wisdom.[37]

Denying their base instincts and worldly desires, devotees would be able to recognize their bodily selves and worldly environments as modalities of shakti, the monistic but self-differentiated spiritual substance that constituted at once individuality, nationality, and humanity. Subjective freedom would lie not in the negation of the mediating authority of Brahmans and idols (the negative freedom of Brahmoism and of civil society), but in the awakening of a spiritual awareness capable of seeing beyond the material particularity of the phenomenal world to its reality as the embodiment of divine spirit.[38]

The social fabric of indigenous society could be understood as a uniform substance in this Tantric discourse, an authentic reality that subsumed the apparently isolated individual of civil society without negating individuality as such. The individual's experience of social disembeddedness was the result of a failure to pierce the veil of *maya* (illusion)—the apparent diversity and ephemerality of phenomenality that causes individuals to experience themselves as separate nodes of consciousness in a world of objects rather than as moments of one indivisible godhead that pervades the universe. The capacity to harness world forces and the nation's immanent power presupposed the capacity to see beyond the fractiousness of individual interests to the underlying unity of an organic social substance that pervaded the phenomenal world of the social and that unfolds itself as self-differentiated through its own self-positing activity (divine play). While classically tied to the philosophical problematic of the relationship of the phenomenally particular and ephemeral to universal essence, shakti was thus being appropriated in the Swadeshi era as the foundational category of an indigenist, idealist sociology that attempted to grasp the substance of national society beyond the commercial, contractual, and associational forms of civil society; that is to say, to grasp the peculiar nature of abstraction in modern society.

That shakti was a core concept of this idealism should not, however, be taken to imply that this discourse was either the special preserve of Shakta sectarians, or that the enthusiasm for it was a simple function of unreconstructed traditionalism on the part of upper-caste Hindus. Aurobindo had had to self-consciously break with his family's Brahmoism to embrace the Tantric Vedantism that would be his hallmark; and many of the key Swadeshi intellectuals had passed through the Brahmo organization. Furthermore, adherents of Bengali Vaishnavism (the worship of Krishna and Radha that was the other great current of Bengali Hinduism) were contemporaneously developing parallel theologico-philosophical formulations. The theology of Vaishnavite devotionalism in Bengal had posited a substantive homology between the relationship between God and the devotee, and the relationship between God and his externalized powers (a homology symbolized above all by Radha, Krishna's lover and also his shakti). Worldly phenomena—in the form of either matter or individual consciousness—were emanations of his powers and hence were constituted by the single substance of his being. Yet the "soul remains a completely separate thing [from God]," explained the important later nineteenth-century guru Bijoy Krishna Goswami, "and it will probably always remain so."[39] The Gaudiya Vaishnavite tradition had generally represented itself as deeply critical of Sankaracharya, for it held that the power (shakti) and the one who possessed that power (Krishna) were not identical despite their common substance. By positing a relationship of *acintyabhedabhed* (inconceivable difference and nondifference) between devotee and deity, Vaishnavism claimed to subsume Advaita Vedanta's critique of the appearance of phenomenal multiplicity as a lower moment in the theological synthesis, and a lower form of spiritual experience than that of loving devotion (*bhakti*) for a divine personality (*ishvar*) who remained necessarily separate from the devotee's self.[40]

Bijoy Krishna Goswami (a collaborator with Siva Chandra in the *Sarva-mangala Sabha*[41]) had been converted to Brahmo theism as a young man, going on to become a sharp critic of idol worship as well as of forms of caste and gender discrimination. But as he increasingly sought to use the traditional devotional forms of Bengali Vaishnavism to communicate the monotheistic message of Brahmoism, he had gradually drifted back into the idioms of Vaishnavite religiosity until, in the face of charges of image worship, he left the Brahmo fold entirely in 1886.[42] His disciples would include no less than four of the most prominent Swadeshi activists—Bipin Chandra Pal, Aswini Kumar Datta (the beloved leader of Barisal), Satish Chandra Mukherjee (ideologue of national education and editor of *The Dawn*), and Manoranjan Guha-Thakurta (the extremist editor of the *Navashakti*).[43] But to Bipin Pal, a former Brahmo engaged in a self-conscious struggle over his guru's legacy, the importance of Bijoy Krishna lay in his recovery of Bengali Vaishnavism's immanent rationality, not through its invocation of theism but through the re-emphasis of an allegedly monistic substratum to its theology: "I myself heard from his own lips that no one could understand the message of Sree Chaitanya Mahaprabhu [the founder of Gaudiya Vaishnavism] who had not acquired a knowledge of Brahman."[44] By positing the doctrine of *acintyabhedabhed*, Vaishnavism claimed to subsume Advaita Vedanta's critique of phenomenal multiplicity, but without negating the reality of the phenomenal as a self-differentiated moment of the divine. Pal thus managed to extract an immanentist monism from the Vaishnavite critique of Sankaracharya. "Every object is a thought of God—materialised;

every man is the Spirit of God—incarnated. So is every nation the manifestation and revelation of a Divine Ideal."[45] "The essential divinity of man,"
Pal explained, "is the central conception of Hinduism," and man's highest
purpose is to realize "his essential divinity, his oneness with God. . . . But
though this is the general characteristic of Hinduism, it is brought out more
prominently in Vaishnavism than perhaps in any other sect or school."[46] This
was because, whereas the Shakta allegedly sought to realize God through the
single medium of one human relationship—the child's love for his mother—
the Vaishnavite sought the sublimation of all human relations and affections
into a spiritual connection with God, leading not only to a richer repertoire
of spiritual practice but also to a vision of "the Spiritual Being manifested in
or as Man."[47] Pal was adopting the Vaishnavite idiom to elaborate an indigenous idealism capable of articulating a unified but differentiated rational
substance of the social against the atomizing principle of "competition,"
which, "economic or otherwise, was a sin against God and man."[48]

A HINDU SOCIOLOGY

"Every evolution is the evolution of an Idea. This central Idea in every organism is what regulates the whole course of its evolution."[49] Both Shaktism and
Vaishnavism were being adopted as the bases of a Hindu idealism that I have
characterized as a discourse of immanentist monism. Instead of negating the
phenomenal in the name of abstract unity, this idealism could recognize the
constitution of the phenomenal through the activity of a divine consciousness immanent to the multiplicity of its forms of appearance. These theological alternatives to abstract monism did not have to be invented in the
late nineteenth century; they drew upon the rich theologico-philosophical
tradition of *vishishtadvaita,* qualified monism. Arguably, these *bhedabhed*
(difference and nondifference) cosmologies came far closer than Advaita to
approximating the mainstream of precolonial Hindu theology in Bengal,
and for that matter, the theological framework of most actual religious practices throughout the nineteenth century.[50] The innovation in this discourse
lay primarily in its application to a new object—social abstraction—rather
than in its specific theological formulations. But to get from the defense of
theological orthodoxy by Rammohun Roy's contemporary Shakta and Vaishnavite critics in the Dharma Sabha to the idealist sociology of the Swadeshi
era did demand more than a debate internal to Hindu textual traditions. It is
hard to understand how we might otherwise derive the rational unfolding of
the Idea in history, which both Aurobindo and Bipin Pal expounded as the

heart of the national ideal, from the conception of divine play, in which the phenomenal world was the fluctuating form of appearance of shakti.[51]

It is therefore hardly surprising to find this Swadeshi-era reconstruction of Hindu idealism being mediated by themes drawn unmistakably from German idealism. Hegel had characterized Hinduism in terms of a dualism that pitched the pure "abstract unity" of Brahma against the "abstract isolation of the world of sense," leading to a correlative duality in forms of worship between self-extinction and "a wild tumult of excess" consequent to an "immersion in the merely natural; with which individuality thus makes itself identical—destroying its consciousness of distinction from Nature." In other words, for Hegel, Hinduism was trapped between a form of unhappy consciousness and a pantheism that stood too proximate to the sensual and was therefore unable to extract the rational idea from phenomenal multiplicity. Hegelianized Vedanta was implicitly framed as an answer to this critique.[52] Bipin Pal could even make it sound as if ancient doctrines of Hinduism were virtually Hegelianism avant la lettre.

> As in higher Christian thought and philosophy the ideal of humanity has grown around the conception of Logos, even so in higher Hinduism the ideal of humanity has grown around the conception of Narayana. Narayana is the Indweller, severally in individual souls, and collectively He is also the Soul, so to say, of the whole human race. And this dual conception of Narayana as manifested in human units and constituting the basal unity and continuity of individual life and consciousness, and as eternally revealing and realising itself—to use Hegelian terminology—in and through the progressive evolution of the collective life and consciousness of the human race, lends a much deeper significance to the Hindu's conception of humanity than is found anywhere outside the very highest level of Christian idealism. But the underlying monistic or pantheistic ideas of Hinduism have lent a strength to the Hindu ideal of humanity both in its individual and collective aspects, which, owing to its essential dualistic emphasis, Christianity has not been able to impart to it in either of these aspects.[53]

The fact that Vedantism was being rearticulated with Hegelian insights in mind should not really strike us as so surprising, given Hinduism's longstanding positioning by German philosophers and Orientalists as the ancestor of modern idealism;[54] the ascendancy of philosophical idealism in Britain at the end of the nineteenth and beginning of the twentieth centuries;[55] the contemporary crypto-Hegelian reconstruction of other theological traditions such as Japanese Buddhism;[56] and the explicit Hegelianism of Hiralal Haldar and Brajendranath Seal, arguably the most influential philosophers in Bengal at the turn of the century.[57] But just as the internal logic of Hindu theology cannot explain the development of this new Hindu idealism at the end of the nineteenth century, neither can this appeal to German philosophical concepts stand in as a sufficient cause—for, as I have consistently tried to emphasize, intellectual lineages will not do to explain the resonance of particular conceptual frameworks to particular subjects in particular historical contexts.

That Hindu idealism was being understood in Swadeshi discourse as preeminently social in its reference marked it as profoundly modern, despite the archaic sources of its idiom. The declaration of Swami Vivekananda (who stood alongside Bankim as the other great ideological precursor of Swadeshi thought) that social work was the highest path to self-realization represented a crucial break even from his guru, Ramakrishna, who had been deeply suspicious of "philanthropy" as a potential form of worldly attachment. "Dare you say that you have the power to do good to others?" demanded Ramakrishna of Bankim on the one occasion of their meeting. "Those who want to build hospitals and dispensaries and are satisfied with that, are also good people, but they are of a different grade. The real devotee seeks nothing but God."[58] The real measure of charity was not its efficacy, but only the degree to which it was undertaken in a spirit of nonattachment, as a means of serving God, and realizing God in one's life as a real (indeed, sensible) presence. The intense, sensual immediacy of the relationship between man and God—which in turn mediated the Tantric relationship between man and the phenomenal world (understood as shakti), and even the relationship between man and man—was interrupted by Vivekananda's interposition of the category of society, which in mediating the relationship between men could also stand in as the medium of one's devotion to God.

> The individual's life is in the life of the whole, the individual's happiness is in the happiness of the whole; apart from the whole, the individual's existence is inconceivable;—this is an eternal truth, and is the bed-rock on which the eternal is built. To move slowly towards the infinite whole, bearing a constant feeling of intense sympathy and sameness with it, being happy with its happiness and being distressed in its affliction, is the individual's sole duty. . . . This is the law of Nature; and who can throw dust in her ever-watchful eyes? None can hoodwink society and deceive it for any length of time. However much there may have accumulated heaps of refuse and mud on the surface of society,—still, at the bottom of those heaps the life-breath of society is ever to be found pulsating with the vibrations of universal love and self-denying compassion for all.[59]

Bipin Pal made this identical point from a Vaishnavite standpoint:

> The message of [Bijay Krishna's] earlier Brahmoism was the brotherhood of man, which formulated itself in a propaganda of social amelioration. The mes-

sage of his later Vaishnavism was the divinity of man, which transformed the service of man into a living service of God, and worked out a noble transfiguration in all human relations and social activities.[60]

In passages like these, society had become an embodiment of the universal rather than, as it had been for Ramakrishna, an instance of phenomenal form that exercised a strong pull away from the immediate striving to see God.[61]

The newness of this reconception of Hindu idealism as a social discourse is marked not least by the absence of any term in Sanskrit that could adequately denote the modern concept of *society* that lay at the heart of both Vivekananda's and the Swadeshists' concerns. Trying to account for this lexical deficiency in the Sanskrit tradition, Daya Krishna has recently observed:

> This [absence of a word for *society*] is perhaps because what we call society today was not a natural unit, but an artificial, logical construction from existing groups for which there were a myriad of names. The terms varna, jati, kula, sangha, sreni, gana, puga, vrat, *naigam, samuha, parisad, carana* found in the *Smrti* literature of India refer to actually existing and functioning organizations which deal with familial, commercial, civic, craft and administrative functions. The idea of something overarching all of these and interrelating them was indicated by such concepts as *loka, parampara, dharma vyavahara* (in the sense of law) and *rajya.*[62]

If classical Indian thought tended to see the social order as a scale of concrete institutions structured in relation to a transcendental cosmic order, the concept of society in the modern world seems to index something more fundamental than this cumulative scale of forms. Yet this lexical absence is not a civilizational peculiarity of the subcontinent, for historians have also drawn attention to the modernity of the concept of society in both Europe and Japan.[63] It is surely thus necessary to account not for the specific absence of an appropriate lexical item in any particular language or tradition, but rather for the modern emergence of the need for such a term. How, in other words, can we specify the historicity of this *natural unit* that *society* has become today?

The class-interest analyses that have dominated the critical historiography of modern Bengal have commonly interpreted the political turn to religious idioms in the Swadeshi era as the compound result of, on the one hand, an incomplete modernization on the part of the educated middle class themselves, and on the other, their manipulation of popular religious icons to mobilize a mass political base in the context of an enduringly precapitalist social order.[64] In this, historians have drawn broadly on the form of ideology critique pioneered by the younger Marx, who had famously sought to turn Hegelian idealism—which "always converts the Idea into the subject and the particular actual subject . . . into the predicate"—"on its head," by showing that the subject of historical process was not the Idea, but rather the concrete, alienated worker laboring under conditions of bourgeois private property.[65] In the standard reading of this argument, idealist philosophers become sophisticated apologists for class society, resolving its contradictions at an abstract level while leaving them intact in reality. In this tradition of ideology critique, the political turn to religious idioms is interpreted as a means for the educated middle class to pursue hegemony by conflating their class interests with those of the people at large. As Barbara Southard argued, however, this approach falters in the face of the socially limited popular appeal of a Shakta religious symbolism closely associated with higher-caste religious practices—a limitation amply confirmed by the Swadeshists' ultimate failure to win broad-based popular support for the Swadeshi project. Reiterating the same instrumental logic that she had criticized in others, however, Southard proceeded instead to contend that the appeal to this specific religious idiom must therefore represent a more limited attempt to forge an alliance between the urban, Western-educated middle class and the rural upper castes, who both generally shared this common religious heritage.[66]

While it was an openly avowed aim of the new Swadeshist program to appeal to a broad-based constituency through the deployment of a religious idiom, the interest-based instrumentalism of this kind of analysis still gets us no closer to understanding either why Swadeshists should have thought that this was the appropriate modality for communicating with that constituency, or the apparent sincerity with which the nationalist leadership itself appeared to pursue their agenda not merely as public performance, but as a genuine ethical imperative in their own personal lives. Such a commitment is amply evidenced by Aurobindo's transformation after the subsidence of the Swadeshi movement into the famous yogi of Pondicherry.[67] We need to ground both the near universality and the conceptual specificity of the turn to the idiom of Vedantic idealism in something more fundamental than the imperative of mass mobilization.

As Moishe Postone has underlined, Marx's mature critique of Hegelian idealism was of a fundamentally different nature from the more familiar mode of critique that his earlier work represented. In capitalist society, labor's peculiar role as a socially mediating activity necessarily relates each instance of concrete labor to the totality of social labor as abstract human labor. It is this peculiar form of abstract mediation (the mediation of social interdependence by the totality of productive labor) that is reified through the category of society. Modern society is not to be understood primarily as an association of individuals bound by contract, or as a cumulative scale of institutions and arrangements as in Daya Krishna's premodern society. Since in capitalist society, labor forms the most fundamental mediation between individual and individual, it is correlatively abstract labor, that historically peculiar quality of labor under capital, that therefore constitutes the substance of the social whole. For this kind of Marxian approach, society cannot simply be assumed as a foundational, given framework of social-scientific or social-theoretical analysis. Rather, it becomes a category that is grounded in the structures of practice constitutive of, and constituted by, alienated social labor.[68] While Marx's later critique still turned on the grounding of abstract categories in real social practices, it also recognized that abstract human labor was a structure of social practice that had no specific concrete subject. In other words, the "identical subject-object" of history was not any specific class, but rather (as Hegel had suggested precisely by adopting the abstract categories of idealism) coercive structures of practice that did not directly depend on the volition of individual or class agents for the reproduction of its movement—even if, as concrete totality, it could never be distinct and separate from those individual or class agents either (since it was continually reconstituted by their labor, and at another level of abstraction, continually prone to crisis). Marx's mature "materialism" did not mean reducing abstraction to an obfuscation or legitimation of concrete social relations and agents. Rather, it meant grounding this (real) abstraction in the historically determinate structures of mediating practice that Marx denominated capital. The "rational core" of Hegel's philosophy was precisely its idealistic apprehension of the abstractness of the subject of modern history, even as it misrecognized that subject as transhistorical Spirit.[69]

The idealist idiom of Swadeshi discourse, I suggest, articulated this very same insight into the nature of social mediation when it began Vedantism's dialogical relationship with Hegelianism. "Behind the best work lies a quiet super-consciousness—knowledge that the work itself is not the great thing but the spirit that speaks in it," explained Aurobindo in 1909. "Nationality will be the synthesis of all righteous forms of effort."[70] By juxtaposing the deeper truth and spiritual primacy (*sattva*) of the social organism to the maya (illusion) and *tamas* (darkness and inertness—the quality of maya that obfuscates its real spiritual substratum) of both the culture of civil society and the inessential (*asar*) selfish interests that structured it, Swadeshi discourse was struggling to develop an indigenous philosophical language with which to grasp the nature of the social as something more fundamental and more abstract than an assemblage of individuals or a scale of institutional forms.[71] Swadeshi ideology consistently turned on the systematic opposition of substance, spiritual freedom, labor, production, and wealth to form, material attachment, consumption, exchange, and value. It is not through the abstractness per se of its idealist philosophical language that Swadeshi ideology marked itself as modern—indeed, most of its philosophical lexicon was explicitly and deliberately drawn from precolonial Hindu textual traditions—but rather through its redeployment of the premodern lexical forms of this abstraction as means of thinking essentially social problematics.[72] Following the broad impulse of Bankim's culturalism, Swadeshists sought to grasp indigenous social organization as grounded in a higher form of rationality that not only rose above the rank superstition or otherworldliness of which Hinduism had been so often accused but also superseded the liberal rationality of free exchange in civil society. Repudiating the superficial (Western) understanding of society as an association of atomistic individuals, Swadeshists located a more fundamental substratum in which an organic social solidarity was expressed immanently within practical activity itself. The Hindu social order could be understood (in its essential spirit if not always in its corrupt practice) as a form of ethical life grounded in the rationality of practical activity. Whereas the West had proven incapable of grasping this, and the babu had also been drawn into this inauthentic superficiality, popular Hinduism continued to express this underlying truth. In effect, this politics affirmed the rationality of the productive peasant household (a complex of noncontractual ethical relationships that formed the productive basis of the Indian nation) as the standpoint for a critique of exchange (the exploitative, impersonal, and atomizing superstructure imposed by Western colonialism). Swadeshists were thus able to translate the rarified theologico-philosophical conception of immanentist monism into a concrete political and economic project, as well as a vision of national history, by elaborating the abstruse philosophy of immanentist monism into a politics of the indigenous producer.

POLITICAL ECONOMY

For the new nationalists of the Swadeshi era, it was not simply an opposition of individual and society that was at stake, for the generality of the category society does not quite capture the concrete specificity of the *nation-form*, which, they insisted, constituted society's natural organic unit, and was therefore the proper subject of the aspiration to historical and political self-realization.[73] "God is one, and Humanity is also one," Bipin Pal acknowledged. "But, at the same time, as the Divine Unity is not an undifferentiated but a self-differentiated Unity, even so the unity of the human race is also a unity which exists in and realises itself through endless varieties—some personal and individualistic and some national and collectivistic."[74] Manu Goswami has compellingly and nonfunctionalistically grounded the spatial structure underlying Indian nationalist discourse—and its recuperation of the ancient geographical imagination of *bharatvarsha*—in the contradictions of the process of infrastructural integration that took place under British rule in the second half of the nineteenth century. As part and parcel of the attempt to lock the subcontinent more firmly into the dual role of producer of primary goods for export on the one hand and consumer of British manufactures on the other, the rapid extension of infrastructures of transportation and communication in the post-Mutiny era, at the very same time as more tightly articulating Indian practices of production and consumption with the world market, also created a more integrated economic space within the subcontinent. This bounded social and economic space was articulated through the categories of nation and national economy, and against the international structure of imperial domination and exchange. The politics of nationalism demanded an absolute congruence between this nation space and the state structure that was to represent its collective interest.[75]

This bounded national space was the category through which Swadeshi nationalism sought to supersede the cosmopolitan, reformist form of individuality that is constituted within civil or commercial society, where "men in their ordinary utilitarian course of life do not feel called upon to serve any one except themselves" and each individual "is propelled by the inertia of his own individual needs."[76] Unlike the materialistic individual and national selves of the West, the Indian national self recognized that the pursuit of worldly interests, be they political or economic, had meaning only insofar as these ends were subordinated to the higher ends of spirit. In other words, this was a self that grasped its own spiritual substance rather than constantly getting lost in the phenomenality of worldly attachments.[77] The British rulers and Bengali society did not simply square off against each other as commensurable, competing national interests, for whereas the interests of the former were pursued selfishly, the latter sought to pursue its interests through the medium of the universal.[78] When the immanent dynamics of indigenous society are allowed to unfold freely according to their own autonomous logic, individuals living in an organic relation with that society are also given the opportunity to develop freely—as they had in precolonial society when "throughout the villages [of India] every arrangement for the elaboration of humanity [*manushyatvacarca*] was maintained."[79] "Freedom" thus ceases to be a liberal category of individual emancipation from specific relations of authority and subordination, and becomes instead a category of objectification through practical activity. This, I would suggest, is what Bipin Pal meant when he described Indian democratic equality as grounded in "the equality of the divine nature, the divine possibilities and the divine destiny of every individual being," rather than in either a Brahmo reformism that established freedom of individual conscience through the removal of all social authority mediating between the individual and the undifferentiated absolute consciousness, or in a secular discourse of equal rights of the kind that we saw Bankim repudiate around 1880.[80]

By aspiring to become "judges, clerks, deputies and lawyers," wrote a pamphleteer in the heat of the Swadeshi upsurge, Bengalis had been reduced to a "nation of slaves." So long as they continued to crave the wealth and status that followed from this quartet of slave professions, national progress would continue to elude Bengal. In pursuing such service professions, the Bengali sacrificed the greater interest of the country, along with his own independence, by immersing himself utterly in the pursuit of his inessential selfish interests. "We have become accustomed to passing our lives driving about in horse-and-carriage, living in our three-storey mansions and bedecking our families in gold ornaments, and we consider that to be the highest purpose of our lives. We desire only our own luxurious enjoyment and selfish interests, and we know nothing else, and we don't even want to understand anything else. . . . We have become slaves to our narrow selfish interests."[81] For the *Yugantar,* the most extreme of the nationalist papers, the clerks who sold themselves and their children into a bond of servitude had been blinded to the higher interest of the nation because they feared to lose their livelihoods. They depended abjectly on their foreign masters even for their daily sustenance. But "those who live in ease and are addicted to enjoyment and luxury, and are, therefore, selfish" were above all the "obstacles to human society (and) to their own country and religion." They were "thorns" on the path of national liberation that would have to be "picked out."[82]

For the Aurobindo of the Swadeshi era, too, the weakness of modern Bengal lay in the predominance of this "bourgeois type," the "average contented middle-class citizen" who valued wealth, position, comforts, and luxuries above all else. In India, the bourgeoisie had risen to prominence only under British rule, which could not tolerate the statesman or the soldier, and which needed clerks far more than it needed scholars. The British ridiculed the ancient values of self-denial and self-sacrifice and instead held up the successful trader and the professional man as the "crown of humanity." Thus "all the great types which are nurtured on war, politics, thought, spirituality, activity and enterprise, the outgrowths of a vigorous and healthy national existence," were discouraged, and instead a crop of "safe, respectable" bourgeois were raised in their stead. As the bastard children of British rule, these Indian bourgeois sought to distinguish themselves from their countrymen by aping the ways of the English, and unreflectively mouthing their thoughts. "We read of and believed in English economy, while we lived under Indian conditions, and worshipped the free trade that was starving us to death as a nation. We professed notions of equality, and separated ourselves from the people, of democracy, and were the servants of absolutism."[83] As another periodical put it, the Indian bourgeoisie was a class that in "character, ideas, habits and manners, dress, in everything they are altogether unlike those they are professing to represent . . . and know nothing of the real wants and grievances of the country."[84] At the very moment that it made its rarified appeal to the language of rights, this bourgeoisie was clinging hopelessly to the underbelly of a structure of power inimical to the best interests of the nation to which it belonged. To pursue its own interests was therefore the same as pursuing interests that were fundamentally hostile to those of the country as a whole. Indeed, to identify with self-interest was a symptom of disidentification with a nation that represented in its core values a higher form of social consciousness.

That the British state was the institutional instrument of Manchester had attained the status of a truism in debates through the last three decades of the nineteenth century over cotton duties and food grain exports. By the Swadeshi period, to identify Britain in terms of the Napoleonic quip, "a nation of shopkeepers," or in terms of the yet more sinister image of the bloodsucking "vampire," was simply commonplace.[85] "The *feringhis* (foreigners) do two kinds of work in this country—governing and sucking," for it is in the end "the British bureaucrat who stands behind and makes possible exploitation by the merchant."[86] Sakharam Ganesh Deuskar's *Desher katha*, a Bengali-language popularization of the drain of wealth theory—and a general introduction to British "deceitfulness, selfishness, haughtiness and hatred towards other peoples"—was one of the great best sellers of the period, a work that it was "as incumbent a duty of all Bengalis to study as the Gita itself."[87] Selfishness was the British "national characteristic."[88] The Briton, "the greedy son of a needy household," "was a trader in the beginning and he is still a trader," his duties as a sovereign having proven unable to "drive the shopkeeper's instinct out of [his] brain."[89] Belonging to a world that was but "a shop on an enormous scale in which self-interest is the commodity of trade," the English rulers, taking money as the "be-all and end-all of their life," stooped to trade even in "*ganja*, opium and wine."[90] The "habits, manners and customs" of their civilization served only to create "newer and newer artificial wants" and to make "the struggle for existence harder day by day" as, under the "shadow of free trade," they "sucked all the substance out of India."[91]

There was a time when India had been the "Storehouse of the Goddess of Wealth"—before the Englishman came and converted it into a "bazaar of shopkeepers," extracting large profits in his simultaneous roles as "the master, the seller, the purchaser and the tax-collector."[92] Muslim rule had perhaps been barbarous, but having settled in India and made it their home, the Muslims, it was increasingly argued from the 1870s, had been the superior rulers because they had at least not drained the country of its wealth. The four famines of the eighteenth century under the supposedly uncivilized Muslim rule, explained one pamphlet, compared more than favorably with the gradually worsening epidemics of starvation under the British regime of free trade in the nineteenth century. Yet even during this famine-ridden British era there had never been any real shortage of food in India. Rather, in accordance with an argument that had been widely elaborated since the protectionist turn in Bengali opinion in the 1870s, "while fields of grain stand beside our households, we are dying in droves for want of food" because, plundered of its monetary wealth by the British, Indians had lost the power to purchase their sustenance.[93] "The present high prices of rice are due to the exportation of enormous quantities of that article," argued a correspondent in the *Bangabasi*. "It is true that the people get much money thereby, but the purchasing power of that money becomes less owing to the exorbitant rise in the prices of all commodities in the country."[94] Furthermore, cultivators were replacing food grains with jute under the "mistaken" impression that "they derive greater profit from jute than from paddy, because jute brings them more ready money than paddy does." An environmentally unfriendly export crop whose increasingly widespread cultivation in Bengal had been spurred on by international demand, the displacement of the coercive indigo system and the devaluation of the silver rupee, jute became, from the 1870s, a persistent symbol in Bengal of the subordination of indigenous, wealth-producing agriculture to the selfish interests of the foreign market.[95] Whereas food grains represented a potential source of real material wealth

[margin note: Muslim rulers of India]

(and hence autarchic national independence), jute represented only the skewed relation of exploitative exchange.

Alongside the process of spatial differentiation of (in principle) formally equivalent national entities, as Goswami also recognizes, there was also a process of qualitative differentiation between the imperial and national scales of polity. For nationalists, British rule represented a superimposed, parasitical, and unnatural global structure of cosmopolitan exchange.[96] The nation represented, in constitutive contrast to a global sphere of circulation inextricably associated in the South Asian context with the British imperial polity, a natural unit of productive activity and the genuine substance of wealth. The ubiquitous juxtaposition in Swadeshi discourse between fertile fields of grain and recurrent famine, between natural wealth (*"sujala suphala"*[97]) and financial poverty (*"paysar durbhiksha"*[98]), between the hard work of India's masses and their lack of remuneration, articulated the contradictions between production and exchange, between a potentially autarchic national economy and a superimposed global market. "Bengal lost her independence not when the English acquired political power in the country, but only . . . when her people began to depend on foreigners for such necessaries of life as food and clothing. And any country which depends upon a foreign country for food or clothing or any other article of domestic use is a subject country." And elaborating the universalistic implications of this insight one step further, the same editor would add: "In this sense, for England also loss of independence has begun."[99]

The nationalist critique of the absorption of the Bengali middle class in the professional and clerical sectors was undertaken from the perspective of a productionist philosophy of practice—fundamentally continuous with Bankim's *anushilanatattva*—which saw the expansion of human powers taking place through the exercise of those powers. "The individual, standing alone, cannot develop," argued Aurobindo; "he depends on the support and assistance of the group to which he belongs." This "group" (the nation) in turn required an "organisation" (the state), not just to defend it from external attack and internal disorder but also to create the "proper conditions which will give free play for the development of its activities and capacities—physical, moral, intellectual." Unlike the individual, the nation could not afford to specialize, but needed a many-sided development of all "these functions of the organism" in order to remain fit "for the struggle for life." "No government, therefore, can really be good for a nation or serve the purposes of national life and development which does not give full scope for the development of all the national activities, capacities and energies.

Foreign rule is unnatural and fatal to a nation precisely because it throws itself upon these activities and capacities and crushes them down in the interests of its own continued existence."[100] In other words, through the free functioning of the national life, man was to be given the opportunity to "adjust the physical environments in a manner favourable to the expansion of his soul" and thereby "bring forth its latent energy."[101] Both the nation and individual freedom were, in the end, categories of collective practices of self-constitution and world constitution—subjective freedom realized through objectifying practice.

The one-sidedness and ineffectiveness of the babu had developed primarily as a result of the Bengali's exclusion under the colonial regime from the "manly" Kshatriya functions of soldiering and ruling—and, it was nigh universally agreed, they would have to be corrected through a strong emphasis on rigorous gymnastic and martial training. National renewal would heavily rely on a system of pedagogy that would redress the one-sided development of the national character under foreign rule through a comprehensive system of intellectual, moral, spiritual, and physical culture deeply grounded in indigenous traditions.

> Must not the University to which [Indian] children should go for education be an *indigenous* product? . . . Foreign education has failed to make our young men reverent, religious, obedient to their teachers and superiors. Foreign education has failed to produce original men amongst us. . . . Foreign education has not enabled us to be self-reliant, self-dependent, self-sacrificing, patriotic.[102]

Where the official system of education was, from the Indian side, merely a means to respectable (nonmanual) employment, and from the British side, merely a means to produce a service class of clerks and petty functionaries, the revival of the agency of the nation was tied to a program that refused to separate education from the national life—a refusal at the heart of educational boycotts in response to government orders banning student political activity. "Calcutta University is a factory for the manufacturing of slaves," declared a student activist to universal applause at a large student meeting in 1905. "The kind of education that is appropriate for the defense of national life is not given there."[103] Instead, a program of "national education" was called for, which would "harmonise [all our resources] into a system which will be impregnated with the spirit of self-reliance so as to build up men and not machines—national men, able men, men fit to carve out a career for themselves by their own brain-power and resource. . . . So shall the Indian people cease to sleep and become once more a people of heroes, patriots,

[handwritten marginalia: Program of national education]

originators, so shall it become a nation and no longer a disorganised mass of men" (i.e., individuals in civil society).[104] The official education system, it was claimed, positioned Indians as passive consumers of the credentials for respectability in what was commonly referred to as the education machine and the education market. The national system, in contrast, was to provide an education that would produce agents of thought and action, ethically oriented and endowed with the kinds of instrumental knowledge "as are best calculated to develop the material resources of the country and to satisfy its pressing wants."[105] Thus Satish Chandra Mukherjee's first major educational experiment in 1895 was premised on "the efficacy of . . . the great Indian doctrine of *co-operation* and of ethical evolution . . . as calculated to soften the harshness, and rigours of a (competitive) struggle for existence and finally to replace and supplant it," while at the same time also welcoming "all constructive attempts to build up national character along other lines of activity,—such for instance as the *industrial*" (albeit always insisting upon the latter's "being subordinated to the higher interests of humanity, the interests of the progressing soul").[106]

The shallowness of babu liberalism was intimately tied to the flattening of India's economy under a regime of colonial exploitation that tended to stifle the "natural vivacity of the human species."[107] To achieve a vibrant national life necessarily meant awakening the creative energies of the nation, of giving the people scope for the real exercise of the full range of their immanent capacities, and hence of allowing all aspects of humanity to flourish, including the manly virtues that had been suppressed by the narrowness of the Bengali's range of activity under the burden of colonial rule.[108] And fundamental to this possibility was the awakening of the productive forces of the nation. The boycott was "the people's reply to the partition," noted an article in Bipin Chandra Pal's newspaper, *New India*, "and they are determined to sustain the movement not 'until the partition is withdrawn,' but until they have fully developed their own industries and are able to enter the world-market on equal terms with other nations."[109] To this end, Swadeshists took a vow not to purchase or use foreign goods, and instead to support indigenous (*svadeshi*) manufactures even when they were more expensive.[110] Even consumption could be converted into an instrument of national production. All Swadeshi politicians agreed that the structure of free exchange that underpinned liberalism needed to be at least deferred in the name of a protectionism that could establish a level playing field in the face of the political-economic structures of British domination. If the suppression of these forces was the result of a political problem, it was in the realm of politics that a solution needed to be sought; as Bipin Pal consistently argued, "there can be no economics divorced from politics."[111]

Even for Congress Moderates (whose invocation of the discourses of patriotic self-sacrifice and protectionist economics was essentially consistent with the efforts of Chandranath Bose and Bholanath Chandra to rescue the viability of liberal categories through a deferral of free exchange), it was ultimately in the renewal of native industry, the very heart of the Swadeshi boycott campaign, that India's hopes were placed. Bengali Moderates in the Congress, to a much greater degree than their allies in Bombay, gave cautious support to the Swadeshi boycott of British goods, though strictly as a means of applying pressure to the British—through the direct infringement of their financial interests—to revoke the partition. The great political economists of the Congress—Naoroji, Ranade, R. C. Dutt—had accepted that economic renewal was a necessary presupposition for any meaningful political independence. "Is not *Swadeshi* practiced by every civilised country?" demanded R. C. Dutt.[112] They drew on the writings of the critic of Smithian "cosmopolitical economy," Friedrich List, who had argued for the necessity of a strong regime of protectionism to allow weaker economies like those of the German states to develop their productive powers free from the insuperable and crushing competition of British manufactures. The peripheral position from which List had written in 1840s Germany had profound resonance for these critics of colonial exploitation. Moderates tended to defer the structure of equal exchange (rather than negate it outright) through the juxtaposition of natural economic development under conditions of relative equality and the deformative influence of the imbalance of political and economic power expressed by and exercised through imperial rule.[113] In this sense, they sought to salvage the liberal project through the leveling effects of a developmental economics of protectionism, arguing that "liberty and freedom could not possibly mean freedom to foreigners to ruin India's nascent enterprises through unlimited competition and that, in fact, in Indian conditions real liberty would come only through protection and 'artificial nourishment,' while Free Trade meant giving protection to England, the stronger party."[114]

While excoriating their political methods, the "Extremist" critics of the "mendicant," "un-National" Congress who emerged to prominence during the 1890s, drew their economic analysis of colonial rule wholesale from these same Moderate political economists.[115] But this younger generation of nationalists, including Aurobindo Ghose and Brahmabandhab Upadhyay, was more inclined to attack the presuppositions of any liberal categories grounded in the sphere of circulation as fundamentally hostile to India's national interest, and alien to India's national genius. The old-school liberal opposed the boycott as contrary to "the motives and desires . . . that guide men in life" and to "the great economic law of supply and demand," argued Aurobindo; but they forgot that "no real student of economics, who must be a student of life, has ever claimed for the postulates of political economy a binding reference to the man of the nation struggling forward to an act of self-sacrifice by a determined effort of the will."[116] Nationalists saw the boycott of British goods as just one element in an overall program of excluding the British state and British capital from India's national life. To those whom Sumit Sarkar has labeled "constructive Swadeshists," this meant a new spirit of self-reliance and commitment to working for society while foreswearing all assistance from and complicity with the colonial state.[117] (One could easily view this position as an attempt to construct a discrete, indigenous ethical state rooted in social practices, parallel to the merely mechanical functions of the colonial state.) To the leaders of the radical and organized elements of the new movement, the politics of boycott was tied to the necessity of a collective agency to pursue a direct political confrontation with the British rulers and thereby achieve India's *purna svaraj*—total independence and self-determination in every aspect of national life.

As the *Sandhya* explained, "we shall create a new independent system, which will regulate our education, the protection of our lives and our properties, our trade and commerce, our agriculture, our laws and our courts, our rents and our dealings."[118] Extremists reasoned that none of the nationalist programs—neither economic development through Swadeshi enterprise nor popular ethical renewal through national education—could be realistically achieved while India remained politically subordinated to British interests through the machinery of imperial rule. This made the establishment of an independent state as a coordinating agent of national activities—whether through the passive resistance of boycotting British goods, institutions, and social contacts, or through more directly military means—the highest priority of all Swadeshi activities.[119] Where before, India had been victimized by the heteronomous forces of the global market and the alien imperium that embodied it, in the future India would consciously command its own resources as a national subject embodied institutionally in the state. The Extremists proposed, in Aurobindo's formulation, "to establish a popular government which may be relied upon to foster and protect Indian commerce and Indian industry conducted by Indian capital and employing Indian labour."[120] Only thus could the sphere of circulation be rationally subordinated to the productive propensities of the nation. The organic relationship between capital and labor could thereby be overtly grounded in the common substance that constituted both, so that the expansion and accumulation of capital would become the foundation of the growth and development of the nation rather than, as under imperial rule, the cause of its impoverishment and degeneration. If the sphere of circulation was constituted in accordance with the regulative principles of an alien society imposed upon India by foreign rule, then the abolition of that foreign rule and the forms of social practice associated with it (Westernization) also implied the liberation of an indigenous, autonomous, autarchic, and unalienated social organism. Indigenization thus became a politics of productionist autonomy.

In most cases, this negation of civil society was less than absolute. When Bipin Pal argued that the identity of self and not-self was central to Indian thought, he formulated the fundamental principle of Hindu thought more specifically as the privileging of the self as the medium of the universal identity of all creation. "The consciousness of the self as the supreme and central fact in experience, the not-self standing in a relation of eternal and absolute subjection to it, having its value not in itself but in the self alone,—this may, in a word, be said to constitute the essential world-idea of the Hindu race."[121] This self was then to be pursued as a collective interest in a civil society transposed to a specifically global scale of competing national interests, an arena in which the only functioning law was the survival of the fittest, and where a weak nation like India could not survive as a mere assemblage of individuals. Yet the fact that Moderate and Extremist arguments could be conflated and confounded in any particular instantiation or articulation of national political economy should not distract us from recognizing the quite radical disjuncture between their basic principles. In the Moderate version of national political economy, the language of culture and self-sacrifice was being invoked as a supplement to salvage the salience of liberal political, economic, and social categories. In the Extremist argument, national political economy was being invoked as a logical extension of a culturalist imagination that was radically opposed to liberal political, economic, and social categories. For the Moderates, the ultimate aim of national political economy was a vibrant civil society that, because it was impossible under conditions of free trade and imperial rule, would have to be deferred until more favorable circumstances had been established through political means. For the Extremists, the aim of national political economy was an ethical society, which was the determinate negation of the model of self-interested individuality at the core of a reformist, cosmopolitan liberalism.

"It is impossible to save India from destruction now by anything except a combination of the entire Indian people into a great nationality. . . . A Japanese gentleman on one occasion being asked what his religion was, responded that his religion was the religion of Japan. Similarly henceforth every Indian if similarly questioned must reply that his religion is the religion of India."[122] "Men in the mass are strong and capable of wonder-working enthusiasms and irresistible movements," wrote Aurobindo in 1907; "but the individual average man is apt to be weak or selfish."[123] There could be no national redemption through the pursuit of selfish interests. "We have not entered the lists merely to play the *mudi* (grocer). . . . We have often heard the voice from heaven: 'Selfish man, you can have no redemption now; first free the Mother from her bondage, then seek your own deliverance.'"[124] Japan, especially after its victory in the Russo-Japanese war, was ubiquitously invoked as the preeminent example of how an Asian nation could achieve real independence through "the development of its moral and spiritual character" in keeping with national traditions, and through the virtues of "self-sacrifice, self-reliance, and self-nurturance."[125]

> Whatever the outcome of the Russo-Japanese War, this war has a number of lessons to teach a subject nation like us. The first lesson is that we have no reason to despair when it has been possible for this nation to progress so far within so short a period of time. The second lesson is that Japan has demonstrated how much progress man can make within a very short period of time through proper education. The third lesson is that national progress is impossible without the progress of commerce and the arts and sciences. The fourth lesson is that without the development of the national language the nation's progress will be utterly obstructed. The essential message of all these lessons—self-sacrifice and self-renunciation. If Japan had not been initiated into the mantra of self-renunciation, it would never have been able to progress so far.[126]

This capacity for self-sacrifice, in Rabindranath Tagore's view, was grounded in the fact that, instead of being reduced to the status of a dehumanized cog in the military "machine," every Japanese soldier felt in their hearts "a special relationship with the Mikado, and through that tie, with their homeland (*svadesh*)."[127]

It was fundamental to Japanese success that they had armed themselves with the instrumental technologies of the West, but they had taken only as much as was needed and made it a part of their own, without ever allowing these foreign technologies to affect the powerful and dynamic inner life of the people—and this inner life, the national spirit, had enabled Japan to master the instruments of Western technology and thereby carve so preeminent a place for itself in the modern world.[128] Science and technology were useless without a strong national subject capable of subordinating them to its own ends. Such a national subject was to be produced through "the development of Indian thought and learning on which, as on a parent stock, will be engrafted the knowledge of the culture and civilisation of the West."[129] The "secret of Asia," the key to its imminent rebirth, was none other than the ability to "go down to the roots, this gift of diving down into the depth of self and drawing out the miraculous power of the Will, this command over one's own soul."[130]

True Hinduism, "the essence of which consists of self-sacrifice," was at its core "what is called Nationalism" and "is fostered by our social virtues."[131] Against the pettiness of English materialism and "the fighting, the pushing, the materialistic, I was going to say, the cruel democracies of Europe and America," the Swadeshi generation sought to pit an alternative civic discourse that grounded a statist, protectionist economics in the higher culture of indigenous social principles wherein democratic equality was founded on "the equality of the divine nature, the divine possibilities and the divine destiny of every individual being"—on the positive freedom of objectifying activity rather than the negative freedom of emancipation in the sphere of circulation.[132] "The aim of the Congress Party is to bring about a compromise between the indigenous and the foreign, in all things external and internal, material and moral.... The new spirit is one of unalloyed purity and liberty.... The disciples of the new spirit ... are resolved to establish a wholly independent national system."[133] The inner domain of the nation needed to be purged of foreign influence. "Take from the *feringhi* as much as should be taken, and make it part of your own, as Japan has done," declared the *Sandhya*, while at the same time demanding that "the *feringhi* [foreigner[134]] should be ... turned out of the kitchen, of the room of the household deity, of the room where the paddy is husked, of the *ghat* on the edge of the tank, of the place where the religious festivals are held and of the courtyard of the *tol* and *chatuspathi* [traditional schools]."[135] "Hindus in general should practically be Hindus," insisted the *Nayak*, emphasizing the importance of an abstention from foreign habits and clothing as much as from foreign salt and sugar.[136] Tagore, too, was arguing in this period that it was precisely because Bengalis had inverted "the natural relation between the home and the outside world" that they had become like "algae in the current," swept along by alien forces.[137] The nation's "sons" would only be able to banish their effeminate passivity—their "utterly uxorious" submission to the "timid, female" instincts in society[138]—when they came to serve their Mother as real men possessed of a newly virile, and even martial, masculinity that would negate the feminizing structures of colonial civil society.

Only by reestablishing the integrity of this inner domain would it be possible to experience something like real emancipation, freedom, self-determination, and self-realization. Such values were to be realized not through the pursuit of worldly things but through the renunciation of that desire. Although in practice Swadeshi activism overwhelmingly took the form of a practice of consumption, it was a form of consumption that was self-consciously subordinated to the logic of national productivity and that eschewed luxuries in the name of simple necessities. The new freedom conceptualized by Swadeshi Extremism was grounded in a critique of consumption in the name of a political subject who renounced any desire for the fruit of his labor through the practice of nishkam karma (desireless action). In its overtly political-economic form, this emphasis on accumulation through self-sacrificing labor would not only have the more obvious consequence of stemming the flow of money out of the country that resulted from the purchase of foreign commodities, but could also be linked to a theory of capital accumulation through joint stock practices that would combine the small capitals accumulated through self-restraint into more effective magnitudes of investable capital available to society.[139] At a more fundamental ethical level, emancipation was conceived on a profoundly different model from classical liberalism's grounding in free exchange, wherein the pursuit of private interests was validated so long as it remained regularized in accordance with law and the rights of others. "Freedom . . . is not want of restraint, but self-restraint; freedom is not want of regulation, but self-regulation; freedom is not want of determination, but self-determination."[140] "There is a world of difference between a *bania* (trader) and a *Vedantist*," argued the *Navashakti*; and identifying most emphatically as the latter, the Extremists wanted the real substance of "autonomy, not certain rights; independence, not happiness; emancipation, not self-gratification."[141] Swadeshi nationalists inseparably welded an ethical critique of the (heteronomous) desiring subject of civil society with a political economy of accumulation through renunciatory practice—using the latter to extend the practical scope of the former. They were elaborating a mode of political subjectivity adequate to serving a nation conceived as a productive organism.

Against the debilitating practice of freedom through exchange in an alien sphere of circulation, Swadeshi discourse counterposed an alternative political and ethical imperative: "There is only one way to prevent our intelligence, our heart, and our sensibility (*ruci*) being sold off on a daily basis for a pittance: we must consciously, forcefully, dynamically and totally become what we ourselves are."[142] Whatever the differences of emphasis among the new Extremist periodicals of Bengal, "whether the *Bande Mataram* or *New India* or vernacular journals like the *Yugantar*, the *Nabasakti* or the *Sandhya* ... they are united by a common faith and a common spirit; a common faith in India, not in an Anglicised and transmogrified nation unrecognisable as Indians."[143] While "a strong central authority" was necessary to act as "a means of self-expression and united actions, a chief organ and nerve-centre with subsidiary organs acting under and in harmony with it," its actions and policy could not be guided by principles external to the society it was to represent and govern.[144] As Aurobindo's *New Lamps for Old* had already adumbrated, the basis for such a politics would need to be found in the immanent propensities of Indian society, in its traditions of man-making and ethical life.[145]

The earlier identification with the French model of a socially generalized liberal culture was soon sidelined: the more Aurobindo grappled with Indian circumstances and conditions, the more the need to ground politics in the life of the people implied the necessity of subjecting that politics to a rationality that was not, in any classical sense, liberal.[146] "If a nation were an artificial product that could be made, then it might be possible for one nation to make another. But a nation cannot be made,—it is an organism which grows under the principle of life within.... The nation-builder, Cavour or Bismarck, is merely the incarnation of a national force which has found its hour and its opportunity.... But the process ... is one of growth and not of manufacture."[147] To reconnect with these immanent propensities of the collective life, the educated people of the land would have to "wander about the villages and pathways in search of that heart of the country," so as to reacquaint themselves with the illiterate masses through "intimate intercourse, sympathy and service."[148] They would have to "give up imitating the English and discover such means for the attainment of our objects as are suited to our national character and situation."[149] "A genuine leader of the country or of society becomes the ruler of every man's heart by increasing his affective relations with the entire people of every class in the country down to the very meanest. He can never, like our leaders today, screw up his face and refer to the common people as a 'mass' ... The economic and spiritual desires of every man and woman in society are present in his heart. The ideal of the whole society can be grasped just by looking at him."[150]

Instead of forming associations and holding meetings on an alien and (for most Indians) alienating Western model, they would have to turn to the traditional forms to which the people could relate—*mela* (fairs), *jattra* (a form of theater), *kirtan* (Vaishnavite hymns), and *kathakata* (professional storytelling).[151] Only then could they draw on the true power of the country; not the babus, but the "thousands upon thousands of common people" whose "bodies are very strong," who are independent, among whom "the living ideals of the homeland are fully alive," and who are the "chief support for the establishment of national self-rule."[152] When a "natural bond of unity" has been reestablished between intellectual and manual labor, "then what the head will decide the hand will carry out."[153]

NATIONAL HISTORY

In 1912, Pramathanath Mukherjee, a disciple of Siva Chandra Vidyarnava Bhattacharya, published his major treatise on the philosophical foundations of national education, *India: Her Cult and Education,* a work conceived and begun some time around 1907 or 1908 while he was a member of the faculty at the Bengal National College.[154] "Life must be lived in matter in such a fashion," he had therein explained, "that it may rise to master it at last: the conditions of possible spirituality are (a) recognition of matter, (b) co-ordination of matter and (c) conquest and conversion of matter. In its primary presentation, matter is an alien order to be obeyed and borne with, in its final representation it is a submissive vehicle of life's expression—the interval between the two is long and eventful like history itself."[155] The history of India had thus been none other than the (re)appropriation of nature by spirit through human activity. "The soul is the centre of a radiation which is the universe itself; it is the Reality that *appears* as the world. . . . The Source makes an eject of itself in its own emanation. . . . From the Spirit's point of view [history] is conquest and not *adaptation:* the Spirit cannot think of adapting itself to its own echo, reflex, eject."[156] The institutions and ideals of Hindu society, founded on "*realistic idealism*" and moved by "*spiritual automobility,*" were ideally suited to create a new social order in which economic and political institutions were subordinated to the dynamic unfolding of human spiritual self-realization.[157]

The discourse of spirituality that pervaded the Swadeshi movement can be seen as a discourse of what in Hegelian terms would be understood as the objectification of spirit—and by extension, in Marxian terms, a discourse of labor. "Economics and politics, and social and domestic life and the arts and crafts of culture and civilisation,—all these we need, all these we must have, but they must always be subordinated to the demands of the inner life,—

must work together for the unfolding of the life of the soul, which is truly an unfolding of the life of God in man."[158] A critique of the isolated individual of civil society—the "abstract cosmopolitan" who views the particularities of national history from the debilitating perspective of an illusory "outside" to time and place—was undertaken in the name of a subject who, through his practical activity, shares a common substance with his fellow men and with a physical environment inscribed by the nation's collective history. "The unfolding of man's capacities takes place while working," observed Benoy Kumar Sarkar while still a young acolyte of Satish Chandra Mukherjee. "Everyone begins work first, and then discovers and nourishes their own capacities in the process of striving and through efforts to perform tasks."[159] In this he was not only following the *anushilanatattva* elaborated by Bankim, but also implicitly invoking Swami Vivekananda. "All the actions that we see in the world, all the movement in human society, all the works that we have around us, are simply the display of thought, the manifestation of the will of man," Vivekananda had written. "Machines or instruments, cities, ships, or men-of-war, all these are simply the manifestation of the will of man; and this will is caused by character, and character is manufactured by Karma"—where "Karma," it is specially noted, was to be understood "in its widest sense" of work or activity in general.[160] This is what made it possible for Vivekananda to argue that the Sudra, the caste whose role was labor, was "the real body of society"—and moreover, to famously declare that the time would come when this constitutive role of labor in society would be concretely realized in its overt organization—"when there will be the rising of the Sudra class, *with their Sudra-hood* . . . when the Sudras of every country, with their inborn Sudra nature and habits,—not becoming in essence Vaisya [traders] or Kshatriya [warriors], but remaining as Sudras [workers],—will gain absolute supremacy in every society."[161] In such a society, the spiritual dimension of existence would, in terms of the social logic of idealism, have been fully realized. (Although what this formulation obscured was the continued reliance on the Brahman to guarantee that the self-realization of the Sudra was not a descent back into illusion—a tension that, as we shall see in the next chapter, would be resolved in two radically different ways in the post-Swadeshi era.)

The nation, as the collective embodiment of both living and objectified labor, was not "a mere *word*, a mere *abstraction*, a mere *idea*," explained Bipin Pal. "It is something very tangible, something very concrete. It is both word and thought, both an idea and its symbol and manifestation,—it is both abstract and concrete."[162] Consequently, the basis of the new politics, rather than being "evolved out of the head" of the individual reformer on the basis of purely abstract precepts, had to "be sought for in the past history and evolution of the nation itself," where the process and logic of the successive concrete manifestations of the "regulative idea" of the nation could be seen unfolding. "A right understanding of the meaning and purpose of Indian history"—history understood not as a catalogue of dates and names but as "the science of comparative history and sociology as well as the general philosophy of history"—is, therefore, the "primary duty of every nation-builder in modern India. . . . Patriotism that does not feed upon history is like religion that rejects the help of the scriptures—rootless, fanciful, unreal."[163] Swadeshi Nationalism's *nation* was, from the perspective of the argument I have been pursuing in this book, the reified embodiment of the abstractness that concrete laboring activity embodied. If the nation was thus the negation of the social and temporal vacuum of a civil society inhabited by atomized individuals pursuing their own personal ends, *history* was the specific mode of temporality in which the collective substance of the nation had been constituted though the process of objectification through labor.[164] The alien quality of abstract labor—its appearance as a form of social mediation external to the individual subject and embodied in the act of exchange in the sphere of circulation—was substantialized in the colonial context in terms of an allegedly Western propensity to pursue materialistic ends in a spirit of utilitarian individualism. A foreign rule that cloaked mercantile interests in the regularities of the rule of law was thus understood to underpin the impersonal structure of civil society. The overthrow of foreign rule would not just remove an oppressive regime as such. More fundamentally, it would negate the alien quality of abstract mediation in the sphere of circulation in the name of a concrete collective subject that constituted itself through the active (and hence agential) process of concrete labor. The nation would cease to be the servant of (foreign) capital, and become instead the historical embodiment of capital's constitutive activity and substance (spiritualized labor). The culmination of this process of self-realization was, in the view of most Swadeshists both Moderate and Extremist, the development of modern industry in the hands of indigenous capital ("to the almost complete exclusion," as Bipan Chandra noted, "of interests purely commercial").[165]

We can now begin to understand the new turn toward the people in terms more fundamental than—though not necessarily exclusive of—an argument about the hegemonic aspirations of any particular social group. That politicians like Aurobindo were claiming for the new middle class a position of moral-social leadership does not need to be demonstrated, for it is quite explicit in his writings. My project here is to grasp the more fundamental social logic in which the rationality of such a claim to leadership could be grounded. By seeking to found the new politics on the immanent propensities and latent dynamics of the nation, Swadeshi nationalism imagined the possibility of elaborating a vision of political autonomy and national development out of the dynamic temporality of capital. At the same time, by resuming their organic connection with that nation, Swadeshists saw themselves as negating the heteronomous forces that structured their existence in civil society; a heteronomy identified in terms of the superimposition of the alien and exploitative practices of exchange in civil society upon a social organism whose immanent potential for rationality resided in its productive propensities (the appropriation of nature to human ends). Rather than standing alone as individuals in civil society confronting an external realm of necessity constituted by colonial capital, Swadeshists instead sought to channel the forces of indigenous society by identifying themselves with the nation understood as the collective subject of a history of objectification. By reintegrating themselves as the political center and intellectual "head" to the social "body," they would draw together the scattered energies of the nation into a self-consciously coordinated organism actively pursuing its own logic of development. The Indian nation could claim such an autonomous dynamic development because the temporality of capital was construed as already inhering in the precolonial history of the nation, in its social practices and its systems of thought, even in its (Aryan) "racial" constitution. Against the historical particularity of modern practices of free exchange (what Vivekananda called the age of the Vaishya) was posited the historical universality of the laboring subject. Such a subject did not negate the particularity of national history and indigenous society in the name of cosmopolitan individuality—and yet neither did it have to negate the universally human in the name of this particularity, for universality inhered in the very act of labor that had constituted India's particularity.

The concept of culture that Swadeshists appropriated from Bankim indexed a practice whereby individuals developed their own active powers in the world as a function of their ethical and spiritual development and also realized their organic connection with the social whole of which they were a part. If the social world was constituted through a collective history of labor, then the concrete laboring activity of each individual assumed the character of a homogeneous moment in an organic process. This provides us, I would suggest, with a key theoretical insight for understanding why the discourse of culture appears to have taken such an ethnographic turn in the late nineteenth century. The practice of culture, as elaborated by Bankim, represented the rejection of the emancipatory rationality of exchange in the sphere of circulation, a practice that constituted only the negative freedom of an individual pursuing his own interests in a realm of necessity that seemed to confront him as an external means to his own ends. In contrast, culture represented the means to a positive freedom whereby the rationality of the abstract-universal was to be approached through concrete practices that simultaneously constituted the ethical self, and the capacity of that ethical self to command nature to its own spiritual ends.

The ethnologization of culture represented the integration (or, as Bankim and the Swadeshists might have put it, the *re*integration) of the individual's cultivation of worldly agency and ethico-spiritual development into the dynamic, concrete temporal dimension of history, the unfolding process of the nation's collective subjective appropriation of the environment to its own spiritual nature. The culture of India in the collective sense—"all that she has stored up of knowledge, character and noble thought in her immemorial past," in Aurobindo's words[166]—had represented, as Bankim made clear, a cumulative process whereby the nation had cultivated its capacity to liberate itself from subjection to the heteronomous forces of nature (whether in the form of environmental determinism, maya, or nature worship). Culture necessarily represented a process simultaneously of universalization and of particularization—the first because concrete labor embodied the substance of abstract labor; the latter because, as concrete activity, it always embodied it historically in specific ways. As Satish Chandra Mukherjee put it when introducing his system of "higher culture," the "spirit of universalism, the very breath of all progress upwards, is not inconsistent with, but is highly co-operant towards a special study of systems of thought and belief which is equally necessary to a special evolution of each individual spirit. Each race, therefore, should cultivate this double line of progress."[167]

India's spiritual predisposition was its privilege. In Western societies, the relations among the self-interested individuals who constituted society were regulated by mechanical institutions:

> All political ideals must have relation to the temperament and past history of the race. The genius of India is separate from that of any other race in the world, and perhaps there is no race in the world whose temperament, culture and ideals are so foreign to her own as those of the practical, hard-headed, Pharisaic, shopkeeping Anglo-Saxon. The culture of the Anglo-Saxon is the very antipodes of Indian culture. . . . His ideals are of the earth, earthy. His institutions are without warmth, sympathy, human feeling, rigid and accurate like his machinery, meant for immediate and practical gains. The reading of democracy which he has adopted . . . is the most sordid possible, centred on material aims and void of generous idealism. . . . If [India] is to model herself on the Anglo-Saxon type she must first kill everything in her which is her own.[168]

Unlike Anglo-Saxon social institutions, the prescribed practices of Hinduism tied man to man organically by pointing the individual constantly toward the truth of a higher unity. "The Hindu social order [*hindudharma*] shows us a way of getting beyond the small-scale relationships of the household and the village and feeling a connection of unity between each of us and the world."[169] India's social institutions were the medium of the nation's history of objectification, not merely utilitarian instruments for the regulation of relations among atomized individuals pursuing selfish ends. They were, insofar as they were properly fitted to their time (culture, not custom), instances of the concrete historical realization of the abstract, rather than arbitrary and oppressive forms of authority that should be negated in the name of the cosmopolitan subject of reform. Caste, for example, had originally been "conceived as a distribution of duties" and was thus in principle a "socialistic institution," despite its "later perversions" that now necessitated its "transformation."[170] Similarly, "the Hindu doctrine of the *Guru*" was an institutional means, grounded in the historical continuity of succession (*parampara*), of mediating the approach of particular individuals to the unity of the godhead that was also the unity of society.[171] "Hindu society" had been engaged for thousands of years in gathering the "collective strength of society" through the genius of such social institutions, a form of strength far superior to mere force of arms—a dormant force that "permeates our life in every aspect of it" and has merely awaited awakening.[172] As a result, the "Indian labourer is a much higher being in civilisation and moral culture than a European labourer," for "his mind is impregnated with the same high ideas of religion, morality, truth, peace and self-control as guide the actions of his fellow-countrymen belonging to the higher classes."[173] Whereas the "West is full of interest in phenomena," it was with India that the future of the world rested, Aurobindo declared, because of its capacity to pierce the veil of particularity and see the single moving spirit that underlay the outward appearance of diversity.[174] This was the basis of India's ability to "go to the roots" and "draw out the miraculous power of the Will" with which its new nationalism, "the politics of the twentieth century," would combat a rootlessly alien and spiritlessly materialistic foreign regime.[175] In this sense, the "movement of which the first outbreak was political, will end in a spiritual consummation," as Asia teaches Europe how to overcome the shallowness of its social and political imagination and thereby attain an ethical collective life.[176] Once again, India was to be the world's guru.

———— ✳ ————

CHAPTER SIX

Reification, Rarification, and Radicalization

[handwritten margin note: Anushilan associated with physical and martial training and ultimately terrorism]

BANKIM'S term, *anushilan*, did not stick as Bengali's standard equivalent for the English word *culture*. It would become deeply associated with Swadeshi-era secret societies dedicated primarily to physical and martial training—and, as time went on, to terrorism.[1] The Anushilan Samiti (Culture Societies) of Calcutta and Dhaka rose to great prominence in the Swadeshi and post-Swadeshi eras as centers of revolutionary activity.[2] The term, *anushilan*, perhaps in part had become too deeply implicated in the Swadeshi movement's collapse into secret-society terrorism, and quietly retreated, outside of this more specific political identification, to its more general sense of *practice*. Searching for a new word from the Sanskrit lexicon to translate the higher conceptual ambitions of culture, and thereby to root it in Indian intellectual tradition, Bengali writers soon came down to two leading contenders. The first, *krishti*, connoted the idea of *cultivation*—identical in this respect to the Latin word, *cultura*. The other word, *sanskriti*, was understood to mean something more like *purification*. Both these words had emerged into widespread circulation by the 1920s.[3] But by the 1930s, Rabindranath Tagore, grandson of Dwarkanath, son of Debendranath and Bengal's most prominent litterateur, had launched his rather extraordinary campaign to displace *krishti* from the Bengali lexicon and establish the supremacy of *sanskriti* in conventional usage.[4]

[handwritten margin note: Sanskriti, "purification"]

Tagore's identification of culture with art and literature, and his sense that there existed a profound cleavage between these noninstrumental activities and the exigencies of daily life, represented a profound break from the culturalist tradition that Bankim had inaugurated. Bankim's concept of

176

[handwritten margin note: Tagore identifies culture with art and literature, profound break of Bankim's culturalist tradition]

anushilan had drawn its vitality and plausibility from its claim to have deep roots in the practices of everyday life. The ideal of *anushilan* would surely have been to transform even the mundane activity of cultivating the soil into a practice of cultivating humanity. It thus represented the transfiguration of everyday life rather than its negation. In this sense, the double entendre of *krishti* could not have been more appropriate—for reasons that went far beyond merely reproducing the etymology of its English equivalent. So how was Tagore able to succeed, on the basis of nothing more than his personal prestige and the persuasiveness of his case, in driving *krishti* into relative marginality? The subsidence of both *anushilan* and *krishti* as synonyms for *culture* cannot be adequately explained purely in terms of Tagore's personal influence. The purpose of this chapter will be to clarify the transformed circumstances under which only *sanskriti* could function as an adequate Bengali equivalent for *culture*. Post-Swadeshi Bengali intellectuals felt increasingly compelled to rethink the foundations of cultural practice in response to an anxiety provoked by the interruption of the identification of Swadeshi culture with the life of the people. This expulsion of culture from the life of the people—from life circumscribed by material needs and wants—is what *sanskriti* specifically named. To this end, I examine the ways in which the failure of the Swadeshi movement impacted the coherence of the culture concept by focusing on a series of different kinds of responses: first, aestheticism; second, antimodernism; third, bhadralok communalism; fourth, Pakistanism; and finally, Marxism.

SANSKRITI

While the Tagore family had supported Swadeshi ideals for decades, Rabindranath Tagore had doubts from the beginning about the seriousness of the "'agitation'-wallahs" and "the childishness of boycott."[5] Yet he cooperated with the other leaders of the movement as one of the foremost Swadeshi ideologists whose essays, songs, oratory, and educational work carried great moral and emotional weight among educated Hindus. By the end of 1907, however, disillusioned by the outbreak of communal conflict and the turn to terrorist violence, he had quietly withdrawn from the movement and would go on to voice his concerns publicly in a series of extremely unpopular essays published the following year.[6]

The government, he had begun by acknowledging in the first of his 1908 interventions, was deliberately trying to drive a wedge between Hindu and Muslim Bengal by partitioning the province.[7] This it had done by partition-

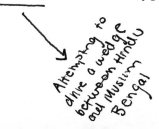

Attempting to drive a wedge between Hindu and Muslim and Bengal

ing the eastern part of Bengal proper where the Muslim populace became ever more numerically preponderant with every passing year—"that part of the country which is rich in crops and full of paddy and money, where the natives have strength in their bodies and courage in their hearts, whose vitality has not been sucked dry by malaria and poverty"—from the poorer western part where Hindus predominated. The government recognized that the Bengali Hindus were united, but it also recognized that the sense of solidarity stopped at the boundaries that separated them from Muslims, from their own lower castes, and from the other less educated peoples of the Bengal Presidency (Biharis, Oriyas, and Assamese). In this sense, however, the colonial strategy of divide and rule was only exploiting and exacerbating divisions that were already present. When the Partition was finalized, educated Bengalis had responded with a virtually exclusive emphasis on boycott, thereby seeking to make their anger known to the government and challenge its authority. What they did not do, Tagore observed critically, was direct their efforts toward ensuring that the social bonds that had connected Hindus and Muslims remained strong despite the political stress. To make matters worse, though, the boycott undertaken in the name of the indivisibility of Bengali national unity had come to function as the chief instrument for further driving the two communities apart. Educated Hindus had made the boycott of foreign goods obligatory, enforcing it through intimidation and the threat of social boycott. They had demanded that the lower classes maintain it despite the recognized hardship involved, arguing that this was a sacrifice ultimately in the people's best interests. When the people resisted, the educated Hindus had responded with uncomprehending anger. But why should the lower classes believe that the educated Hindus had their ultimate best interests in mind? Hadn't educated Hindus always treated Muslims and Namasudras with contempt? The imposition of boycott was not just experienced as a harsh inconvenience by the lower classes; the very imperiousness of the demand encoded the thoughtless arrogance of the educated Hindus toward the rest of the people. It could therefore be no surprise when the people began to respond to the Swadeshi program with undisguised hostility, and Muslims and Namasudras began buying imported salt and cloth even when it was more expensive than the nationally produced alternative.

  It was not that Tagore disagreed with the Swadeshist claim that the promotion of national economic self-reliance was indeed in the entire country's best interest. And he really did not question that it was the ignorance of the lower classes that prevented them from recognizing this fact. But it was, he insisted, both a moral obligation and a practical necessity for the educated classes to win the people over to the national cause, rather than to force them merely to obey their dictates. Instead of going to the people and explaining how boycott would ultimately improve their lives, however, these educated Hindus had communicated only a desire to vanquish the English, asserting the need for popular support for the boycott if that end was to be accomplished. It was inevitable and natural that the people would respond to the subsequent intimidation and threats with anger and active hostility. The only way in which Swadeshi ideals could be salvaged was by convincing the people in their hearts rather than merely coercing them. This in turn could only be accomplished if the educated classes could convince the people that Swadeshi ideals genuinely did represent the best interests of the people as a whole. "A brother can indeed accept hardship for a brother, but it just doesn't happen that a person will give up part of his home as soon as someone turns up saying 'brother' without any basis. The common folk of this country don't know us to be their brothers, and even now they have seen no evidence in our conduct that brotherly sentiments towards them really are alive in our hearts."[8] What was needed was a display of love, respect, and service on the part of educated Hindus that would express a genuine feeling of brotherhood with the uneducated Muslims and Namasudras. In the absence of such patient endeavor, the "nation" of the educated Hindus did not really include the entire people whom they claimed to represent. The outcome of this hollowness at the heart of Swadeshi activism was, Tagore argued, a spiritual and moral vacuum. Having embraced hatred and anger at the expense of a full reverence for humanity as an end in itself, Swadeshism looked, in the face of the growing popular hostility to the movement, to a Western practice of politics whose amoral instrumentalism could no longer measure the proper proportion between ends and means, and finally collapsed into the anomic phantasmagoria of terrorist violence.[9]

The ideal of an ethical and autonomous national community at the heart of Swadeshi nationalism had failed, from Tagore's perspective, because it had been unable to carry the people with it. But his critique of the movement, it needs to be emphasized, was undertaken using the standards of the Swadeshi ideal. A community founded on coercion could never be an ethical community. Loudly declaring national solidarity was no substitute for working to realize an authentic national solidarity. The anti-babu nationalist had ended up looking more and more like a babu at heart after all, attached to an abstract India rather than the real India of diverse communities and unlettered peasants, and contemptuously divorced from the life of the people even as his rhetoric proudly proclaimed his identification with the nation as a whole. By identifying coercion as the core issue, Tagore seemed to be saying that the problem with the Swadeshi movement was that it was not in the end Swadeshi enough. Profoundly disillusioned with Swadeshi politics, Tagore withdrew from Calcutta to continue his educational experiments at Shantiniketan, a property in Bolpur that his father had purchased in the 1860s to be the site of an ashram.

In 1902, still an enthusiastic Swadeshi activist, Tagore had founded a school at Shantiniketan modeled on the forest hermitages of ancient India where young men had passed their period of *brahmacarya*, the first of the four scripturally prescribed stages of life (*caturashrama*), in residence with their guru teachers. There was a far more fundamental ideal underlying the revival of brahmacarya by diverse Swadeshi educational innovators like Rabindranath Tagore, Satish Chandra Mukherjee, and Brahmabandhab Upadhyay than merely a formal nod to national tradition. On the contrary, Tagore explained in "The Problem of Education" (his programmatic outline of what the new national program of instruction should look like, composed in 1906 in response to a request that he draw up a constitution for the college to be established by the new National Council of Education), merely reviving the ancient school system without adapting it to India's present needs would be to institute as pointless and formalistic an imitation as the Western-style education they were trying to replace.[10] Brahmacarya was to be a practice through which the subjectivity of the nation's young men could be formed free from the artificial multiplication of the desire for superfluities.

> To speak of maintaining *brahmacarya* should not imply mere physical auster-
> ity. . . . All the inner propensities, while still in an undeveloped state, receive an
> untimely birth under artificial influences. As a result, there is only a squandering
> of powers and the mind becomes weak and unfocused. Against this it is abso-
> lutely necessary to safeguard the authenticity of [the young man's] nature from
> the untimely awakening of his faculties and the rude excitations of luxurious
> indulgence.[11]

The blossoming of inner propensities would take place in a manner that was simultaneously highly disciplined (in relation to the sensuality of consumption), yet highly individual (in the sense that each student would strive to freely develop his own specific capacities). The result would be that "a refined sensibility regarding ethical conduct [dharma] would be imparted naturally. . . . Moral precepts are not superimposed on life like an external ornament; life is rather built up with righteousness [dharma] within it, and in this way righteousness is not posited as hostile to life, but rather is rendered internal to it."[12] Such a national system of pedagogy aimed to produce a cultivated subject for whom private interest would no longer be pitted against the common good, and for whom morality was the enabling principle of life rather than an external limit to action—making for a truly ethical community grounded in the organizing principles of indigenous society.

In Europe, the Western model of education was integrated into the social system, so that "man becomes man while remaining within society."[13]

> But where the school cannot assimilate into the society around it, what is imposed upon society from the outside is dry and lifeless. What we get out of it, we get through suffering, and the resultant knowledge is useless to us. We cannot see any connection between what we learn by rote from ten till four, and our lives, the human beings around us, and our homes. There is no relationship between their education at school and what their fathers, mothers, brothers and friends discuss at home. . . . So we need to abandon the Western model; for Western history and Western society is not ours. We have to understand clearly what ideals have captivated the minds of the people of our country through the years, and what has filled our country's hearts with pleasure [*ras*].[14]

Tagore, the national educationist, was quite clear that this school was intended to fulfill the double ideal of Swadeshi ideology: to realize the subjective autonomy of the individual through labor and to reintegrate the educated classes back into the metabolic life of the nation understood as a productive organism. At the basis of Tagore's program at this time lay a pedagogical instantiation of his Swadeshi critique of mendicancy.[15] Instead of relying on government, he would explain in a 1906 address on the newly formed National College, Indians needed to understand "that the homeland is our field of action, and we ourselves are its most important agents." The students should therefore "feel within their own hearts the union of the life of this school with the life of the entire Bengali people," to make of it a center for gathering the collective power of the country to work toward national ends.[16] In Shantiniketan too, according to its original program, students would be taught to attend to "our country's ancient ideals concerning the renunciation of luxury, self-discipline, obedience to rules, and devotion to the guru," as the ethical foundations of a political subjectivity adequate to national consciousness and service.[17]

Central to Tagore's attempt to recover the ancient forest hermitage as a model for modern pedagogy had been his argument that, to elicit the ideal subject of an ethically constituted national society, it was crucial that the student be removed from the artificial environments of the city, the office, and the classroom. The disciplining and standardizing function of colonial institutions operated as factories to render the individual merely a homogeneous dehumanized cog in a mechanical system. Furthermore, such artificial environments of "brick, timber and stone" removed the student from a direct relationship with nature, in whose sublimity the divine unity of creation was most readily experienced.[18] In Shantiniketan, in contrast, the student was free to explore the natural world that surrounded him, in a process of sensory appropriation that transcended mere consumption. "If possible," Tagore explained in 1906, "there should also be a little fertile land attached to the school; from this land will be gathered the food needed by the school, and the students will assist with the labor of cultivating it. There will be cows for milk and ghee and so on, and the students will have to join in their tending. In their breaks from study, they will do the gardening with their own hands, turn the soil at the base of the trees and water them, and build fences. In this way they will be establishing not just an emotional [*bhaber*] relationship with nature, but also a relationship of labor [*kajer*]."[19]

Tagore would continue to insist, in the wake of his break with the Swadeshi movement in 1907, on the central need to educate young men in a natural and simple environment far from the social conventions, urban environments, and colonial institutions where the direct relationship with nature became attenuated by the interposition of material superfluities, artificial needs, and empty abstractions. Tagore wanted his students at Shantiniketan to educate their senses before they undertook the intellectual work of formal abstraction. Mother's milk "is their first introduction to the great truth that man's true relationship with the world is that of personal love and not that of the mechanical law of causation."[20] Instead of seeking to sever that intimate relationship at the earliest opportunity, Tagore wanted his students to climb trees and not just to study them—much to the consternation of the disciplinarian headmaster who "believes in an impersonal knowledge of the tree because that is science, but not in a personal experience of it."[21] Whereas the human environment's artificialities, habits, and conventions presented reality as inert objectivity and obscured the plenitude of the student's experience of the oneness of creation, the direct and sensual encounter with the unshaped and unaltered natural world allowed the student to develop a truly spiritual orientation to that world. The student so educated saw the world as the living embodiment of the divine unity rather than as a mere instrument for his rational purposes.

For this reason, students must not only live surrounded by nature, but they must also live in simple poverty, for "poverty is the school in which man had his first lessons and his best training. . . . Poverty brings us into complete touch with life and the world, for living richly is living mostly by proxy, thus living in a lesser world of reality. . . . Wealth is a golden cage in which the children of the rich are bred into artificial deadening of their powers."[22] The history of the appropriation of nature is not only the unfolding of man's spiritual self-realization but also of his distancing from truth by the interposition of human invention. Therefore it was necessary that "men should have some limited period of their life specially reserved for the life of the primitive man," so that, as soon as they are born, they are not "pounced upon by the society of cultivated habits" and lost among the "meaningless miscellanies" and "accumulations" of civilized society.[23] Every generation would have the opportunity to experience the universality of the human life force before submitting to the inevitable discipline of social norms and functional specialization. "I felt clearly that what was needed was not any particular material object, not wealth or comfort or power, but our awakening to full consciousness in soul freedom, the freedom of life in God, where we have no enmity with those who must fight, no competition with those who must make money, where we are beyond all attacks and above all insults."[24]

There remained in this post-Swadeshi educational philosophy clear thematic continuities with Tagore's earlier commitment to Swadeshi culturalism. In Swadeshi discourse, the nation embodied a history of the appropriation of nature to free subjectivity. As Tagore had suggested, precolonial society had been able to provide for its own needs through an established set of institutions ensuring the regular appropriation of nature to human ends, while "arrangements for the cultivation of humanity were maintained in every village." To restore this indigenous social order, Bengalis would as a nation have to "consciously, forcefully, dynamically and completely become what we ourselves are" through a renewed reliance on the immanent logic of Hindu dharma.[25] Tagore's emphasis on the encounter with the natural world, through playful encounter and manual labor, followed from a sense that the educated Bengali needed to be restored to a direct relationship with nature if he was to achieve a form of subjectivity adequate to the kind of (productive) nation he sought to represent and lead. Yet these continuities should not distract us from a profound disjuncture. In the post-Swadeshi encounter with nature, the universality of man is only achieved through the removal of man from civilized society. The nation's history of appropriating nature to human ends is actually an obstacle to the realization of a universal, free subjectivity, rather than its precondition, because in civilized society one lives by proxy, a reliance on the labor of others, which must necessarily narrow the scope of individual human activity. Whereas in the Swadeshi period the encounter with the spiritual unity of nature was inseparably tied to the need to recognize the spiritual unity of society, in this post-Swadeshi period, it is nature rather than society that embodies the spiritual unity of creation. The universality of humanity can therefore no longer be a social fact, but rather becomes a hypostatized truth that stands juxtaposed to the formalistic and instrumental structures of life in civilized society.

It was certainly not the case that through this move Tagore was giving up the core Swadeshi commitment to a Hegelianized Vedanta.[26] In fact, at the heart of his educational primitivism was the belief that it was only through rendering the student's experience of nature more direct that the primacy of man's relationship to nature—his essential identity with the natural world realized in the acts of appropriation and creation—could be made conscious. Following directly in the line of Bankim and Vivekananda, Tagore would insist in his 1910 essay on "Spiritual Realization through Action" ("Karmayog"), that those who considered worldly action to be a form of spiritual bondage failed to understand that the "soul [atma] needs external action to be free, precisely because its freedom cannot exist within itself."

> The more man acts, the more does he make the invisible within himself visible, the more does he bring his own distant future into being. In this way, man is only defining himself—it is himself that man is able to see from different perspectives within his various actions, within the state, and within society. . . . [Our spiritual self] undertakes actions for which there is no necessity whatsoever and which are not needed for our livelihood, because it wants freedom. . . . When man cuts down the brambles and thickets and prepares a garden, the beauty that he liberates from ugliness is his own inner beauty—he cannot realize freedom internally unless he can set it free externally. The good that man sets free from within the bonds of woe when he establishes law in the midst of the willfulness of society, is the good of his own inner life. If he cannot realize freedom externally, then he cannot win freedom in his heart either. So it is his own power [shakti], his own beauty, his own goodness, his own soul that man frees from bondage through his various actions.[27]

The resultant conception of freedom remained profoundly Hegelian in its understanding of nishkam karma (desireless action); freedom was not the license of intoxication, but rather, just as the sweetness of the poet's effusions are structured by meter, so too does the spiritual man realize the joy of his freedom within the bounds of the law.[28] In principle, Tagore remained committed to a conception of society as the expression of a higher spiritual unity grounded in the collective externalization of man's inner life through the appropriation of nature.

For man, the best opportunity for such a [spiritual] realization has been in men's Society. It is a collective creation of his, through which his social being tries to find itself in its truth and beauty. . . . Unless it degenerates, it ever suggests in its concerted movements a living truth as its soul, which has personality. In this large life of social communion man feels the mystery of Unity. . . . From that sense of Unity, men came to the sense of their God.[29]

Man's work was not merely born of relentless exigency, but also of the bliss of activity in itself. As a result, as civilization has unfolded, he has continuously invented new needs for himself, and new forms of activity.[30] Through this collective work of creation he discovers the spiritual truth of unity.

But the blossoming of civilization had been a double-edged sword. On the one hand, its efflorescence was the highest expression of man's spiritual nature as the gradual realization in tangible reality of the truth of the divine unity of all creation. On the other hand, the process of that reappropriation of nature to spirit also created an environment so baroque in its elaboration that civilized man could easily lose sight of the fundamental purpose and impulse of society.

In a society, the production and circulation of materials, the amassing and spending of money, may go on, as in the interminable prolonging of a straight line, if its people forget to follow some spiritual design of life which curbs them and transforms them into an organic whole. . . . Human society is for the best expression of man, and that expression, according to its perfection, leads him to the full realization of the divine in humanity. When that expression is obscure, then his faith in the Infinite that is within him becomes weak; then his aspiration cannot go beyond the idea of success. His faith in the Infinite is creative; his desire for success is constructive; one is his home; and the other is his office. With the overwhelming growth of necessity, civilization becomes a gigantic office to which the home is a mere appendix.[31]

Action that was born only out of need was fundamentally driven by the desire for the fruit of that action. The man who is immersed exclusively in such action quickly mistakes accumulation as the real purpose of work, forgetting that it is in work, as the creative activity of self-expression, that man realizes his spiritual nature. Civilization becomes the very opposite of itself—instead of expressing man's spiritual nature, its endless elaboration of new needs and boundless material accumulations instead obstruct his capacity to recognize himself in his product. And, crucially, this trajectory is no longer a peculiarity of the West; the theme of the inversion of home and world, inside and outside, authenticity and babuism that already featured so prominently in his earlier writings no longer correlates, as it did then, with *deshi* and *bideshi,* the indigenous and the foreign.[32]

[While society remained in principle the highest expression of the universality of man's spirit, the performative function of society in Tagore's post-Swadeshi culturalism was consistently as the negation of unity, as the realm of narrowness, dehumanization, competition, and conflict—precisely those qualities of Western society that indigenous society had been supposed to fundamentally negate] Furthermore, even as the poor toiling laborer became one of Tagore's favorite tropes for symbolizing India's sublime beauty, the burden of this spiritual myopia fell most fundamentally on the poor and oppressed, for it was they who were most tightly hemmed in by the forces of material necessity, who had no respite or leisure for the purer practice of free creativity.

[handwritten margin note: Toiling laborer as symbol of India's sublime beauty]

> The predominance of the pursuit of success gives to society the character of what we call *Shudra* in India. . . . The name Shudra symbolizes a man who has no margin round him beyond his bare utility. The word denotes a classification which includes all naked machines that have lost their completeness of humanity, be their work manual or intellectual. They are like walking stomachs or brains, and we feel, in pity, urged to call on God and cry, "Cover them up for mercy's sake with some veil of beauty and life!"[33]

Tagore here identified society as "Shudra" with exactly the opposite sense of Vivekananda's usage two decades earlier; the victory of the Shudra as such represented the descent of man into rank materialism and utilitarianism, rather than the self-realization of man as the active embodiment of spirit. Unlike many of his contemporaries, Tagore did not articulate this critique of popular propensities in a spirit of contempt or hostility. He was sympathetic to the material aspirations of the poor. Educated Hindus, he argued, should welcome Muslim demands for educational and vocational advancement. Only when the Muslim community had achieved its own sense of dignity and self-reliance would communal harmony be possible—not as the dissolution of communal difference, but as a negotiated relationship between equals. By supporting Muslim efforts at self-improvement, the Hindu community could undercut the spirit of animosity and competition that drove those efforts, opening the space for Muslim striving to become an endeavor of collective self-realization rather than communal competition, and thereby creating the conditions under which communal relations could become genuinely amicable across the enduring differences.[34]

Tagore's recognition of the Shudra propensities of the people did not lead him directly into a narrowly elitist hostility to popular aspirations. It opened up the space for him to elaborate a scathing critique of Indian society, reappropriating many of the themes of the pre-Swadeshi reformist critique of indigenous society (and indeed of liberal critiques of his own romantic portrayal of traditional society a few years earlier[35]) to his new vision of active individual and collective self-realization through practice.[36] In the face of the violence and popular hostility that had emerged in the course of Swadeshi mobilization, Tagore felt compelled to acknowledge that Indian society was pervaded with inequalities and maladaptions—caste discrimination, gender exclusion, economic exploitation, petty jealousies, sectarian rivalries and, overarching all of these, the immoveable despotism of unreflective custom. "Having seen all this at first hand," he would write in 1908, "I no longer feel any desire to idealise the Hindu samaj [society] through delusions pleasant to the ear, but ultimately suicidal—a big contrast indeed—to the *Swadeshi Samaj* of just four years before."[37] In the first of his political novels, in which he dramatized his break with the Swadeshi leadership, Tagore's main character, Gora—an ultraorthodox neo-Hindu nationalist to whom India's dharmic order represents the concrete embodiment of abstract divinity—confronts the realities of the traditional rural society as an urban stranger and discovers there that, though every one of the villagers "had a simple faith in popular customs . . . they drew no strength at all in the realm of action from this bondage to society and this reverence for custom." It rather served only to leave them "terrified, helpless and powerless to determine their own best interests."[38] There was, he argued, a fundamental lack of fit between the Swadeshist's still-abstract conception of India's Hindu nationhood, and the realities on the ground—a failure of conception and commitment that was at the root of the Swadeshi movement's coercive and terrorist response to the challenge of Muslim dissent. "If India is a reality, then it must contain Muslims within it," Tagore's fictional alter ego, Nikhilesh, objects in the face of Swadeshi activities on his estate in the author's second major political novel, *Ghare baire* (*The Home and the World*, 1915-16). Sandip, the Swadeshi leader, having failed to win the Muslims with rhetoric, replies cynically, "That may be, but we need them to know their place, and to keep them there forcibly. Otherwise they will resist us."[39]

The post-Swadeshi Tagore was not simply retreating back to a pre-Swadeshi reformist liberalism; the figure of man that Tagore held up as the standpoint of his new philosophy remained fundamentally a creature defined by his own self-constituting activity. But Tagore no longer felt it plausible, in the face of Swadeshi's failure to carry the people with it, to ground the standpoint of this cultural critique in indigenous society—but only in the ancient Vedic texts and long-lost forest ashrams of India's high tradition, as one privileged moment in a cosmopolitan history of striving for universal human self-realization. It was precisely from the Shudra propensities of society—not just Western society or its babu epigone—that Shantiniketan was to become a refuge: a natural environment "where life is simple" so that students can freely exercise their physical and intellectual capacities without resorting to "living by proxy"; "surrounded by fullness of leisure" so that students can engage in nonpurposive creative activity outside the material constraints of necessity; and providing "ample space and pure air and profound peace of nature" so that students can feel nature's innate spiritual substance outside of the narrowing confines of mechanical habit, social convention, and formal education.[40] Shantiniketan reconstituted the Swadeshi ideal of an ethical community grounded in the common substance underpinning self-constituting practice—but as a voluntary cultural heterotopia from a society that was relegated to the operations of self-interest and instrumentalism.

"I felt sure that what was most necessary was the breath of culture," Tagore wrote of Shantiniketan, "and no formal method of teaching."[41] By this he meant a concrete education of the senses that partook of the spiritual, rather than the dull acquisition of abstract systems of formal knowledge that would remain bound to the material and utilitarian. As another of Tagore's fictional alter egos was to put it years later, "As with a lotus-like diamond, the stone itself is called learning, and the beads of light that fall from it are called culture. The stone has weight, the light has brilliance."[42] An aesthetic appreciation of the particular was, perhaps counterintuitively, the highest expression of universality, for only then did man recognize in the other not the empty abstraction of a universal objectivity but his own soul.[43] Such spiritual unity was not grounded in sameness, but in the harmony that interlinks the diversity of particularities in the world. Through the practice of culture, the fractiousness of the world could be transcended, Tagore was suggesting, without the coercive violence of abstraction. In its constant juxtaposition of the personal, the tangible, the concrete, and the particular to the merely formal or abstract, Tagore's post-Swadeshi reconstruction of cultural critique can be properly characterized as aestheticist, for it is "the principle of unity" within concrete form that is "the true principle of art."[44] Artistic practice was the basis of Tagore's vision of cosmopolitan man because it represented nonpurposive activity, undertaken without the compulsion of external necessity, for its own sake. It was, in other words, a model of pure practice—nishkam karma—available to every educated man in the form of literature and music. Tagore would become emblematic of the post-Swadeshi reconfiguration of the conceptual logic of Swadeshi discourse not just because of the prestige of his 1913 Nobel Prize. His aestheticization of culture made it available to every middle-class Bengali as a means to overcome the babu condition without sacrificing the tedious yet necessary security of employment.[45] The Nobel Prize served primarily, in this context, to grant the cosmopolitan impulse of post-Swadeshi Bengali culture a truly cosmopolitan status.

Seen from this vantage point, Tagore's curious war against the inoffensive word *krishti* in the 1930s takes on a new significance as a condensation of the post-Swadeshi turn of Bengali culturalism. The ascendancy of *sanskriti* over both *anushilan* and *krishti* represents the self-conscious withdrawal of Swadeshi discourse from the domain of material life. It presents culture as the disentanglement of man's spiritual life from his materiality. Tagore's aestheticization was not the only way to do this—on the contrary, as we shall see in this chapter, post-Swadeshi cultural discourse could also take either antimodernist or communalist forms. But at the root of the emergence of all these discourses was a peculiarly post-Swadeshi anxiety about the emergent disjuncture between culture and the popular. If post-Swadeshi culture was destined to become a language of class, and even communalism, in the Bengal of the 1920s and 1930s, it would do so not primarily as a language of mobilization per se, but rather of defeat and involution. The way in which the problematics of class and community were experienced, and the various discursive resolutions that were worked out, can only be understood as meaningful through the refractive lens of Swadeshi ideology.

THE CONTAGION OF MATERIALISM

In the last two decades of the nineteenth century, Pramatha Nath Bose had established himself as a prominent and articulate exponent of the increasingly sharp Moderate critique of British rule.[46] In his acclaimed 1894 survey, *A History of Hindu Civilization during British Rule,* he had praised the development of a liberal-reformist intellectual culture under the British, while sharply criticizing the immiserating effects of free trade under the inequitable conditions of colonial domination. This early Bose was deeply critical of Hindu social institutions such as caste, which, having become detached from genuine Hindu religious ideals through a process of formalistic atrophy, had suppressed the free development of individual character, individual initiative, and individual enterprise in the pursuit of private interests.[47] But at the

Caste

same time, following the trenchant critique of deindustrialization and the drain of wealth under the British, elaborated most famously in Bengal by his father-in-law R. C. Dutt, he argued for the necessity of protectionist tariffs to nurture Indian industries, of coordinated efforts to promote modern technologies of production, and, unquestionably his best-known intervention, of the development of technical education programs that would provide specialized scientific knowledge for industrial ends. Without these deliberate interventions, the scope of human life had been rendered too narrow for any vibrant liberal culture to flourish in the servile political-economic context of colonial India.[48] To salvage the liberal project of emancipation, Bose, like other Bengali Moderates, was suggesting that the free operation of the global sphere of circulation would have to be suspended through a collective intervention on behalf of the nation. The individualistic pursuit of private interests would have to be hybridized with a discourse of patriotic, self-sacrificing labor if the liberal vision was to be rendered viable. Without superseding selfish interests, it would be impossible to lay the groundwork for India's industrial development; and without industrial development, India would be unable, in the face of the crushing competition of cheaper imports from developed economies, to enjoy the self-sustaining social and economic vibrancy that was the prerequisite to a healthy liberal culture.[49] The Moderate program for national renewal was thus a "synthesis" that would energize Hindu civilization with Western vigor, while tempering the harshness of Western civilization with "higher principles."[50]

In reality, Bengali Moderates had by the turn of the century lost their faith in the miraculous efficacy of mendicant appeals to British conscience.[51] But Bose was nevertheless suspicious of the Extremist argument that there could be a directly political solution to India's economic subjection. Whereas Extremists were arguing that the revival of India's national life was impossible while subject to the machinery of British rule, Bose argued that there could be no viable form of political autonomy until its foundations had been laid in economic vitality.[52] Correlatively, he also remained more equivocal in his attitude toward liberal individualism and the pursuit of private interests; a "happy combination of ardent patriotism and calculating commercialism" could provide the crucial motivation for effective and sustainable Swadeshi enterprise.[53] But there was always a sharper edge to Bose than this comfortable vision of synthesis. Throughout the Swadeshi era, he enjoyed a paradoxical status as an incisive critic of the romantic advocacy of the revival of India's handicraft industries and of the uncritical celebration of the emancipatory promise of modern industrial development.

As early as 1901, Bose was endorsing a thoroughly Carlylean understanding of modern industry as the very cornerstone of Western civilization's soullessly commercial orientation, reducing men from their status as
rational agents of labor to mere instruments of production. By cheapening
production, Western industry had undermined the viability of India's manufactures, driving an overwhelming proportion of Indians to a debilitating
dependence on the land. At the same time, by raising expectations about the
standard of living, industry promoted an inexcusable "sacrifice of necessaries to luxuries, of substance to shadow," sharpening the struggle for animal
existence, undermining moral progress in the name of the selfish interests
of the consuming subject, and deepening the discontent of the have-nots.
Furthermore, the application of scientific knowledge to the invention of
laborsaving machinery inevitably led to overproduction, which meant that
new markets had constantly to be found beyond the frontiers of the industrialized nations, creating a self-reproducing system that demanded the
exploitative extension of Western commercial interests to every corner of
the globe. Armed with these same formidable technologies, the West had
ruthlessly preyed upon India in the name of civilizational progress, even as
it had undermined its independence.[54]

Bose also publicly, and unpopularly, rejected the practicability of reviving handicraft industries (a common enthusiasm of Swadeshists). India's
best hope for independence and self-determination was to continue working
to undermine the economic foundations of imperialism's essentially commercial interests through constructive efforts at indigenous industrial development. In the face of plentiful and cheap industrially produced imports,
traditional manufactures could not possibly succeed.[55] Bose had become
convinced that "the most important step in our industrial regeneration" was
the promotion of scientific and technical knowledge.[56] When, in 1906, the
nationalist leadership set out to develop a practical and institutional agenda
for national education, Bose focused his energies on technical instruction,
joining the Society for the Promotion of Technical Education and its Bengal
Technical Institute (funded by the Moderate Taraknath Palit), rather than
the more radical National Council of Education and its Bengal National
College.[57]

Spiritual freedom was grounded in a primary release from animal necessity. Yet the West's industrialism, and its consequent imperialism, had rendered industrial development an external necessity for the maintenance even
of India's bare animal existence. Since 1901, Bose had acknowledged in no
uncertain terms that industry, rather than freeing humanity from bondage

to nature, inherently tended to intensify the struggle for animal existence, while undermining society's ethical foundations. India's spiritual autonomy thus depended on the prior satisfaction of animal necessities that could only be satisfied, under modern colonial conditions, by a system of production that inherently tended to undermine spiritual autonomy. Swadeshi idealism had posited India's spirituality as the condition of possibility for a subjective freedom that would allow the nation to command nature to genuinely human ends. So long as industry was seen simply as an extension of the nation's history of appropriating nature to national subjectivity, there was no conflict between this spirituality and material development. But Bose was threatening to undermine the logic of Swadeshi ideology by questioning the possibility of the spiritual reappropriation of the technologies of the materialist West. Despite his consistent efforts to suppress these tensions under a continued rubric of synthesis, we can sense a lurking anxiety that synthesis was less a matter of transcendence and supersession than an ad hoc accommodation of incommensurable forces. Bose was profoundly sympathetic with both the political-economic and the culturalist dimensions of the Swadeshi program, but he seemed less and less sure about how to render them compatible, let alone mutually reinforcing.

Bose had shared the Swadeshi faith in the capacity of patriotic fervor and proper organization to compensate for the disadvantages of political and economic subjection.[58] But by 1908, the Swadeshi movement had petered into abatement as a popular movement, and its attempts at founding indigenous enterprises had not borne much fruit. Without a strong ethical program directing students to national service, it seemed that technical education could just as easily produce technicians for European concerns as it could for Swadeshi ones. "Remember," he advised students in 1909 with a tinge of reproof, "there is a world of difference between mercenary soldiers and soldiers motivated by patriotism."[59] In reality, both the Bengal National College and the Bengal Technical Institute were suffering from a dearth of enrollments. "It did not take long for the enthusiasm which had been exhibited for the Council in 1906 to die down," he would recall jadedly. "Education which cannot be stamped into current coin and be exchanged for the good things of the world commands but little value now."[60] Bose was merely articulating a ubiquitous diagnosis when he attributed national education's failure to the narrow vocational interests of students and their guardians.[61] In the face of this crisis Bose supported the merger of the Bengal Technical Institute into the National Council in 1910.[62] This incorporation of technical education into a wider humanistic syllabus was unquestionably appealing to Bose in the face of his deepening moral concerns about the resilience of India's spiritual orientation in the face of the materialist offensive of self-ishness, consumption, and Westernization.[63] In reality, however, even this merger merely presaged the reduction of the Council to a technical institution without any students enrolled in its humanistic program.[64]

Ironically, these disappointments seem to have been instrumental in pushing Bose ever deeper into the idiom of Swadeshi nationalism at the very moment when the Swadeshi movement was collapsing. Even those Western values that appeared virtuous in reality cloaked a degraded moral sensibility; where the West spoke of "freedom" and "equality" and "democracy," what it meant was only an equality of opportunity in (and hence the further generalization of) the struggle for animal existence.[65] Where it spoke of "national culture," it meant not a genuine cultivation of higher spiritual values (love, benevolence, nonviolence, cooperation), but the exultation of "matter above spirit, of egotism above altruism, and of patriotism above humanitarianism."[66] Every consideration of the relations between different nations, classes, and even individuals was debased to the level of interests, boiling down to a single question: "in the highly expressive though somewhat exaggerated language of Carlyle, 'Can I kill thee, or canst thou kill me.'"[67]

In the wake of Swadeshi's failure, the former equivocal liberal of the Moderate Congress seemed to have become an avenging angel of culturalist indigenism. India needed to draw on the tradition established by Swami Vivekananda, which, according to Bose, placed central emphasis neither on political efforts nor social reform, but rather on the cultivation of a moral disposition centered on "inner knowledge, renunciation, non-violence, non-greediness, humility, and spiritual realization through action [karmajog]."[68] From 1913 until his death in 1934, Bose wrote obsessively to denounce the Westernization of neo-Indians (the babus), propounding a wholesale return to the traditional values of Hindu civilization. Bose now argued that the "Positive Method" of Swadeshi—by which he meant industrial development—could not possibly succeed without the complementary force of a "Negative Method."[69] The Negative Method involved the embrace of the ancient values of renunciation and simplicity. Instead of endlessly striving for a better standard of living, Indians needed to release themselves from the desire for sense gratification through absurd and superfluous luxuries and focus on providing for their basic nutritional requirements. This embrace of simplicity and renunciation would not only release India from its dependence on foreign imports but also make possible the accumulation of small capitals that together over time could form an adequate social fund for effective industrial ventures. These ventures would have to be strictly limited, but "the thing to see is to have industries without Industrialism, capital without Capitalism, and desire to accumulate without Mammonism"—in other words, to have the productive side of capital that underwrote subjective agency while restraining the forces of consumption and commerce that locked India into heteronomous subjection.[70] If industry was not to undermine the renunciatory values that were indispensable to the possibility of its emergence, it had to be directed solely to the production of the necessities of basic social reproduction rather than to general commercial ends, becoming a powerful instrument used to release man from his servility to the base struggle for animal existence through the cooperative provision of his animal needs.

All civilizations, Bose argued, passed though three natural stages in the course of a complete efflorescence: first, subjection to material forces; second, an attempt to master these heteronomous forces through the power of the intellect; and third, the development of a genuine ethical culture that exists in a delicate state of equilibrium with the provision of material wants.[71] India had, centuries ago, attained a higher synthesis that subsumed within itself the baser, materialistic concerns that exclusively drove Western civilization, but in subordinate, equilibrated counterpoint to the higher ideals of its "ethical and spiritual culture."[72] To seek a synthesis with a materialistic modern West trapped in a protracted civilizational adolescence was to destabilize the equilibrium of India's social order in favor of its baser part—the very part that was already getting the upper hand under colonial conditions. "The cultured classes among the Ancients whether in the East or in the West kept aloof from industrial and commercial pursuits, whereas those among the Modern are steeped in them. Modern culture has become as unlike ancient culture, as Bottom transformed was unlike his former self."[73]

As one contemporary reviewer perceptively observed, this three-stage historical model "seems to me to be parallel to the threefold division of mental properties adopted in the philosophical literature of India, viz., Tamasika, Rajasika and Satvika, the one following being higher than the one preceding it. . . . It is not improbable that the author was unconsciously influenced by his recent study of Indian Philosophy to adopt this threefold staging."[74] Bose was indeed very much working from within the conceptual logic of Swadeshi discourse. Beneath all the antimodernist bluster, he was trying to restore the coherence of Swadeshi ideology through the back door, through the ever more thorough subordination of its political-economic logic to the program of ethical culture. Yet at the heart of India's third-stage, syntheti-

Rejection of Western modernism

cally equilibrated civilization, there remained two fundamentally distinct developmental trajectories. "Cosmic" development, meaning the material evolution of civilizations, had been fundamentally driven by man's universal "desire for the superfluous in respect of his physical wants." This is the classic political-economic narrative that had grounded the reformist tendencies of his earlier *History*. This trajectory of development was "directed not towards the wants of the inner life, but towards those of the outer life. . . . The process of material evolution is that of strife and competition, and is governed by the law of survival of the fittest." In contrast, "non-cosmic" progress, the development of the inner life of humanity as a spiritual end in itself through a regime of "real artistic, intellectual and ethical culture," had "been evolved by a process different from, and partly antagonistic to that by which the desire for material progress has been satisfied." In other words, the temporal trajectory of noncosmic "progress" was distinct from, and even contradictory to, the mechanical process of cosmic "evolution."[75]

And it is here that there emerges a distinctly post-Swadeshi mode of culturalism. "In every civilized community"—even in old India at its civilizational apex—"there is a numerical preponderance of the individuals who are worked upon by forces making for material development. There is, therefore, a natural tendency in all civilizations towards excessive materialism and all that it connotes—inordinate luxury, greed, lust, and strife."[76] Furthermore, Indian civilization's higher synthesis of cosmic and noncosmic forces could be mapped socially as a subordination of the inherent materialism of "the people" to the spiritual ideals cultivated and disseminated by a cultural elite excluded from all moneymaking pursuits.[77] While Bose accepted the Swadeshi opposition of Western and Indian civilizations as essentially material and spiritual respectively, he simultaneously complicated that external opposition by superimposing a homologous opposition internal to Indian society.

> According to Hegel the history of mankind is a history of the "necessary development of the free spirit through the different forms of political organizations . . ." This conclusion is based upon what appears to be an incorrect interpretation of sociological phenomena. Inequality and restriction of freedom are the necessary concomitants of differentiation of function and, therefore, of social progress. . . . The abiding progress of a community depends upon whether the influence of the wise and the good, the individuals in the third stage [of civilization], preponderates over the influence of the numerically larger classes in the lower stages, whether the upward force exerted by the former is stronger than the downward impulse of the latter.[78]

If we see in this (admittedly banal) critique of "Hegel" an implicit critique also of Hegelianized Vedanta, it becomes clear that Bose's new formulation had moved away profoundly from the Swadeshi ideal of national self-realization. If Swadeshi discourse had sought to lay the foundations of its new cultural politics in the indigenous social and cultural forms that organized the life of "the people"—as the locus of at least the germ of a form of cooperative ethical sociality antithetical to commercial society and materialistic individualism—Bose's new synthesis made that mode of indigenism far more problematic by establishing the category of culture primarily on the basis of an antithesis to popular propensities. He thereby structurally identified "the people" with the materialism of the West.

It is certainly true that Bose would never abandon a profound attachment to the romantic ideal of the Indian village as a site of social harmony, in contrast to the city, where social relations had been reduced to cash nexus. "One of the most important lessons which history teaches is that civilizations whose soul lay in large commercial cities ... have been of a more or less ephemeral character.... The reason of this is that city civilizations cannot properly fulfill the essential condition for the survival of a civilization, namely, the attainment and maintenance of an equipoised condition between the forces making for material progress and those leading to ethical culture."[79] But when Bose advocated the *panchayat* system of village self-government as superior to the Western system of representational government, his advocacy rested on his critique of democracy as a political form that placed governance in the hands of those least morally and spiritually equipped for the job. While Edwin Montagu and Lord Chelmsford were outlining the institutional seeds of representational self-governance, Bose looked to the traditional panchayat as an arena where the counsel of the cultured prevailed over the voices and demands of the many: "it was a scheme of communal village life," Bose would approvingly cite E. B. Havell, "in which each section of the community and each individual member of it took their allotted shares of work for the common weal, not under the compulsion of an autocrat or of a ruling caste, but by a clear perception of mutual advantage, and a voluntary recognition of superior intellectual leadership."[80] It was, in other words, in the village, and only on the scale of the village, that one might now find the living embodiment of Bankim's Positivist-Hindu polity. Such an appeal to the village did not then constitute a reiteration of the Swadeshi appeal to a politics of the people as "national" politics. Rather, it represented a fundamental retreat from the realm of "national" politics in a juxtaposition of the authenticity of "cultural swaraj" (village self-determination) to the inauthenticity of "political swaraj" (national-

[Margin annotation: Romanticized image of the Indian Village]

ist politics).[81] Where Swadeshi had seen culture consuming the space of the political, Bose saw culture being inevitably hollowed out by its engagement with the political. National politics had been irredeemably compromised as a colonial arena essentially constituted for the pursuit of private or sectional interests (the nation that the Montagu-Chelmsford Reforms of 1919 wanted to call forth into the arena of representation). There could be no more egregious symptom of the pursuit of political ends than communalism. "The ties of mutual service and sympathy which bind together the different classes in the village are rudely severed in the town where cash nexus forms the sole bond between them. Hindu-Moslem riots are seldom heard of in villages. They occur chiefly in towns."[82]

While the external standpoint of Bose's critique of Western materialism appears at first glance to invoke a nationalist standpoint, behind this apparent continuity with Swadeshism lurked a subtle but important discontinuity. Bose's later culturalism was preoccupied with keeping popular materialism in check. Culture and material life were reconstituted as fundamentally distinct and perduring dimensions of the social. The cultural elite would no longer serve to mediate the relationship of individuals, the national organism, and the absolute so as to transfigure daily life; rather, they would serve to contain the irremediably selfish and sensuous propensities of the majority through moral authority. At the root of his retreat from the political was a fundamental anxiety about the immanent propensity for moral degeneration on the part of the materialistic masses. If Swadeshism looked to the people to cure the babu of his babuism, Bose seemed rather to focus on the threat of moral infection the babu's contagious materialism posed to the people. The pursuit of material interests and pleasures, it seemed, was a profoundly transmissible disease. The problem was not merely that India could not, by its very nature, become like the West, but also that it so easily could. Bose, it seems, had rediscovered the universality of the self-interested individual posited by liberals and utilitarians—but as a threatening, insurgent substructure of India's social order, bursting forth not only among the Anglicized, educated elite, but also in the equally dangerous form of demands for communal representation and rural reform.

THE SELFISH MUSLIM

The fact that the respectable classes proved in the long run unable to withstand the socioeconomic pressures of private interests (such as the need for respectable employment as the means to livelihood) represented a fundamental challenge to the viability of the Swadeshi agenda. Yet this dimension of Swadeshi's failure could not provoke a fundamental crisis in itself. The demoralizing recognition of the pervasive preoccupation with selfish vocational interests on the part of students and their guardians seems, if anything, to have helped push Bose's Moderate political-economic commitments deeper into the ethical dimensions of Swadeshism. Swadeshism had from its inception posited itself as an attempt to overcome the selfish materialism of the babu through the application of a superior form of political and spiritual will, and the failure of that will to overcome babuism was, while a galling political defeat, still a defeat fully comprehensible within the terms of the conceptual oppositions of Swadeshi discourse.

But Swadeshi nationalism had done more than juxtapose babu selfishness to the national will. It had positioned babuism as a rootless transplantation of Western materialism, and the national will as the political expression of an organic, historical nation. As we have seen in the previous chapter, Aurobindo Ghose had made it perfectly clear from his first foray into the public sphere in the early 1890s that the new politics would ground itself in the immanent propensities of the nation, drawing from the realm of "the popular" both the core of its social ideals and the substance of its capacity to act politically. If I have argued against interpretations of Swadeshi ideology that reduce it to an instrument of class mobilization, this is not to obviate the central importance of popular mobilization to Swadeshi ideology. Swadeshi nationalists sought to draw their political strength from the life of the people, to enroll the nation as their armies in the fight against the alien colonizers, to reforge their fractured identity with an authentic folk life. Mobilization may not have been the wellspring of Swadeshi ideology, but it was certainly one of its most compelling logical correlates.

To this end, despite their general commitment to an emphatically Hindu neo-Vedantic idealism, nationalist leaders made ecumenical overtures to Muslims one of the highest priorities of their public campaigns. The first census of Bengal, taken in 1872, had revealed that 48 percent of the region's population was Muslim—and by the 1891 census, Muslims outnumbered Hindus.[83] Furthermore, Muslims were numerically preponderant in the eastern districts—the areas that had been partitioned off to create the new province in 1905, and the areas (outside of Calcutta) that would see by far the most active Swadeshism. It hardly made much sense, then, to think that a popular movement in these districts could afford to exclude the Muslim population as somehow alien to national aspirations, even if the nation's default identity remained unmistakably Hindu. Bipin Pal would embrace what he called a "composite patriotism," combining his neo-Vedantic Vaishnavite

Hinduism with an espousal of the simultaneous, separate, and complementary development of each religious community in India along the lines of its own immanent cultural logic. A young Benoy Kumar Sarkar argued that there was "no conflict of religion between Hindus and Muslims"; since both faiths shared a commitment to "renunciation" as the universal principle of "natural religion," communal hostility was best understood as a symptom of the failure of religiosity in the face of materialism and self-interest.[84] Rabindranath Tagore, who composed countless Swadeshi anthems celebrating Hindu-Muslim brotherhood, had famously promoted *rakhi bandhan*, the exchange of auspicious friendship bracelets across boundaries of class, caste, or creed to symbolize Bengali national unity in the face of the 1905 partition. And Aswinikumar Dutt had gone to significant lengths in both word and conduct to build political trust between Muslims and Hindus in Barisal.[85] Crucial to this whole effort was the attribution of the origins of Bengal's Muslim masses and their syncretic religious practices to conversion among the lower Hindu castes in the era of Mughal conquest—making Muslims not only children of the Mother by adoption but by blood too.[86]

Some Muslims did unquestionably respond to these overtures, despite the Hindu-revivalist emphasis of much Swadeshi discourse. Abdur Rasul and Liakat Husain emerged as prominent Swadeshists with Extremist leanings. The Bengal Mahomedan Association (established in 1906) and the Indian Musalman Association (established in 1907) were both intended to act as pronationalist counterorganizations to the new propartition Muslim League (founded in 1906).[87] Muslim participation in Swadeshi meetings—both in the audience and on the podium—was common, especially during the first wave of enthusiasm.[88] Nonetheless, the prominence of the anti-Swadeshi campaigns of the Muslim press (most notably the *Mihir-o-Sudhakar*, the Muslim paper with by far the largest circulation) and of the more prestigious and powerful Muslim leadership (headed by Nawab Salimullah of Dhaka and Syed Nawab Ali Chaudhuri of Mymensingh) soon outstripped their Swadeshist rivals.[89] This collaboration produced both the Simla deputation of 1906, which pressed the sympathetic new viceroy, Minto, to recognize the distinctness of Muslim interests from those of "an unsympathetic [Hindu] majority," and the subsequent formation of the All-India Muslim League.[90]

The fading of Swadeshi passions, coupled with the widespread absence of Muslim sympathy for the Swadeshi cause, provoked a profound crisis in Swadeshi ideology. Swadeshi leaders became increasingly ambivalent, combining an overall commitment to a noncommunal conception of national integrity (without which Bengal could only be an empty shell) with the sometimes thinly disguised—and for that matter, the sometimes completely overt—deployment of communal stereotypes to explain the willingness of the anti-Swadeshi movement to cooperate with the British against the national interest. This stereotype of "the Muslim" was a compound product of overlapping histories, but what it indexed above all was the failure of "the people" to transcend the impulses of civil society and live up to the ideological burden that Swadeshi ideology had ascribed to them.

Muslims as a Sectional Interest

"The Mahommedan population is the preponderating element in this [new] Province, and this being the case, they are entitled to the first consideration of the Government," Nawab Salimullah explained in 1906. "Government had now fully and clearly realised that an inadequate proportion of places in the gift of government has fallen to the lot of the Mahommedans. . . . The separation has offered us many facilities which we did not possess before."[91] This claim was the culmination of two decades of nascent Muslim political organization among the urban *ashraf* of Bengal.[92] It was also one of the prime (if somewhat retrospective) justifications of the partition—that by creating a Muslim-majority province out of eastern Bengal and Assam, new opportunities would be, and in fact were, created for Muslims, freer from the crushing competition of the high-caste Hindus who had dominated the professions and services throughout the nineteenth century.[93]

W. W. Hunter's 1871 intervention in Anglo-Indian opinion, *The Indian Musalmans,* had sought to interpret the widespread activities of various Islamic reform movements in India as a "chronic conspiracy within our territory."[94] But in elaborating the outlines of this "conspiracy," he also sought to interpret sympathetically the genuine grievances of Muslims against the British regime, to communicate "a knowledge of the not ignoble motives which lead men, sincerely good according to their own lights, into treason."[95] Drawing from his experiences in eastern Bengal, he focused his explanation on the remnants of a decaying Muslim aristocracy "drag[ging] on a listless existence . . . sinking deeper and deeper into a hopeless abyss of debt, till the neighbouring Hindu money-lender fixes a quarrel on them, and then in a moment a host of mortgages foreclose, and the ancient Musalman family is suddenly swallowed up and disappears forever."[96] This impoverished condition was the result, Hunter explained, of the fundamental displacement of the Muslim aristocracy from the sources of their status and livelihood in the precolonial era: with the accession of the British, they could obviously no longer dominate the military; they were displaced from their (alleged) position at the top of the land revenue hierarchy by the recognition of a proprietary interest in the (mostly Hindu) zamindars; their role in the administration of justice was undercut by the replacement of Persian by English as the language of the courts; and most fundamentally, their access to public employment was impeded by a system of public instruction ill-adapted to their needs.[97] While Hindus had adapted to the new regime as easily as they had to the old, thereby achieving outright dominance of the respectable professions, the aristocratic sensibilities and religious strictures of a supposedly once-dominant race had prevented Muslims from doing the same, while the government, having found in the rising Hindu educated middle class an adequate supply of clerks, had neglected educational institutions adapted to Muslim needs.[98]

Hunter's prescription was a concerted effort on the part of the British to direct educational efforts at a disaffected Muslim population with a propensity for treasonous religious fanaticism. His arguments, along with arguments of prominent Calcutta Muslims organizing for the first time into associations, were directed to sympathetic ears.[99] In the wake of the so-called Great Wahabi Case of 1870,[100] the British government, recognizing in the category, Muslim, the widespread disaffection represented by the Mutiny of 1857 and the enduring attractiveness of Islamic reformism and jihad, passed (just a few months after Hunter's book was published) a Resolution on Muslim Education. This inaugurated a new age of pro-Muslim policy in Bengal's educational system, which focused on making ordinary schools more palatable to Muslims on the one hand, and on taking control of indigenous Muslim schools to introduce a greater emphasis on secular studies on the other.[101] Later, during the 1880s and 1890s, this initiative would be expanded, in response to further Muslim demands for demographically proportionate representation in education and public employment, to include a system of scholarships for Muslim students at all levels of instruction, an effort to popularize education at the mass level beyond the narrow circles of the urban *ashraf,* and attempts to redress the underrepresentation of Muslims in government service.[102] This new approach was part of an overall strategy to build up an educated class of loyalist Muslims who would regard themselves as a social interest distinct from Hindus and dependent on British favor, thereby simultaneously countering the increasingly critical Hindu middle class that claimed to speak for the national interest and effecting a wholesome influence over the ignorant and fanatical lower orders of Muslim society.[103] Hindus were fully aware of this and resented it: "The late Lieutenant-Governor, Sir George Campbell, made the Mahomedans of this province more conceited than ever," complained the *Education Gazette* in 1876. "Though not educated as much as the Hindus, they aspire to the privilege of attaining equal appointments in public service, and reproach Government with injustice if their undue aspirations are not granted"—this despite the fact that "in some respects the Mahomedan is rather viewed with even more favor than the Hindu."[104]

By positing Muslim interests as distinct from and even hostile to those of the educated Hindus, the British were able to position themselves as the neutral arbiters of an irremediably fractured society. All factions attempted to demonstrate the unrepresentativeness of their rivals by implicating them in a politics of self-interest. The Salimullah party would denounce prominent Swadeshi Muslims as paid agents of the Hindu elite as often as Swadeshi propagandists would point to the Nawab's financial connection with the British (who had bailed him out of debt to now-hostile Hindu creditors). Swadeshi leaders, in turn, had always taken care to include Muslim leaders on the podium to undercut the attacks of the Salimullah camp. For Salimullah and the British, to unmask the Hindu agenda of Swadeshi as an extension of babu class interest was to negate their claims to speak for a singular national interest. For Swadeshists, to unmask the discourse of Muslim separatism as a British conspiracy of "divide and rule" was to show that the communal separation of "Muslim interests" from those of the national community as a whole was an artificial construct purveyed by a self-interested government and its self-serving agents.[105] It did not take any timeless Hindu prejudice to activate this critique. The great Muslim Swadeshist, Abdur Rasul, speaking as president of the Bengal Provincial Conference at Barisal, equally reviled the sectional selfishness of the Muslim elite:

> Some of the Mohammedans have been told that the Partition is for the benefit of the Mohammedans because a lot of Mohammedans will get appointments. The cause of the downfall of the Mohammedans has been due to always looking after their individual interests at the expense of the interests of the whole community. Some of them will get Government posts so they must support Partition, no matter what happens to the interests of the dumb millions of their community. . . . The Mahommedans always thought that they were the favourites of the Government and whether they paid much attention to education or not they would be provided for. How sadly mistaken they have been, they know now to their cost.[106]

This was nothing but the familiar Swadeshi critique of the babu transposed to the Muslim context. But the increasing transposition of the babu-characteristics of selfishness and dependency onto the Muslim made one major difference to the logic of Swadeshi ideology: what before was a matter of internal reform could now become an external Other.

The Muslim as Selfish Peasant

Whatever the legitimacy of the competing conspiracy theories proposed on both sides of the struggle, these well-known developments of high politics were unquestionably only part of the story of the increasing communalization of the Swadeshi issue. That there was more going on was made clearer in 1906–7 in the Mymensingh and Tippera districts by the eruption of what were the first episodes in the dynamic of violent communal conflict that would sweep over Bengal in the subsequent decades.[107] Both sides would attempt to contain the implications of these riots through the extension of conspiratorial frameworks that reduced politics to sectional interests; and both sides' interpretations indexed complex histories to underpin their plausibility.

The Swadeshists blamed the Nawab and his army of hired mullahs and "Mohamedan Goondas" and "Badmashes" for inciting "ignorant low-class Mahomedans" to acts of violence against innocent, respectable Hindus with the complicity and approval of the British.[108] There can be little doubt that the British did consciously manufacture and manipulate competition between the two communities—so much so that three prominent moderate Muslim leaders had complained to Viceroy Minto about the pro-Muslim bias of the authorities following the Comilla riots.[109] Nor can there be much doubt that Nawab Salimullah, whatever his public denials, was connected to the mullahs who had so often appealed to his authority in inciting anti-Hindu sentiment in the subsequently riot-afflicted areas.[110] The anti-Swadeshists and the British, meanwhile, tended to interpret the riots as the result of Hindu activists trying to coerce lower castes and Muslims into observing a boycott for which they had little sympathy and which was the cause of considerable economic hardship. That there was some coercion on the part of young Hindu activists and local zamindars is widely acknowledged. Coercion was, after all, only a short step beyond the openly avowed Swadeshi policy of social boycott, the ostracization of anyone who did not observe the ban on foreign goods. "A certain amount of ill-feeling between the Hindus and Mahommedans continues in parts of the Mymensingh district," a Home Department report explained in October 1906 following the first outbreaks of trouble there, "and the Hindu landlords of Iswarganj and Nandail are reported to be putting pressure on their Mahommedan tenants." More specifically, zamindars were levying substantial fines on tenants found to be assisting Maulvi Samiruddin, a local firebrand who preached the "rescue" of Muslim servants and prostitutes from Hindu masters, and who was closely linked to the incidents in April and May of that year. That Muslim tenants resented such impositions was also clear: "The Mahommedans of Silchar . . . resolved that they would not join the Hindus in their disloyal attitude but would use imported salt and other goods and would refrain from using country products as by this means the boycott would be defeated."[111]

Yet there are good reasons to question whether the incidents of attempted coercion that sometimes acted to spark communal conflict in the Swadeshi years were more than catalytic in importance.[112] The credibility of this anti-Swadeshi argument about coercion ultimately rested on the complex social configuration of eastern Bengal, the heartland of Swadeshism and the site of the riots. In 1859, the government of Bengal undertook its first significant attempt to bolster the position of ryots against the absolute proprietary rights of zamindars by passing a law that recognized a right of occupancy (unless explicitly set aside by private contract) to those who had cultivated the same land for twelve continuous years, restricting rent enhancement for such tenants, and revoking the almost unlimited power of distraint that zamindars had enjoyed for decades.[113] When Act X of 1859 had been passed, its effects were differentiated according to the varied structures of agrarian land control that characterized the diverse subregions of Bengal. Its greatest effect was on the fertile, deltaic parts of (mostly eastern) Bengal, where rural society was composed of a comparatively homogeneous class of smallholding, cash-cropping cultivators who were predominantly Muslim (alongside considerable numbers of low-caste Namasudras), and an overlay of rentier, creditor, and professional groups in the towns and cities, who were overwhelmingly Hindu. These latter were tied to the land and the production process primarily through revenue rights in the tenurial structure and capital investments that funded the credit system fundamental to the extensive cash-crop agriculture in the region (most notably, jute).[114] The effect of government efforts to consolidate the occupancy rights of cultivators represented by Act X, and subsequently more effectively by the Tenancy Act of 1885, had most relevance in this region.

The response on the part of eastern Bengal's zamindars was to declare war on occupancy rights as such, which in turn had led to a series of disturbances in the Pabna district in the mid-1870s.[115] In Pabna, more than 50 percent of cultivators had been able to claim occupancy rights under the provisions of the 1859 act.[116] As one local *munsif* explained:

From 1859 the course of legislation has been uniformly in favour of the ryots. Having courts in their immediate vicinity, they have gradually learnt their rights. . . . These circumstances embolden the ryots to assert their rights, and the several decisions of the courts of law here being uniformly in favour of the ryots have still further emboldened them. The combinations are a necessary consequence for a ryot singly cannot cope with zamindars, and therefore they have combined to preserve their rights.[117]

Liberals of the time interpreted such unrest as the result of zamindars' "indiscriminate enhancement of rents" in the wake of the government's 1859 attempt to extend the rule of law to agrarian relations.[118] But both the zamindari interests of eastern Bengal and many of those with nascent neo-Hindu tendencies declared this unrest to be the direct outcome of Act X, which had undermined the paternalistic bonds that had formerly held society together, restraining both unjust enhancements and ryot unrest. This legislation had been the "apple of discord" that had encouraged an increasingly insubordinate tenantry to form combinations and have recourse to legal remedies in the pursuit of its own selfish interests. "Pride and insubordination prevail where formerly there were fear and respect. This change in their relations has been brought about chiefly by Act X of 1859. . . . The riots of the tenantry at Pabna were the outcome of this mischievous policy."[119]

What both sides of this debate implicitly agreed on, however, was the primary orientation of the peasant to the pursuit of economic self-interest—a vision of agrarian society that was intimately tied to the deep involvement of east Bengal's peasantry in cash-crop agriculture. Furthermore, the peasants' orientation to economic self-interest, including their newfound propensity for combination to that end, was frequently interpreted in this framework as a specifically Muslim characteristic. Although there was nothing particularly communal about the tenant movement at Pabna, the degree of congruence between religious and class difference in the district (and in the fertile deltaic parts of Bengal more generally), and the history of Islamic reform movements in rural Bengal more generally, rendered a communalized account of the conflict almost inevitable. More than two-thirds of the convicted ryots at the Pabna trials were Muslim, and most complainants were Hindu. Major newspapers like the *Hindu Patriot* took up the communal explanation.[120] The *Som Prakash*, a major paper with nationalist loyalties, in an 1876 article on the "Need for a Law for the Suppression of Refractory Ryots," would respond to the rumored murder by "the Ferazi Mahomedans of Idilpore" of a police inspector who was looking into the murder of a local zamindar, with the observation that a "Mahomedan tenantry is a source of considerable annoyance to a zemindar. They do not readily pay the rents, and seek every pretext for evading payment." While the specific rumor had not been substantiated, from what he knew of "the Mahomedans in general," the writer was "not disposed to discredit it. They are a most unquiet, selfish, and hard-hearted people; and become furious when forming combinations among themselves. They are easily got up, *as soon as their interests are touched.* This power of unity in sympathy is a remarkable feature of the Mahomedans."[121]

This association of Islam with a troublesome and self-interested peasantry did not entirely lack a historical referent, howsoever chauvinistically and self-interestedly construed. Precolonial syncretic religious culture had never precluded conflict along religious lines, leaving "pre-existing lines of social fracture" that were nevertheless emphatically not the same as the abstractly identitarian communal politics of the high colonial period and beyond.[122] More importantly, however, starting in the early nineteenth century, Bengal had seen the widespread activity of itinerant mullahs propagating reformist ideas that critiqued the practices of both Hanafi orthodoxy and religious syncretism. These movements had hitched themselves explicitly to ryot interests.[123] Faraidism was an indigenous, broadly fundamentalist reform movement that opposed various local practices that smacked of idolatry (such as pirism). Holding British-ruled India to be *dar-ul-harb* (an abode of war), it further demanded the suspension of Friday prayers and Id.[124] But the movement had also from the beginning rooted itself in the concerns of rural Muslims, looking "upon the cause of even the lowest or the poorest amongst them, as the cause of the whole body."

> They not only resist successfully the levy of all extra or illegal cesses by the Zemindars and Talookdars, but with equal ability to pay their land rent, they give much more trouble than others in collecting it—they would withhold it altogether if they dared, for it is a favorite maxim with them, that Earth is God's, who gives it to his people—the land tax is accordingly held in abomination, and they are taught to look forward to the happy time, when it will be abolished.[125]

Faraidis had from the 1840s been prominently involved in the struggle against the indigo system under the leadership of Dudu Miyan, and subsequently played a significant role in the organization and mobilization of the Pabna agrarian league of the 1870s.[126]

Contemporaneously, the Tariqah-i-Muhammadiyah movement, founded by Shah Sayyid Ahmad in northern India and propagated in eastern India under the leadership of Maulanas Wilayet Ali and Inayet Ali, went even further than the Faraidis. Whereas the latter still identified themselves as belonging to the Hanafi school of jurisprudence that was orthodox in Bengal, the Muhammadis took their theological fundamentalism much further by rejecting the final authority of the four orthodox schools of jurisprudence, privileging instead independent judgment (*ijtihad*) founded directly upon the Prophetic tradition. Also, its more active embrace of the *dar-ul-harb* principle led it immediately into the mobilization of a jihad against the Sikh regime in Punjab, and subsequently against British rule (in which they would later be largely joined by the Faraidis).[127] This Tariqah movement, spreading widely in Bengal in the mid-nineteenth century, also explicitly linked the political question to rural concerns, arguing that "when the [English] government is turned out, no more rent is to be paid, and the Mussalmans are to have the '*jote*' [the land-holdings]."[128]

The role of the itinerant mullah in preaching religious reform as a means to communal uplift was crucial to the formation of a Muslim communal identity toward the end of the nineteenth century. More and more rural Muslims were adopting Perso-Arabic names and describing themselves as "Muslims" rather than "Bengalis," an identity whose parochialism was now seen to compromise the integrity of Islam, and which was therefore used exclusively to refer to Hindus. The increasingly ubiquitous Muslim claim to be descended from foreign conquerors was more than a rarified argument addressed to those who would denigrate Muslims as low-caste converts. In fact, there was a massive move throughout rural Bengal to claim foreign ancestry, such that the proportion of the total Muslim population of Bengal implicitly claiming foreign descent through the adoption of Islamic names (most commonly, Sheik) grew from 1.5 percent in the census of 1872, to 99.1 percent in the census of 1891—a transformation that is surely remarkable whether or not we have doubts about the reliability of the census as a gauge of this kind of information.[129] The confluence of agrarian movements with Muslim consciousness raising contributed to the indelible marking of the troublesome and self-interested propensities of the later nineteenth-century Bengali peasant as essentially Muslim characteristics.

Islamic reformism grew increasingly moderate in outlook in the 1870s as, under the leadership of Maulana Karamat Ali's Ta'aiyuni movement (an early offshoot of the Tariqah movement that restored the authority of the four schools), reformists increasingly accepted the British regime as *dar-ul-Islam*, and eschewed political confrontation in favor of the internal reform of rural socioreligious practices as the path to Muslim uplift.[130] When the Tenancy Act of 1885 had effectively ended the kind of agrarian struggle that the Pabna events had represented, consolidating the displacement of rent-based surplus extraction by credit-based systems, the sense of immediate threat from Muslim "fanaticism" had gone into a degree of abeyance. But the preoccupation with an emergent stereotype of "the Muslim" remained firmly in place.[131] The Tenancy Act had confirmed the political strength of a ryot class increasingly affluent thanks to jute cultivation, itself a common Swadeshi symbol of Bengal's economic subordination to foreign interests and commercial society. The selfish and violent Muslim remained an enduringly spectral threat that would leap back into new and dangerous prominence as Swadeshists lashed out in fury in the wake of the 1907 riots at Jamalpur: "You do not know [the Muslims] for what they are," growled the *Sandhya*. "*When their interests are jeopardized* they are ready to become demons. The stroke of this boycott has made dogs of them."[132]

The anti-Swadeshi explanations of the outbreak of violence need to be viewed through the lens of these histories. Swadeshi coercion is perhaps a poor explanation of the riots[But while it is implausible for the historian to rely on such instances of coercion as an adequate explanation for the violence of 1906/7, to blame Swadeshi coercion was, in the context of eastern Bengal in 1906/7, precisely to encode rhetorically an explanation in terms of this wider structure of social relations, without courting the social dangers of naming them]This implication was already tacit in the imputation of a Muslim identity to the victims of coercion, because it assumed an alignment of "Muslim" and "peasant" that only made sense in the historical context of eastern Bengal.

The Muslim as Foreign Conqueror

The widespread Muslim identification of the Swadeshi movement as a covert instrument of Hindu interests was more than the obverse correlation of the discourse of Muslim class victimage. The connection that Islamic reformist movements had drawn between Muslim collective upliftment (*svajati* movements[133]) and the purification of religious practices through the suppression of local and/or syncretic usages made the aggressive Hinduism at the very heart of Swadeshi discourse hard for the many Muslims influenced by such reformist ideals to stomach. The most offensive instances are well known: the blasphemous identification of Bengal with the Mother-goddess in the *bande mataram* war cry; the reverence for Bankim, the father figure of Swadeshi, but also the author of some venomously anti-Muslim prose; and the importation of Tilak's celebration of the Maratha hero, Sivaji, enemy of the Mughals. "Everyone, beginning from the poet Iswar Gupta, Rangalal Bandyopadhyay,

[margin note: Muslim class victimage]

novelist Bankimchandra, the poet Hem (Hemchandra Bandyopadhyay), and Nabinchandra right down to the disciples of their disciples, which means any Hindu Tom, Dick and Harry, does not hesitate diabolically to abuse the Muslim race and to vilify their glorious ancestors," explained an article in the *Islam Pracharak* in 1903. "The first word a Hindu author has to write, when taking up his pen, is *Yavana* [a derogatory term for Muslims], otherwise his pen simply does not move. . . . Open your eyes and you will see that each Hindu author is either a second Bankim or a second Nabinchandra, both of whom were enemies of the Muslims. Each one of them are enemies of the *Yavana*."[134] A literary heritage of historical romances centered on the struggle of Hindus to resist (Muslim) foreign conquest, coupled with high-caste Hindu practices of purity (such as the refusal of commensality) which served to freeze out upwardly mobile Bengali Muslims from full respectability (*bhadrata*), were interpreted almost universally among literate Muslims as the outward expression of a fundamental anti-Muslim sentiment. The identification of Swadeshi as a "seditious agitation engineered by interested parties" was an implicit claim that Swadeshi's nation was a Hindu nation with little concern for the welfare of the "alien" (*yavana*) descendants of foreign conquerors.[135]

It is fairly straightforward to trace a direct intellectual lineage running from, say, Bankim's poisonous tirades against the Mughal oppressors of Hindu India to the language of Hindu anti-Muslim communalism that would emerge to increasing prominence in the wake of the Swadeshi era. But the term *yavana* indicated the specificity of the figure of "the Muslim" that Bankim and his generation were writing about: the figure of the Muslim as foreign invader—on the one hand the fanatical, ruthless, and aggressive agent of religious and political oppression; on the other hand the decadent and lustful sensualist of Persian and Turkish excess. With an account that traces the emergence of this historical romance as an imaginative site for vindicating Hindu national valor (supplemented perhaps with reference to high-caste Hindu exclusivity), the history of the anti-Muslim component unfolds with apparently coherent continuity from this primal flaw.[136] Yet the issue of the moral righteousness of Muslim outrage at the sentiments expressed by the Hindu novelists and poets of the Bengal Renaissance should not be conflated with the historical adequacy of this explanation. At least two major qualifications need to be made to this account. First, the increasingly easy conflation of the oppressive Mughal of historical romance with the Muslim as a social identity was presumably premised on the increasing identification on the part of Muslims with a foreign (Islamic) identity central to the reformist movements. Second, and perhaps more importantly, the stereotype of the Muslim that would achieve real importance in the post-Swadeshi era was one that was only partially constructed through this specifically literary history and its preoccupation with imagining national identity through a historical struggle with the Other. It was rather a composite of historically determinate stereotypes: the mendicant Muslim of government favoritism, the selfish Muslim of the agrarian disturbances, the fanatical Muslim of Islamic reformism, and the alien Muslim of foreign descent. The key anti-Muslim epithets—*selfish, fanatical,* and *alien*—each plugged into more than one of these historical determinations, so that one could adopt the historico-literary language of Bankim's virulent denunciation of the *yavana* to attack Muslim selfishness. This was all the more the case because the stereotype of the invading foreigner included such a rich repertoire of sensualism and decadence, plugging into a key constitutive moment in the history of the figure of the babu that was so central to Swadeshi concerns—namely, the cultural Persianization of high-caste Hindus in the eighteenth- and early nineteenth-century urban context.

BHADRALOK COMMUNALISM

Regardless of the rhetorical continuities between the anti-Muslim discourses of Renaissance literature and the anti-Muslim communalism that would emerge in the post-Swadeshi era, the era of educated-Hindu communalism in Bengal really has its roots in the failure of the Swadeshi movement, as refracted through the specific conceptual logic of Swadeshi discourse. Swadeshi discourse's central claim to draw its strength from the life of "the people" was increasingly rendered hollow by the failure of "the people" to respond to its call. Nothing indexed this hollowness more clearly than the increasing turn to secret-society terrorism, which, in Sumit Sarkar's terms, indexed both "the failure to close the age-old gap between the bhadralok and the masses," and the "second, related failure . . . in the region of Hindu-Muslim relations."[137] The Swadeshist strategy of locating all responsibility in the joint machinations of the British and their Muslim agents sought to contain this failure by positing a kind of primal nationalism on the part of Bengal's peasantry, Hindu *and* Muslim, that the Salimullah camp was obscuring with its divisive rhetoric. Yet the diminishing energies of the popular mobilization, the episodes of Hindu-Muslim violence in 1906-7, and the many signs that Muslims were on the whole unsympathetic to the cause of undivided Bengal made this position less and less tenable. Tagore and Bose were not alone in finding the years of Swadeshi's unraveling a watershed for their intellectual and political outlook.

In March 1908, Aurobindo Ghose published an article in the *Bande Mataram* that spoke powerfully to the challenge that this failure to mobilize the realm of the Muslim popular represented for Swadeshi ideology. "It is an ascertained principle of national existence," he explained in a manner entirely consonant with the vision of economic autarchy at the core of Swadeshi political economy, "that only by keeping possession of the soil can a nation persist." While those who control the state and wealth reign only until their virtue has been lost to the corruption inherent in those forms, "the tillers of the soil, ground down, oppressed, rack-rented, miserable, remain, and have always the chance of one day overthrowing their oppressors" to establish "the democracy of peasants." When the British took control of India, however, "the Hindus, who were then the majority of the Bengali-speaking population, began to stream away from the village to the town" in search of government and professional employment under the new Raj. The Hindu community came into a "monopoly of Government service, of the professions, of prestige, wealth and position; but it has lost possession of the soil," sacrificing "its rural root of life to the urban brilliance of its foliage and flowering." The consequence was dire: "If the present state of things is allowed to continue, *the Mahomedan will be the inheritor of the future*, and after a brief period of national strength and splendour the Bengali Hindu, like the Greek, will disappear from the list of nations and remain only as a great name in history." What was most needed then, Aurobindo declared, was a "return to the land. . . . If we train our young men to go back to the fields, we shall secure the perpetuation of the Hindu in Bengal which is now imperiled. . . . To settle more Hindu agriculturists on the land is the first necessity if the Hindu is to survive."[138]

This article was profoundly symptomatic of its times. The most obvious shift in Aurobindo's position is simply that where before he would dismiss communal unrest as an effect of elite manipulation, it now makes sense to him to posit the interests of a "Hindu community" as distinct from those of the "Mahomedans." But the terms in which these different interests are understood also matters: the Hindu community represents an urban phenomenon; the Muslim represents the man on the land. The nationalist has come to confront the productive life of the nation explicitly as a sectional (Muslim) interest, distinct from the national (Hindu) interest. From Aurobindo's perspective, the crisis lies not just in the apparent acceptance of a real split between Hindu-national and Muslim-sectional interests; it lies in the fact that the Muslim-sectional is also identified as the productive agency of Bengal. The national organism of Swadeshi discourse had yoked together the constitution of subjective freedom through culture with the appropriation of nature through labor; this was the very core of the mutually reinforcing relationship it had posited between the cultural and the political-economic elements of its program. But this relationship could only stand firm insofar as the peasant—Vivekananda's *shudra*, the instrumental agent of the self-constituting activity of the nation—could be understood to represent a principle antithetical to the commercial/civil ethos of Western civilization. Naming the peasantry *Muslim* not only marked it as distinct from that organism, it also implicitly marked it as a historical subject motivated by forms of economic and collective self-interest, meanings that had accreted to the stereotype of the Muslim in the histories unfolded above. For Aurobindo in 1908, the only way to resurrect the nationalist project of self-determination was to create a Hindu agriculturalist who could serve as the political-economic expression of the cultural program. That is to say, the free subjectivity of (Hindu) Bengal required an agent of labor to express itself in the world. In the immediate absence of such an agent, Hindus would have to go "back to the land."

Not all peasants were Muslims. Even in eastern Bengal, there was also a sizeable minority of lower-caste Hindu cultivators, among whom the Namasudras were the most numerous and prosperous. Yet while the Namasudra leadership that had emerged in the late nineteenth century, attempting to raise the status of the caste at a time of increasing prosperity, may have had a less prominent voice than the Muslim leadership, they were just as hostile to the Swadeshi cause, reproducing many Muslim strategies of resistance (such as deliberately buying foreign cloth and salt, even when more expensive), and aspiring to the same kinds of government patronage that Muslims enjoyed.[139] The development of lower-caste movements seems to have made less of an impression upon the Swadeshi leadership compared to the more powerful and prominent Muslim movement. This changed only with the approach of the 1911 census, when E. A. Gait, the census commissioner, declared that "depressed classes" would be enumerated separately from Hindus, while Namasudras petitioned for the same kind of separate electoral representation that the Morley-Minto reforms had promised Muslims: "though our religious rites and our observances and social customs are similar to those of high-caste Brahmins, we have not the slightest connection with any of the Hindu communities. . . . Thus we desire to be recognized by the Government as entirely a different community having separate claim to political privileges like Muhammadans."[140] Thus the potential for Swadeshi nationalists to appropriate Namasudra numbers as a numerical and specifi- cally "popular" counterweight to Muslim claims in eastern Bengal was being fundamentally undermined both by the colonial state and by the Namasu- dras themselves.

Interestingly, Bengal would prove the region most resistant to caste-reform legislation in subsequent decades.[141] In this sense, Bengali castism to some extent reiterated the logic of anti-Muslim discourse. Yet the Namasudra would not share the Muslim's fate of becoming the determinate Other of Bengali-Indian nationhood. In the face of a panicked preoccupation with the alleged propensity of Muslims to outbreed Hindus, U. N. Mukherji's widely read pamphlet of 1910, "A Dying Race," argued the necessity of a caste-upliftment movement that, by reducing the exclusivity of the higher castes, would shore up the integrity of the Hindu community against both colonial meddling and its own history of internal discrimination. This was, quite explicitly, to advocate the emulation of the successes of Muslim com- munal mobilization, which had been achieved through religious revival and collective discipline.[142] Observed an adulatory editorial in *The Bengalee* (where "A Dying Race" was first serialized):

> The whole trend of modern thought and of modern institutions is towards the equality of all men and the uplifting of the lower to a higher stratum of society. The Hindu community must adopt the modern conception and by a steady pro- cess of evolution raise the untouchable to the dignity which a Superior Being has conferred upon him. It is no longer a question of morality or right doing. The existence of the Hindu race through all time to come depends upon it. . . . The mind of the community must undergo a transformation—it must silently resolve to treat the "Namasudra" and the untouchable as a brother man and to remove from him the stigma of degradation. If the community will not do that . . . the untouchables, sooner or later—sooner rather than later—permeated with the growing idea of equality and resenting the sense of degradation inflicted upon him as a deliberate affront will bodily embrace that faith—the faith of Islam— where every man has the right divine to be the equal of his fellowman.[143]

Hinduism must negotiate a strained compromise with the demands of the lower castes, incorporating their claims to equality in order to consolidate the Hindu community's roots in the soil. Only thus could Hinduism over- come its old caste prejudices and also the newer discrimination based on education, whereby the "wealth-producing industries which in this country have hitherto been mostly in the hands of the so-called lower castes" had increasingly become a site of social stigma. "The most intelligent members of these industrial castes are fast abandoning their hereditary occupations in the hope of enjoying the social equality of men of higher castes. The industries are naturally being neglected, with the result that wealth is fast passing into the hands of rival communities [a euphemism for Muslims], and the Hindus are getting poorer," explained *The Bengalee* in what amounts to a reiteration of Aurobindo's argument for a return to the land. "And it is poverty which Dr. Mukerjea holds to be the most important and immediate cause of the process of decay which has set in among the Hindus."[144]

The concern about the diminishing proportion of Hindus to Muslims in Bengal was no doubt given political focus by the "colonial engineering" of communal competition through the census.[145] Yet the ways in which Swadeshi nationalists made sense of these institutional effects stemmed from the conceptual logic of Swadeshi discourse. The institutional politics of electoral representation was no doubt very important to Hindu politicians, but the reason that Muslim population growth and lower-caste declassification mattered to the post-Swadeshi Hindus was at least as much because it meant the isolation of culture from the nation's productive metabolism—a national life that had been conceptually relegated to the very realm of interests that Swadeshi discourse had sought to overcome. This is why it seemed to Aurobindo in 1908 that Hindus needed to reestablish a connection with the land to avoid corruption and continue their existence as a living nation. This is also perhaps why it made so much intuitive sense to post-Swadeshi Hindus that Muslim numbers grow faster than Hindu. As both Aurobindo and *The Bengalee* implied, Muslims still had a living and virile connection with nature through laboring activity, whereas Hindus had lost that connection and become effete and babuized. Muslim libidinousness—a classic trope of Renaissance historical romance that would achieve central importance in Hindu communal discourse in Bengal[146]—arguably expressed the fact that this connection with nature was a form of laboring activity tied not to the spiritual constitution of free subjectivity, but rather to selfish desire. This was the truly terrifying quality of the Muslim in the post-Swadeshi bhadralok imagination—that he combined the worst moral failures of the babu (selfishness, sensuality) with the strength and power of productive energies.

In this sense, the life of the people, which Swadeshi discourse had posited as the foundation of the "new politics," came to appear as a social terrain fundamentally alien to the ideals of Swadeshi culture. Muslim communal mobilization, combined with lower-caste mobilization, had robbed the Swadeshi "nation" of its coherence—a coherence that had always been based upon the historically determinate fantasy of a coherent civilizational difference whose contingent coherence we have traced in the preceding chapters. When Aurobindo imagined a return to the land by educated Hindus, he was, on the one hand, still clinging to the feasibility of the Swadeshi project. On the other hand, however, he was implicitly and simultaneously confessing the reality of its demise. He had initially posited the cultural project of self-constitution as the ethico-political form adequate to the productive propensities of the nation. In the post-Swadeshi period, however, it was not just a political-economic agenda that had to be derived as the necessary practical extension of the cultural project, but rather the nation's productive propensities themselves. The standpoint of such a politics was no longer the productive figure of the nation, but rather culture itself, hanging in splendid but awkward ideational isolation.[147] The Swadeshi nation had been outflanked, in the terms of its own logic, by the forces of commercial/ civil society, which now pincered it between two fronts: the British above, and the Muslim popular below.

For Aurobindo, accepting this demise in the face of the fading of enthusiasm and government repression took the form of his retreat to Pondicherry, where, safely beyond British jurisdiction, he turned his attentions to the practice of yoga and a mystical vision of the world's movement toward perfection. "When he came out of jail [in 1908] Sri Aurobindo found the whole political aspect of the country altered; most of the Nationalist leaders were in jail or in self-imposed exile and there was a general discouragement and depression." Upon receiving a divine command, he therefore retreated to the French-held territory of Pondicherry, where, in his own (third-person) account, his "practice of Yoga became more and more absorbing. He dropped all participation in any public political activity, refused more than one request to preside at sessions of the restored Indian National Congress and made a rule of abstention from any public utterance of any kind not connected with his spiritual activities." The inevitability of India's independence rendered his personal involvement superfluous, while the "magnitude of the spiritual work set before him became more and more clear to him." Aurobindo's reconstitution of Swadeshi idealism's ambition to reconstitute the social on cultural principles would now take the exclusive form of a cultural practice whose spiritual efficacy extended to the material world without any inverse relation. His retirement from politics "did not mean, as most people supposed, that he had retired into some height of spiritual experience devoid of any further interest in the world or the fate of India. It could not mean that, for the very principle of Yoga was not only to realise the Divine and attain to a complete spiritual consciousness, but also to take all life and all worldly activity into the scope of this spiritual consciousness and action and to base life on the Spirit and give it a spiritual meaning. In his retirement, Sri Aurobindo kept a close watch on all that was happening in the world and in India and actively intervened whenever necessary, but solely with a spiritual force and silent spiritual action," an agency apparently more efficacious than any other available.[148]

As previously for Pramatha Nath Bose, so too now for Aurobindo; "Science," which had been born as the germ of a higher rationality, now served primarily in the modern world to promote a kind of materialistic "barbarism" expressed in "the pursuit of vital success, satisfaction, productiveness, accumulation, possession, enjoyment, comfort, convenience for their own sake."[149] In the face of a realm of productivity that appeared increasingly antithetical to free subjectivity, yoga ("just another name for culture," as Bankim had observed many years earlier [BR 635]) was a self- and world-constituting activity far beyond the reach of anything so mundane as the squabbling of petty social interests, and had no need for a social foundation in "the land" for its efficacy. Spirit no longer operated through the conscious agency of the patriotic self-sacrificing *karmayogi,* but rather behind the backs of all but the most spiritually self-realized, through the working of an inscrutable providence that could convert even the worst betrayals of the cultural ideal to its own ultimate advantage.[150] Aurobindo, it seemed, could only retain the Swadeshi ideal of a complete subsumption of society into the domain of culture at the cost of a total withdrawal from the political realm, where the fractiousness of interests seemed impossible to contain.

With the shift in standpoint from the productive nation to culture itself, the end of Swadeshi culture inaugurated not a decline in cultural discourses, but rather the beginning of the period when discourses of culture would achieve perhaps their widest proliferation in the life of educated Hindu Bengal. "Culture," declared Deva Prasad Sarvadhikary (a founding member of the National Council of Education) in his 1934 foreword to the first number of the new journal, *Indian Culture,* "is the foundation, the base, and the bedrock of order and orderliness in their broadest and best sense."[151] Looking back over the decades since Bankim's "monumental study of Srikrishna," it seemed to him that he was not alone in giving culture such centrality. "Bengali Vernacular," he observed, "has long been casting about for a suitable name for Culture, and among the many that have been suggested, one finds 'Krishti,' 'Charcha,' 'Sadhana,' 'Alochona,' and 'Anushilan.' The appropriateness and suggestiveness of any of these names need not detain us, except as an index of the widespread desire and demand for the growth and expan-

Yoga

sion of real cultural ideals, ideas, and formulae."[152] This appeal to culture still voiced faith in a quasi-Hegelian historical narrative whereby the "unity of India" remained, in the cited words of the philosopher Surendranath Dasgupta, "essentially one of spiritual aspirations and obedience to the law of Spirit." But looked at more closely, the cultural "Spirit" of the 1920s and 1930s had moved to a safer distance from the crassly material world. What Sarvadhikary really meant by culture was *sahitya,* literature. "'The time of the wise and the intellectual is passed by the pastime of Kavya and Shastras or Literature—worldly and otherworldly.' Here is the key-note of the situation and the seeming pastime is really the cement that goes deep down the foundation and constitutes the bed-rock."[153]

Culture became, as Joya Chatterji has argued, the most important "unifying symbol of bhadralok identity in the first half of the twentieth century."[154] In doing so, we might add, it shifted from being a political ethics that sought to subsume the social, to become the marker of a social boundary. The discourse of bhadralok communalism in this period, Chatterji has shown, revolved around a primal, constitutive opposition of "Hindu culture" and "Muslim barbarism." "If learning is simply knowing how to read and write, there is little difference between Hindu[s] and Muslim[s]," explained the novelist, Saratchandra Chatterjee, in the wake of the Calcutta riots of 1926. "But if the essence of learning is width of the mind and culture of the heart, then there is no comparison between the two communities."[155] Whereas Hinduism is an inclusive religion that breeds tolerance, Islam is by its very nature fanatical—where *fanaticism* simultaneously names coarseness, lustfulness, aggression, selfishness, and, of course, the foreign attachment to Turkey and Arabia that was the essential negation of the Hindu attachment to the *svadesh.*[156] "The Muslims will never truly believe that India's freedom will bring them freedom too. They will only accept this truth when their obsession with their religion weakens. Then they will understand that whatever one's religion, to be proud of fanaticism is a matter of shame, there is no greater barbarism."[157] The Muslim was thus both external to the aspirations of the nation, and qualitatively incapable of participating in its cultural ideals.

For Joya Chatterji, this turn to communal "othering" represented the reemergence of the "old class division between the bhadralok and the chhotolok ... in the guise of a 'communal' difference, between bhadra Hindus and *abhadra* or *itor* Muslims," thus externalizing the otherness of the lower classes in order to consolidate a communal identity that could include the lower castes.[158] Part of this story makes a great deal of sense: Pradip Datta has recently underlined the strategic concerns that linked caste upliftment and the politics of population and representation.[159] But by now it should also be clear that we need to understand the plausibility of this ideological maneuver against a historical background that rendered "the Muslim" both external to the nation and antithetical to its cultural values—"the Muslim" as a figure of sectional self-interest. The transformation of class into community, Chatterji implies, is the result of the manipulation of symbols by a self-interested elite trying to consolidate its collective strength in a field of political contestation defined by the colonial state in terms of religious community. But the social correlation of class and community attributes characteristic of the Hindu communalism of 1920s Bengal was at the same time a strategy adopted from a repertoire of options whose rationality was circumscribed by the logic of a socially constituted ideological terrain. As we have seen, it was the figure of the "Muslim popular" that split apart the unity of Swadeshi discourse, isolating culture from the nation-constituting activity of the laboring classes, and thereby constituting the problematic to which this elite communal ideology was most fundamentally responding. The resultant conception of a "Hindu culture" as antithetical to the Muslim popular was a communal identity that had severed itself profoundly from a standpoint located within the productive life of the nation even as it privileged productive activity as the vehicle of national self-realization.

The nationalism of this new brand of communal consciousness lay in its attempt to reconstitute the discourse of Swadeshi within the confines of an organic Hindu community through the unambiguous ejection of the alien and disruptive Muslim popular from its ranks. In the context of a Muslim-majority Bengal with expanding institutions of political representation, this could only be achieved through an appeal to "All-India" nationalism: "The unadulterated democratic regime that the Hindus wanted on an all-Indian platform was not desired for Bengal," Abul Mansur Ahmad would recall many years later.

The Bengali Hindus were against both majority rule and self-government in Bengal. This of course was a recent mentality among Hindus. From the end of the 19th century through to the beginning of the 20th, Hindu poets and literary and political leaders had promulgated "Bengali nationhood," "Bengali culture," "Bengali autonomy," and so on. Many still believe this. But the moment it became clear that, with the establishment of democracy and the expansion of the franchise, state power would pass into the hands of the Muslim majority, the claims about Bengali nationality and Bengali culture were heard no more. Instead, we began to hear about the "Indian nation," "Indian culture," "Greater-Indian nationhood" [*mahabharatiya mahajati*], and "Aryan civilization."[160]

The parochial foundations of this All-India identification are fully recogniz-
able in the increasing marginalization of Bengal in All-India politics and its
consistently lukewarm response to Gandhian mass-nationalism, especially
after the failure of Non-Cooperation. In the end, as Chatterji has argued, the
educated Hindu Bengalis would ultimately accept the dismemberment of the
national territory whose integrity the Swadeshi generation had considered
sacred, rather than become a minority in a Muslim-majority postindependence state.[161]

MUSLIM CULTURE

Presiding over the East Pakistan Renaissance Convention at Islamiya College in Calcutta in May of 1944, Abul Mansur Ahmad gave articulate voice
to a Bengali-Muslim response to post-Swadeshi Hindu culturalism.[162] In his
audience were just about all of Bengal's most prominent Muslim intellectuals and politicians, as well as some sympathetic leftist Hindus.[163] Ahmad's
presidential address was a manifesto for a specifically culturalist conception
of Bengali Pakistanism. "'Pakistan' is the political demand of the Muslim
League," and "can without a doubt be described as the state-ideal of Muslim
India." Yet, he continued, "whatever the meaning of 'Pakistan' in the judgment of politicians, to literary men its meaning is *tammaduni azadi, sanskritik svaraj*, cultural autonomy" (Urduized Bengali, Sanskritized Bengali, and
transliterated English terms set in apposition to establish their equivalence).
The cultural renaissance to which the society was dedicated represented
"the lightning flash of life on the dead bones of the nation. In the state
and in society, in art and in literature, in trade and commerce, 'renaissance'
means to receive a jolt to every level of life." "Pakistan" represented something much more than a mere political settlement; it was the condition of
Bengali-Muslim collective revitalization and self-realization. "Because no
nation or human society can move forward on the path of progress if it
shuns and ignores its own culture. Those who try that merely imitate, they
do not create. . . . Therefore culture itself is the foundation of every nation's
striving for self-realization [*jiban-sadhanar buniyad*]." And while there might
yet be room for debate about the ultimate political settlement upon British
withdrawal, he contended that there could be no doubt that "Hindus and
Muslims are separate peoples in the field of culture." This was not because
Hindu and Muslim cultures were so profoundly dissonant as to lack any
common ground. "Fundamentally, the culture not just of Hindus and Muslims, but of every people in the entire world is one. But how evident are
the cultural differences between nations!" The abstract cosmopolitanism of

humanism, with its belief that man will "abandon local and national religion and accept a noble, dogma-less religion," carried within its ideal of "mechanical unity or mechanical uniformity" the germ of a "cultural fascism or cultural oppression" that, lacking any "connection with real human life," could not grasp the possibility of "the human communities of the various regions and climes . . . unfold[ing] themselves on the basis of their own religion and culture."

The differences that divided Bengali Hindus from Bengali Muslims despite their common language were ultimately rooted in religious difference. "The Hindus and Muslims of India are not one people, and nor do they have a common culture. . . . The relationship between the tree and the seed is the same as that between religion and culture." But following the same logic, cultural differences also divided Bengali Muslims even from other South Asian Muslims. "Just as the tree and the seed are not the same, however, nor are religion and culture. Religion can traverse geographical borders; but culture cannot ignore geographical borders. Rather the roots of culture reside within those borders. So there is a border between Eastern and Western Pakistan. Eastern Pakistan is a territorial entity. The natives of Eastern Pakistan are an autonomous and distinct people from the other peoples of India and from their religious brethren in Western Pakistan." Ahmad thus set out to ground the political autonomy of Muslim Bengal in a vision of its cultural autonomy. "The political freedom of nations will undoubtedly be the watchword of the imminent age. But the significance of that political self-rule will be the free, original, unhindered blossoming of nations. The core principle of this blossoming is *tammaduni azadi* or cultural autonomy. The name of this is Pakistan."[164]

We cannot but recognize the history of post-Swadeshi culturalism in Ahmad's understanding of "Hindu culture."

> Hindu religion is the religion of renunciation, of otherworldliness and of the sages and saints. So the culture of the Hindus is also the culture of renunciation, love and devotionalism. The foundation of this culture is the worship of symbols. Therefore the artistic heart of the Hindu is a worshipper of beauty. . . . Beauty- and symbol-worshipping, this cultivated mind has freely espoused the principle of "art for art's sake." . . . Gradually through the brush of the artist the great and noble founding principles of Hindu culture—renunciation, otherworldliness, devotion and love—were aestheticized, making [the] womanly love [of Radha for Krishna] its center.[165]

Such an account of Hindu culture would have been incomprehensible in the Swadeshi era, when Hinduism was surely nothing if not the religion of collective agency. But despite its misrecognition of Tagorean aestheticism as the essence of a timeless Hinduism, it constituted a rather acute diagnosis of the rarified trajectory of Bengali culturalism by the time he was speaking in the 1940s. Ahmad's invocation of "culture" as the living antithesis of a soulless cosmopolitanism, as the instrument of a profound revitalization of collective life, and as the founding principle of autonomous self-determination was at one level merely another instantiation of what should by now be a rather familiar Bengali culturalism. His insistence on the necessity of an original, creative culture grounded in the ideals of Bengali-Muslim life was supposed to be the Muslim answer to the "highly developed literature" that had emerged "from the literary men of the age from Vidyasagar and Bankimchandra to Rabindranath and Saratchandra."[166] It was his central contention that this was an exclusively Hindu tradition. "The national conception of every nation centers on its own tradition. No nation will find inspiration in that literature as long as it is not composed on the basis of that tradition."[167] Since this literature was devoid of allusions or references to Islamic history and literature, he would conclude that "the Muslims are not the creators of this literature, the Muslims are not its subject-matter, its spirit is not Muslim, and even its language is not the language of the Muslims" thanks to the Sanskritization and correlative de-Persianization of Bangla's so-called chaste literary idiom constructed by the great Hindu litterateurs of the nineteenth century.[168] Nonetheless, it is clear that Ahmad was envisioning a cultural production (*tammadun*) that was, in some sense, to be parallel to that same Hindu tradition (*sanskriti*) precisely through its discovery of its own original voice and its rootedness in the realities of Bengali-Muslim society. He was speaking as the inheritor of a tradition of twentieth-century Muslim literary activism that stemmed from a pervasive feeling among Muslim members of the (noncommunal) Bangiya Sahitya Parishad (Academy of Bengali Literature) that they were the "poor cousins" of Bengali literature, who needed a parallel but independent institutional space to "gather strength" before they could participate as full members of the literary mainstream.[169]

Before we dismiss Ahmad's intervention outright as the mechanical appropriation and reiteration of a discourse of authenticity already well established in the more prestigious literary and intellectual circles of Hindu educated society, however, we need to consider at least a few important qualifications. At one level, Ahmad was positing Hindu and Muslim cultures as formally equivalent national collectivities, both pitched against the threatening uniformity of an abstract cosmopolitanism. But just as post-Swadeshi thinkers had struggled to deracinate the culture concept in the face of the indifference and even hostility of its own popular foundations, so too was Ahmad elaborating a three-dimensional structure of differentiation. The classically colonial structure of Swadeshi thought, with its opposition of Indian culture to Western commerce, was being challenged in the post-Swadeshi period by a communal imagination according to which the differences within Indian society were understood to be just as qualitative and asymmetrical as the difference between colonizer and colonized that had been so fundamental to Swadeshi idealism. It was not just that Hindus and Muslims were homologous collectivities distinct from each other, while both being qualitatively distinct from the West's commercial civilization. Rather, if East was to West as culture was to commerce, then Hindu was to Muslim as culture was to barbarism. Structurally, the selfishness of the Muslim aligned him with the selfishness of the European. In Ahmad's speech, while the difference between colonizer and colonized has been displaced as the central problematic (even while still very much taken for granted), the Hindu/Muslim difference was of constitutive significance. But in taking seriously the category of Muslim culture, he was doing something quite distinct from mainstream Bengali culturalism; he was arguing on the one hand for a potential symmetry between formally equivalent Hindu and Muslim collectivities (both being cultural in their constitution), and on the other hand reinscribing in quite different terms an asymmetrical and qualitative difference between Hindu and Muslim cultures.

When Ahmad set down to the crucial task of identifying the *differentia specifica* of Hindu and Muslim forms of culture, he seemed if anything to have been attempting a recuperation of the social ambitions of Swadeshi-era idealism in the face of the involution of post-Swadeshi culturalism.

> Howsoever noble the ideals of renunciation, otherworldliness, devotion and love may be, they are not the life-ideals of the Muslims. Just as the religion of the Hindus is the religion of renunciation, otherworldliness and the sages and saints, so is the religion of the Muslims the religion of justice, equity, struggle and martyrdom. While the symbolistic, beauty worshipping, aestheticist Hindu culture is person-centered . . . Muslim culture, with its commitment to right and justice and its orientation to welfare, is in fact society-centered. In the judgment of the Muslim then, art is not for art's sake, art is for society's sake. As a result of this united welfare-orientation, the Muslims are fundamentally action-oriented, not devotionalistic.[170]

If Hindu culture was identified in terms of a popular Vaishnavite aestheticism, Muslim culture was on the contrary still replete with expansive energy for social transformation. If Hindu culture had collapsed into atomized individualism, Muslim culture was grounded in the grand old Swadeshi values of action orientation and collective life. Was Ahmad saying that "Muslim" was to "Hindu" as "Swadeshi" was to "post-Swadeshi"? Was he simply reversing the Hindu-communalist structure, making Muslims the bearers of a higher culture and consigning the Hindus to the status of inveterate individualists and crypto-Europeans? Not quite. Hindu individualism remained, even in Ahmad's account, distinctly cultural in form, far from the liberal individualism of rights and interests. In contrast, Muslim socialism contained at its very core the liberal categories of rights and interests. "Muslim social structure is not founded on renunciation or otherworldliness, or on offerings and tithes. Muslim social structure is founded on justice and equity." Woman does not represent mystical renunciative devotion to the Muslim, but rather a "female human being" whose heart "can be won through justice and equity, through rights and equality, like all other members of society."[171] Thus Muslim society was fundamentally oriented toward the very concern for rights and interests that Hindu aestheticism, inwardness, and otherworldliness sought to transcend.

We can now see the peculiarity of Ahmad's intervention; he was identifying the ethical and political categories of the sphere of circulation as the defining characteristics of a specifically Muslim "culture" embodied in the life practices of eastern Bengal's cash-cropping peasantry—even though culture had been a category whose historical function in Bengal had been to negate the ethical and political categories of the sphere of circulation. Furthermore, he was not doing this in the tradition of the old Moderate Congress, where culture acted as an ethical supplement to rescue the salience of liberal categories to colonial society. He was identifying equality and justice as the intrinsic substance of Muslim culture. Ahmad shared post-Swadeshi culturalism's identification of the Bengali Muslim, the productive peasant who had so terrified Aurobindo in 1908, with the values of the sphere of circulation, but, on the basis of this very same recognition of the Muslim as producer, sought to identify these values in turn as forms of culture. This represented a strikingly different resolution of the dilemmas of post-Swadeshi culturalism.

THE MARXIST TRANSFORMATION

If the trajectory of post-Swadeshi culturalism had served systematically to obfuscate the already opaque practical foundations of Bengali culturalism, an alternative trajectory of post-Swadeshi political discourse sought to render those foundations at least partially more transparent. The post-Swadeshi turn to a more rarified conception of culture was a defensive maneuver, formulated from within the conceptual logic of Swadeshi ideology, in response to popular energies that it could not encompass or harness. But if what we might call the "rightist" renunciation of the popular as a realm of insurgent material interests represented the dominant trajectory of the post-Swadeshi period, it by no means exhausted the possible responses to this crucial conjuncture. In these same years there emerged in Bengal an explicitly "leftist" political project. Instead of renouncing the popular, this leftist tradition sought to reconceptualize culturalist categories in a manner that might accommodate the structuring logic of popular political energies. Ahmad was able in the early 1940s to finally synthesize his unwavering commitment throughout the 1930s to the agrarian class politics of tenants and cultivators with a communally defined culturalism that had been developing separately in his literary pursuits, because his conception of "Bengali-Muslim culture" combined the dynamism of the cultural imagination of Swadeshism with a peculiar sensitivity to the interests of the agrarian producing classes that the category Bengali Muslim was understood to name.[172] But in bringing the practical realities of productive activity into the domain of culture, the leftist project risked bursting the limits of this culturalism asunder, recuperating the realm of popular interests to the culturalist project of autonomous self-determination, yet also potentially renouncing the entire idiom of spirituality in favor of an aggressive Marxist materialism. Like many strands of the dominant rightist discourse we have discussed, this Marxist alternative, which had already begun to emerge in the 1920s, would take a radical turn toward cosmopolitanism; but this cosmopolitanism was grounded not in the abstraction of culture from popular life, but in the identification of productive activity as a universally constitutive element of social reproduction. One need not take every claim of this new Marxism to heart to see that it represented in some sense a de-sublimation of culturalist idealism: it finally rendered explicit the social foundations of idealist discourse in the practice of labor even if it was unable to grasp labor as anything other than the essence of humanity; and it developed the universalistic impulse of Swadeshi thought even as it sought to conceptualize a viable popular politics in the specific historical conjuncture of the Swadeshi movement's recent failure.

The biographical links between Swadeshism and Marxism are very far from exhausting the latter's origins even among intellectuals—one immediately thinks of Muzaffar Ahmad's recollections of the marginality of some vague Swadeshi sympathies to his own consciousness, with his deep involvement in the Bengali Muslim Literature Society instead being his path into political involvement.[173] Nor are biographical connections necessary to the kind of argument I want to make. If the plausibility of Swadeshi idealism's categories depended not merely on the predominance of a discursive regime, but more fundamentally on its domain of social reference, then the problematic that Swadeshi idealism faced was one constituted at a more general level than that of the Swadeshi political activist as such. Yet biographical connections are numerous: many secret-society revolutionaries would drift into the communist camp in the course of the 1920s, starting with the ultimate celebrity of Bengali Marxism, M. N. Roy, whose life in politics began with a deep investment in neo-Hindu politics in the tradition of Bankim and Vivekananda, and had as its practical condition of possibility a two-decade-long commitment to the revolutionary project of Swadeshi- and post-Swadeshi-era secret societies that led him overseas in search of arms and money. Necessary or not, such biographical connections give us a useful way of entering into the intimacy of the relationship between two ideological frameworks that give every outward appearance of being diametrically opposed.

Narendranath Bhattacharya had been active in secret societies since around 1901 or 1902, joining the Anushilan Society under Barin Ghose (Aurobindo's brother) in 1905 (but gradually shifting his allegiance to the Yugantar group under Jatin Mukherjee from around 1910), and had also enrolled as a student in the Swadeshi National Education program from 1906. In 1915, after two arrests, a failed attempt at gun smuggling and the death of Jatin in a shootout, Narendranath left India in search of material assistance for the revolutionary struggle from a Germany at war with Britain, traveling through Southeast Asia to Japan, China, the United States (where he assumed the name by which he is remembered, Manabendranath [M. N.] Roy, and began reading Marx initially with a view to refuting materialism), and thence to Mexico (where he began to embrace a more systematic Marxism and founded the Communist Party of Mexico), before finally heading off to join the Comintern in 1919.[174] He would not return to India until 1930, whereupon he was promptly imprisoned.

By his own recollection, "cultural nationalism is a prejudice that dies very hard," and its hold on his thought would persist for some years after he had embraced socialist ideals and Marxist "dialectics."[175] Writing in Mexico in 1918, Roy still elaborated a classically Swadeshi understanding of India's history and mission.

India began life in the dim past, questioning the reason for her existence. Since that time, the moral and intellectual life of India has been based on the ability and courage to respond to these questions. Each of the various sects and philosophical schools interpret the question of existence in its own way. The mutually agreed solution arrived at constitutes the spirit and culture of India: "That which exists is One—men call Him by many names." I am the subject—the creation, with its apparent diversity is the object and enables me to find unity in diversity. And in the end to be the centre of creation, which is nothing but a creation of mine; and being my creation, it cannot exist without me.... This concept of the unity of the universe, the realization of the identity of the individual with cosmic existence, is India's contribution to the progress of humanity.[176]

"The Indian did not worry about the form or constitution of his country's government so long as he could continue to advance towards social and intellectual perfection. He did not wish to become a slave to exaggerated necessities."[177] [Armed with this core spiritual insight, ancient India had embarked on the elaboration of a "well-defined social system" that "contained many of the principles of modern socialism" in its recognition of "the concept of equality and unity of human beings," and the development of "trade and industry" that promoted "progress and prosperity."][178] "The fertility of the soil and dexterity of the people were able to satisfy all the country's needs, until the greedy Europeans arrived. The English in particular robbed the people of all their wealth, all the products of their daily work and of their soil."[179] The British had beggared the subcontinent, first by extracting enormous amounts of bullion from India as booty from its conquest, thereby underwriting Britain's own rise to prosperity, and subsequently by exploiting the legendary fertility of India's soils for commercial export at the expense of its starving masses, systematically destroying its industries, transferring the "home charges" to Britain, and rendering it dependent on imported British manufactures.[180]

    There is absolutely nothing in this that departs from the classical formulations of Swadeshi idealism outlined in the previous chapter. But even though he was many miles away, Roy was not unaffected by the collapse of the movement; with the nationalist revolutionaries arrested and his former guru dead, he realized that his mission to Germany had been rendered pointless, and he struggled to resolve the tension between loyalty to his old comrades and "an intelligent choice of a new ideal."[181] By 1919, writing under the direct influence of Marxist thought, Roy was already beginning to make some key transitions in his thinking. "By nature, education and centuries of culture, the Indians as a race are peaceable, and averse to shedding blood,"

he would explain, clearly still drawing on the nationalist ideological regis-
ter. "English capitalists, taking advantage of this well-known characteristic,
initiated a kind of exploitation, merciless, cruel and efficient, which is calculated to annihilate the entire Indian people." These "English capitalists"
depended on the exploitation of Indian labor to compensate for their losses
in their struggle with the British workers, who in turn failed to recognize,
in their support of imperialism for the sake of minor gains, that they would
never overcome capitalist exploitation so long as Britain controlled India.
The struggle between the British exploiter and the Indian productive organism translates into the world-historical struggle between capital and labor,
so that the struggle for Indian independence ceases to be merely a *"local
affair, having for its end and purpose the creation of another egoistic nationalism,"* and rather becomes *"a factor in world politics."* "English capital," after
all, "is more than mere English capital—it represents at once the epitome
and bulwark of the capitalistic system thruout [*sic*] the world. . . . The liberation of India is more than a mere act of abstract justice; it signifies a long
step towards the redemption of the world from the jaws of the capitalistic
system."[182]

It is not difficult to see how continuous these claims are with the classic Swadeshist critique of exploitation. But there is also a key difference
that we see emerging in the major texts composed after Roy's transition to
Marxism in the early 1920s. Where Swadeshism had turned on a *national*
difference—the materialism of the European and the spirituality of the
Asian—the *sociological* determination of exploiter and exploited emphasized
the class difference within the structure of Indian society. It is true that
Swadeshism had already struggled with the difference between the classes—
but only as a problem of separation or deracination. And on the right, men
like P. N. Bose were also struggling with the problem of class. For the Marxist Roy, however, the relationships between Britain and India, between British capitalists and labor, and between Indian capitalists and labor were all
structurally analogous; national liberation was now rendered meaningless
in the absence of a corresponding social revolution. Where Swadeshism had
envisaged the cooperative development of the national organism through
the harmonious subordination of Indian labor to Indian capital, Roy could
no longer embrace the national economy as the standpoint of his critique of
imperialism once he had argued that the *"increase to national wealth means
the enrichment of the native propertied class, and the enrichment of this class
means the expropriation and pauperization of the producing class."*[183] The subject of labor, still rather loosely conceived in terms of an amalgamation of

peasants and proletarians, was no longer the national organism, but rather a class subject. *"We want a Swaraj which will guarantee to the worker the full value of what he produces. . . . The worker is the producer of all wealth. Those who produce food for all should not go hungry. Those who manufacture cloth should not go naked. Those who build palatial houses and prosperous cities should not live in dens and holes like animals."*[184]

The aspiration to political and economic self-determination on the part of this class subject represented the negation of the selfish interests characteristic of civil society, the target of Swadeshi criticism. Yet this vision of collective self-determination was nonetheless at the same time an expression of social interests; through the realization of the collective interest of the producing classes in socialism, the overcoming of the selfish interests of the exploiting classes could be achieved. Where the dominant response to the popular energies that had been partly responsible for the failure of Swadeshi had been to renounce the people's shudra propensities, and Aurobindo had recoiled from the figure of the Muslim popular precisely because of the terrifying and explosive combination of self-interest and productive energy it represented, the leftist alternative was instead to recuperate these popular energies as the basis of its politics. Not, of course, in their raw form, as expressions of particular social interests; but through their sublimation into a politics of antiexploitation from the standpoint of production. If then it became necessary to renounce the spiritual idiom of Swadeshi discourse this was surely because Roy was self-consciously embracing the materialism of the shudra classes. The activity of the nation became the labor of the working class. Roy would mirror the rightist turn to cosmopolitanism as a symptom of the irremediable fracturing of the national organism, identifying the universality inherent in a sociological determination of class rather than the universality inherent in an abstracted conception of culture. That Roy's Marxism was elaborated far from Bengal in the cosmopolitan circles of Mexico, Berlin, and Moscow in no way compromises this basic point. These categories always had been cosmopolitan in their fundamental structure. Starting with Bankim, they had derived the primacy of the concrete—the nation as a political, social, and ethical category of particularity—from universalistic principles. And Roy's ability to translate Swadeshi nationalism into Marxist internationalism was premised on the fact that the materialist discourse of Marxism was expressing something fundamental about the idealist logic underpinning Swadeshism—that it had always been, unbeknownst to itself, a discourse of labor.

"When, as a school boy of fourteen, I began my political life," Roy would recall in 1946, "I wanted to be free.... In those days we had not read Marx. We did not know about the existence of the proletariat. Still, many spent their lives in jail and went to the gallows.... They did not have the dream of Communism. But they had the human urge to revolt against the intolerable conditions of life.... I began my political life with that spirit, and I still draw my inspiration rather from that spirit than from the three volumes of *Capital* or three-hundred volumes by the Marxists. That is the basic urge of freedom, which created this world of men, which created the feudal as well as the capitalist world, an which will create a still better world of which we are dreaming."[185] What Roy's desublimation of the logic of culturalism also makes clear is that the core categories of his Marxism remained deeply complicit with their culturalist roots through the validation of laboring activity both as the standpoint for a critique of exploitation and as the practical foundation of subjective autonomy. The laboring subject retains its ontological status even when it is downgraded from the operations of spirit to the strictly material actuality of the productive activities of mere human beings. Beneath the formalistic regularities of exchange still lay, in this leftist vision, the substantial bedrock of productive activity; and if the superimposition of market functions and bourgeois class domination could be removed, then the rational principle of productive activity would be fully realized. That is why even Roy's politics never aspired to rise above the act of expropriating the means of production from the exploiting classes in order to restore them to the producing classes, both proletarian and peasant, through national-popular ownership. Seen in this light, it is perhaps unsurprising, firstly, that when Marxism began to build a more broad-based support among middle-class Bengalis in the 1930s and 1940s, it was as in a spirit of antiformalist romanticism;[186] and secondly that, when Roy ultimately came to renounce orthodox Marxist theory as a form of objectivist determinism, it was in the name of a "radical humanism" that reasserted the centrality of subjective emancipation.

CONCLUSION

———— ✳ ————

Universalistic Particularisms and Parochial Cosmopolitanisms

AT THE END of this narrative we have seen the proliferation of concepts of culture in post-Swadeshi Bengal not as the result of the triumph of culturalist ideology, but as a process of involution inextricably bound up with its defeat as a sociopolitical project. At the same time though, most of the strands of post-Swadeshi thought that we have traced share a striking tendency toward a newly expansive form of cosmopolitanism. Swadeshi culturalism had been deeply grounded in the socioeconomic bifurcation of a specifically colonial social order, with civilizational difference at the core of its ideological structure. Post-Swadeshi ideological trajectories, in contrast, all displayed what can only be described as a postcolonial impulse [By this, I don't mean that they were articulated in a postcolonial historical context; nor do I mean to imply the equally false suggestion that they abandoned the ideal of national independence as a key ideological objective] I mean that, whereas Swadeshi culture presumed a colonial relation as the sine qua non of its very coherence, these post-Swadeshi discourses did not fundamentally rely on the fact of colonialism for their intelligibility. As the example of Satyajit Ray makes clear, the conceptual structure of Tagorean cosmopolitanism would be largely unaffected by the fact of British withdrawal; and the same could certainly be said of M. N. Roy's Marxism.

To call the post-Swadeshi discourse of culture *postcolonial* is to suggest that although culturalist discourse's emergence to prominence in Bengal was inextricably tied to the circumstances of the colonial relation in eastern India in the second half of the nineteenth century, that should not be taken to imply that the logical moment of closure for its history must necessarily be 1947. On the contrary, the postcoloniality of Bengali culturalism was generated, I am suggesting, from the critical moment of Swadeshism's self-diagnosed failure. Just as we have traced the impulse to national particularism in the late nineteenth and early twentieth centuries to structures of social organization that were anything but regionally particular, so too must we remember that the (specifically culturalist) impulse to cosmopolitanism that we see intensifying from the 1910s was rooted in regional social dynamics. This is not just a function of my own personal contrariness. It is rather once again to underline the necessity of understanding that the local/global dyad is always produced in each context of its articulation, and that the local specificity of Bengali culturalism therefore in no way negates its structural relationship to other equally specific forms of culturalism elsewhere. The universalistic categories of capitalist modernity do not occupy some global stratosphere that confronts the particularity of regional lifeworlds from the outside, but are constituted in dialectical intimacy with those regional particularities. From the critical-Marxist perspective of this book, the fact of this precocious postcoloniality presents no fundamental difficulty of interpretation. On the contrary, its seeds really lie in the elaboration of Swadeshi discourse itself—in its complex articulation of the antinomies of the commodity form as a condensation of abstract and concrete labor. Expressive of these more fundamental forms of social mediation, culture could remain a vital discursive category in colonial and postcolonial Bengal so long as Bengali society remained bound by the structures of alienated social labor.

The advent of an explicit Marxism in early twentieth-century India may have been enormously important in opening up more sophisticated ways of thinking about exploitation and domination (questions that had certainly been blunted by the nationalist focus on Western domination), but it cannot be understood as a triumphal unveiling of the essential and universal truth of class exploitation without recognizing that class, however crucial politically, is neither the foundational nor the ultimate category of Marxian analysis. Among other things, the aim of this book has been to show that Marxian theory should not be dismissed as the variant of developmentalist historicism that it undoubtedly was in the hands of an M. N. Roy, and is fully capable of grasping the ostensibly antimodern trajectory of so much colonial ethical, social, and political discourse.

At a time of culturalist and discursivist hegemony in the humanistic disciplines, many readers will undoubtedly argue that such a theoretical project necessarily involves the violent subordination of Indian difference to European forms of theoretical and historical consciousness. To grasp Indian difference through the categories of Western theory is, it is increasingly assumed, like trying to type in mittens. But it was Bengalis who found in "their own" intellectual traditions resources to articulate a theoretical convergence with categories of modern European thought. This must be understood not primarily in terms of symbolic or epistemic violence, but more fundamentally as a possibility grounded in social transformations under the impact of the region's incorporation into capitalist society. In other words, the conditions under which modern social-scientific abstractions have come to be applicable to Bengal were produced in Bengal; if the modern West has constantly seen culture in Bengal, this cannot be separated from the fact that modern Bengal has come to present itself as cultural. The relations of colonizer and colonized in the era I study cannot be adequately grasped in the immediacy of their ethnic or racial content (as one culture or civilization superimposed upon another), but must be understood as two positions within the bilateral totality of a colonial society. What this ultimately means is that the history I have told about modern Bengal also presumes as its correlate an increasingly unfamiliar way of framing modern European intellectual history: that is to say, in terms of a historical process in which modern European intellectual history ceases to be European precisely to the extent that it expresses modern categories of practice that are global in their logic and salience. The adjective *modern* here refers not primarily to a sensitivity on the part of historical subjects to the temporal disjuncture between past and present, but to a temporal disjunction instantiated by the practical subsumption of Bengali society into global structures of social mediation that are best understood, in epochal terms, as capitalist.

At the core of this book has been an attempt to reframe the intellectual history of the modern non-West in a manner that departs fundamentally from discourse-theory and from the more familiar varieties of materialist criticism. The conceptual frameworks within which the historical subjects who feature in the foregoing narrative operate, have been presented neither as autonomous determinations of history nor as the abject flotsam of an economic infrastructure. They are understood as determinate thought forms that take their meaning and their plausibility from specific structures of social practice, and yet in turn set in motion distinct and even potentially contradictory political and ethical projects (for example, liberal reform and cultural renewal) that draw upon the potentialities of different moments of the total social process. Culture emerges from this study as a *subjective moment* of capitalist society—a category that is at once inadequate insofar as it is posited dogmatically and positively (without mediations), yet irreducible insofar as it names a crucial moment of social reproduction. If the problematic of culture is, as I have suggested in chapter 2, the problematic of subjectivism, this book seeks to reframe the cultural as sociohistorically constituted subjectivity.[1] The intellectual history of modern Bengal is, from this perspective, always and necessarily much more than "just" intellectual history. To the extent that categories of thought are not just formal concepts, but rather are constituted in relation to determinate objects through the mediating agency of practical activity, intellectual history properly understood becomes a key entryway to grasping the deep historicity of modern Bengali society. Genealogical histories of discourse will never suffice if we want to capture this social dimension of intellectual history. And if I have convinced my readers of nothing else, I hope that I have persuaded them that there are crucial questions of colonial intellectual history that contemporary idealist, institutionalist, and naively materialist paradigms have systematically elided—perhaps because they are so ill equipped to handle them.

Notes

CHAPTER ONE

1. Udayan Gupta, "The Politics of Humanism: An Interview with Satyajit Ray," *Cineaste* 12, no. 1 (1982): 24–29; Shyam Benegal, *Benegal on Ray: Satyajit Ray, a Film* (Calcutta: Seagull, 1988), 112.

2. See Henri Micciollo, *Satyajit Ray* (Lausanne: Éditions L'Âge d'Homme, 1981), 271.

3. See Robin Wood, *The Apu Trilogy* (New York: Praeger, 1971), 17.

4. Folke Isaksson, "Conversation with Satyajit Ray," *Sight and Sound* 39 (Summer 1970): 114–20; George Sadoul and Satyajit Ray, "De film en film," *Cahiers du Cinéma* 175 (February 1966): 53–56, 76–79.

5. Firoze Rangoonwalla, *Satyajit Ray's Art* (Delhi: Clarion, 1980), 131–32.

6. Chidananda Das Gupta, *Satyajit Ray: An Anthology of Statements on Ray and by Ray* (New Delhi: Directorate of Film Festivals, Ministry of Information and Broadcasting, 1981), 35.

7. Isaksson, "Conversation with Satyajit Ray," 119. Ray would explicitly renounce any faith in leftism a couple of years later (Christian Braad Thomsen, "Ray's New Trilogy," *Sight and Sound* 42 [Winter 1972/73]: 31–33). By 1982 he was also denying any significant social role for film (Gupta, "Politics of Humanism," 27).

8. Niharranjan Ray, *Krishti, kalcar, sanskriti* (Calcutta: Jijnasa, 1978), 1–2.

9. Ray, *Krishti, kalcar, sanskriti*, 2.

10. Ibid., 4.

11. Ibid., 7.

12. See Dipesh Chakrabarty, *Provincializing Europe: Postcolonial Thought and Historical Difference* (Princeton, NJ: Princeton University Press, 2000), 170–72.

13. Cited from Clinton B. Seely's translation, in his *A Poet Apart: A Literary Biography of the Bengali Poet Jibanananda Das, 1899–1954* (Newark: University of Delaware Press, 1990), 193–94.

14. Amblan Datta, "Shantiniketan," in *Amader Shantiniketan: Shatabarsher Aloya*, ed. Sutapa Bhattacharya (Shantiniketan: Subarnarekha, Bengali year 1407 [ca. 2000]), 5–6; Bhudev Chaudhuri, "Visva-Bharati: A Poet's Vision: Withering!" in *Visva-Bharati, Platinum Jubilee, 1921–1996* (Shantiniketan: Visva-Bharati, 1997), 74–83; quotations are on pp. 75, 78.

15. I borrow the notion of translative equivalency from Lydia H. Liu, *Translingual Practice: Literature, National Culture, and Translated Modernity; China, 1900–1937* (Stanford, CA: Stanford University Press, 1995), whose introduction offers a salutary call for a specifically historical study that goes "beyond the deconstructionist stage of trying to prove that equivalencies do not exist" and instead looks "into their *manner of becoming*" (16).

16. Ray explicitly accepted the burden of representing "not just Indian cinema, but also Indian history, the Indian social phenomenon" to the rest of the world, and was fully aware that "the foreigner's curiosity about the Orient" was key to the marketability of his films, and consequently that the universalistic spirit of his humanism was only appealing when clothed in exotic garb. Peter Cargin and Bernard Cohn, "Entretien avec Satyajit Ray," *Positif* 112 (January 1970): 19-28; Das Gupta, *Satyajit Ray*, 135; Satyajit Ray, *Our Films, Their Films* (Calcutta: Orient Longman, 1976), 40-43.

17. This study thus takes as its theoretical point of departure Marx's very Hegelian discussion of method in the *Grundrisse: Foundations of the Critique of Political Economy (Rough Draft)* (London: Penguin, 1973), 100-102.

18. Homi Bhabha, *The Location of Culture* (London: Routledge, 1994), 34.

19. See Sharmishta Gooptu, "The Glory That Was: An Exploration of the Iconicity of New Theatres," *Comparative Studies of South Asia, Africa and the Middle East* 23, nos. 1, 2 (2003): 286-300.

20. Joseph Levenson, *Confucian China and Its Modern Fate; A Trilogy* (Berkeley: University of California Press, 1968).

21. See Partha Chatterjee, *Nationalist Thought and the Colonial World: A Derivative Discourse?* (London: Zed Books, 1986), chap. 1.

22. Anil Seal, *The Emergence of Indian Nationalism: Competition and Collaboration in the Later Nineteenth Century* (Cambridge: Cambridge University Press, 1968); and Anil Seal et al., eds., *Locality, Province, and Nation: Essays on Indian Politics, 1870-1940* (Cambridge: Cambridge University Press, 1973).

23. Rajat K. Ray, "Political Change in British India," *Indian Economic and Social History Review* 14, no. 4 (1977): 503 (emphasis in original).

24. Antonio Gramsci, *Selections from the Prison Notebooks* (New York: International, 1971), 377.

25. Sumit Sarkar, *Swadeshi Movement in Bengal, 1903-1908* (New Delhi: People's Publishing, 1973), 512.

26. Quentin Skinner, *Visions of Politics,* vol. 1, *Regarding Method* (Cambridge: Cambridge University Press, 2002).

27. See especially Benedict Anderson's ubiquitous work, *Imagined Communities: Reflections on the Origin and Spread of Nationalism* (London: Verso, 1991). For a compelling critique of Anderson's "ideal-typical" (as distinct from "sociohistorical") model of modularity, see Manu Goswami, "Rethinking the Modular Form: Toward a Sociohistorical Conception of Nationalism," *Comparative Studies in Society and History* 44, no. 4 (2002): 770-99.

28. This Western will to power and its role in distorting representations are thematized classically in Edward Said, *Orientalism* (New York: Pantheon, 1978); and more specifically with respect to India in Ronald B. Inden, *Imagining India* (Cambridge, MA: Blackwell, 1990).

29. For a critique of the anthropological culture concept from this kind of Saidian perspective, see Lila Abu-Lughod, "Writing against Culture," in *Recapturing Anthropology: Working in the Present,* ed. Richard G. Fox (Santa Fe, NM: School of American Research Press, 1991), 137-62. The postcolonialist conception of cultural colonization can be read as a condensation, in varying degrees according to different authors, of the Foucauldian analysis of discontinuous discursive regimes of truth; Gramsci's notion of "hegemony"; Bourdieu's conception of "symbolic violence" (the imposition of a cultural arbitrary by an arbitrary power, elaborated in Pierre Bourdieu and Jean-Claude Passeron, *Reproduction in Education, Society and Culture* [London: Sage, 1990]); Fanon's analysis of the psychology of colonial domination; and Louis Althusser's theory of "interpellation" in his essay on "Ideology and Ideological State Apparatus (Notes towards an Investigation)," in *Lenin and Philosophy and Other Essays* (New York: Monthly Review Press, 2001). *Epistemic violence* is Gayatri Chakravorty Spivak's term: see *A Critique of Postcolonial Reason: Toward a History of the Vanishing Present* (Cambridge, MA: Harvard University Press, 1999).

30. Spivak, *Critique of Postcolonial Reason,* 199, 211.

31. For an important text that privileges the pedagogical moment, see Gauri Viswanathan, *Masks of Conquest: Literary Study and British Rule in India* (London: Faber and Faber, 1990); and for the brilliant founding moments of the "colonial knowledge" model, see Bernard Cohn, *An Anthropologist among the Historians and Other Essays* (Delhi: Oxford University Press, 1987). For a recent sophisticated critique of the hypostatizing tendencies of postcolonial critiques of "Western modernity," see Frederick Cooper, *Colonialism in Question: Theory, Knowledge, History* (Berkeley: University of California Press, 2005).

32. See, especially, Chakrabarty, *Provincializing Europe;* Ranajit Guha, "Dominance without Hegemony and Its Historiography," in *Subaltern Studies VI: Writings on South Asian History and Society,* ed. Ranajit Guha (Delhi: Oxford University Press, 1992); and Gyan Prakash, *Another Reason: Science and the Imagination of Modern India* (Princeton, NJ: Princeton University Press, 1999).

33. Chatterjee, *Nationalist Thought,* 40.

34. Ibid., chap. 2.

35. Ibid., 168-69.

36. Partha Chatterjee, *The Nation and Its Fragments: Colonial and Postcolonial Histories* (Princeton, NJ: Princeton University Press, 1993), 6.

37. Chatterjee, *Nation and Its Fragments,* 13.

38. The critique of Chatterjee elaborated in this paragraph partly parallels Manu Goswami's acute analysis in *Producing India: From Colonial Economy to National Space* (Chicago: University of Chicago Press, 2004), 21-27.

39. Chatterjee, *Nation and Its Fragments,* 11, 237.

40. Ibid., 235-37.

41. Ibid., 6.

42. Ibid., 236.

43. Ibid., 235.

44. Goswami, *Producing India,* 25.

45. Chatterjee, *Nation and Its Fragment,* 197-99 (emphasis added).

46. Chatterjee, *Nationalist Thought,* 38.

47. On Okakura in Calcutta, see Stephen Hay, *Asian Ideas of East and West: Tagore and His Critics in Japan, China, and India* (Cambridge, MA: Harvard University Press, 1970).

48. The argument of this book is most deeply indebted theoretically to Moishe Postone, *Time, Labor, and Social Domination: A Reinterpretation of Marx's Critical Theory* (Cambridge: Cambridge University Press, 1996). For the most lucid discussion of the inadequacies of base-superstructure models to Marx's approach, see Derek Sayer, *The Violence of Abstraction: The Analytic Foundations of Historical Materialism* (Oxford and New York: Blackwell, 1987).

49. Norbert Elias, *The Civilizing Process,* trans. Edmund Jephcott (Cambridge, MA: Blackwell, 1994).

50. Karl Marx, *Capital: A Critique of Political Economy,* vol. 1 (London: Penguin Classics, 1990), 92.

51. Marx, *Capital: A Critique of Political Economy,* vol. 1, 90.

52. This point is central to the argument of William H. Sewell Jr., "A Theory of Structure: Duality, Agency, and Transformation," in *Logics of History: Social Theory and Social Transformation* (Chicago: University of Chicago Press, 2005), 124-51.

53. Chakrabarty, *Provincializing Europe,* chap. 1.

54. Guha, "Dominance without Hegemony," 220 (emphasis in original).

55. Ibid., 271 (emphasis in original).

56. The example of agriculture will be taken up in more detail in the following chapter. For a suggestive discussion of the transformations in caste-based marriage in later colonial Bengal, see Rochona Majumdar, "Looking for Brides and Grooms: Ghataks, Matrimonials, and the Marriage Market in Bengal, c. 1875-1940," *Journal of Asian Studies* 63, no. 4 (2004): 911-35.

CHAPTER TWO

1. In *History and Class Consciousness*, trans. Rodney Livingstone (Cambridge, MA: MIT Press, 1971), 27-45; quotation is on p. 34 (emphasis in original).

2. The prominent English Comtean, Frederic Harrison, for instance, wrote good-humoredly of Arnold's "fiddlestick, or sauerkraut, or culture (call it as you please)," in "Culture: A Dialogue," *Fortnightly Review* 2 (July-December 1867): 603-14.

3. In *Über Pädagogik* (Langensalza: Hermann Beyer and Sons, 1883), Kant refers in §1 to "Unterweisung nebst der Bildung," and in §7 to "Kultur (so kann man die Unterweisung nennen)." Mendelssohn's contrastive definitions in his essay "Über die Frage, was heißt aufklären?" are cited in Rudolph Vierhaus, "Bildung," in *Geschichtliche Grundbegriffe: Historisches Lexikon zur politisch-sozialen Sprache in Deutschland*, 8 vols., ed. Otto Brunner, Werner Conze, and Reinhart Koselleck (vol. 1; Stuttgart: Ernst Klett, 1972), 1:508.

4. See Anthony La Vopa, *Grace, Talent, and Merit: Poor Students, Clerical Careers, and Professional Ideology in Eighteenth-Century Germany* (Cambridge: Cambridge University Press, 1988), esp. chap. 9; Vierhaus, "Bildung."

5. Jörg Fisch, "Zivilisation, Kultur," in *Geschichtliche Grundbegriffe: Historisches Lexikon zur politisch-sozialen Sprache in Deutschland*, 8 vols., ed. Otto Brunner, Werner Conze, and Reinhart Koselleck (vol. 7; Stuttgart: Klett-Cotta, 1992), 7:685, 700-703; Philippe Bénéton, *Histoire de mots: Culture et civilisation* (Paris: Presses de la Fondation Nationale des Sciences Politiques, 1975), 30. The *OED* cites Wordsworth's *Preludes* (1805) as the earliest example of this stand-alone usage in English, but one could certainly find significantly earlier examples.

6. Lucien Febvre, "*Civilisation:* Evolution of a Word and a Group of Ideas," in *A New Kind of History*, ed. Peter Burke (New York: Harper and Row, 1973), 219-57; and Emile Benveniste, "Civilization: A Contribution to the History of the Word," in *Problems in General Linguistics*, trans. Mary Elizabeth Meek (Coral Gables, FL: University of Miami Press, 1971), 289-96.

7. See Fisch, "Zivilisation, Kultur," 679.

8. Sigmund Freud, *The Future of an Illusion*, trans. W. D. Robson-Scott (London: Hogarth Press, 1943), 7n1.

9. La Vopa, *Grace, Talent, and Merit*, 264-78.

10. Norbert Elias, *The Civilizing Process*, trans. Edmund Jephcott (Cambridge, MA: Blackwell, 1994), 3-28.

11. Fisch, "Zivilisation, Kultur," 681-82, 714-15, 722n246, 749-52; Bénéton, *Histoire de mots*, chaps. 4-5.

12. In fact, it is worth noting that Elias began his discussion with the more nuanced recognition that "the function of the German concept of *Kultur* took on a new life in the year 1919," but that in doing so it was reactivating and reappropriating an older conceptual antithesis that had its "concrete point of departure" in the "significantly different" historical context of the late eighteenth century. See Elias, *Civilizing Process*, 7. This was a nuance to which Herbert Marcuse was also drawing attention more or less contemporarily, and without at all reducing the concept to its nationalistic homology: "Although the distinction between civilization and culture may have joined only recently the mental equipment of the social and cultural sciences, the state of affairs that it expresses has long been characteristic of the conduct of life and the weltanschauung of the bourgeois era" (Herbert Marcuse, "The Affirmative Character of Culture," in *Negations: Essays in Critical Theory* [Boston: Beacon Press, 1968], 88-133). Meanwhile, T. C. W. Blanning has recently restated the importance of the eighteenth-century conceptual opposition between Frenchness and Germanness in his *The Culture of Power and the Power of Culture: Old Regime Europe, 1660-1789* (Oxford: Oxford University Press, 2003), 232-65.

13. David Blackbourn has briefly but suggestively linked the emergence of cultural discourses in late nineteenth-century Germany to the economic instability of the Great Depression of 1873-96,

and thereby helped to locate the specificities of these discourses within an international frame, in "The Discrete Charm of the Bourgeoisie: Reappraising German History in the Nineteenth Century," in *The Peculiarities of German History: Bourgeois Society and Politics in Nineteenth-Century Germany*, ed. David Blackbourn and Geoff Eley (Oxford: Oxford University Press, 1984), 206-21. On the role of Treitschke in leading the shift in German attitudes toward England from the 1870s, see Charles E. McClelland, *The German Historians and England: A Study in Nineteenth-Century Views* (Cambridge: Cambridge University Press, 1971), part 4. Fritz Ringer has given the best-known account of the German academy's renewed emphasis on the culture-civilization dichotomy in the later nineteenth century, in *The Decline of the German Mandarins: The German Academic Community, 1890-1933* (Middletown, CT: Wesleyan University Press; Hanover, NH: published by University Press of New England, 1990).

14. Raymond Williams has provided the classic account of the English tradition of cultural criticism in *Culture and Society, 1780-1950* (New York: Columbia University Press, 1983).

15. John Morrow, ed., *Coleridge's Writings*, vol. 1, *On Politics and Society* (Princeton, NJ: Princeton University Press, 1991), 176.

16. Matthew Arnold, *Culture and Anarchy* (Cambridge: Cambridge University Press, 1963), 48-49.

17. Bénéton, *Histoire de mots*, 56-59, 73-76.

18. Jean Starobinski, *Blessings in Disguise; or, The Morality of Evil* (Cambridge, MA: Harvard University Press, 1993), chap. 1.

19. See Jan Goldstein, "Mutations of the Self in Old Regime and Postrevolutionary France," in *Biographies of Scientific Objects*, ed. Lorraine Daston (Chicago: University of Chicago Press, 2000), 86-116. Cousin, Bénéton notes (*Histoire de mots*, 56-57), was also instrumental in introducing the French public to the philosophies of Fichte, Schelling, and Hegel.

20. See Francois Guizot, *General History of Civilization in Europe from the Fall of the Roman Empire to the French Revolution* (New York: D. Appleton, 1928).

21. A. L. Kroeber and Clyde Kluckhohn, *Culture: A Critical Review of Concepts and Definitions* (New York: Vintage, 1963), 29-30.

22. John Stuart Mill, "On Liberty," in *The Collected Works of John Stuart Mill*, vol. 21, *Essays on Equality, Law, and Education* (Toronto and Buffalo: University of Toronto Press; London: Routledge and Kegan Paul, 1984); and see also Wilhelm von Humboldt, *The Limits of State Action* (Cambridge: Cambridge University Press, 1969).

23. John Stuart Mill, "Civilization," in *The Collected Works of John Stuart Mill*, vol. 28, *Essays on Politics and Society* (Toronto and Buffalo: University of Toronto Press; London: Routledge and Kegan Paul,, 1977), 117-47.

24. Fraser Neimann, ed., *Essays, Letters, and Reviews by Matthew Arnold* (Cambridge, MA: Harvard University Press, 1960), 105; Arnold, *Culture and Anarchy*, 75, 82, 95-97.

25. See David Lloyd and Paul Thomas, *Culture and the State* (New York and London: Routledge, 1998).

26. Stefan Collini has written persuasively concerning the ubiquity of anxieties about the social consequences of the generalized pursuit of self-interest in Britain in the second half of the nineteenth century, noting Victorian social critics' "obsessive antipathy to selfishness" and their "constant anxiety about the possibility of sinking into a state of psychological malaise or anomie, a kind of emotional entropy assumed to be the consequence of absorption in purely selfish aims," in *Public Moralists: Political Thought and Intellectual Life in Britain, 1850-1930* (Oxford: Clarendon Press, 1991), 65.

27. Kroeber and Kluckhohn, *Culture*, 26.

28. Wilhelm von Humboldt, *On Language: On the Diversity of Human Language Construction and Its Influence on the Mental Development of the Human Species* (Cambridge: Cambridge University Press, 1999), 34; Kroeber and Kluckhohn, *Culture*, 26.

29. Humboldt, *On Language*, 34-35.

30. Ibid., 35.

31. Ibid., 30.

32. Ibid., 23, 30-31.

33. La Vopa, *Grace, Talent, and Merit*, 272.

34. Humboldt, *On Language*, 34.

35. Immanuel Kant, *Critique of Judgment*, trans. Werner S. Pluhar (Indianapolis: Hacket, 1987), §83, 319, translator's interpolations.

36. Immanuel Kant, *Critique of Pure Reason*, trans. Norman Kemp Smith (Houndmills, NY: Palgrave Macmillan, 2003), 575 (A 709-10, B 737-38).

37. Immanuel Kant, "Idea for a Universal History from a Cosmopolitan Point of View," in *On History: Immanuel Kant*, ed. Lewis White Beck (New York: Macmillan, 1963), 21.

38. Raymond Geuss makes this claim in "Kultur, Bildung, Geist," in his *Morality, Culture, and History: Essays on German Philosophy* (Cambridge: Cambridge University Press, 1999), 33-34.

39. Kant, *Über Pädagogik*, §§3-4 (my emphasis).

40. See Robert B. Pippin, *Idealism as Modernism: Hegelian Variations* (Cambridge: Cambridge University Press, 1997), chaps. 3 and 4; Allen W. Wood, *Kant's Ethical Thought* (Cambridge: Cambridge University Press, 1999); and Yirmiahu Yovel, *Kant and the Philosophy of History* (Princeton, NJ: Princeton University Press, 1980).

41. Immanuel Kant, "Conjectural Beginning of Human History," in Beck, ed., *On History*, 60-63.

42. Kroeber and Kluckhohn, *Culture*, 29.

43. Ibid., 284. Proceeding from this anthropological universalization of culture, the older part-whole relationship of culture and civilization could be reversed, so that civilization could specify that subset of cultures that had achieved certain levels of technical advancement. See, for example, Robert Redfield, "Civilizations as Things Thought About," in *Human Nature and the Study of Society: The Papers of Robert Redfield*, vol. 1, ed. Margaret Park Redfield (Chicago: University of Chicago Press, 1962), 367-71.

44. Raymond Williams appears to be partly responsible for the ubiquity of this misrepresentation. See *Keywords: A Vocabulary of Culture and Society* (New York: Oxford University Press, 1983), 89.

45. Johann Gottfried von Herder, *Reflections on the Philosophy of the History of Mankind*, abridged ed. (Chicago: University of Chicago Press, 1968), 100-101; and cf. Fisch, "Zivilisation, Kultur," 708-12.

46. Herder, *Philosophy of the History of Mankind*, 110-11.

47. Ibid., 84 (my emphasis).

48. In Kroeber and Kluckhohn, *Culture*, 35-38.

49. Fisch, "Zivilisation, Kultur," 746-48.

50. George W. Stocking Jr., *Race, Culture, and Evolution: Essays in the History of Anthropology* (New York: Free Press, 1968), 72-73.

51. Sigmund Freud, *Civilization and Its Discontents* (New York and London: W. W. Norton, 1961), 36-50.

52. Sigmund Freud, *New Introductory Lectures on Psychoanalysis* (New York: W. W. Norton, 1965), 100.

53. Adam Kuper, *Culture: The Anthropologists' Account* (Cambridge, MA: Harvard University Press, 1999), chap. 2.

54. See Carl Pletsch, "The Three Worlds Concept and the Division of Social Scientific Labor, Circa 1950-1975," *Comparative Studies in Society and History* 23, no. 4 (1981): 565-90.

55. Claude Lévi-Strauss, *The Savage Mind* (Chicago: University of Chicago Press, 1966), 66-70, 130-31.

56. Roy Boyne, "Culture and the World System," *Theory, Culture and Society* 7, nos. 2 and 3 (1990): 57-62.

57. See Elman R. Service, *A Century of Controversy: Ethnological Issues from 1860 to 1960* (Orlando, FL: Academic Press, 1985), chap. 16.

58. Geuss, "Kultur, Bildung, Geist," 36-37; Kroeber and Kluckhohn, *Culture*, 47; Ringer, *Decline of the German Mandarins*.

59. Heinrich Rickert, *Science and History: A Critique of Positivist Epistemology* (Princeton, NJ: D. Van Nostrand, 1962). See also Andrew Arato, "The Neo-Idealist Defense of Subjectivity," *Telos* 21 (1974): 108-61.

60. Bronislaw Malinowski, *Argonauts of the Western Pacific: An Account of Native Enterprise and Adventure in the Archipelagoes of Melanesian New Guinea* (London: Routledge, 1922), 60-62.

61. Ian Hunter, *Culture and Government: The Emergence of Literary Education* (London: Macmillan, 1988).

62. Lloyd and Thomas, *Culture and the State*, 16-20.

63. Ibid., 3-5.

64. Ibid., 15.

65. Ibid., 118.

66. Williams, *Culture and Society*, xviii.

67. Andrew Sartori, "Emancipation as Heteronomy: The Crisis of Liberalism in Later Nineteenth-Century Bengal, *Journal of Historical Sociology* 17, no. 1 (2004): 56-86.

68. Boris Jakim and Robert Bird, trans. and eds., *On Spiritual Unity: A Slavophile Reader; Aleksei Khomiakov and Ivan Kireevsky* (Hudson, NY: Lindisfarne Books, 1998), 187-88, 213.

69. Kroeber and Kluckhohn, *Culture*, 53-54; Frank Fadner, *Seventy Years of Pan-Slavism in Russia: Karazin to Danilevskii, 1800-1870* (Washington, DC: Georgetown University Press, 1961), 314-38; Andrzej Walicki, *The Slavophile Controversy: History of a Conservative Utopia in Nineteenth-Century Russian Thought* (Notre Dame, IN: University of Notre Dame Press, 1989), chaps. 12 and 13.

70. In Walicki, *Slavophile Controversy*, 529, where the author cites Williams to draw a direct parallel between Slavophilism and the British tradition of cultural criticism.

71. *Bunka* was widely understood in the Meiji period to be an abbreviation of *bunmeikaika*. By the 1920s, however, it had been clearly established as the translative equivalent of *Kultur*, and (on the model of *Kultur/Zivilisation*) it could be opposed to *bunmei*, or the material civilization with which the Meiji era was associated. In China, the character (*kanji*) used in Japan for *bunka* was then "translated back" into its classical Chinese equivalent, *wen-hua*, to allow the classical term to do the new work of translating the concept of culture. See Douglas Howland, *Borders of Chinese Civilization: Geography and History at Empire's End* (Durham, NC: Duke University Press, 1996), 294n37; Liu, *Translingual Practice*, 32-34, 239.

72. Howland, *Borders of Chinese Civilization;* Tessa Morris-Suzuki, "The Invention and Reinvention of 'Japanese Culture,'" *Journal of Asian Studies* 54, no. 3 (1995): 762-63.

73. Howland, *Borders of Chinese Civilization*, 65.

74. Prasenjit Duara, "The Discourse of Civilization and Pan-Asianism," *Journal of World History* 12, no. 1 (2001): 99-130; Stephen N. Hay, *Asian Ideas of East and West: Tagore and His Critics in Japan, China, and India* (Cambridge, MA: Harvard University Press, 1970); Liu, *Translingual Practice;* Morris-Suzuki, "Invention and Reinvention of 'Japanese Culture.'"

75. See Duara, "Discourse of Civilization"; Morris-Suzuki, "Invention and Reinvention of 'Japanese Culture,'" 762.

76. Dipesh Chakrabarty, *Provincializing Europe: Postcolonial Thought and Historical Difference* (Princeton, NJ: Princeton University Press, 2000); Liu, *Translingual Practice;* Tejaswini Niranjana, *Siting Translation: History, Post-Structuralism, and the Colonial Context* (Berkeley: University of California Press, 1992); Vicente L. Rafael, *Contracting Colonialism: Translation and Christian Conversion in Tagalog Society under Early Spanish Rule* (Ithaca, NY: Cornell University Press, 1988).

77. Chakrabarty, *Provincializing Europe*.

78. Roman Jakobson, "On Linguistic Aspects of Translation," in *Theories of Translation: An Anthology of Essays from Dryden to Derrida*, ed. Rainer Schulte and John Biguenet (Chicago: University of Chicago Press, 1992), 144-51.

79. For the distinction between sense and meaning, see Lev Vygotsky, *Thought and Language* (Cambridge, MA: MIT Press, 1986), chap. 7.

80. Ferdinand de Saussure, *Course in General Linguistics* (New York: McGraw-Hill, 1966), 114-17.

81. See, for example, William F. Hanks, *Language and Communicative Practice* (Boulder, CO: Westview, 1996); *Language and Communication* 23, nos. 3-4 (2003), "Words and Beyond: Linguistic and Semiotic Studies of Sociocultural Order," a special issue edited by Paul Manning; and especially Webb Keane's contribution, "Semiotics and the Social Analysis of Material Things," 409-25. Paul Manning's work has been especially helpful to me in formulating the problem at hand more clearly: see especially his "Owning and Belonging: A Semiotic Investigation of the Affective Categories of a Bourgeois Society," *Comparative Studies in Society and History* 46, no. 2 (2004): 300-325.

82. In this reading of Marx, I am following Moishe Postone, *Time, Labor, and Social Domination: A Reinterpretation of Marx's Critical Theory* (Cambridge: Cambridge University Press, 1996).

83. Adam Smith, *An Inquiry into the Nature and Causes of the Wealth of Nations*, 2 vols. (Chicago: University of Chicago Press, 1976), esp. 1:15-19. It is worth noting that Smith reiterates this same fundamental point in his other great work, *The Theory of Moral Sentiments* (New York: Cambridge University Press, 2002).

84. Smith, *Wealth of Nations*, 1:17.

85. Karl Marx, *Capital: A Critique of Political Economy*, vol. 1 (London: Penguin Classics, 1990), 166.

86. Marx, *Capital: A Critique of Political Economy*, 1:64-65.

87. In fact, just as Smith distinguished real price from nominal and market price, Marx's category of exchange value does *not* correspond to the economic category of price, which is a form of appearance that further obscures the functioning of the value form. Whereas value is a category that seeks to grasp analytically the structure of social interdependence, price is a category that seeks to describe the actual quantities involved in particular exchanges without speaking to the conditions under which exchange assumes fundamental importance. The trajectory of the three volumes of *Capital* from value to price and surplus value to profit does not express an overarching attempt to develop a more adequate price theory (as was argued both by classical Marxists like Rosa Luxemburg and early critics of Marx like Eugen von Böhm-Bawerk), but rather to grasp how the underlying structures of modern society take on forms of appearance that disguise their essential determinations. See Postone, *Time, Labor, and Social Domination*, 132-35.

88. Rajat Kanta Ray, *Social Conflict and Political Unrest in Bengal, 1875-1927* (Delhi: Oxford University Press, 1984), 53.

89. Gopalacandra Ray, *Anya ek bankimcandra* (Calcutta: De's Publishing, 1979), 23, 59-60.

90. Karl Marx, *Grundrisse: Foundations of the Critique of Political Economy (Rough Draft)* (London: Penguin, 1973), 410 (emphasis in original).

91. Marx, *Grundrisse*, 459-60 (emphasis in original).

92. Ibid., 409-10 (emphasis in original).

93. The theoretical argument that follows is most fundamentally indebted to the writings of Jairus Banaji; see "Capitalist Domination and the Small Peasantry: The Deccan Districts in the Late Nineteenth Century," *Economic and Political Weekly* 7, no. 33-34 (special number) (1977): 1375-404; Jairus Banaji, "Modes of Production in a Materialist Conception of History," *Capital and Class* 3 (1977): 1-44; Jairus Banaji, "The Fictions of Free Labour: Contract, Coercion, and So-Called Unfree Labour," *Historical Materialism* 11, no. 3 (2003): 69-95.

94. Hameeda Hossain, *The Company Weavers of Bengal: The East India Company and the Organization of Textile Production in Bengal, 1750-1813* (Delhi: Oxford University Press, 1988).

95. On the rationale driving the Permanent Settlement, see Ranajit Guha, *A Rule of Property for Bengal: An Essay on the Idea of Permanent Settlement* (Durham, NC: Duke University Press, 1996).

96. Rajat Datta, *Society, Economy, and the Market: Commercialization in Rural Bengal, c. 1760-1800* (New Delhi: Manohar, 2000), 16 (emphasis in original).

97. On the rent offensive, see Sugata Bose, *The New Cambridge History of India*, III, 2, *Peasant Labour and Colonial Capital: Rural Bengal since 1770* (Cambridge: Cambridge University Press, 1993), 114-19.

98. Rajat Kanta Ray, *Social Conflict and Political Unrest in Bengal, 1875-1927* (Delhi: Oxford University Press, 1984), 13.

99. See Sugata Bose, *Agrarian Bengal: Economy, Social Structure, and Politics, 1919-1947* (Cambridge: Cambridge University Press, 1986), chaps. 2 and 3.

100. Amales Tripathi, *Trade and Finance in the Bengal Presidency, 1793-1833* (Calcutta: Oxford University Press, 1979), 155.

101. Bose, *Agrarian Bengal*, 58.

102. My discussion of indigo production is drawn from Bose, *Peasant Labour and Colonial Capital*, 45-52; Benoy Chowdhury, *Growth of Commercial Agriculture in Bengal, 1757-1900* (Calcutta: Indian Studies Past and Present, 1964), 1:73-203; Blair B. Kling, *The Blue Mutiny: The Indigo Disturbances in Bengal, 1859-1862* (Philadelphia: University of Pennsylvania Press, 1966); and Chittabrata Palit, *Tensions in Bengal Rural Society: Landlords, Planters, and Colonial Rule, 1830-1860* (Calcutta: Progressive, 1975), chaps. 4 and 5.

103. Bose, *Peasant Labor and Colonial Capital*, 74.

104. Quotation cited from ibid., 47.

105. Ibid., 51-52; and Chowdhury, *Growth of Commercial Agriculture*, 1:192-203.

106. Bose, *Peasant Labour and Colonial Capital*, 53; ibid., 52-63; B. B. Chaudhuri, "Growth of Commercial Agriculture in Bengal, 1859-1885," *Indian Economic and Social History Review* 7, nos. 1 and 2 (1970): 25-60, 211-51.

107. This complaint, coupled with the declaration that indigo would no longer be cultivated regardless of the terms of the contract or the remunerativeness of the crop, was voiced repeatedly and ubiquitously by cultivators. See the Minutes of Evidence, *Report of the Indigo Commission, 1860*.

108. "Condition of the Serving Class," editorial of May 14, 1857, *Hindu Patriot*, cited from Chowdhury, *Growth of Commercial Agriculture*, 1:200.

109. Chowdhury, *Growth of Commercial Agriculture*, 1:198.

110. Bose, *Peasant Labour and Colonial Capital*, 119-22; Palit, *Tensions in Bengal Rural Society*, chap. 6.

111. Minutes of Evidence, *Report of the Indigo Commission, 1860*, 101.

112. Bose, *Peasant Labour and Colonial Capital*, 86.

113. Ibid., 122-30.

114. J. B. P., "Rustic Bengal," *Calcutta Review* 59, no. 117 (1874): 180-214; quotations are on pp. 200-201 (emphasis added).

115. Bose, *Agrarian Bengal*.

116. Datta, *Society, Economy, and the Market*, esp. chap. 4.

117. Cited from Datta, *Society, Economy, and the Market*, 220.

118. Bose, *Peasant Labour and Colonial Capital*, 118; Chowdhury, *Growth of Commercial Agriculture*, 1:175.

119. Bose makes this quite explicit in his analysis of rural credit mechanisms; see *Agrarian Bengal* and *Peasant Labour and Colonial Capital*, chap. 4.

120. Samita Sen, *Women and Labour in Late Colonial India: The Bengal Jute Industry* (Cambridge: Cambridge University Press, 1999), 74-83.

121. Bose, *Agrarian Bengal*, 11-18, Bose, *Peasant Labour and Colonial Capitalism*, 93-95.

122. C. R. Marindin in Lord Dufferin's *Report on the Condition of the Lower Classes of Population in Bengal* (1888), cited from Sen, *Women and Labour*, 84-85.

123. Sen, *Women and Labour*, 81.

124. Bose, *Peasant Labour and Colonial Capital*, 99.

125. Ibid., 97-103.

126. Sen, *Women and Labour*, 54-65, 83-88.

127. Robert Tucker, ed., *The Marx-Engels Reader*, 2nd ed. (New York and London: W. W. Norton, 1978), 154-55.

128. This is more than theoretical lip service. That historically constituted subjectivity is a consequential moment of social reproduction becomes quite clear when we focus on its transformative potential. Subjects constitute sociohistorical structures through their actions, yet their actions are not formed in the metaphysical vacuum of absolute freedom, but rather "under circumstances directly found, given and transmitted from the past" (Tucker, ed., *Marx-Engels Reader*, 595). These circumstances being contradictory, the formation of subjectivity within capitalist society does not in the least imply the Durkheimian thesis that such subjectivities are therefore in harmony with social homeostasis. To take just a single example directly from *Capital*: the workers' full recognition of their status as commodity owners in the sphere of circulation where they sell their labor power gives rise to the demand for a shorter working day. It is by engaging in the sale of their labor power that the workers discover that they are commodity owners, and hence, as "bourgeois subjects," both free and equal. Meanwhile, liberal capitalist subjects, insofar as they are operating within the logic of equal exchange, can in principle be persuaded to support the claims of the worker to a shorter workday. Yet insofar as the capitalist is concerned to ensure the continuous expansion of their capital, the capitalist must also resist the limitation of the workday, demanding the full value of the day's labor power they have purchased. This in turn leads to a struggle between right and right that can only be settled through the contingencies of political struggle. The worker and the bourgeois, both treated in *Capital* systematically as "personifications of economic categories" rather than as simple empirical categories, are instances of historically constituted subjectivities that both reproduce and transform capitalist society. See Marx, *Capital: A Critique of Political Economy*, vol. 1, 92, 340-44.

129. Theodor W. Adorno, "Subject and Object," in *The Essential Frankfurt School Reader*, ed. Andrew Arato and Eike Gebhardt (New York: Continuum, 1997), 497-511.

130. See especially Adorno's introductory essay in Theodor W. Adorno et al., *The Positivist Dispute in German Sociology*, trans. Glyn Adey and David Frisby (Aldershot: Avebury, 1976), 1-67.

131. See Reinhart Koselleck, "Begriffsgeschichte and Social History," in his *Futures Past: On the Semantics of Historical Time*, trans. Keith Tribe (Cambridge, MA: MIT Press, 1985), 73-91.

132. Georg Lukács, "What Is Orthodox Marxism?" in *History and Class Consciousness*, 1-26.

133. The Habermasian critique of Marxism as a (subjectivist) philosophy of labor thus becomes a critique of much of the Marxist tradition (of which I take Lukács to be one of the most brilliant expressions), but does not apply to the critique of labor that Marx made possible. See Postone, *Time, Labor, and Social Domination*, 226-60.

134. The discussion of Lukács that follows seeks to elaborate on Postone's critique in *Time, Labor, and Social Domination*, 71-83; and his "Lukács and the Dialectical Critique of Capitalism," in *New Dialectics and Political Economy*, ed. Rob Albritton and John Simoulidis (Houndsmill, Basingstoke, and New York: Palgrave Macmillan, 2003).

135. Lukács, "Reification and the Consciousness of the Proletariat," in *History and Class Consciousness*, 83-222; quotation is on p. 121.

136. Lukács, "Reification and the Consciousness of the Proletariat," 110.

137. Ibid., 110.

138. In ibid., 136.

139. In ibid., 136-37.

140. In ibid., 139 (emphasis in original).

141. Georg Lukács, *Goethe and His Age* (New York: Grosset and Dunlap, 1969).

142. For a suggestive discussion of the relationship of Lukács's early writings to his mature theory, see Gyorgy Markus, "Life and the Soul: the Young Lukács and the Problem of Culture," in *Lukács Reappraised*, ed. Agnes Heller (New York: Columbia University Press, 1983), 1–26. Herbert Marcuse made a very similar argument in his essay on "The Affirmative Character of Culture," tracing the emergence of a genuinely critical humanism in the later eighteenth century through its subsequent collapse into an affirmative conception of culture as the resolution of contradiction through the inner formation of individual bourgeois subjectivity. Culture's drift into idealism, Marcuse argued, was the result of an attempt by the newly dominant bourgeois classes to contain the critical energies of the humanistic vision of total personality by sequestering its practice of autonomous human self-realization as far as possible from the contradictory practices of actual capitalist social relations. This circumscription of the domain of cultural activity transformed culture from a critical concept that stood in constitutive contradiction with capitalist society into an affirmative or noncontradictory one that sought simply to exist alongside it. Herbert Marcuse, "The Affirmative Character of Culture," in his *Negations: Essays in Critical Theory* (Boston: Beacon Press, 1968), 88–133. Alongside Marcuse's ultimately Williamsesque defense of culture as the negative principle of modern capitalism, however, is a more ambivalent attitude that, even as it holds up the figure of man as the affirmation of social totality (culture as the rationality of productive activity), explicitly recognizes that Marx's politics turned not on the liberation of labor from exploitation, but rather, and more fundamentally, on the "abolition of labor." See Herbert Marcuse, *Reason and Revolution: Hegel and the Rise of Social Theory* (Boston: Beacon Press, 1960), 287–95. But, still aligning reason with Hegel's conception of totality, Marcuse seemed never quite capable of realizing the implications of this argument, reaffirming the culturalist conception of "humanity" explicitly in his recuperation of Schiller in *Eros and Civilization: A Philosophical Inquiry into Freud* (London: Ark, 1987), chap. 9. On totality as a category of capitalist society rather than the rational principle negating capitalist society, see Postone, *Time, Labor, and Social Domination*, 71–83.

143. This is also, in the end, the core of Lloyd and Thomas's critique of Williams's attachment to the figure of man. But whereas they would dissolve this figure into a strategy of class domination, I would rather seek to understand the historical availability of the concept more fundamentally in terms of its social constitution through the structuring practices of capitalist modernity.

144. Lukács, *History and Class Consciousness*, 134.

145. Postone, *Time, Labor, and Social Domination*.

CHAPTER THREE

1. D. A. Washbrook, "India, 1818–1860: The Two Faces of Colonialism," in *The Oxford History of the British Empire*, vol. 3, *The Nineteenth Century*, ed. Andrew Porter (Oxford and New York: Oxford University Press, 1999), 395–421; and see also C. A. Bayly, *The New Cambridge History of India*, II, 1, *Indian Society and the Making of the British Empire* (Cambridge: Cambridge University Press, 1988).

2. David Kopf, *The Brahmo Samaj and the Shaping of the Modern Indian Mind* (Princeton, NJ: Princeton University Press, 1979), 9–10.

3. Barun De, "The Colonial Context of the Bengal Renaissance," in *Indian Society and the Beginnings of Modernization*, ed. C. H. Philips and M. D. Wainwright (London: SOAS, 1976); Barun De, "A Historiographical Critique of Renaissance Analogues for Nineteenth-Century India," in *Perspectives in Social Science*, vol. 1, *Historical Dimensions*, ed. Barun De (Calcutta: Oxford University Press, 1977); Sumit Sarkar, "Rammohun Roy and the Break with the Past," in *Rammohun Roy and the Process of Modernization in India*, ed. V. C. Joshi (Delhi: Vikas, 1975), 46–68; Asok Sen, *Iswar Chandra Vidyasagar and His Elusive Milestones* (Calcutta: Riddhi-India, 1977); Asok Sen, "The Bengal Economy and Rammohun Roy," in Joshi ed., *Rammohun Roy and the Process of Modernization*. See also Partha Chatterjee, *Nationalist Thought and the Colonial World: A Derivative Discourse?* (London:

Zed Books, 1986), 22-28; and Brian Hatcher, "Great Men Waking: Paradigms in the Historiography of the Bengal Renaissance," in *Bengal: Rethinking History; Essays in Historiography*, ed. Sekhar Bandyopadhyay (New Delhi: Manohar, 2001), 135-63.

4. Chatterjee, *Nationalist Thought and the Colonial World*, was a crucial intervention in this respect.

5. Anthony Pagden, *Peoples and Empires: A Short History of European Migration, Exploration, and Conquest, from Greece to the Present* (New York: Modern Library, 2003), 168-69.

6. Thomas Edwards, *Henry Derozio* (Calcutta: Riddhi-India, 1980), 111-20.

7. Hugh Urban, *The Economics of Ecstasy: Tantra, Secrecy, and Power in Colonial Bengal* (Oxford: Oxford University Press, 2001); and see also Urban's translations of many Kartabhaja and Sahebdhani songs in the companion volume, *Songs of Ecstasy: Tantric and Devotional Songs from Colonial Bengal* (Oxford: Oxford University Press, 2001).

8. On liberalism in the wider imperial context, see Thomas C. Holt's masterpiece, *The Problem of Freedom: Race, Labor, and Politics in Jamaica and Britain, 1832-1938* (Baltimore: Johns Hopkins University Press, 1992); Catherine Hall, *Civilising Subjects: Metropole and Colony in the English Imagination, 1830-1867* (Chicago: University of Chicago Press, 2002); Thomas Metcalf, *The New Cambridge History of India*, III,. 4., *Ideologies of the Raj* (Cambridge: Cambridge University Press, 1995); Bernard Semmel, *The Rise of Free Trade Imperialism: Classical Political Economy, the Empire of Free Trade and Imperialism, 1750-1850* (Cambridge: Cambridge University Press, 1970); and Eric Stokes, *The English Utilitarians and India* (Delhi: Oxford University Press, 1989). For prominent accounts of the emergence of the conception of the empire as British, Protestant, maritime, and free in the early modern period, see David Armitage, *The Ideological Origins of the British Empire* (Cambridge: Cambridge University Press, 2000), and Jack P. Greene, "Empire and Identity from the Glorious Revolution to the American Revolution," in *Oxford History of the British Empire: The Eighteenth Century*, ed. P. J. Marshall (Oxford: Oxford University Press, 2001). Steve Pincus's forthcoming book, *The First Modern Revolution*, will challenge some of the assumption of this literature in terms more consonant with the approach of this work. For a more general discussion on the contemporary historiography of British liberalism and the empire, and a critique of its constructivist and culturalist tendencies, see Andrew Sartori, "The British Empire and Its Liberal Mission," *Journal of Modern History* 78, no. 3 (2006): 623-42.

9. Karl Marx, *Capital: A Critique of Political Economy*, vol. 1 (London: Penguin Classics, 1990), 280; Karl Marx, *Grundrisse: Foundations of the Critique of Political Economy (Rough Draft)* (London: Penguin, 1973), 241-45.

10. Marx, *Grundrisse*, 245.

11. Steve Pincus, "Neither Machiavellian Moment nor Possessive Individualism: Commercial Society and the Defenders of the English Commonwealth," *American Historical Review* 103, no. 3 (1998): 705-36; quotations are on pp. 707-8.

12. See, for example, Brian A. Hatcher, *Idioms of Improvement: Vidyasagar and Cultural Encounter in Bengal* (Calcutta: Oxford University Press, 1996), and Bruce Carlisle Robertson, *Raja Rammohan Ray: The Father of Modern India* (Delhi: Oxford University Press, 1995), 154-55.

13. A. F. Salahuddin Ahmed, *Social Ideas and Social Change in Bengal, 1818-1835* (Leiden: Brill, 1965); Rajat Datta, *Society, Economy, and the Market: Commercialization in Rural Bengal, c. 1760-1800* (New Delhi: Manohar, 2000), chap. 3; Blair B. Kling, "Economic Foundations of the Bengal Renaissance," in *Aspects of Bengali History and Society*, ed. Rachel Van M. Baumer (Honolulu: University Press of Hawaii, 1975), 26-42; S. N. Mukherjee, *Calcutta: Essays in Urban History* (Calcutta: Subarnarekha, 1993), 117-31.

14. Manu Goswami, *Producing India: From Colonial Economy to National Space* (Chicago: University of Chicago Press, 2004).

15. See, for example, Amales Tripathi, *Trade and Finance in the Bengal Presidency, 1793-1833* (Calcutta: Oxford University Press, 1979); Sugata Bose, *The New Cambridge History of India*, III,

2, *Peasant Labour and Colonial Capital: Rural Bengal since 1770* (Cambridge: Cambridge University Press, 1993), 45-52; Kling, "Economic Foundations of the Bengal Renaissance;" Blair B. Kling, *Partner in Empire: Dwarkanath Tagore and the Age of Enterprise in Eastern India* (Berkeley: University of California Press, 1976).

16. William Bolts, *Considerations on India Affairs; Particularly Respecting the Present State of Bengal and Its Dependencies* (London, 1772), vii.

17. Bayly, *Indian Society and the Making of the British Empire,* 68-76; Kling, "Economic Foundations of the Bengal Renaissance;" Kling, *Partner in Empire,* chap. 2; Tripathi, *Trade and Finance,* 201-7; Washbrook, "The Two Faces of Colonialism," 410-11.

18. Cited from Kling, "Economic Foundations of the Bengal Renaissance," 38-39.

19. Rammohun certainly understood "India" as a subcontinental entity—but, emphasizing the diversity of its population, characterizes it as an "empire" rather than an organic entity. See Jogendra Chunder Ghose, ed., *The English Works of Raja Rammohun Roy* (New Delhi: Cosmo, 1982), 295, 389 (hereafter cited in text as *EW* followed by page reference).

20. C. A. Bayly, *The Birth of the Modern World, 1780-1914: Global Connections and Comparisons* (Malden, Oxford, and Carlton: Blackwell, 2004), 293.

21. E.g., Sarkar, "Rammohun Roy and the Break with the Past."

22. Jatindra Kumar Majumdar, ed., *Raja Rammohun Roy and Progressive Movements in India: A Selection from Records (1775-1845)* (Calcutta: Art Press, 1941), 447-48, 450-51.

23. See, for example, the many endorsements from the liberal press in Majumdar, ed., *Rammohun Roy and Progressive Movements;* and the glowing praise he received from Jeremy Bentham and his giddy reception in Europe, in Sophia Dobson Collet, *The Life and Letters of Raja Rammohun Roy,* ed. Dilip Kumar Biswas and Prabhat Chandra Ganguli (Calcutta: Sadharan Brahmo Samaj, 1962), 302-411, 488-92.

24. Hatcher, *Idioms of Improvement,* 196-206.

25. Mrityunjay Vidyalankar, *Vedanta chandrika,* in *Mrityunjay-granthabali,* ed. Brajendranath Bandyopadhyay (Calcutta: Ranjan, 1939), 191-213 (an English translation is also appended to the volume); D. H. Killingley, "Vedanta and Modernity," in *Indian Society and the Beginnings of Modernisation, c. 1830-1850,* ed. C. H. Philips and Mary Doreen Wainwright (London: SOAS, 1976), 127-40; Robertson, *Rammohan Ray,* 154-55.

26. On the fundamental distinction between the spontaneous impulse to sensual pleasure and the "element of reflection and calculation" implied by the term *interest,* see Albert O. Hirschman, *The Passions and the Interests: Political Arguments for Capitalism before Its Triumph* (Princeton, NJ: Princeton University Press, 1977), 32.

27. Sarkar, "Rammohun Roy and the Break with the Past," 53-55; A. F. Salahuddin Ahmed, "Rammohun Roy and His Contemporaries," in Joshi, ed., *Rammohun Roy and the Process of Modernization,* 99-101.

28. See Robertson, *Rammohan Ray,* 170.

29. Salahuddin Ahmed, *Social Ideas and Social Change,* 8-10; Majumdar, ed., *Rammohun Roy and Progressive Movements,* 437-39.

30. Majumdar, ed., *Rammohun Roy and Progressive Movements,* 411-12, 438-39.

31. Bose, *Peasant Labour and Colonial Capital,* 47.

32. Tripathi, *Trade and Finance,* 186.

33. Majumdar, ed., *Rammohun Roy and Progressive Movements,* 457-58; *EW* 284.

34. Cited from Robertson, *Rammohan Ray,* 48. On his enthusiasm for France, see Collet, *The Life and Letters,* 306-8.

35. C. A. Bayly, "Rammohun Roy and the Advent of Constitutional Liberalism in India, 1800-1830," *Modern Intellectual History* 4, no. 1 (2007): 25-41.

36. Collet, *Life and Letters,* 331-35.

37. Cf. Ted Koditschek, "Imagining a British India: History and the Reconstruction of Empire,"

from *Towards a Greater Britain? Liberal Imperialism and the Historical Imagination, 1800-1885* (unpublished manuscript).

38. See Collet, *Life and Letters*, 385-87.

39. Bayly, "Rammohun Roy."

40. See ibid., on the extraordinary cosmopolitanism of Roy's liberalism.

41. Rama Prasad Chanda and Jatindra Kumar Majumdar, eds., *Raja Rammohun Roy: Letters and Documents* (Delhi: Anmol, 1987), 95, 141-44, 255-72. Tapan Raychaudhuri has argued that the joint-family form had only become normative in the first place for upper-caste Bengali Hindus in the second half of the eighteenth century, in "Norms of Family Life and Personal Morality among the Bengali Hindu Elite, 1600-1850," in Baumer, ed., *Aspects of Bengali History and Society*, 13-25.

42. Chanda and Majumdar, eds., *Rammohun Roy*, xx-xlii; Carlisle, *Rammohan Ray*, 11-12, 22-23.

43. See Chakrabarty, *Provincializing Europe*, chap. 8. If Radhakanta Deb, his conservative rival, saw Rammohun's endeavor to spiritualize worldliness as innovation driven by the self-interested pursuit of respectability by a Brahman who had fallen from his ritual obligations, it was not because his position had been built on different foundations—his family had also risen to wealth and power through Company service—but because he had decided to equilibrate the threat of moral anomie inherent in the worldly pursuits that had made his grandfather so rich, with the moral respectability of lineage and piety. Cf. Syamalendu Sengupta, *A Conservative Hindu of Colonial India: Raja Radhakanta Deb and his Milieu (1784-1867)* (New Delhi: Navrang, 1990), chap. 1; and Robertson, *Rammohan Ray*, 149-58.

44. See Tripathi, *Trade and Finance*, chap. 5.

45. Bolts, *Considerations on India Affairs*, vi.

46. Cited from Kling, *Partner in Empire*, 71.

47. Cited from ibid., 74.

48. Cited from Bimanbehari Majumdar, *History of Political Thought from Rammohun to Dayanand (1821-84)*, vol. 1, *Bengal* (Calcutta: University of Calcutta Press, 1934), 164; cf. Kling, *Partner in Empire*, 58-59.

49. Chris Bayly has drawn attention to this previously neglected aspect of Roy's representational politics in "Rammohun Roy," 34-36.

50. While he did attend Brahmo services in the 1820s, he alone would arrive informally attired, refusing to intrude the worldliness of his office dress into the worship of God, "to whom we should always appear in the simplest and humblest garb" (Kling, *Partner in Empire*, 22-23).

51. Mukherjee, *Calcutta*, 129; Kling, *Partner in Empire*, 42-44, 198-212.

52. Kling, *Partner in Empire*, 11-12.

53. Ibid., 232-33.

54. Two graduate students at the University of Chicago, James Vaughn and Spencer Leonard, are currently working on dissertations that deal with the centrality of Whig radicalism, and its ultimate defeat in the 1780s to the development of British territorial empire in India.

55. Kling, *Partner in Empire*, 27, 32-36, 50-72, 76, 156-62; Majumdar, ed., *Rammohun Roy and Progressive Movements*, 437-39.

56. Nemai Sadhan Bose, *Racism, Struggle for Equality, and Indian Nationalism* (Calcutta and Los Angeles: KLM, 1981); Kling, *Partner in Empire*, 163; Chittabrata Palit, *Tensions in Bengal Rural Society: Landlords, Planters, and Colonial Rule, 1830-1860* (Calcutta: Progressive, 1975), chap. 4.

57. Kling, *Partner in Empire*, 171, 176-77.

58. Majumdar, *History of Political Thought*, 166.

59. Kling, *Partner in Empire*, 176.

60. Majumdar, *History of Political Thought*, 171.

61. Goutam Chattopadhyay, ed., *Awakening in Bengal in Early Nineteenth Century (Selected Documents)*, vol. 1 (Calcutta: Progressive, 1965), xxxix-xl; Majumdar, *History of Political Thought*, 170-71.

62. Kling, *Partner in Empire*, 177-79.

63. Salahuddin Ahmed, *Social Ideas and Social Change*, 40-51; Majumdar, *History of Political Thought*, 91-92, 110-11.

64. *The Englishman*, May 1836, cited from Majumdar, *History of Political Thought*, 79-80.

65. Majumdar, *History of Political Thought*, 88, 90-91, 100-101, 112; Chattopadhyay, ed., *Awakening in Bengal*, 389-99.

66. Peary Chand Mitra, "The Zemindar and the Ryot," *Calcutta Review* 6, no. 12 (1846): 305-53; quotation is on p. 316.

67. Mitra, "Zemindar and the Ryot," 316 (emphasis in original).

68. Ibid., 311-16, 342.

69. Ibid., 307 (emphasis in original).

70. Ibid., 318, 325-27, 336-37.

71. Ibid., 334.

72. Ibid., 316-17, 327, 334, 338, 343, 352.

73. Salahuddin Ahmed, *Social Ideas and Social Change*, 42.

74. Majumdar, *History of Political Thought*, 116-20; Chattopadhyay, *Awakening in Bengal*, 401-2.

75. Sarkar, "Rammohun Roy and the Break with the Past."

76. Sengupta, *A Conservative Hindu*, 90-94; Kling, *Partner in Empire*, 166-67; Majumdar, *History of Political Thought*, 163-68.

77. Cited from Kling, *Partner in Empire*, 223.

78. Amiya Bagchi, *Private Investment in India, 1900-1939* (Cambridge: Cambridge University Press, 1972), 165-81; Amiya Bagchi, "European and Indian Entrepreneurship in India, 1900-1930," in Ray, ed., *Entrepreneurship and Industry*, 157-96; Goswami, *Producing India*; Manu Goswami, "From *Swadeshi* to *Swaraj*: Nation, Economy, Territory in Colonial South Asia, 1870-1907," *Comparative Studies in Society and History* 40, no. 4 (1998): 609-36; Kling, *Partner in Empire*, chaps. 9-10; John McGuire, *The Making of a Colonial Mind: A Quantitative Study of the Bhadralok in Calcutta, 1857-1885* (Canberra: Australian National University, 1985); Maria Misra, *Business, Race, and Politics in British India, c. 1850-1960* (Oxford: Clarendon Press; New York: Oxford University Press, 1999); Rajat Kanta Ray, *Social Conflict and Political Unrest in Bengal, 1875-1927* (Delhi: Oxford University Press, 1984), 11-21; Narendra Krishna Sinha, "Indian Business Enterprise: Its Failure in Calcutta (1800-1848)," in *Entrepreneurship and Industry in India (1800-1947)*, ed. Rajat Kanta Ray (Delhi: Oxford University Press, 1994), 70-82.

79. Tithi Bhattacharya, *The Sentinels of Culture: Class, Education, and the Colonial Intellectual in Bengal* (New Delhi: Oxford University Press, 2005).

80. Ray, *Social Conflict and Political Unrest*, 13.

81. For histories of the economic doctrines undergirding the Permanent Settlement and its utilitarian alternative, see Ranajit Guha, *A Rule of Property for Bengal: An Essay on the Idea of Permanent Settlement* (Durham, NC : Duke University Press, 1996), and Eric Stokes, *The English Utilitarians and India* (Delhi: Oxford University Press, 1989). For general introductions to the new policies, see S. Ambirajan, *Classical Political Economy and British Policy in India* (Cambridge: Cambridge University Press, 1978), 110-29; S. B. Cook, *Imperial Affinities: Nineteenth-Century Analogies and Exchanges between India and Ireland* (New Delhi: Sage, 1993), chap. 3; and Dietmar Rothermund, *Government, Peasant, and Landlord in India: Agrarian Relations under British Rule, 1865-1935* (Wiesbaden: Franz Steiner, 1978), 49-57. On Sir Henry Maine, see George Feaver, *From Status to Contract: A Biography of Sir Henry Maine, 1822-1888* (London: Longmans 1969), and Maine's own essays in *Village-Communities in the East and West* (New York: Henry Holt, 1880). And on John Stuart Mill, see Lynn Zastoupil, *John Stuart Mill and India* (Stanford, CA: Stanford University Press, 1994), and Mill's review, "Maine on Village Communities," in *Collected Works of John Stuart Mill*, vol. 30, *Writings on India* (Toronto and Buffalo: University of Toronto Press; London: Routledge and Kegan Paul, 1990), 224-25.

82. Bose, *Peasant Labour and Colonial Capital,* chap. 2; B. B. Chaudhuri, "Growth of Commercial Agriculture in Bengal, 1859-1885," *Indian Economic and Social History Review* 7, nos. 1 and 2 (1970).

83. "An Amended Rent Law," *Calcutta Review* 41 (1865): 161.

84. "The Relations of Landlord and Tenant in India," *Calcutta Review* 39 (1864): 111.

85. This argument is made in more detail in Andrew Sartori, "Emancipation as Heteronomy: The Crisis of Liberalism in Later Nineteenth-Century Bengal," *Journal of Historical Sociology* 17, no. 1 (2004): 56-86.

86. Bose, *Racism, Struggle for Equality, and Indian Nationalism,* chap. 3; Majumdar, *History of Political Thought,* 174-85; P. N. Singh Roy, ed., *Chronicle of the British Indian Association (1851-1952)* (Calcutta: British Indian Association, ca. 1965).

87. Kling, *Partner in Empire,* 162-65.

88. See Holt, *Problem of Freedom.*

89. Sunjeeb Chunder Chatterjee, *Bengal Ryots: Their Rights and Liabilities* (Calcutta: K. P. Bagchi, 1977), 12-13.

90. Cited from Majumdar, *History of Political Thought,* 278-79.

91. Goswami, *Producing India,* chap. 7.

92. Cited from Majumdar, *History of Political Thought,* 283.

93. Goswami, *Producing India,* 218-19.

94. Majumdar, ed., *Rammohun Roy and Progressive Movements,* 87-90.

95. Salahuddin Ahmed, *Social Ideas and Social Change,* 40-49.

96. Kopf, *Brahmo Samaj,* 166.

97. Chakrabarty, *Provincializing Europe,* 218-23.

98. Kshetra Gupta, ed., *Madhusudan racanabali* (Calcutta: Sahitya Samsad, 1965), 241-54.

99. Becharam Chattopadhyay, *Griha Karma* (1864), cited from Bhattacharya, *Sentinels of Culture,* 85.

100. See Jayanta Gosvami, *Samajcittre unabingsha shatabdir banglar prahasan* (Calcutta: Sahityashri, 1974), 463-518.

101. The discussion of Bankim that follows is largely drawn from Sartori, "Emancipation as Heteronomy."

102. Sir Henry Yule, *Hobson-Jobson: A Glossary of Colloquial Anglo Indian Words and Phrases, and of Kindred Terms, Etymological, Historical, Geographical and Discursive* (New Delhi: Rupa, 1986), 44.

103. Bishnu Basu, ed., *Bankim racanabali: Sahitya samagra* (Calcutta: Tuli-Kalam, ca. 1986), 249-56 (hereafter cited in text as *BR* followed by page reference).

104. Bankimchandra Chatterjee, *Essays and Letters* (Calcutta: Bangiya Sahitya Parishad, 1940), 68.

105. Chatterjee, *Essays and Letters,* 68-69.

106. Ibid.

107. Sudipta Kaviraj, *The Unhappy Consciousness: Bankimchandra Chattopadhyay and the Formation of Nationalist Discourse in India* (Delhi: Oxford University Press, 1998), 58-67.

108. Chatterjee, *Essays and Letters,* 67.

109. Interestingly, Bankim seems to have been drawing here on an old Kartabhaja trope, the *bhab-bajar* (marketplace of material things—in contrast to the marketplace of love), when he refers in this passage to the *bhaber bajar* (marketplace of essences, marketplace of sentiments, or marketplace of the imagination). In fact, Bankim was an avid collector of old Vaishnava songs, most likely including ones from heterodox traditions. See Shyamali Cakrabarti, *Bankimcandrer shilpa o sangiter jagat* (Calcutta: Aruna, 1990), 100-108.

110. Chatterjee, *Essays and Letters,* 68.

111. Kaviraj, *Unhappy Consciousness,* 50-51.

112. For the classic account of these political associations that naturalizes the category of inter-

est in its explanation of the emergence of nationalist politics, see Anil Seal, *The Emergence of Indian Nationalism: Competition and Collaboration in the Later Nineteenth Century* (Cambridge: Cambridge University Press, 1971), chap. 5.

113. Sisir Kumar Das, *The Artist in Chains: The Life of Bankimchandra Chatterji* (New Delhi: New Statesman, 1984), 113-14.

114. Sureshchandra Samajpati, ed., *Bankim prasanga* (Calcutta: Nabapattra, 1982), 122.

CHAPTER FOUR

1. In *New Essays in Criticism* (Calcutta: Papyrus, 1994), 13-84; quotation is on pp. 72-73.

2. Brajendranath Seal, "The Neo-Romantic Movement in Literature," in *New Essays in Criticism* (Calcutta: Papyrus, 1994), 73.

3. Seal, "Neo-Romantic Movement," 35.

4. Ibid., 39-40.

5. Ibid., 32.

6. Tithi Bhattacharya, *The Sentinels of Culture: Class, Education, and the Colonial Intellectual in Bengal* (New Delhi: Oxford University Press, 2005).

7. We can also arguably see in the preceding formulation of his theology a hint of Tantrism (a concept explained in more detail in chapter 5); that is to say, the mundane world of individual souls and material objects comes awfully close on this reading to being an instantiation of the divine rather than its illusory veil and, hence, negation. This is a less speculative association than it might at first appear: Rammohun was closely associated in his early life with a Tantric ascetic by the name of Nandakumar Vidyalankar. See Rama Prasad Chanda and Jatindra Kumar Majumdar, eds., *Raja Rammohun Roy: Letters and Documents* (Delhi: Anmol, 1987), xxviii-xxix.

8. Karl Marx, *Grundrisse: Foundations of the Critique of Political Economy (Rough Draft)* (London: Penguin, 1973), 84, 241-42.

9. Devendranath Tagore, *The Autobiography of Maharishi Devendranath Tagore,* trans. Satyendranath Tagore and Indira Devi (Calcutta: S. K. Lahiri, 1909), 25.

10. Tagore, *Autobiography*, 46-51.

11. Ibid., 39.

12. Ibid., 23, 83.

13. Ibid., 18.

14. For an outline of the major themes and positions voiced by the *Tattvabodhini Patrika* during its forty years of publication, see Amiya Kumar Sen, *Tattwabodhini Patrika and the Bengal Renaissance* (Calcutta: Sadharan Brahmo Samaj, 1979).

15. Tagore, *Autobiography*, 24.

16. Devendranath Tagore, *Atmatattvavidya* (Knowledge of the Essence of Self). (Calcutta: Brahma Samaj, 1818 *shak* [ca. 1896]).

17. Tagore, *Atmatattvavidya*, 13-14.

18. Ibid., 49.

19. Tagore, *Autobiography*, 36.

20. Tagore, *Atmatattvavidya*, 1.

21. Ibid., 65.

22. Ibid., 104.

23. Ibid., 99.

24. Ibid., 24.

25. Akshaykumar Datta, *Bahya bastur sahit manab prakritir sambandha bicar* (Calcutta: Sanskrit Press, 1860).

26. Jogesh Chandra Bagal, ed., *Bankim Rachanavali: Collection of English Works* (Calcutta: Sahitya Samsad, 1969), 200-201.

27. Bagal, ed., *Bankim Rachanavali*, 204-5 (emphasis in original).

28. Ibid., 212.

29. Ibid., 210-11.

30. Ibid., 213.

31. Much of this work was first published serially in *Nabajiban* from 1884 to 1886. For the complete text of 1888, see *BR* 584-679.

32. This work was initially serialized from 1884 to 1886 in *Pracar*, a journal Bankim founded in 1884 to propagate his new religious vision. The first edition in book form came out in 1886, and was superseded by a much-expanded second edition in 1892 (*BR* 407-583).

33. See the preface to the first edition of *Krishnacarittra* (*BR* 1032).

34. For the classic scholarly elaboration of the theology of Bengali Vaishnavism, see S. K. De, *Early History of the Vaishnava Faith and Movement in Bengal* (Calcutta: K. L. Mukhopadhyay, 1961). For a broader historical sweep, see Ramakanta Chakravarti, *Vaisnavism in Bengal, 1486-1900* (Calcutta: Sanskrit Pustak Bhandar, 1985). Bankim does not make the great figures of the Gaudiya tradition explicit targets in *Krishnacarittra*, probably for reasons of propriety.

35. See Partha Chatterjee, *Nationalist Thought and the Colonial World: A Derivative Discourse?* (London: Zed Books, 1986), 58-59; and Sudipta Kaviraj, *The Unhappy Consciousness: Bankimchandra Chattopadhyay and the Formation of Nationalist Discourse in India* (Delhi: Oxford University Press, 1998), chap. 3.

36. Niharranjan Ray (*Krishti, kalcar, sanskriti* [Calcutta: Jijnasa, 1978], 32) has suggested that this everyday and practical orientation is built into the very etymology of *anushilan*. Bankim, however, infused the term with its newly political and social (as distinct from ritual) significance.

37. While Bankim was critical of the otherworldly asceticism of yogis, he also described "yoga" as "just another name for a method of culture" (*BR* 635).

38. George W. Stocking Jr., *Race, Culture, and Evolution: Essays in the History of Anthropology* (New York: Free Press, 1968), 82-83, 97-98.

39. This notion that all of creation was pervaded by the divine presence might seem at first glance to contradict Bankim's primary emphasis on a personal, embodied deity. In fact, however, this is actually one case where Bankim was probably directly drawing on the theological resources of Gaudiya Vaishnavite tradition. The doctrine of *acintyabhedabhed* (inconceivable difference and nondifference) will be discussed in the following chapter.

40. Cf. Chatterjee, *Nationalist Thought and the Colonial World*, 55; Tanika Sarkar, "Imagining Hindurashtra: The Hindu and the Muslim in Bankim Chandra's Writings," in *Contesting the Nation: Religion, Community, and the Politics of Democracy in India*, ed. David Ludden (Philadelphia: University of Pennsylvania Press, 1996), 162-84.

41. Jogesh Chandra Bagal, ed., *Bankim racanabali, pratham khanda: Samagra upanyas* (Calcutta: Sahitya Samsad, 1970), 728-30. "Bande mataram" ("Hail to the Mother"), Bankim's famous patriotic hymn, was first introduced in this novel, sung by the ascetics: Bagal, ed., *Bankim racanabali: samagra upanyas*, 725-28. It has often been pointed out that this *shakta* iconography sits rather oddly in the context of the Vaishnavite creed of these ascetics.

42. Dipesh Chakrabarty, *Provincializing Europe: Postcolonial Thought and Historical Difference* (Princeton, NJ: Princeton University Press, 2000), chap. 8.

43. Bankim frequently vacillates about the nation for which he spoke: *Bande mataram* clearly implies that it is Bengal, while elsewhere he speaks of *bharatbarsa*, or India.

44. John Morrow, ed., *Coleridge's Writings*, vol. 1, *On Politics and Society* (Princeton, NJ: Princeton University Press, 1991), 172-76.

45. See John Morrow, *Coleridge's Political Thought: Property, Morality, and the Limits of Traditional Discourse* (New York: St. Martin's Press, 1990).

46. Sir John R. Seeley, *Ecce Homo* (London: Dent, 1969), esp. chap. 9.

47. Sir John R. Seeley, *Natural Religion* (Boston: Roberts Brothers, 1882), chap. 1.

48. Seeley, *Natural Religion*, 138.

49. Ibid., 125, 150-71.

50. See "Religion and the State" and "Religion and the Church," in Seeley, *Natural Religion,* 172-224. For a general account of Seeley as a thinker in the National Church tradition, see R. T. Shannon, "John Robert Seeley and the idea of a National Church: A study in churchmanship, historiography, and politics," in *Ideas and Institutions of Victorian Britain: Essays in Honour of George Kitson Clark,* ed. Robert Robson (London: G. Bell and Sons, 1967), 236-67.

51. Mill's *System of Logic* (1843) had been instrumental in disseminating the epistemological theses of Comte in Britain "at a time when his name had not yet, in France, emerged from obscurity" (J. S. Mill, *Autobiography* [Boston: Houghton Mifflin, 1969], 164). In the 1850s, a number of translations of Comte's works became available, and "by about 1880 . . . Comte's system was undeniably in the domain of public acquaintance." See W. M. Simon, *European Positivism in the Nineteenth Century: An Essay in Intellectual History* (Ithaca, NY: Cornell University Press, 1963), chap. 3.

52. For Bankim's early comments on Mill and Comte, see his obituary, "John Stuart Mill" (*BR* 880-83).

53. See Simon, *European Positivism,* chap. 2; Geraldine Forbes, *Positivism in Bengal: A Case Study in the Transmission and Assimilation of an Ideology* (Calcutta: Minerva, 1975).

54. For an outline of these general themes, see especially the second volume of *The Positive Philosophy of Auguste Comte, Freely Translated and Condensed by Harriet Martineau, in Two Volumes* (London: Trübner, 1875).

55. Forbes, *Positivism in Bengal.*

56. Herbert Marcuse, *Reason and Revolution: Hegel and the Rise of Modern Social Theory* (New York: Humanities Press, 1963), 323-88; Leszek Kolakowski, *The Alienation of Reason: A History of Positivist Thought* (New York: Anchor, 1969), 45-69; and the long editorial introduction to Gertrud Lenzer, ed., *Auguste Comte and Positivism: The Essential Writings* (Chicago: University of Chicago Press, 1975).

57. For Comte's criticisms of political economy, see his *Positive Philosophy of Auguste Comte,* 2:51-54, 299-300; more generally, see chaps. 1 and 10.

58. Comte, *Positive Philosophy of Auguste Comte,* 2:326, 399-400.

59. Ibid., 2:399-402.

60. Ibid., 2:305; and cf. Seeley, *Ecce Homo,* chap. 10.

61. See, for example, Auguste Comte, *A General View of Positivism* (London: W. Reeves, 1851), 10-13.

62. Comte, *Positive Philosophy of Auguste Comte,* 2:35-36, 388-98.

63. See P. J. Cain and A. G. Hopkins, *British Imperialism, 1688-2000* (Harlow: Pearson Education, 2002), chaps. 3 and 4; Martin J. Wiener, *English Culture and the Decline of the Industrial Spirit, 1850-1980* (Cambridge: Cambridge University Press, 1981).

64. See Bipin Chandra, *The Rise and Growth of Economic Nationalism in India: Economic Policies of Indian National Leadership, 1880-1905* (New Delhi: People's Publishing House, 1966), chap. 6.

CHAPTER FIVE

1. Gaganchandra Hom, "Sucana" ("Introduction"), *Alocana: Dharma, samaj o niti bishayak masik pattrika* 1, no. 1 (1806 *Shak* [1884]): 2.

2. Umeshchandra Datta, "Samajgati o tahar parinam" ("Social Progress and Its Telos"), *Alocana* 1, no. 1 (1806 *Shak* [1884]): 13-22.

3. Curzon to Max-Müller, July 26, 1899, cited from Amales Tripathi, *The Extremist Challenge: India between 1890 and 1910* (Bombay: Orient Longmans, 1967), 85.

4. Sumit Sarkar, *The Swadeshi Movement in Bengal, 1903-1908* (New Delhi: People's Publishing House, 1973), 9-20; Tripathi, *Extremist Challenge,* chap. 3.

5. Aurobindo Ghose, *Bande Mataram: Early Political Writings* (Pondicherry: Sri Aurobindo Ashram, 1972), 20.

6. Ghose, *Bande Mataram,* 16-17.

7. Ibid., 16, 18.

8. Ibid., 43.

9. Ibid., 20-21.

10. Ibid., 21.

11. Ibid., 26-27, 39.

12. Ibid., 29.

13. Ibid., 13, 30.

14. Ibid., 30, 38-39.

15. Ibid., 31-32.

16. Ibid., 45.

17. Ibid., 54.

18. Ibid., 46.

19. Aurobindo's idealist bent was already evident in the Plato-inspired dialogues he composed when he was around eighteen years old: *Sri Aurobindo Birth Centenary Library*, vol. 3, *The Harmony of Virtue, Early Cultural Writings* (Pondicherry: Sri Aurobindo Ashram Trust, 1972), 1-64. For one prominent example of the common misreading of *New Lamps for Old* as a more "materialist" text written under the influence of Aurobindo's recent schooling in Europe ("the cradle and the citadel of materialism"), see Tripathi, *Extremist Challenge*, 116.

20. Ghose, *Bande Mataram*, 38-39.

21. Bipin Chandra Pal, "Nation-Building," in *Writings and Speeches* (Calcutta: Yugayatri, 1954), vol. 1, part 2, 27.

22. Bipin Chandra Pal, *Character Sketches* (Calcutta: Yugayatri, 1957), 242.

23. Bipin Chandra Pal, *Swadeshi and Swaraj: The Rise of New Patriotism* (Calcutta: Yugayatri Prakashak 1954), 17-19.

24. Pal, *Swadeshi and Swaraj*, 17.

25. Rabindranatha Thakura, "Svadeshi samaj," in *Rabindra racanabali* (Calcutta: West Bengal Government, Bengal year 1368 [ca. 1961]), 12:683-702; quotation is on pp. 690-91.

26. Pal, *Character Sketches*, 65-66; and see also 238-39.

27. Pal, *Swadeshi and Swaraj*, 252.

28. Ibid., 289.

29. Pal, "Nation-Building," *Writings and Speeches*, 27-33; Pal, *Swadeshi and Swaraj*, 290-92; Pal, *Character Sketches*, 50-51.

30. See Partha Chatterjee, *The Nation and Its Fragments: Colonial and Postcolonial Histories* (Princeton, NJ: Princeton University Press, 1993), chap. 3.

31. Jeffrey Kripal has explicated Ramakrishna's basic Tantric orientation in *Kali's Child: The Mystical and the Erotic in the Life and Teachings of Ramakrishna* (Chicago: University of Chicago Press, 1998). Perhaps the best-known explicit late nineteenth-century defense of Tantra came from the charismatic saint, Sivachandra Vidyarnava: see Sir John Woodroffe's famous edited volume, *Principles of Tantra: The Tantra-tattva of Sriyukta Siva Candra Vidyarnava Bhattacarya Mahodaya*, trans. J. Majumdar (Madras: Ganesh, 1978); and for biographical details about Sivachandra, and his relationship with Woodroffe, see Kathleen Taylor, *Sir John Woodroffe, Tantra and Bengal: "An Indian Soul in a European Body"?* (Richmond: Curzon Press, 2001), 98-108.

32. In what follows, I focus solely on the ways in which *shakta* theorists assimilated the Vedanta system of philosophy to their practice for the simple reason that this came to be the most important theological issue in the nineteenth and twentieth centuries. I am not thereby implying that Shaktism grew out of Vedanta, or that this had always been its primary philosophical orientation.

33. Woodroffe, *Principles of Tantra*, 1:164-74; 2:34-44.

34. Ibid., 1:123-34.

35. *Sandhya*, May 13, 1907, *Reports on Native Papers, Bengal*, hereafter *RNPB*, No. 20 of 1907.

Indicative of the iconic status of Bankim and his *Anandamath* in the Swadeshi era was the Bankim Utsab, or Bankim Festival, that was organized by the *Bande Mataram Sampraday* in Kanthalpur, his birthplace and a place of nationalist pilgrimage, on April 21, 1907. Haridas Mukherjee and Uma Mukherjee, eds., *Sri Aurobindo and the New Thought in Indian Politics* (Calcutta: K. L. Mukhopadhyay, 1964), xxiii.

36. Aurobindo's pamphlet, "Bhawani Mandir," is an especially clear statement of this pervasive Swadeshi image. On the Mother as the "visible representation of the Eternal Spirit of the Indian Race," see Pal, "The Durga Pujas" and "Mataram in Bande Mataram," in *Swadeshi and Swaraj*, 103-12, 292-95.

37. Pal, *Swadeshi and Swaraj*, 104-5.

38. Aurobindo had no time for spiritual practices until some of his friends in Baroda induced him to try yoga as a means for acquiring practical powers (Peter Heehs, *The Bomb in Bengal: The Rise of Revolutionary Terrorism in India, 1900-1910* [Delhi: Oxford University Press, 1993], 72).

39. Jnanendra Mohan Datta and Manmath Nath Mukhopadhyaya, eds., *Sadhana: Prabhupad mahatma shrishribijaya krishna gosvami jiur amritopadesh* (Howrah: Srianil Baran Deuti, 1991), 114.

40. For a detailed discussion of the complex theology of *acintyabhedabhed*, see S. K. De, *Early History of the Vaishnava Faith and Movement in Bengal* (Calcutta: K. L. Mukhopadhyay, 1961).

41. Taylor, *Sir John Woodroffe*, 99.

42. David Kopf, *The Brahmo Samaj and the Shaping of the Modern Indian Mind* (Princeton, NJ: Princeton University Press, 1979), 219-27.

43. Sarkar, *Swadeshi Movement in Bengal*, 28.

44. Bipin Chandra Pal, *Memories of My Life and Times*, vol. 2, *1886-1900* (Calcutta: Yugayatri Pakashak, 1951), 190. Pal's increasing attraction to immanent monism was grounded initially in Ralph Waldo Emerson, and subsequently deepened by readings in classical Hindu scriptures (120-22, 132-35). Pal seemed to have been self-consciously involved in a struggle over his guru's legacy in emphasizing the rational purity of Bijoy Krishna's alleged adherence to Advaita monism: see his criticism of the guru's "new Hindu" disciples (i.e., those who had not passed through the rationalizing influence of the Brahmo Samaj) and the "atmosphere of medieval faiths and ideals" which they sought to create around him (190-95, 213).

45. Pal, *Swadeshi and Swaraj*, 288-89.

46. Pal, *Character Sketches*, 257.

47. Pal, *Memories*, vol. 2, *1886-1900*, 161-65, 182-83.

48. Ibid., 212.

49. Pal, "Nation-Building," *Writings and Speeches*, 30.

50. Ron Inden goes so far as to suggest that strict monism never really constituted the basis of any premodern Hindu religious practice. See his *Imagining India* (Cambridge, MA: Blackwell, 1992), 105ff.

51. See Surendranath Dasgupta, *Indian Idealism* (Cambridge: Cambridge University Press, 1962), 53-54. Aurobindo, like Bipin Pal, would also refer to the national struggle as part of a process whereby "the purpose of God is worked out and the idea shapes itself into an accomplished reality" (*Bande Mataram*, 717).

52. G. W. F. Hegel, *The Philosophy of History* (New York: Dover, 1956), 157.

53. Pal, *Character Sketches*, 261.

54. The most famous instance of this kind of argument was, of course, Arthur Schopenhauer's enthusiasm for the Upanishads and Buddhism. The argument had been most recently and influentially reformulated by Schopenhauer's student, Paul Deussen, as, for example, in his "On the Philosophy of the Vedanta in Its Relations to Occidental Metaphysics: An Address Delivered before the Bombay Branch of the Royal Asiatic Society, 25 February 1893," in his *Outlines of Indian Philosophy* (Berlin: Karl Curtius, 1907), 45-65.

55. Frank M. Turner, "The Triumph of Idealism in Victorian Classical Studies," in his *Contesting*

Cultural Authority: Essays in Victorian Intellectual Life (Cambridge: Cambridge University Press, 1993), 322–61.

56. For a reading of late nineteenth-century Japanese Buddhist thought that is suggestive of Hegelianization, see James Edward Ketelaar, *Of Heretics and Martyrs in Meiji Japan: Buddhism and Its Persecution* (Princeton, NJ: Princeton University Press, 1990), chaps. 4 and 5.

57. Hiralal Haldar's Hegelianism is lucidly and succinctly expressed in "Some Aspects of Hegel's Philosophy," *Philosophical Review* 5, no. 3 (1896): 263–77; and "The Conception of the Absolute," *Philosophical Review* 8, no. 3 (1899): 261–72. By 1903, when republishing earlier Hegelian essays in literary criticism, Brajendranath Seal had renounced an orthodox Hegelianism on account of its Eurocentrism, instead arguing that "historical comparison implies that the objects compared are of co-ordinate rank and belong more or less to the same stage in the development of known culture." See Seal, *New Essays in Criticism* (Calcutta: Papyrus, 1994), 9–12; Kopf, *Brahmo Samaj*, 62; and Wilhelm Halbfass, "India and the Comparative Method," *Philosophy East and West* 35 (January 1985): 3–15.

58. *Life of Sri Ramakrishna, compiled from various authentic sources* (Almora: Advaita Ashrama, 1948), 507–9.

59. Swami Vivekananda, "Modern India" (1899), in *The Complete Works of the Swami Vivekananda*, vol. 4 (Almora: Advaita Ashrama, 1932), 371–413; quotation is on p. 396.

60. Pal, *Character Sketches*, 257–58; see also 75–76.

61. For Kripal, Vivekananda's advocacy of Advaita Vedanta makes his thought fundamentally irreconcilable with Ramakrishna's Tantrism. Yet Vivekananda's articulation of Advaita was heterodox in crucial ways: he espoused not *jnan-yog* (union with God through gnosis), but *karma-yog* (union with God through worldly activity or work) as the path best suited to the vast majority of people. This meant "making use of all the bondages [of the world] themselves to break those very bondages," an approach that was much more indebted to Ramakrishna's Tantrism than Kripal acknowledges. See Kripal, *Kali's Child*, 25–27, 170–75; Vivekananda, *Karma-Yoga*, in *The Complete Works of the Swami Vivekananda*, vol. 1 (Almora: Advaita Ashrama, 1931), 96–97.

62. Daya Krishna, *The Problematic and Conceptual Structure of Classical Indian Thought about Man, Society, and Polity* (Delhi: Oxford University Press, 1996), 157–58. Swarupa Gupta's recent attempt to root modern Bengali notions of nationhood in a precolonial conception of *samaj* misses Krishna's crucial distinction by eliding precisely the category of society. See "Notions of Nationhood in Bengal: Perspectives on *Samaj*, 1867–1905," *Modern Asian Studies* 40, no. 2 (2006): 273–302.

63. Keith Michael Baker, "Enlightenment and the Institution of Society: Notes for a Conceptual History," in *Main Trends in Cultural History: Ten Essays*, ed. Willem Melching and Wyger Velema (Amsterdam: Rodopi, 1994), 95–120; Daniel Gordon, *Citizens without Sovereignty: Equality and Sociability in French Thought, 1670–1789* (Princeton, NJ: Princeton University Press, 1994), esp. chap. 2; and Douglas Howland "Society Reified: Herbert Spencer and Political Theory in Early Meiji Japan," *Comparative Studies in Society and History* 42, no. 1 (2000): 67–86.

64. Having no framework for viewing religious consciousness as anything other than either a regressive historical holdover in an incomplete modernity, or as a cynically manipulated banner for mass mobilization, Sumit Sarkar tended to interpret the Swadeshi discourse of spirituality—when he interpreted it at all—in this light: "The caste-ridden imagination of the neotraditionalist Hindu bhadralok found solace in the dream of a stratified society with provision explicitly made for the 'maintenance or support of higher castes of workers devoted to the discovery or spread of truths' [quoting Satish Chandra Mukherjee]—a Brahman aristocracy of the intellect exempt as always from manual toil" (*Swadeshi Movement in Bengal*, 107–8). Partha Chatterjee's reading of Gandhi in *Nationalist Thought and the Colonial World* (London: Zed Books, 1986) also views the religious idiom of his political discourse in much the same, if less harshly phrased, terms.

65. Loyd D. Easton and Kurt H. Guddat, eds., *Writings of the Young Marx on Philosophy and Society* (New York: Anchor Books, 1967), 159.

66. Barbara Southard, "The Political Strategy of Aurobindo Ghosh: The Utilization of Hindu Religious Symbolism and the Problem of Political Mobilization in Bengal," *Modern Asian Studies* 14, no. 3 (1980): 353–76.

67. In fact, Southard observed that Aurobindo "already saw himself as the instrument of divine will" as early as 1905 ("Political Strategy of Aurobindo Ghosh," 364). See also Heehs, *The Bomb in Bengal*, 65–73.

68. See Theodor Adorno, *Introduction to Sociology* (Stanford, CA: Stanford University Press, 2000). Even a category as fundamental as society can therefore only be applied transhistorically with important caveats. Moishe Postone has argued that, "because both the interaction of humanity with nature and essential social relations are mediated by labor in capitalism, the epistemology of this mode of social life can be formulated in terms of categories of alienated social labor. The forms of interaction with nature and of human interaction, however, vary considerably among social formations. Different formations, in other words, are constituted by different modes of social constitution. This, in turn, suggests that forms of consciousness *and* the very mode of their constitution vary historically and socially. Each social formation, then, requires its own epistemology." Postone, *Time, Labor, and Social Domination: A Reinterpretation of Marx's Critical Theory* (Cambridge: Cambridge University Press, 1996), 259. As Sheldon Pollock complementarily observes from a classicist's perspective, studies of premodernity have tended to rest "upon a set of beliefs about the relation of culture and power (whether as instrumental reason, legitimation, or ideology) that have been formed in the age of capital in order to make sense of it. . . . It is no easy matter . . . to theorize a premodern world without deploying the theoretical presuppositions—the only ones we have—forged by modernity. . . . It thus remains unclear to me what warrants such presuppositions in understanding a different—potentially radically different—world of the nonmodern non-West." Pollock, "The Cosmopolitan Vernacular," *Journal of Asian Studies* 57 (February 1998): 6–37; quotation is on p. 32.

69. Postone, *Time, Labor, and Social Domination*, 71–83.

70. Sri Aurobindo Ghose, "Paramhamsa Dev and His Birthday Utsav" (1909), reprinted in *Amrita Bazar Patrika*, March 11, 1932.

71. See, for example, Pal, *Swadeshi and Swaraj*, 69, 241; Ghose, *Bande Mataram*, 60–71, 710–13.

72. See Marcel Stoetzler, "Postone's Marx: A Theorist of Modern Society, Its Social Movements, and Its Imprisonment by Abstract Labor," *Historical Materialism* 12, no. 3 (2004): 261–83; from pp. 275–77.

73. See Ghose, *Bande Mataram*, 296–99, 304–8.

74. Pal, *Character Sketches*, 259.

75. Manu Goswami, *Producing India: From Colonial Economy to National Space* (Chicago: University of Chicago Press, 2004).

76. Ghose, *Bande Mataram*, 703–4.

77. Pal, "Nation-Building," *Writings and Speeches*, 29.

78. See Pal, *Swadeshi and Swaraj*, 12–17.

79. Thakura, "Svadeshi Samaj," 686.

80. Pal, *Swadeshi and Swaraj*, 201.

81. Kshitinath Das, *Shiksha sankat* (Calcutta: Published by the author, 1906), 2–7.

82. *Yugantar*, February 1, 1908, *RNPB*, No. 6 of 1908; *Yugantar*, March 7, 1908, *RNPB*, No. 11 of 1908.

83. Aurobindo Ghose, "The Bourgeois and the Samurai" (1906 or 1907), *Sri Aurobindo: Archives and Research* 2 (April 1978): 1–18.

84. *Sri Sri Vishnu Priya-o-Ananda Bajar Patrika*, January 10, 1907, *RNPB*, No. 2 of 1907.

85. See, for example, the poem, "The Vampire," in the *Khulnavasi* of September 21, 1907, *RNPB*, No. 39 of 1907.

86. *Sandhya*, November 16, 1906, *RNPB*, No. 47 of 1906; Ghose, *Bande Mataram*, 120.

87. Sakharam Ganesh Deuskar, *Desher katha* (Calcutta: Published by the author, 1904), 5-7; *Murshidabad Pratinidhi*, April 24, 1906, *RNPB*, No. 21 of 1906.

88. *Hitavadi*, May 4, 1906, *RNPB*, No. 19 of 1906.

89. *Sandhya*, January 8, 1907, *RNPB*, No. 2 of 1907; *Basumati*, March 23, 1907, *RNPB*, No. 13 of 1907.

90. *Daily Hitavadi*, October 29, 1907, *RNPB*, No. 44 of 1907; *Sonar Bharat*, December 21, 1907, *RNPB*, No. 52 of 1907.

91. *Navasakti*, March 20, 1908, *RNPB*, No. 13 of 1908; *Charumihir*, January 9, 1906, *RNPB*, No. 3 of 1906.

92. *Howrah Hitaishi*, July 7, 1906, *RNPB*, No. 28 of 1906.

93. Jyoti Lal Mukherji, *Svadeshi brata* (Calcutta: Svadeshi Pracharini Sabha, 1906). The *Hindu Hitoishini* (March 2, 1878), for example, wrote of the "spectacle ... of famine raging in the land, while exportation [of food grains] is as brisk as ever"—*RNPB*, No. 10 of 1878. The "drain of food wealth" argument was common from the 1870s and already was linked to the production of "indigo, jute, and other commodities, which find sale in foreign markets"—*Bharat Sangskarak*, January 1, 1875, *RNPB*, No. 1 of 1875. Cf. Bipin Chandra, *The Rise and Growth of Economic Nationalism in India: Economic Policies of Indian National Leadership, 1880-1905* (New Delhi: People's Publishing House, 1966), 162-67.

94. *Bangabasi*, June 6, 1908, *RNPB*, No. 24 of 1908.

95. *Howrah Hitoishi*, July 6, 1907, *RNPB*, No. 28 of 1907; *Samajdarpan*, April 13, 1908, *RNPB*, No. 17 of 1908; *Bangabasi*, June 6, 1908, *RNPB*, No. 24 of 1908. The critique of jute cultivation as an expression of Bengal's economic subordination was exacerbated from the mid-1870s by the depreciation of silver (and with it India's silver-standard rupee), which gave a substantial boost to cash-crop exports, yet at the very same time underlined the unequal nature of the exchange. See, for example, *Nababibhakar*, January 25, 1886, *RNPB*, No. 5 of 1886. On the general satisfaction of the Congress leadership with the depreciation of the rupee, see Chandra, *Rise and Growth of Economic Nationalism*, chap. 7. On the rise of jute, see Sugata Bose, *The New Cambridge History of India*, III, 2, *Peasant Labour and Colonial Capital: Rural Bengal since 1770* (Cambridge: Cambridge University Press, 1993), 53; on the depreciation of silver, see Dietmar Rothermund, *An Economic History of India from Pre-Colonial Times to 1991* (London: Routledge, 1993), 42-44; on the new turn of India's economy generally toward production of primary products for export in the later nineteenth century, see B. R. Tomlinson, *The Economy of Modern India, 1860-1970* (Cambridge: Cambridge University Press, 1993), 51-53; and for a brilliant synthetic analysis of the structural implication of the subcontinent in global structures of capitalism see Goswami, *Producing India*.

96. The normative standpoint of this critique was in principle as applicable to social structures within England as it was to the Indian context. Thus, if the English were brutish, barbarous, and above all selfish, it "is only when this sinful people will be taken severely to task by the labourers of their country that they will be roused to their senses" (*Hitabadi*, May 4, 1906, *RNPB*, No. 19 of 1906).

97. "Well-watered, fertile," the second line of Bankim's song, *Bande mataram*.

98. "Scarcity of money," as distinct from any genuine "scarcity of rice (*dhan caler durbhiksha*)" (Mukherji, *Svadeshi brata*, 6).

99. *Medini Bandhab*, April 11, 1906, *RNPB*, No. 17 of 1906.

100. Ghose, *Bande Mataram*, 306-7.

101. Aurobindo Ghose, "Religion and Politics" (1907), in Mukherjee and Mukherjee, *New Thought in Indian Politics*, 128-30; quotation is on p. 129.

102. Satish Chandra Mukherjee, "The Dawn and the Bhagavat Catuspathi," *The Dawn* 1, no. 12 (1898): 353-56; quotation is on p. 354.

103. This student-based movement drove the founding of the National Council of Education.

Students declared a boycott of government-run educational institutions and called for the founding of a national university, forcing the Swadeshi leadership to develop alternative institutional arrangements. See Kedarnath Das Gupta, *Shikshar andolan* (Calcutta: Published by the author, 1905), esp. 6-10. Sumit Sarkar emphasizes the importance of the student movement in driving the national education initiative (*Swadeshi Movement in Bengal*, 158-64).

104. Ghose, *Bande Mataram*, 718.

105. *Report of the National Council of Education, Bengal, 1907*, Appendix G, "Memorandum of Association" (1906). See also Das, *Shiksha sankat*, esp. 6-7: "Education is for knowledge, not for earning an income."

106. Mukherjee, "The Dawn and the Bhagavat Catuspathi," 355-56 (emphasis in original). For an account of the national education movement that emphasizes the role of Satish Chandra Mukherjee, see Haridas Mukherjee and Uma Mukherjee, *The Origins of the National Education Movement (1905-1910)* (Calcutta: Jadavpur University, 1957).

107. *Daily Hitavadi*, March 25, 1907, *RNPB*, No. 13 of 1907.

108. See, for example, Aurobindo Ghose, "Religion and Politics" (1907), in Mukherjee and Mukherjee, *New Thought in Indian Politics*, 129.

109. *New India*, August 25, 1906, *RNPB*, No. 36, Part 2 (on Native-Owned English Newspapers in Bengal) of 1906.

110. See Sarkar, *Swadeshi Movement in Bengal*, chap. 2, for a more detailed analysis of the economic program.

111. Pal, *Swadeshi and Swaraj*, 219-49.

112. As reported in *The Bengalee*, January 3, 1906, *RNPB*, No. 1, Part 2 (on Native-Owned English Newspaper in Bengal) of 1906.

113. Chandra, *Rise and Growth of Economic Nationalism*, 146, 169-70, 729, and more generally chaps. 4, 6, 14, and 15; Goswami, *Producing India*, chap. 7.

114. Chandra, *Rise and Growth of Economic Nationalism*, 727.

115. Sarkar, *Swadeshi Movement in Bengal*, 97.

116. Aurobindo Ghose, "Why the Boycott Succeeded" (1907), in Mukherjee and Mukherjee, *New Thought in Indian Politics*, 126-27.

117. On the distinction between the "constructive" and the political or "Extremist" strands of Swadeshi thought, see Sarkar, *Swadeshi Movement in Bengal*, chap. 1.

118. *Sandhya*, September 20, 1906, *RNPB*, No. 40 of 1906.

119. Aurobindo Ghose's 1907 series of articles on "The Doctrine of Passive Resistance" were widely acknowledged as the great programmatic statements of that position. See Ghose, *Bande Mataram*, 83-123. Aurobindo, whose allegiance to passive resistance was more pragmatic than principled (97-98), was also linked to secret societies committed to more directly military means of overthrowing the British—an approach most representatively voiced by the *Yugantar*.

120. Ghose, *Bande Mataram*, 91.

121. Pal, "Nation-Building," *Writings and Speeches*, 27-28.

122. *Daily Hitabadi*, October 25, 1907, *RNPB*, No. 44 of 1907.

123. Ghose, *Bande Mataram*, 113.

124. *Sandhya*, August 13, 1907, *RNPB*, No. 33 of 1907.

125. Nagendrachandra Som, "Japani akhyanamala" ("Japanese Tales"), *Prabasi* 4, no. 6 (Bengali year 1311 [1904]): 313-18; Rasiklal Gupta, "Japan sambandhe kaekti katha" ("A Few Words about Japan"), *Bandhab* (Bengali year 1311 [1904]): 10-17 and 68-76. The sense of identification with Japan was so strong that Japanese goods were widely regarded as "swadeshi." See Muzaffar Ahmad, *Myself and the Communist Party of India, 1920-1929* (Calcutta: National Book Agency, 1970), 9-10.

126. Debiprasanna Raychaudhuri, "Atma-bali o atma-bili" ("Self-Sacrifice and Self-Commitment"), *Nabyabharat* 22, no. 4 (Bengali year 1311 [1904]): 219-23; quotation is on p. 219.

127. Thakura, "Svadeshi samaj," 690.

128. Thakura, "Svadeshi samaj"; *Sandhya*, January 10, 1907, *RNPB*, No. 3 of 1907.

129. *Report of the National Council of Education, Bengal, 1908*, 15–16.

130. Ghose, *Bande Mataram*, 468–69.

131. *Nayak*, January 4, 1908, *RNPB*, No. 2 of 1908; *Motherland*, June 5, 1907, *RNPB*, No. 24, Part 2 (on Native-Owned English Newspapers in Bengal) of 1907.

132. Pal, *Swadeshi and Swaraj*, 201.

133. *Sandhya*, September 1, 1906, *RNPB*, No. 36 of 1906.

134. *Feringhi*, a derogatory term for a European, seemed in Swadeshi discourse to connote the specifically selfish and mercenary figure of colonial oppression. See, especially, the extended mock etymology of the word in the *Sandhya*, November 23, 1906, *RNPB*, No. 49 of 1906: *"feringhis* are men who demand a *fee* (money) on any and every occasion. . . . There is no nation of *feriwallahs* (hawkers) on earth like the *feringhis."* It is possible that this connotation draws from the term's origins in the precolonial era of trade with the Portuguese. See the entry on the term in Sir Henry Yule, *Hobson-Jobson: A Glossary of Colloquial Anglo Indian Words and Phrases, and of Kindred Terms, Etymological, Historical, Geographical, and Discursive* (New Delhi: Rupa, 1986), 352–54.

135. *Sandhya*, January 8, 1907, *RNPB*, No. 2 of 1907; *Sandhya*, January 10, 1907, *RNPB*, No. 3 of 1907.

136. *Nayak*, January 4, 1908, *RNPB*, No. 2 of 1908.

137. Thakura, "Svadeshi samaj," 687.

138. Ibid., 699–700.

139. See, for example, Aswinikumar Datta's address to the 1907 Provincial Congress at Barisal, in Priyanath Guha, *Yajna bhanga ba barishol pradeshik samitir itihas* (Calcutta: Published by the author, 1907), appendixes, 9; and Binaykumar Sarkar, "Svadesh sebak" ("Servant of the Homeland"), *Nabyabharat* 25, no. 5 (Bengali year 1314 [1907]): 249–79; from pp. 256–57.

140. Pal, *Swadeshi and Swaraj*, 147.

141. *Navashakti*, August 13, 1907, *RNPB*, No. 33 of 1907.

142. Thakura, "Svadeshi samaj," 701.

143. Aurobindo Ghose, "The Heart of Nationalism" (late 1907 or early 1908), *Sri Aurobindo: Archives and Research* 2, no. 2 (1978): 110.

144. On how the British had systematically destroyed the old coordinating centers of indigenous social power, see Ghose, *Bande Mataram*, 314–18. On the importance of central authority even to those who de-emphasized direct political confrontation with the British regime, see Thakura, "Svadeshi samaj," 693–98.

145. Ghose, *Bande Mataram*, 121.

146. See Tripathi, *Extremist Challenge*, 64.

147. Ghose, *Bande Mataram*, 309.

148. *Navashakti*, February 5, 1908 and February 6, 1908, *RNPB*, No. 7 of 1908.

149. *Yugantar*, April 8th, 1906, *RNPB*, No. 15 of 1906; *Nayak*, May 9th, 1908, *RNPB*, No. 20 of 1908.

150. Sarkar, "Svadesh sebak," 259.

151. Ibid., 687–89.

152. Ibid., 261–62.

153. *Navashakti*, February 5, 1908 and February 6, 1908, *RNPB*, No. 7 of 1908.

154. Swami Pratyagatmananda Saraswati (Pramathanath Mukhopadhyaya [Mukherjee]), *India: Her Cult and Education, The Complete Works of Swami Pratyagatmananda Saraswati*, vol. 1 (Chanduli: Saranam Asram, 1980). On the origins of this project in the Swadeshi era, see the *Report of the National Council of Education, 1908*, 17–18.

155. Swami Pratyagatmananda, *India: Her Cult and Education*, 38.

156. Ibid., 69–72.

157. Ibid., 18, 65–69 (emphasis in original).

158. Pal, *Swadeshi and Swaraj*, 82.

159. Binoy Kumar Sarkar, "Bange nabayuger nutan shiksha" ("The New Education of the New Age in Bengal"), in *Sadhana (bibidha prabandha)* (Calcutta: A. Banerjee, Bengali year 1320 [ca. 1913]), 1–2.

160. Vivekananda, *Karma-Yoga*, 27–30.

161. Vivekananda, "Modern India," 401 (emphasis in original).

162. Pal, *Swadeshi and Swaraj*, 84–87; quotation is on p. 85.

163. Pal, "Nation-Building," *Writings and Speeches*, 25–26, 30–31; "The Message of Indian History," *Writings and Speeches*, 37–41; quotation is on p. 37.

164. For a more detailed exposition of the relationship between these structures of temporality and the logic of the commodity form, see Postone, *Time, Labor, and Social Domination*, 291–98.

165. Chandra, *Rise and Growth of Economic Nationalism*, 170, chaps. 2 and 3. As I shall discuss in the following chapter, however, this espousal of modern industry was itself a topic of internal controversy among Swadeshi Nationalists.

166. Ghose, *Bande Mataram*, 718.

167. Satish Chandra Mukherjee, *The Dawn* 1 (March 1897): 1.

168. Ghose, *Bande Mataram*, 903.

169. See, for example, Thakura, "Svadeshi samaj," 680–83.

170. Ghose, *Bande Mataram*, 536–37.

171. Pal, *Character Sketches*, 67–76.

172. *Sandhya*, February 14, 1906, *RNPB*, No. 7 of 1906.

173. *Sandhya*, August 2, 1906, *RNPB*, No. 32 of 1906.

174. Ghose, *Bande Mataram*, 712–13.

175. Ibid., 91, 468–69.

176. Ibid., 465–69, 799–801.

CHAPTER SIX

1. Sumit Sarkar, *The Swadeshi Movement in Bengal, 1903–1908* (New Delhi: People's Publishing House, 1973), chap. 9; Peter Heehs, *The Bomb in Bengal: The Rise of Revolutionary Terrorism in India, 1900–1910* (Delhi: Oxford University Press, 1993).

2. Sarkar, *Swadeshi Movement in Bengal*, 471–78.

3. Niharranjan Ray, *Krishti, kalcar, sanskriti* (Calcutta: Jijnasa, 1978), chap. 1.

4. Ray, *Krishti, kalcar, sanskriti*, 1–2.

5. See his letter to Dinesh Chandra Sen, November 17, 1905, in Krishna Dutta and Andrew Robinson, eds., *Selected Letters of Rabindranath Tagore* (Cambridge: Cambridge University Press, 1997), 61–65.

6. For the generally hostile reaction to Tagore's criticisms, see *Basumati*, April 25, 1908, *RNPB*, No. 18 of 1908; *Bande Mataram*, May 27, 1908, *RNPB*, No. 23 of 1908, Part 2; *Nayak*, June 6, 1908, *RNPB*, No. 24 of 1908.

7. Rabindranatha Thakura, "Sadupay" ("Righteous Means"), in *Rabindra racanabali* (Calcutta: West Bengal Government, Bengal year 1368 [ca. 1961]), 12:826–33.

8. Thakura, "Sadupay," 829.

9. See ibid., 832–33. Tagore's critique of terrorism as a flawed attempt at a political shortcut to resolving the country's problems was further elaborated in an equally important essay of 1908, "Path o patheo" ("Ways and Means"), in *Rabindra racanabali*, 12:974–91.

10. Thakura, "Shikshasamasya" (1906), in *Rabindra racanabali*, 11:559–72; quotations are on p. 561. The Bhagavat Catuspathi, the experimental school founded by Satish Chandra Mukherjee in 1898, also had as its "*primary object . . .* the regulation of the daily life and habits of the scholar under a system of Hindu discipline according to the orthodox plan of Gurugrhabasa or residence

with the Guru at his Asrama and under his complete control" in accordance with the *brahmacarya* system. See Mukherjee, "The Dawn and the Bhagavat Catuspathi," *The Dawn* 1, no. 12 (1898): 353 (emphasis in original).

11. Thakura, "Shikshasamasya," in *Rabindra racanabali*, 11:563.

12. Ibid., 11:563-64.

13. Ibid., 11:560.

14. Ibid., 11:561.

15. This critique was elaborated most systematically in "Svadeshi samaj," in *Rabindra racanabali*, 12:683-702.

16. Thakura, "Jatiya bidalaya" (1906), in *Rabindra racanabali*, 11:572-79; quotations are on pp. 574-75.

17. Thakura, "Shantiniketan brahmacaryasram: Pratham karyapranali" (1902), in *Rabindra racanabali*, 11:817-24; quotation is on p. 818.

18. Thakura, "Shikshasamasya," in *Rabindra racanabali*, 11:560, 563-64.

19. Ibid., 566.

20. Rabindranath Tagore, "My School," in *Personality* (New York: Macmillan, 1917), 137-79; quotation is on p. 138.

21. Tagore, "My School," in *Personality*, 144-45.

22. Ibid., 148-49.

23. Ibid., 149-50.

24. Ibid., 158-59.

25. See Thakura, "Svadeshi samaj," esp. 686, 692, 701.

26. This comes out quite clearly in what in English are perhaps his best-known synthetic essays, *Sadhana: The Realization of Life* (New York: Macmillan, 1913).

27. Thakura, "Karmayog," from *Shantiniketan*, in *Rabindra racanabali*, 12:383-93; quotations are on pp. 385-86.

28. Thakura, "Karmayog," 384-85.

29. Rabindranath Tagore, "The Poet's Religion," in *Creative Unity* (New York: Macmillan, 1922), 21.

30. Thakura, "Karmayog," 386-87.

31. Tagore, *Creative Unity*, 21-23.

32. Tagore, "Svadeshi samaj," esp. 687.

33. Tagore, *Creative Unity*, 23.

34. Rabindranath Tagore, "Hindu University" (1911), in *Towards Universal Man* (New York: Asia Publishing House, 1961), 141-57; from pp. 144-47.

35. Prithvishchandra Ray, for example, was a prominent politician in the Indian Association who had challenged Tagore's claim that Indian society had been capable of either readily providing for its own material prosperity or arranging for the cultivation of humanity, in "'Svadeshi samaj'—byadhi o cikitsa," *Prabasi* 4, no. 4 (Bengali year 1311 [1904]): 221-36; esp. 227.

36. Tagore would retain the Swadeshi critique of the negative freedom of the sphere of circulation. See, for example, his essays on "The Modern Age" and "The Spirit of Freedom," in *Creative Unity*, 109-36.

37. Letter to Manoranjan Bandyopadhyay, July 1908, cited in Tapati Dasgupta, *Social Thought of Rabindranath Tagore: A Historical Analysis* (New Delhi: Abhinava Publications, 1993), 139-40.

38. Rabindranatha Thakura, *Gora*, in *Rabindra upanyas-sangraha* (Calcutta: Visvabharati, 1990), 768-69. Gora, the eponymous main character (modeled on Brahmabandhab Upadhyay), gradually comes to realize the limits of village society in chaps. 20, 26, and 67 of the novel.

39. Thakura, *Rabindra upanyas-sangraha*, 917. On Tagore's critique of compulsion, see also the conversation about cow killing between Nikhilesh and his tenants, 941-42.

40. Tagore, "My School," in *Personality*, 164-65.

41. Ibid., 170.

42. Thakura, *Shesher kabita* (1928–29), in *Rabindra upanyas-sangraha*, 1108.

43. Tagore, "The World of Personality," in *Personality*, 55–96; from p. 88.

44. Tagore, "What Is Art?" in *Personality*, 9–54; quotations are on p. 31.

45. See Dipesh Chakrabarty, *Provincializing Europe: Postcolonial Thought and Historical Difference* (Princeton, NJ: Princeton University Press, 2000), 170–72.

46. Upon returning in 1880 to a position with the Geological Survey of India, from an almost six-year sojourn in England where he had (unprecedentedly) focused his studies on the natural sciences, Bose soon became a regular visitor to the household of R. C. Dutt, the greatest of Bengal's political economists. Wedding Dutt's oldest daughter, Kamala, in 1882, Bose married into the heart of Calcutta's political and cultural elite in a ceremony attended by, among others, Surendranath Banerjea, Bankimchandra Chatterjee and a young Rabindranath Tagore. Pramatha Nath Bose, "Reminiscences and Reflections of a Septuagenarian—IV & V," *Amrita Bazar Patrika*, January 24, 1932; Jogesh Chandra Bagal, *Pramatha Nath Bose* (Calcutta: Elm, 1955), chaps. 4 and 5.

47. Pramatha Nath Bose, *A History of Hindu Civilization during British Rule*, 3 vols. (1894; New Delhi: Asian Publishing House, 1978), 3:ii; Pramatha Nath Basu, "Hindudharmmer nabajiban," in *Bibidha prabandha* (Calcutta: S. K. Lahiri, b.s. 1299 [1893]), 1–14.

48. Bose, *History*, 1:lxxviii–xcv; Basu, "Upay ki?" in *Bibidha prabandha*, 14–27. Bose's pamphlet, *Technical and Scientific Education in Bengal* (Calcutta: S. K. Lahiri, 1886), was widely considered the founding manifesto of the technical education movement.

49. Bose, *History*, 3:Introduction.

50. Bose, *History*, 1:xxx–xxxiii, xlv–xlix, lxiv–lxx.

51. Sarkar, *Swadeshi Movement in Bengal*, 32.

52. Pramatha Nath Bose, "Rectorial Address, Bengal Technical Institute (1909)," in *Essays and Lectures on the Industrial Development of India and Other Indian Subjects* (Calcutta: W. Newman, 1917), 64–74; esp. pp. 70–71.

53. Bose, *Essays and Lectures*, 72.

54. Pramatha Nath Bose, "Western Science from an Eastern Standpoint," *Westminster Review* 156, no. 2 (1901): 207–19.

55. Bose, "The Possibilities of Handloom Weaving in India" (1906), *Essays and Lectures*, 42–48; see also, in the same volume, "Industrial Development of India" (1891), 1–16; "Industrial Development by Indian Enterprise" (1906), 17–26; and "Address at the Second Indian Industrial Conference" (1906), 49–63.

56. Bose, "Reminiscences—IV & V."

57. P. N. Bose, "Reminiscences and Reflections of a Septuagenarian—VII," *Amrita Bazar Patrika*, March 15, 1932; Bagal, *Pramatha Nath Bose*, chap. 10; Haridas Mukherjee and Uma Mukherjee, *The Origins of the National Education Movement (1905–1910)* (Calcutta: Jadavpur University, 1957), 47–50.

58. See especially Bose, "Plea for a Patriotic Movement" (1903), *Essays and Lectures*, 27–41.

59. Bose, *Essays and Lectures*, 73–74.

60. Bose, "Reminiscences and Reflections—VII."

61. S. C. Roy, a young national educationist from Rangpur, recalled that, "After the first few months of excitement was over ... difficulties began to arise before our guardians and students which they did not foresee. They found, for instance, that they must give up all hope of being provided into any of the Government or other offices if they came out with the hall mark of the so-called National University. School and College education in those days was received by our students ostensibly with a view to qualifying themselves for government and other offices." *The Story of My Times* (Calcutta: The Bengal Journals, 1934), 84–85.

62. See "National Council of Education," *The Bengalee*, June 2, 1910; Bose, "Reminiscences and Reflections—VII;" Bose, *Essays and Lectures*, 64–65, 75–86.

63. Pramatha Nath Bose, *National Education and Modern Progress* (Calcutta: Kar, Majumder and Co., ca. 1921), 12–22.

64. Benoy Kumar Sarkar, *Education for Industrialization: An Analysis of the Forty Years' Work of Jadavpur College of Engineering and Technology (1905-1945)* (Calcutta: Chuckervertty Chatterjee, 1946), 94-99; Mukherjee and Mukherjee, eds., *National Education Movement,* 169-78; Bagal, *Pramatha Nath Bose,* 105-8.

65. Pramatha Nath Bose, *The Illusions of New India* (Calcutta: W. Newman, 1916), 170-73; Pramatha Nath Bose, *Epochs of Civilization* (1913; New Delhi: Asian Education Services, 1978), 313-17.

66. Pramatha Nath Bose, "The Root Causes of the Present War," *Modern Review* 17, no. 3 (1915): 320-23.

67. Bose, *Epochs,* 295.

68. Pramathanath Basu, *Svami Bibekananda* (Calcutta: Udbodhan Karyalay, Bengali year 1368 [ca. 1961, originally published ca. 1919]), 16.

69. Bose, *Illusions.*

70. Bose, "Root Causes of the Present War," 323.

71. This is the central thesis of Bose, *Epochs.*

72. Bose, *Epochs;* Pramatha Nath Bose, "Can Hindu Civilization be Synthetised?" *Modern Review* 20, no. 3 (1916): 314-16; quotation is on p. 315.

73. Bose, *National Education and Modern Progress,* 14.

74. Jitendralal Bose, "The Epochs of Civilization," *Modern Review* 15, no. 1 (1914): 29-35; quotation is on p. 32.

75. Bose, *Epochs,* 26-28; Bose, "Can Hindu Civilization be Synthetised?" 315.

76. Bose, *Epochs,* 207.

77. Ibid., 166-211.

78. Ibid., 313-15.

79. Pramatha Nath Bose, "Reminiscences of a Septuagenarian—XIII," *Amrita Bazar Patrika,* October 5, 1932.

80. Pramatha Nath Bose, *The Montagu-Chelmsford Reform Scheme—A Constructive Criticism* (Calcutta: W. Newman, 1918), 2; Pramatha Nath Bose, *Swaraj—Cultural and Political* (1929; New Delhi: Usha, 1986), 69.

81. Bose, *Swaraj.* Bose also published a series of letters in the *Amrita Bazar Patrika,* applauding Gandhi's emphasis on questions of Hindu-Muslim unity, removal of untouchability, temperance, and hand spinning and hand weaving, but questioning his giving them a political bias, an approach that threatened to undermine the basis of India's nationality (Bagal, *Pramatha Nath Bose,* 147-48).

82. Bose, *Motagu-Chelmsford Reform Scheme,* 7-8; Pramatha Nath Bose, *Hindu-Muslim Amity* (Calcutta: Elm Press, n.d. [ca. 1924]), 15-16; Bose, *Swaraj,* chap. 5.

83. Tazeen M. Murshid, *The Sacred and the Secular: Bengal Muslim Discourses, 1871-1977* (Calcutta: Oxford University Press, 1995), 28.

84. Benoy Kumar Sarkar, "Svadeshi sebak" ("Servant of the Homeland"), *Nabyabharat* 25, no. 5 (Bengali year 1314 [1907]): 249-79; quotations are on pp. 262-63.

85. Sarkar, *Swadeshi Movement in Bengal,* 419-24, chap. 6; Bipin Chandra Pal, *Swadeshi and Swaraj: The Rise of New Patriotism* (Calcutta: Yugayatri Prakashak 1954), 5-12.

86. Murshid, *The Sacred and the Secular,* 30.

87. Wakil Ahmad, "Kalikata musalman sabha-samiti," *Bangladesh Asiatic Society Patrika* 12, no. 1 (1994): 29-80; from pp. 57-60.

88. Sarkar, *Swadeshi Movement in Bengal,* 424-36.

89. Ibid., 428, 444; Rajat Kanta Ray, *Social Conflict and Political Unrest in Bengal, 1875-1927* (Delhi: Oxford University Press, 1984), 185-89.

90. Amales Tripathi, *The Extremist Challenge: India between 1890 and 1910* (Bombay: Orient Longmans, 1967), chap. 5.

91. Shan Muhammad, ed., *The Indian Muslims: A Documentary Record,* vol. 1, *Founding of the Muslim League* (Meerut: Meenakshi Prakashan, ca. 1983), 131.

92. Sufia Ahmed, *Muslim Community in Bengal, 1884-1912* (Dacca: Published by the author, 1974), chap. 3.

93. On social and educational advances in the later nineteenth century, and British policies of Muslim advancement, see Ahmed, *The Bengal Muslims*, chap. 5; Murshid, *The Sacred and the Secular*, 59-64; Ahmed, *Muslim Community in Bengal*, chap. 1, part 2, and 286-95; Ray, *Social Conflict and Political Unrest*, 186-89.

94. W. W. Hunter, *The Indian Musalmans* (1871; Lahore: The Premier Book House, 1964), chap. 2.

95. Hunter, *Indian Musalmans*, 108-9.

96. Ibid., 115-17. For a sense of the commonness of this theme at this time, cf. Murshid, *The Sacred and the Secular*, 47-48.

97. Hunter, *Indian Musalmans*, 117ff.

98. Ibid., 132-43.

99. On the activities and agenda of Abdul Latif's Mahomedan Literary Society, see Dr. Md. Mohar Ali, ed., *Autobiography and Other Writings of Nawab Abdul Latif Khan Bahadur* (Chittagong: Mehrub Publications, 1968). On Ameer Ali's organization, see Muhammad Yusuf Abbasi, ed., *Annals of the Central National Mahommedan Association, 1878-1888* (Islamabad: National Institute of Historical and Cultural Research, 1992).

100. The British pursued a series of prosecutions, collectively referred to as the "Wahabi trials," from 1863 to 1870. See Muin-ud-Din Ahmad Khan, ed., *Selections from Bengal Government Records on Wahhabi Trials (1863-1870)* (Dacca: Asiatic Society of Pakistan, 1961).

101. Ahmed, *The Bengal Muslims*, 140; Murshid, *The Sacred and the Secular*, 59-61.

102. Ahmed, *Muslim Community in Bengal*, 51-53, 132-41; Ahmed, *The Bengal Muslims*, 141-43, 148-50, 155-58. On the genesis of the figure of the "backward Muslim," see Sanjay Seth, "Constituting the 'Backward but Proud Muslim': Pedagogy, Governmentality, and Identity in Colonial India," in *The Unfinished Agenda: Nation Building in South Asia*, ed. Mushirul Hasan and Nariaki Nakazato (New Delhi: Manohar, 2001), 129-49. For a concise summary of the new (pragmatic) attitude of loyalty to the British, see P. Hardy, *The Muslims of British India* (Cambridge: Cambridge University Press, 1972), chap. 4.

103. Ahmed, *The Bengal Muslims*, 147-48.

104. *Education Gazette*, November 10, 1876, *RNPB*, No. 47 of 1876.

105. Sarkar, *Swadeshi Movement in Bengal*, 419, 435-36; Tripathi, *Extremist Challenge*, 161, 166; and for a prominent example of the Swadeshi counter-response, see Aurobindo Ghose, "The Comilla Incident" (1907), *Bande Mataram*, 209-14.

106. Priyanath Guha, *Yajna bhanga ba barishol pradeshik samitir itihas* (Calcutta: Published by the author, 1907), appendixes, 37-38.

107. For detailed accounts of the riots, see Sarkar, *Swadeshi Movement in Bengal*, 444-64; Suranjan Das, *Communal Riots in Bengal, 1905-1947* (Delhi: Oxford University Press, 1991), chap. 2.

108. See, for example, Aurobindo Ghose's articles, "The Comilla Incident," "Bureaucracy at Jamalpur," and "The East Bengal Disturbances," in *Bande Mataram*, 208-14, 285-86, 369-72.

109. Tripathi, *The Extremist Challenge*, chap. 5; Sarkar, *Swadeshi Movement in Bengal*, 451-52.

110. Sarkar, *Swadeshi Movement in Bengal*, 453-54.

111. Muhammad, ed., *The Indian Muslims*, 121.

112. Sarkar, *Swadeshi Movement in Bengal*, 449-51; Das, *Communal Riots in Bengal*, 41-42.

113. For a fuller discussion, see Andrew Sartori, "Emancipation as Heteronomy: The Crisis of Liberalism in Later Nineteenth-Century Bengal, *Journal of Historical Sociology* 17, no. 1 (2004).

114. Sugata Bose, *Agrarian Bengal: Economy, Social Structure, and Politics, 1919-1947* (Cambridge: Cambridge University Press, 1986).

115. See Kalyan Kumar Sen Gupta, *Pabna Disturbances and the Politics of Rent, 1873-1885* (New Delhi: People's Publishing House, 1974), 15, 31.

116. Sen Gupta, *Pabna Disturbances*, 12–14.

117. Cited from Ray, *Social Conflict and Political Unrest*, 63.

118. "Agrarian Outrages in the Pubna District," *The Bengalee*, July 5, 1873; "The Rent Bill," *The Bengalee*, May 15, 1875.

119. *Dacca Prakash*, December 26, 1875, *RNPB*, No. 1 of 1876; Joy Kissen Mukherjee, "Ryot and Zamindar," Letter to the Editor, *Friend of India*, October 16, 1873, reprinted in Sen Gupta, *Pabna Disturbances*, Appendix F, 184–87.

120. Sen Gupta, *Pabna Disturbances*, 50–53.

121. *Som Prakash*, November 6, 1876, *RNPB*, No. 47 of 1876 (emphasis added).

122. C. A. Bayly, "The Pre-History of 'Communalism'? Religious Conflict in India, 1700–1860," *Modern Asian Studies* 19, no. 2 (1985): 177–203; quotation is on pp. 202–3.

123. Hardy, *Muslims of British India*, 50–60.

124. For detailed accounts of Faraidism, its theology, organization, and involvement in political movements, see Muin-ud-Din Ahmad Khan, *History of the Fara'idi Movement in Bengal (1818-1906)* (Karachi: Pakistan Historical Society, 1965); and Muhammad Mohar Ali, *History of the Muslims of Bengal*, vol. 2 (Riyadh: Imam Muhammad Ibn Saud Islamic University, 1988).

125. Report No. 50 of 1847, from J. Dunbar, Dhaka Divisional Commissioner, to F. J. Halliday, Secretary to the Government of Bengal, March 18, 1847, reprinted in Ali, *History of the Muslims of Bengal*, 445–49; quotations are on pp. 446, 448; Ahmed, *The Bengal Muslims*, chap. 2.

126. See Ranajit Guha, *Elementary Aspects of Peasant Insurgency in Colonial India* (Delhi: Oxford University Press, 1992), 172–73.

127. On the Tariqah movement, its theological and organizational difference from the Faraidi movement, and the theological distinctions that separate both these movements from Wahabism, see Ahmad Khan, *History of the Fara'idi Movement*, xxxvi-lxxvii.

128. Cited from Ahmed, *The Bengal Muslims*, 44.

129. Murshid, *Sacred and the Secular*, 30–31, 37–41; Ahmed, *The Bengal Muslims*, chap. 4. The gradual acceptance of Bengali as a Muslim language—after a period of enthusiasm for promoting Urdu—was not in the first decade of the twentieth century an embrace of localism, but rather an embrace of communal solidarity that could only be pragmatically achieved through a language understood by the majority of Muslims. See Ahmed, *The Bengal Muslims*, 119–32.

130. On the central importance of Maulana Keramat Ali, who in the 1860s and 1870s organized a series of major theological debates over the status of British rule to promote a new moderation among reformists on the issue of British rule, see Ahmad Khan, *History of the Fara'idi Movement*, lii-lviii, lxxiii-lxxvii, 89–103; Ahmed, *The Bengal Muslims*, 52–53; and "Abstract of Proceedings of the Mahomedan Literary Association, 1870," in Mohar Ali, ed., *Autobiography of Abdul Latif*, 107–39.

131. It is also possible that this was further compounded by the contemporaneous rise, in northern and western Bengal (and arguably, though to a significantly more qualified extent, also in eastern Bengal) of predominantly Muslim *jotedars* (wealthier peasants controlling the actual production process on the ground) as increasingly powerful figures in rural society. For the argument that the jotedar phenomenon was regionally specific to northern Bengal, see Bose, *Agrarian Bengal*, chap. 1. For the argument that this framework can still be applied in a more qualified way even to eastern Bengal, see Rajat Kanta Ray, "The Retreat of the Jotedars?" *Indian Economic and Social History Review* 25 (1988): 237–47, and Joya Chatterji, *Bengal Divided: Hindu Communalism and Partition, 1932-1947* (Cambridge: Cambridge University Press, 1994), 58–61. Looking through the older historiographical lens of tenure hierarchy (subinfeudation), Partha Chatterjee has noted that "the common perception about a predominantly upper-caste Hindu landlord class and a predominantly Muslim peasantry" is of limited statistical validity as a general characterization for east and north Bengal (though certainly much more valid in the heartland of east Bengal). Unlike the Hindu gentry, however, Muslim jotedars "had risen from the ranks of the rest of the peasantry . . .

[and] were socially part of the peasant community." Partha Chatterjee, *Bengal, 1920–1947: The Land Question* (Calcutta: K. P. Bagchi, 1984), 126–29.

132. *Sandhya*, April 30, 1907, *RNPB*, No. 18 of 1907 (emphasis added).

133. *Svajati* (one's own people) was the Muslim counterterm to *svadesh*.

134. Cited from Mustafa Nurul Islam, *Bengali Muslim Public Opinion as Reflected in the Bengali Press, 1901–1930* (Dhaka: Bangla Academy, 1973), 142–43.

135. "Resolution Passed by Mymensigh Anjuman in Support of the Partition of Bengal," September 1906, in Muhammad, ed., *The Indian Muslims*, 125.

136. Tanika Sarkar, "Imagining Hindurashtra: The Hindu and the Muslim in Bankim Chandra's Writings," in *Contesting the Nation: Religion, Community, and the Politics of Democracy in India*, ed. David Ludden (Philadelphia: University of Pennsylvania Press, 1996).

137. Sarkar, *Swadeshi Movement in Bengal*, 75–91.

138. Aurobindo Ghose, "Back to the Land," *Bande Mataram*, 732–35 (emphasis added).

139. Sekhar Bandyopadhyay, *Caste, Protest, and Identity in Colonial India: The Namasudras of Bengal, 1872–1947* (Richmond: Curzon Press, 1997), chap. 3.

140. Cited from Bandyopadhyay, *Caste, Protest, and Identity*, 84.

141. Chatterji, *Bengal Divided*, 191–92.

142. Pradip Kumar Datta, *Carving Blocs: Communal Ideology in Early Twentieth-Century Bengal* (New Delhi: Oxford University Press, 1999), chap. one. Mukherji's pamphlet was originally published as a series of articles in *The Bengalee* in 1909.

143. "A Dying Race," *The Bengalee*, September 25, 1909.

144. "Hindu Samaj," *The Bengalee*, June 8, 1910.

145. Datta, *Carving Blocs*, 24–26.

146. See, for example, Datta, *Carving Blocs*, chap. 4.

147. This is to give a significantly more determinate content to Sumit Sarkar's account of how "moments of strain and frustration" increased the "otherworldly pull of religion" leading "the revolutionary leader" to become "the yogi of Pondicherry." *Swadeshi Movement in Bengal*, 315–16.

148. *Sri Aurobindo Birth Centenary Library*, vol. 26, *On Himself, Compiled from Notes and Letters* (Pondicherry: Sri Aurobindo Ashram, 1972), 34–38.

149. *Sri Aurobindo Birth Centenary Library*, vol. 15, *Social and Political Thought* (Pondicherry: Sri Aurobindo Ashram, 1970), 70–73.

150. For the earliest elaborations (1915–18) of this post-Hegelian master-narrative, see *The Human Cycle* and *The Ideal of Human Unity*, in *Sri Aurobindo Birth Centenary Library, vol. 15*.

151. Sir Deva Prasad Sarvadhikary, "Culture and Order," *Indian Culture* 1, no. 1 (1934): 1.

152. Sarvadhikary, "Culture and Order," 3, 5.

153. Ibid., 3.

154. Chatterji, *Bengal Divided*, 155.

155. Cited from Chatterji, *Bengal Divided*, 174; and see chapter 4 generally. In this passage, "culture" is *kalcar* in the original Bengali.

156. Chatterji, *Bengal Divided*, 175–78.

157. Cited from Chatterji, *Bengal Divided*, 175. Appendix 1 (269–74) is a complete translation of this speech.

158. Chatterji, *Bengal Divided*, 177. *Bhadra* means *refined, cultivated*, and is a term defining a kind of social respectability. *Abhadra*, *unrefined*, is its opposite. *Itor lok*, the *lower people*, and *chotolok*, the *little people*, are those beyond the pale of *bhadrata*, respectability, and refinement.

159. Datta, *Carving Blocs*, chap. 1.

160. See Abul Mansur Ahmad, *Amar-dekha rajnitir panchas bachar* (*Fifty Years of Politics That I Have Seen*), in *Abul Mansur Ahmad Racanabali*, vol. 3, ed. Rafikul Islam (Dhaka: Bangla Academy, 2001), 97.

161. Chatterji, *Bengal Divided*, esp. chap. 6.

162. A fuller discussion of Ahmad's speech and its historical location is to be found in Andrew Sartori, "Abul Mansur Ahmad and the Cultural Politics of Bengali Pakistanism," in *From the Colonial to the Postcolonial: India and Pakistan in Transition,* ed. Dipesh Chakrabarty, Rochona Majumdar, and Andrew Sartori (Delhi: Oxford University Press, 2007), 119-36.

163. Ahmad, *Amar-dekha rajnitir panchas bachar,* 145.

164. Abul Mansur Ahmad, "Mul sabhapatir abhibhashan" ("Address of the First President"), *Masik Mohammadi* 17, nos. 10-11 (Bengali year 1351 [1944]): 437-44; quotations are on pp. 437-39.

165. Ahmad, "Mul sabhapatir abhibhashan," 442.

166. Ibid.

167. Ibid., 443.

168. Ibid., 442-43.

169. Ahmad, "Kalikata musalman sabha-samiti," esp. 63-69; Saiyad Emdad Ali, "Dhaka purba-pakistan sahitya-sangsad, dvitiya barshik adhibeshan: Jatiya sahitya svarup" ("Dhaka East Pakistan Literature Society, Second Annual Meeting: The Originality of National Literature"), *Masik Mohammadi* 17, no. 7 (Bengali year 1351 [1944]): 307-11; quotations are on p. 309.

170. Ahmad, "Mul sabhapatir abhibhashan," 442.

171. Ibid., 442-43.

172. This argument is elaborated in Sartori, "Abul Mansur Ahmad."

173. Muzaffar Ahmad, *Myself and the Communist Party of India, 1920-1929* (Calcutta: National Book Agency, 1970), 7-13, 23-27.

174. For fuller accounts of M. N. Roy's early career as a nationalist, see M. N. Roy, *Memoirs* (Delhi: Ajanta, 1984), part 1; Samaren Roy, *The Restless Brahman: Early Life of M. N. Roy* (Bombay: Allied Publishers, 1970); and Sibnarayan Ray, *In Freedom's Quest: A Study of the Life and Works of M. N. Roy (1887-1954),* vol. 1, *1887-1954* (Calcutta: Minerva, 1998).

175. Roy, *Memoirs,* 59, 215.

176. M. N. Roy, *India: Her Past, Present and Future* (1918), in *Selected Works of M. N. Roy,* vol. 1, *1917-1922,* ed. Sibnarayan Ray (Delhi: Oxford University Press, 1987), 91-92.

177. Roy, *India,* 142-43.

178. Ibid., 95-96, 106.

179. Ibid., 143.

180. Ibid., 109-24.

181. Roy, *Memoirs,* 35.

182. M. N. Roy, "Hunger and Revolution in India" (1919), in Ray, ed., *Selected Works of M. N. Roy,* vol. 1, 157-58 (emphasis in original).

183. M. N. Roy, *What Do We Want?* (1922), in Ray, ed., *Selected Works of M. N. Roy,* vol. 1, 513 (emphasis in original).

184. Roy, *What Do We Want?* 504-5 (emphasis in original). It is worth noting, in case it is not clear enough from *Capital,* that Marx had gone out of his way to explicitly repudiate the claim that the working class was the producer of all wealth (a claim that is symptomatic of Roy's enduring culturalism) on the very first page of his *Critique of the Gotha Program* (Moscow: Progress, 1970).

185. M. N. Roy, *New Orientation* (Delhi: Ajanta, 1982), 121-22.

186. See Rajarshi Dasgupta, "Rhyming Revolution: Marxism and Culture in Colonial Bengal," *Studies in History* 21, no. 1, n.s. (2005): 79-98.

CONCLUSION

1. Moishe Postone, *Time, Labor, and Social Domination: A Reinterpretation of Marx's Critical Theory* (Cambridge: Cambridge University Press, 1996), 184, 224-25.

Index

acintyabhedabhed, 148
Act X of 1859, 204, 205
Adam, William, 91
Adelung, Johann, 36
Adorno, Theodor W., 61–62
Advaita Vedanta: nondualism of, 78, 112, 113, 145; Rammohun Roy on, 78, 82, 112, 113; Debendranath Tagore's rejection of, 114; and Vaishnavite immanentist monism, 148; Vivekananda's advocacy of, 256n61
agency: subjective freedom versus worldly, 111–17, 134, 135. *See also* autonomy
Age of Reason (Paine), 94
Age of Reform, 68–69, 90
agriculture. *See* cash crops; peasant society
Ahmad, Abul Mansur, 218, 219–23, 224, 268n162
Ahmad, Muzaffar, 224
Alocana, 136
Althusser, Louis, 236n29
Anandamath (*The Abbey of Bliss*) (Bankimchandra Chatterjee), 109, 124, 145, 254n35
Anderson, Benedict, 11, 236n27
anthropological culture, 34–40, 122–23
anti-Catholicism, British, 82
anticlericalism, British, 82
antimissionary mobilization, 102, 114
anushilan: Bankimchandra Chatterjee founds new humanism on concept of, 110, 117, 119–20, 134, 176–77, 252n36; displacement

as equivalent for *culture*, 176, 177, 189; doctrine of culture (*anushilanatattva*), 43, 122, 160, 171; Swadeshi-era secret societies associated with, 176
Anushilan Samiti (Culture Societies), 176, 225
Apu trilogy (Ray), 1–2
Arnold, Matthew: Aurobindo compares French with, 141; Aurobindo influenced by, 142; on better liberalism, 30; Bankimchandra Chatterjee compared with, 122; on culture, 26, 28, 37, 42, 142, 238n2
Atmiya Sabha (Friendly Society), 77
Aurobindo Ghose (Ghosh): on the bourgeois type, 157–58; in boycott in response to partition of Bengal Presidency, 137, 163–64, 166; on culture of India, 174; on grounding politics in life of the people, 169, 198; liberalism criticized by, 139–42; on middle-class leadership, 172; and Muslim popular, 211, 228; New Lamps for Old series, 139, 141–42, 169; on passive resistance, 259n119; Plato-inspired dialogues of, 254n119; productionist philosophy of practice of, 160–61; on rational unfolding of Idea in history, 149–50, 154; on return to land for Hindus, 211, 214, 215; Tantric Vedantism embraced by, 147; transformation into yogi of Pondicherry, 153, 215–16, 257n67; on Western materialism versus Indian spirituality, 175; yoga practiced by, 215, 255n38

269

autonomy: in antinomic logic of culture, 41; Pramatha Nath Bose on, 190, 192; Bankimchandra Chatterjee and creation of autonomous national subject, 134; of culture, 26, 30–34, 38, 47; global resonance of subjective, 67; of human subjectivity, 39, 40; Pakistanism as, 219, 220; productionist, 165; in Swadeshi political vision, 173; in Rabindranath Tagore's educational philosophy, 181

babu: Pramatha Nath Bose on, 193, 197; in capitalist transformation of Bengali society, 52; effeminacy attributed to, 43, 103–4; existence grounded in civil society, 118, 135; Muslims compared with, 202–3; satirizing, 101–8; superficial Western conception of society of, 155; Swadeshi view of, 161, 162, 198; Western learning of, 104, 107
Bahya bastur sahit manab prakritir sambandha bicar (A Consideration of the Relationship between Human Nature and External Matter) (Dutt), 116
Banaji, Jairus, 53, 57, 58, 242n93
"Bande mataram" ("Hail to the Mother") (Bankimchandra Chatterjee), 145, 208, 252n41
Bande Mataram (periodical), 169, 211
Bandyopadhyay, Bhabanicharan, 102
Bandyopadhyay, Hemchandra, 209
Bandyopadhyay, Rangalal, 208
Banerjea, Surendranath, 138, 263n46
Bangabasi, 159
Bangiya Sahitya Parishad, 221
Bangladesh (East Pakistan): construction of Bengali-Muslim literature, 8, 221; Pakistanism, 219–23
Bayly, C. A., 72, 77, 87
Bengal: capitalism in peasant society, 51–60; caste-reform legislation resisted in, 213–14; enthusiasm for things Japanese in, 17; financial crisis of 1847–48, 95–96; first census of, 198; import of British manufactured goods and export of primary products, 96, 97; liberalism in nineteenth-century, 22, 68–108; metropolitan economic fluctuations affect, 54–55, 75; partition of Bengal Presidency, 137, 162, 177–78, 198, 200, 202; Permanent Settlement, 69, 84, 85, 93–94, 97; political marginalization of, 8, 219; textile manufacturing in, 53. See also Bengali

culturalism; Bengali culture; Bengal Renaissance; Calcutta; Swadeshi movement; Young Bengal
Bengal British India Society, 92, 93, 94, 99
Bengalee, The, 213–14
Bengal Hurkaru, 95–96
Bengali culturalism: of Aurobindo, 142; Bengali appropriation of Western culture concept, 19; of Pramatha Nath Bose, 193, 195; Bankimchandra Chatterjee in establishment of, 22–23, 111; coherence of conceptual logic of, 6; emerges as reaction against liberalism, 6, 43–44, 68; Marxist desublimation of, 224, 229; as misrecognition of global capitalist structures, 5–6; a new approach to, 17–21; Pakistanism as response to Hindu culturalism, 219–23; post-Swadeshi thought as postcolonial, 230–32; of Rabindranath Tagore, 176–77; as translatable across geographical and linguistic boundaries, 7–8
Bengali culture: assimilated to language of distinction and prestige, 24; bhadralok, 8, 9, 24, 51, 111, 210–19; Bankimchandra Chatterjee's doctrine of culture, 43–44; effeminacy attributed to, 103–4; high culture of colonial provenance, 8; "Hindu culture" distanced from Muslim popular, 24, 211, 217–18; as historical problem, 1–24; Rabindranath Tagore as ultimate icon of, 3; who is a Bengali, 8. See also babu; Bengal Renaissance
Bengali Muslim Literature Society, 225
Bengal Mahomedan Association, 199
Bengal National College, 181, 191, 192, 263n61
Bengal Renaissance: and Bankimchandra Chatterjee's neo-Hindu revivalist turn, 109–10; continuity in conventional narrative of, 7; "great men" of, 6; liberalism of, 68, 73; Muslim attitude toward, 209; as story of failure, 69–70
"Bengal's Peasants" (Chatterjee), 106, 108
Bengal Technical Institute, 191, 192–93
Bentham, Jeremy, 30, 73, 94, 141
Bentinck, Lord William, 68, 85, 89
Bhabha, Homi, 7
bhadralok: communalism of, 210–19; discourse of culture and, 24; education as social distinction for, 111; emphasized in histories of colonial South Asia, 9; and meaning of Bengali, 8; salaried employment for, 51
bhadrata, 97, 141

Bhagavad Gita, 23, 43, 110, 120, 121
Bhagavata purana, 121
Bhagavat Catuspathi, 261n10
bharatvarsha, 156
Bhattacharya, Siva Chandra Vidyarnava, 145-46, 170
Bhattacharya, Tithi, 97, 111
"Bhawani Mandir" (Pal), 255n36
Bildung, 26, 31-32, 45
Black Act, 91, 99
Blackbourn, David, 238n13
Blanning, T. C. W., 238n12
Blue Mutiny, 55, 97
Boas, Franz, 37, 39
Bolts, William, 75, 89
Bombay Gazette, 76
Bose, Chandranath, 100, 163
Bose, Pramatha Nath, 189-97; on classes, 227; on education, 191, 192-93; *A History of Hindu Civilization during British Rule,* 189; on industrialism, 190-92, 194; marries Dutt's daughter, 263n46; on *panchayat* system, 196-97; on return to traditional Hindu values, 193-95; on romantic ideal of Indian village, 196-97; on science, 191, 216; and Swadeshi movement, 192, 193, 194-95, 197, 198, 210-11; three-stage historical model of, 194
Bose, Sugata, 55, 58, 85
Bourdieu, Pierre, 236n29
brahmacarya, 180
Brahmans: Bankimchandra Chatterjee on role of, 122; Rammonhun Roy's opposition to, 79-80; in self-realization of the Sudras, 171; Tantrism and, 147
Brahmo Sabha (Assembly of God), 77, 90, 92
Brahmo Samaj: deepening experiential conflict between objectivity and subjectivity in, 112; Bijoy Krishna Goswami and, 148; Pal in rethinking, 143, 144; Debendranath Tagore in revival of, 114, 116
British empire: Bengali liberalism and, 68-108; Pramatha Nath Bose on appeals to British conscience, 190; in Bankimchandra Chatterjee's satire of the *babu,* 106; imagining possibility of a liberal, 89; liberal ideology of, 73; M. N. Roy on British rule, 226, 227; Rammonhun Roy's loyalty to British rule, 86-88; satirical representation of the Briton, 102; Swadeshi criticism

of British rule, 158-60. *See also* East India Company
British Indian Association, 99, 108
British India Society, 91
Brougham, Lord, 91
Buckingham, James Silk, 86
Buddhism, 112, 121, 150
bunka, 44, 241n71
bunmeikaika, 44, 241n71
Burckhardt, Jacob, 27

Caitanyaites, 121
Calcutta: Anushilan Samiti in, 176; capitalist social transformation in, 71, 72; civil society of, 76; commercial society of, 74-75; Das's poems on, 4; in dual economy of India, 97; financial crisis of 1847-48, 95-96, 98; heterodox religious developments in, 72-73; as key center of imperially-constituted commercial society, 75, 76; Muslims organizing associations in, 201; Okakura Tenshin's visit to, 17; and partition of Bengal Presidency, 137, 198; reified as essentially "white," 22, 97; riots of 1926, 217; sharpening racial lines in, 96-97
Calcutta Journal, 86
Calcutta Review, 56
Calcutta University, 161
Campbell, Sir George, 97, 202
capitalism: Bengali culturalism as misrecognition of global structures of, 5-6; Pramatha Nath Bose on capital without, 194; capital as self-positing and self-expanding value, 49-50; community imagined as anti-capitalist, 14-15; Congress criticism of, 101; continuity of transmission of indigenous practices fractured by, 21; culture and abstract mediation in, 47-51; culture as subjective moment of capitalist society, 232-33; culture concept as contingent upon, 47; culture discourse as response to global, 129; as driving beyond national barriers and prejudices, 52; as epochally particular constellation of social practices, 18; fundamental contradiction of, 64; Indian transition to, 71-72; Marxist transition narrative of, 70; Marx's sociohistorical approach to, 18-19; non-Western historical actors influenced by, 8; in peasant society, 51-60; precolonial South Asian conceptual apparatus contextu-

capitalism (*continued*)
ally resituated by, 20; M. N. Roy on Indian independence struggle as struggle against, 227; universalistic categories of, 231. *See also* commercialization; commodity exchange; laissez-faire

Carlyle, Thomas, 191, 193

Carr, Tagore and Company, 115

cash crops: capitalism in peasant society, 54, 55–56, 57, 58–59; jute, 55–56, 57, 98, 159–60, 208, 258n95; Muslims and, 204, 205, 223. *See also* indigo

cash-rent, 54

caste: Pramatha Nath Bose on, 189; Bankimchandra Chatterjee on functions of, 122; Bankimchandra Chatterjee on inequalities of, 105; Partha Chatterjee's analysis of, 15; lower-caste movements, 212; reform legislation, 213–14; Swadeshi view of, 175; Tagore on, 187; Young Bengal disregards rules of, 102, 104. *See also* Brahmans; Sudras (Shudras)

Chakrabarty, Dipesh, 20, 45–46, 47, 124

Chakrabarty, Tarachand, 92

Chandra, Bholanath, 100–101, 163

Chatterjee, Bankimchandra: Ahmad on Muslim answer to literature of, 221; *Anandamath* (*The Abbey of Bliss*), 109, 124, 145, 254n35; anti-Muslim views of, 208, 209, 210; "Bande mataram" ("Hail to the Mother"), 145, 208, 252n41; Bankim Festival, 254n35; "Bengal's Peasants," 106, 108; at Bose-Dutt wedding, 263n46; as collector of Vaishnava songs, 250n109; Comte as influence on, 23, 43, 129, 131, 133, 135; culture and habit distinguished by, 119, 123; culture concept used as foundation for ethical and political action, 22–23; doctrine of culture of, 43–44, 160, 171; *Equality*, 105, 108; on Hinduism as natural religion, 121–22, 128, 133; Hindu revivalist turn of, 23, 109–10, 117–22, 129, 135; on industrialism, 134; on Krishna, 121, 123, 132; *Krishnacarittra* (*The Life of Krishna*), 118, 121, 216, 252n32; liberalism of, 105, 106, 107; nationalism of, 122–26, 252n43; on political economy, 108, 135; *Pracar* founded by, 252n32; Ramakrishna's criticism of, 151; on religion as moral integration, 131–32; on salaried employment, 51; satire of the *babu*, 103–7; on sources of civilizational

development, 106; on subjective freedom versus worldly agency, 111–12, 116–17, 134; in systematization of Bengali culturalism, 22–23, 111; Rabindranath Tagore breaks with culturalism of, 176–77; turns against liberalism, 22, 108, 117; "What Is Humanity?," 111–12, 116; on yoga, 216

Chatterjee, Partha: on Gandhi's religious idiom, 256n64; on *jotedars*, 266n131; on nationalism, 12–15, 16

Chatterjee, Saratchandra, 217, 221

Chatterjee, Sunjeeb, 99–100

Chatterji, Joya, 217, 218, 219

Chaudhuri, Syed Nawab Ali, 199

children, unpaid agricultural labor by, 58, 59

China, 44–45

Christianity: antimissionary mobilization, 102, 114; Bankimchandra Chatterjee on ethical idealism of, 124; colonial identification of civilization with, 128; National Church movement, 127, 129, 130; versus natural religion for Bankimchandra Chatterjee, 121, 128

Church and State (Coleridge), 126–27

Church of Humanity, 129

Cicero, 27

civilisation, 27, 28, 29

civilization: Asian, 45; Pramatha Nath Bose on urban, 196; Pramatha Nath Bose's three-stage historical model, 194; colonial identification of Christianity and, 128; culture versus, 26–30, 31, 44; emergence of term, 27; identification with colonizer, 11; Tagore on unfolding of, 185

Civilizing Process, The (Elias), 18, 238n12

civil society: of Calcutta, 76; Bankimchandra Chatterjee grounds subjectivity in Hinduism not, 23, 118–19, 133, 135; colonial seen as externally imposed, 51; culturalist response to Indian functionaries entering, 43; as domain of heteronomy, 137; Hindu nationalist critique of, 139; in liberal view of practical activity, 51; Marxist criticism of selfish interest in, 228; Marx on rights and, 73; nationalist organicism contrasted with, 146; Pal on cosmopolitan religious reformers and, 143; patrilineage versus, 124; Rammohun Roy on colonial, 88–89; Swadeshi criticism of, 154, 156, 162, 165, 168, 171, 173, 228; Tantrism and, 147 class: Aurobindo on narrow class interests, 141; Aurobindo on the bourgeois type, 157–58; and community in Hindu communalism, 218; as not ultimate category of Marxist analysis, 231; in post-Swadeshi discourse, 189; M. N. Roy on, 227–28, 229; Swadeshi movement and, 138. *See also* caste; proletariat

clerisy, 126–27

Cohn, Bernard, 237n31

Coleridge, Samuel, 28, 126–27

Collini, Stefan, 239n26

colonialism: capitalism in peasant society, 51–60; colonizer/colonized distinction as constituted by rather than constitutive of constellations of colonial society, 7; commercialization seen as colonial imposition, 98; historiographical impasse of anticolonialism, 9–17; institutions as factories to Tagore, 181. *See also* British empire; postcolonialism

commercialization: of capital and product markets, 98; East is to culture as West is to commerce, 222; of peasant agriculture, 72, 98; as reaching deep into fabric of Bengali society, 72; Roy's support of, 85; seen as colonial imposition, 98

commodity exchange: abstract labor in, 49; as determining subjective propensities and objective circumstances, 60; in liberal conceptions of individuality and society, 73; Marx on rights and, 73; relationship between individuals in, 50; in rural Bengal, 54–55, 58; Smith on naturalness of, 48

community: *bhadralok* communalism, 210–19; imagined as antimodernist, antiindividualist, and anticapitalist, 14–15; in post-Swadeshi discourse, 233; Swadeshi ideal of ethical, 188

Comte, Auguste, 129–31; atheism of, 129, 131; Bankimchandra Chatterjee draws on, 23, 43, 129, 131, 133, 135; on division of labor, 131, 133

Condillac, Étienne, 29

Congress: Aurobindo's criticism of, 139–40, 141; liberalism of, 99, 108; national developmentalism of, 101; protectionism advocated by, 101, 163; Swadeshi criticism of, 167

Congreve, Richard, 129

cosmopolitanism: the abstract cosmopolitan, 171, 221; Ahmad on, 221; and historical universality of the laboring subject, 173; Marxist, 224; Pal on Brahmo Samaj and, 143; of post-Swadeshi thought, 230–32; Ray's cosmopolitan humanism, 1, 5, 230, 236n16; M. N. Roy on rightist, 228; Swadeshi attempt to transcend reformist individualism of, 156; Rabindranath Tagore on, 188–89

Cousin, Victor, 29

credit, 55, 56–57

critical theory, 63

cultivation: Aurobindo on, 140; and *Bildung*, 45; Bankimchandra Chatterjee equates *anushilan* with, 43–44, 110, 119–20; civilization contrasted with, 28, 32; culture as synonymous with, 26; in humanistic understanding of culture, 34; *krishti* associated with, 3, 176; Schiller on, 64, 65; of specialized knowledge for Bankimchandra Chatterjee, 132–33

culturalism: and anthropological culture, 39; beyond Marxist, 60–67; and liberalism as distinct ideological paradigms, 6, 7, 29–30, 51; nationalism's quest to fashion modern national culture, 14; practical activity constitutes substance of social whole for, 50–51; as response to global capitalism, 129; transnational dimension of, 5. *See also* Bengali culturalism

culture: and abstract mediation in capitalism, 47–51; Ahmad on relation of religion to, 220; anthropological, 34–40, 122–23; antinomic logic of, 40–41; *anushilan* as equivalent of *culture*, 43, 110, 119–20, 134, 176, 177, 189, 216; Arnold on, 26, 28, 30, 238n2; autonomy of, 26, 30–34, 38, 47; biology contrasted with, 37; Bankimchandra Chatterjee contrasts habit with, 119, 123; Bankimchandra Chatterjee on transfiguring custom into, 135; versus civilization, 26–30, 31, 44; concept development beyond the West, 43–47; concept represents unified conceptual field, 21; cultural difference versus cultural diversity, 7; East is to culture as West is to commerce, 222; emerges as free-standing concept, 27; etymology of English word, 26–27; as global concept, 4–5, 17–18, 21, 25–67; as historically specific

culture (*continued*)
  yet universal, 47; humanistic understanding
  of, 34–35, 122–23; imposition of concept on
  rest of world, 11; Lukács's conception of, 63,
  65–66; Marcuse on affirmative character of,
  245n142; pluralization of, 36; *sanskriti* versus *krishti* for translating term, 3, 176, 189;
  structuralist, 38; as subjective moment of
  capitalist society, 232–33; Swadeshi movement's concept of, 173–74; Rabindranath
  Tagore's aestheticization of, 3, 176–77,
  188–89; toward a theory of formation of
  concept of, 40–67; translating term in Asian
  languages, 5; on underdeterminedness of
  human subjectivity, 21–22, 26, 47, 67; as
  way of linking human subjectivity with
  practical activity, 6; Western genealogy
  of concept of, 17. *See also* Bengali culture;
  culturalism
Culture and Society (Williams), 42
Curzon, Lord, 136–37
custom: Bankimchandra Chatterjee on
  transfiguring into culture, 135; Tylor distin-
  guishes culture from, 37, 123; universalistic
  political economy contrasted with native,
  97–99, 137

Dalhousie, Lord James, 69
Danilevsky, Nicolai, 44
dar-ul-harb, 206, 207
Das, Jibanananda, 4
Dasgupta, Surendranath, 217
Datta, Aswini Kumar, 148, 260n134
Datta, Pradip, 217–18
Datta, Rajat, 53–54
De, Barun, 69, 70, 71, 75
Deb, Radhakanta, 88, 95, 102, 114, 248n43
debt, 55, 56, 58
deindustrialization, 53, 69, 190
democracy: Aurobindo on the bourgeois type
  and, 158; Bengali Hindus and Muslim
  majority, 218; Pramatha Nath Bose on, 196;
  limits on democratization in India, 69
Derozians: *India Gazette*'s criticism of, 102;
  Rammohun Roy criticized by, 81. *See also*
  Young Bengal
Derozio, Henry Louis Vivian, 92, 102
Desher katha (Deuskar), 158
determinism: reductionist, 38–39; M. N. Roy
  on orthodox Marxist, 229

Deuskar, Sakharam Ganesh, 158
Deussen, Paul, 255n54
devotion, 120–21, 123–24, 133–34, 147
Dhaka, 176
dharma, 119, 126, 134, 136, 180, 183
Dharma Sabha, 149
Dharmmatattva: Anushilan (*The Essence of
  Religion: Culture*) (Bankimchandra Chat-
  terjee), 118
Dilthey, Wilhelm, 38
Dinajpur, 58
discourse theory, 231, 232
"drain of wealth" theory, 100, 158, 190
Dudu Miyan, 206
Dutt, Akshay Kumar, 116–17, 134, 199
Dutt, Michael Madhusudan, 102, 103
Dutt, Romesh Chandra, 101, 163, 190, 263n46
"Dying Race, A" (Mukherji), 213

East India Company: and Age of Reform, 69;
  and Bengali textile industry, 53; and Bengal
  Renaissance, 69; Calcutta as key center of
  imperially-constituted commercial society,
  75; Charter renewal of 1833, 75; free trade
  advocates' criticism of, 75, 84, 91; and
  liberalism, 71; in social transformation of
  Lower Bengal, 71–72; Dwarkanath Tagore's
  opposition to, 90; Young Bengal on, 93
East Pakistan. *See* Bangladesh (East Pakistan)
East Pakistan Renaissance Convention, 219
Ecce Homo (Seeley), 127, 131
Economic History of India (Dutt), 101
economy, political. *See* political economy
education: *babu*'s Western learning, 104, 107;
  Pramatha Nath Bose's program for, 191,
  192–93; limits on Indian universal, 69; for
  Muslims, 201–2; as social distinction, 111;
  Swadeshi program for, 161–62, 181, 192,
  225; Rabindranath Tagore's program for,
  180–84, 188; Western model of, 181
Education Gazette, 202
effeminacy, 103–4
Elias, Norbert, 18, 28, 238n12
Emerson, Ralph Waldo, 255n44
equality: Aurobindo on, 142; Pramatha Nath
  Bose on, 193, 195; Bankimchandra Chatterjee on, 105, 108; Marx on commodity
  exchange and, 73; Mukherjee on, 94–95;
  Pal on, 157; Rammohun Roy's egalitarianism, 82–83; Swadeshi movement on, 167;

Rabindranath Tagore on Indian inequalities, 187
Equality (Chatterjee), 105, 108
exchange value, 49, 50, 242n87
Expansion of England, The (Seeley), 127
Extremists: Pramatha Nath Bose on, 190; culturalist national political economy of, 101, 163-65, 168-69; on development of modern industry, 172

family labor, unpaid, 52, 55, 58-59
famines, 159-60, 258n93
Faraidism, 206
female inheritance, 83
feringhis, 158, 167, 260n134
Fisch, Jörg, 36
food shortages, 159-60
Foucault, Michel, 21, 41, 42, 67, 236n29
France, 140-41, 142, 169
freedom: Aurobindo on, 142, 161; Pramatha Nath Bose on, 191-92, 193, 195; Hindu nationalism on subjective freedom through labor, 139; Marx on commodity exchange and, 73; negative and positive conceptions of, 29-30, 115-16, 147; as renunciation of desire for Bankimchandra Chatterjee, 120; M. N. Roy on basic urge to, 229; Swadeshi conception of, 157, 168, 174; Rabindranath Tagore's conception of, 184; worldly agency versus subjective, 111-17, 134, 135
free trade: Aurobindo on the bourgeois type and, 158; in Bengali opposition to East India Company privileges, 75; Bankimchandra Chatterjee's defense of, 106; Congress Moderates abandon, 101, 163; Rammohun Roy as free trader, 84, 99; Swadeshi opposition to, 162, 168; Dwarkanath Tagore as free trader, 90
Freud, Sigmund, 27, 37

Gait, E. A., 212
Gandhi, Mohandas, 219, 264n81
Gaudiya Vaishnavism: Bankimchandra Chatterjee and, 121, 252n34, 252n39; heterodox challenges to, 72; and immanentist monism, 147-49
Geisteswissenschaften, 39
Geist und Natur, 31
Germanism, 26
German philosophy: Hindu and German

idealism, 150; Lukács's analysis of classical, 63-64. *See also* Hegel, Georg Wilhelm Friedrich; Kant, Immanuel
Geuss, Raymond, 33
Ghare-Baire (The Home and the World) (Ray), 2-3
Ghare-Baire (The Home and the World) (Tagore), 2-3, 187
Ghose, Barin, 225
Ghosh, Jogendra Chandra, 108
Goethe, Johann Wolfgang von, 117, 120
Gora (Tagore), 187, 262n38
Goswami, Bijoy Krishna, 148, 151-52, 255n44
Goswami, Manu, 14-15, 75, 96, 100, 101, 156, 160
Gramscianism, 10, 14, 236n29
"great man" theory of history, 6
Great Wahabi Case, 201, 265n100
Guha, Ranajit, 20
Guha-Thakurta, Manoranjan, 148
Guizot, François, 29
Gupta, Iswar, 208
gurus: emergence of new type of, 144; Swadeshi view of, 175

habit, Bankimchandra Chatterjee contrasts culture with, 119, 123
Haldar, Hiralal, 150, 256n57
handicraft industries, revival of, 190, 191
Harrison, Frederic, 238n2
Hatcher, Brian, 80
Havell, E. B., 196
Hegel, Georg Wilhelm Friedrich: Pramatha Nath Bose and view of human history of, 195; critique of Kantian subjectivism, 61; on Hinduism, 150; Marx's criticism of idealism of, 153-54; Marx's dialectical approach influenced by, 63; moves from abstract to concrete, 6; Schiller's emphasis on cultivation and, 65; Swadeshi ideology influenced by, 23, 170, 184. *See also* Hegelianism
Hegelianism: and culture concept, 38; Hegelianized Vedanta, 150, 154, 184, 196
Hem, 209
Herder, Johann Gottfried, 35-36
Hindi cinema, 1-2
Hindu College, 92, 101, 102
Hinduism: Anglo-Saxon institutions contrasted with practices of, 175; in Aurobindo's culturalism, 142; *bhadralok* communal-

Hinduism (*continued*)
ism, 210-19; Pramatha Nath Bose as critical of social institutions of, 189; Pramatha Nath Bose on traditional values of, 193-95; Bankimchandra Chatterjee on otherworldliness of, 106; Bankimchandra Chatterjee on universalism of, 123-24; Bankimchandra Chatterjee's Hindu revivalist turn, 109-10, 117-22, 135; as culture, 109-35; Hegel's characterization of, 150; heterodox movements in Calcutta, 72-73; "Hindu culture" distanced from Muslim popular, 24, 211, 217-18; Hindu-Muslim violence, 197, 203-5, 210; Hindu nationalism, 125, 128, 138-39; Hindu revivalism, 17, 23, 44; Hindu sociology, 149-55; lower-caste Hindu peasants, 212; as natural religion for Bankimchandra Chatterjee, 121-22, 128, 133; on nondualism of self and not-self, 144, 165; Pakistanism as response to Hindu culturalism, 219-23; and pro-Muslim policy in education, 201-2; as religion of renunciation, 199, 220, 222; versus Rammohun Roy's monotheism, 78-84; in Swadeshi ideology, 137; Debendranath Tagore's theological reformism, 113-16; Young Bengal's criticism of, 92. *See also* Gaudiya Vaishnavism; Tantrism; Vedantism
Hindu Patriot, 56, 205
historischen Kulturwissenschaften, 39
History and Class Consciousness (Lukács), 63
History of Hindu Civilization during British Rule, A (Bose), 189
Hobson-Jobson, 103
Humboldt, Wilhelm von, 31-33
Hume, Joseph, 91
Hunter, Ian, 41-42, 63
Hunter, W. W., 200-201

idealism: culture as antithesis of Marxist materialism, 65; in Hindu sociology, 149-55; Marxist desublimation of culturalist, 224; Marx's criticism of Hegel's, 153-54; Mukherjee on realistic, 170; Swadeshi, 151, 154-55, 192, 198, 215, 225, 226
Ideals of the East, The (Okakura), 17
ideology critique, 153
idolatry, 79-81, 88, 101, 113, 114, 117, 148
Imagined Communities (Anderson), 11, 236n27
Inden, Ron, 255n50
India: as "bazaar of shopkeepers" under

British rule, 159; capitalist transformation in, 71-72; import of British manufactured goods and export of primary products, 96, 97, 156; increasing racial divide in, 96-97, 99; spiritual predisposition of, 174-75; versus West as custom versus political economy, 98-99, 137; Western materialism versus Indian spirituality, 195; Western theory and Indian difference, 231-32; and the West seen as incommensurable, 118. *See also* Bengal
India: Her Cult and Education (Mukherjee), 170
India Gazette, 101-2
Indian Association, 108
Indian Culture, 216
Indian Musalman Association, 199
Indian Musalmans, The (Hunter), 200-201
Indian Mutiny, 69, 97, 201
Indian National Congress. *See* Congress
indigo: Blue Mutiny against, 55, 97; capitalism in peasant society, 55, 56, 57, 243n7; collapse of system, 95, 98; commercialization of agriculture, 72; Faraidi opposition to system of, 206; native participation in British commercial activity, 75; Rammohun Roy as advocate of, 84-85; Dwarkanath Tagore as advocate of, 91
Indigo Commission, 56
individualism: Ahmad on Hindu, 222-23; Aurobindo on, 140; Pramatha Nath Bose on, 190; commodity exchange in liberal conception of, 73; community imagined as antiindividualist, 14-15; Comte and, 129; Swadeshi movement and, 138, 155, 156, 172
Indu Prakash, 139
industrialism: Pramatha Nath Bose on, 190-92, 194; capitalist transformation and industrialization distinguished, 51-52; deindustrialization, 53, 69, 190; limits on industrialization in India, 69; Nehru's support for industrialization, 1; Swadeshi movement on indigenous industry, 172; Victorian critique of, 134. *See also* manufacturing
intellectual history, 5, 233
Islam. *See* Muslims
Islam Pracharak, 209

Jakobson, Roman, 46
Jalsaghar (The Music Room) (Ray), 2

Jamaica, 99
Jamalpur, 208
Jana Aranya (*The Middleman*) (Ray), 2
Japan, 44–45, 150, 166–67, 259n125
jotedars, 58, 266n131
jute, 55–56, 57, 98, 159–60, 208, 258n95

Kant, Immanuel: anthropological conception
   of culture and, 40; on culture, 33–34; Hege-
   lian critique of subjectivism of, 61; Herder
   and concept of culture of, 36; on *Kultur* and
   Bildung, 26, 238n3; unresolvable unknow-
   able content in system of, 64
Karamat Ali, 207, 266n130
Kartabhajas, 72–73
Khan, Mehboob, 1
Kireevsky, Ivan, 44
Kling, Blair, 95
Kluckhohn, Clyde, 31, 34–35, 36, 37, 39
Koselleck, Reinhart, 62
Krishna, 121, 123, 132, 147, 148
Krishna, Daya, 152, 154
Krishnacarittra (*The Life of Krishna*) (Bankim-
   chandra Chatterjee), 118, 121, 216, 252n32
krishti: anushilan and, 177; cultivation associ-
   ated with, 3, 176; as equivalent of *culture*,
   3, 176, 216; marginalization of, 3, 176,
   177, 189
Kroeber, Alfred, 31, 34–35, 36, 37, 39
Kultur: and *Bildung*, 26, 45; as civilization, 27,
   29; Freud on, 37; Kant on, 33–34; versus
   Zivilisation, 28, 31–32, 45, 238n12, 241n71
Kultur der Renaissance, Die (Burckhardt), 27
Kuper, Adam, 37–38

labor: abstract, 49–50, 153–54, 172, 174; as
   basis for sustainable mode of worldly
   agency for Bankimchandra Chatterjee, 135;
   Pramatha Nath Bose on modern industry
   and, 191; Comte on division of mental and
   material, 131, 133; Hindu nationalism on
   subjective freedom through, 139; laborer
   as trope for India's beauty for Tagore, 186;
   Muslim, 214; M. N. Roy on, 227–28, 229,
   268n184; Sudras as, 171; Swadeshi view
   of, 165, 170, 172, 173, 174; in Rabindranath
   Tagore's educational philosophy, 182, 183.
   See also proletariat
laissez-faire: Chandra's denunciation of, 101;
   Bankimchandra Chatterjee and turn away

from, 134; first articulation of Bengali
   critique of, 99
Landholders Society, 91, 92, 95, 99
La Vopa, Anthony, 28, 32
Leont'ev, Konstantin, 44
Levenson, Joseph, 9
Lévi-Strauss, Claude, 38
Liakat Husain, 199
liberalism: Arnold's call for a better, 30;
   Aurobindo's critique of, 139–42; Bengali
   culturalism as reaction against, 6, 43–44,
   68; British empire and Bengali, 68–108; of
   Bankimchandra Chatterjee, 105, 106, 107;
   Bankimchandra Chatterjee turns against, 22,
   108, 117; and commercial society, 73, 107;
   Congress attempts to salvage, 163; crisis of,
   76, 95–101; and culturalism as distinct ideological paradigms, 6, 7, 29–30, 51; defined
   in terms of practical activity in society
   organized on basis of commodity exchange,
   50–51; in 1830s and 1840s, 89–95;
   emergence of English, 73–74; Extremist
   negation of, 165; liberal mode of satire,
   105; nineteenth-century Bengali, 22; of
   Rammohun Roy, 77–89, 113; in second half
   of nineteenth century, 99, 101; Swadeshi
   critique of, 168; universalistic values of, 129
List, Friedrich, 163
Liu, Lydia H., 235n15
Lloyd, David, 42–43, 63, 245n143
Locke, John, 29, 124
love of country, 125
Lukács, Georg, 25, 63–66, 244n133

Macaulay, Thomas, 68, 91, 99
Mahaprabhu, Chaitanya, 148
Maine, Sir Henry, 97
Malinowski, Bronislaw, 39–40
"man": grounding in categories of capitalist
   society, 63; Victorian ideology and cultural
   trope of, 41, 43
Manchester, 134, 158
Manning, Paul, 242n81
manufacturing: Bose calls for development of,
   100; Bankimchandra Chatterjee on industrialism, 134; India as importer of British
   manufactured goods, 96, 156; revival of
   handicraft industries, 190, 191
"Manushyatva ki?" ("What Is Humanity?")
   (Bankimchandra Chatterjee), 111–12, 116

Marcuse, Herbert, 238n12, 245n142
Marx, Karl: on capitalism driving beyond national barriers and prejudices, 52; on commodity as "cell-form" of modern society, 19; on commodity production and exchange determining subjective propensities and objective circumstances, 60; criticism of Hegel's idealism, 153–54; Hegel's conception of self-moving activity as core of dialectic of, 63; materialism of, 65, 154; moves from abstract to concrete, 6; sociohistorical approach to capitalism of, 18–19; on value, 48–50. *See also* Marxism
Marxism: Bengali, 223–29; class as not ultimate category of, 231; Gramscianism, 10, 14, 236n29; historicist-developmentalist, 20; beyond Marxist culturalism, 60–67; materialism of, 65, 154, 224, 228; nationalism as interpreted by, 10; Swadeshi movement and Bengali, 24, 223–25, 228; transition narrative of capitalism of, 70
materialism: Aurobindo on, 140; Pramatha Nath Bose on, 190, 194, 196, 197; civilization and, 28; Hindu nationalist critique of, 139; of industrial society, 134; late-nineteenth-century debate over spiritualism and, 111–17; Marxist, 65, 154, 224, 228; Seeley on worship of visible things versus, 128; Shudra, 186, 228; Swadeshi criticism of, 156, 167, 172, 175, 198
Mendelssohn, Moses, 26
Mihir-o Sudhakar, 199
Mill, James, 93
Mill, John Stuart: Chatterjee Bankimchandra on the *babu* and, 107; Chatterjee Bankimchandra renounces influence of, 108, 117, 120; Comte's thought popularized by, 130, 253n51; on culture, 42; on custom in Indian society, 97, 99; on negative and positive freedom, 29–30
Minto, Lord, 199, 203, 212
Mitra, Peary Chand, 93, 98, 100, 105
Moderates: Pramatha Nath Bose as Moderate, 189, 190, 193; Moderate Congress support for protectionism, 101, 163; new politics versus liberalism of, 142, 165
modernity: assimilation of Western concepts in developing world, 11; Pramatha Nath Bose on, 194; community imagined as antimodernist, 14–15; European evolution rejected as general model, 20; nationalism's quest to fashion modern national culture, 14; Rammohun Roy as founding figure of Bengali colonial, 77; the subaltern becomes a horizon to Western, 12; universalistic categories of capitalist, 231; the West associated with, 9
modernization: and Bengal Renaissance, 69–71; identification with colonizer, 11; modernizing universalism, 70; Nehru's support for, 1
monism: immanentist, 142–49, 155; qualified, 149; Rammohun Roy's nondualism, 78–79, 112–13, 115; Debendranath Tagore's opposition to, 114
Montagu-Chelmsford Reforms, 196, 197
Mookerjee's Magazine, 100
Morley-Minto reforms, 212
Mukherjee, Dakshinaranjan, 94–95
Mukherjee, Jatin, 225
Mukherjee, Pramathanath, 170
Mukherjee, Satish Chandra: and class analysis of religious idioms, 256n64; as disciple of Bijoy Krishna Goswami, 148; as educational innovator, 162, 180, 259n106, 261n10; ethnologization of culture of, 174; Benoy Kumar Sarkar as student of, 171
Mukherji, U. N., 213, 214
Mukhopadhyay, Bhudeb, 108
Mundal, Santosh, 56
Muslim League, 199, 219
Muslims: anti-Muslim epithets, 210; Bankimchandra Chatterjee on Muslim conquest of India, 124; education for, 201–2; foreign ancestry claimed by, 207; "Hindu culture" distanced from Muslim popular, 24, 211, 217–18; Hindu-Muslim violence, 197, 203–5, 210; Islam versus natural religion for Bankimchandra Chatterjee, 121; itinerant mullahs propagate reform among, 206–7; libidinousness attributed to, 214; Muslim conquerors' violations of property rights, 86; nationalist overtures toward, 198–99; Pakistanism as response to Hindu culturalism, 219–23; and partition of Bengal Presidency, 137, 177–78, 198, 200, 202; as peasants, 203–8, 212; Perso-Arabic names adopted by, 207; as sectional interest, 200–203; selfishness attributed to, 197–210, 222; Swadeshi boycott opposed

by, 178–79, 187, 199, 203–4, 208, 210–11;
Swadeshi view of Muslim rule, 159, 208–10;
Rabindranath Tagore on supporting self-
improvements of, 186

Namasudras: Act X assists, 204; separate
representation sought by, 212–13; Swadeshi
boycott resisted by, 178–79, 212
nation: nation-as-mother concept, 124; Pal
on organic constitution of, 144; Swadeshi
conception of, 155–56, 172, 183. *See also*
nationalism
National (Broad) Church movement, 127, 129,
130
National Council of Education, 180, 191,
192–93, 216, 258n103
nationalism: All-India, 218–19; of Bankimchandra Chatterjee, 122–26, 252n43;
conceptual structure of indigenist, 136–75;
double bind of, 16–17; Hindu, 125, 128,
138–39; historiographical impasse of, 9–17;
Japanese influences on Indian, 17; Marxist
interpretation of Indian, 10; methodological, 75; political economy of, 100–101, 139;
quest to fashion modern national culture,
14. *See also* Swadeshi movement
Nationalist Thought and the Colonial World
(Chatterjee), 12
Nation and Its Fragments, The (Chatterjee), 13
natural religion, 121–22, 127–28, 133, 199
Natural Religion (Seeley), 127–28
nature: Muslims' connection to, 214; in Tag-
ore's educational philosophy, 182–84
Natur und Geist, 31
Navashakti, 148, 168, 169
Nayak, 167
Nehru, Jawaharlal, 1
neo-Kantianism, 38
neo-Romanticism, 110, 111
New India, 162, 169
New Lamps for Old series (Aurobindo), 139,
141–42, 169
Newman, John Henry, 127
Nietzsche, Friedrich, 29
nishkam karma, 119–20, 133, 168, 184, 188–89
Nivedita, Sister, 17

objectivity: commodity production and
exchange as determining subjective propensities and objective circumstances, 60–61;

cultural specificity of forms of subjectivity
versus sociological, 11; and nature in Rabindranath Tagore's educational philosophy,
182; as necessarily and irreducibly mediated by subjectivity, 61–62; Rammohun Roy
on subject/object mediation, 112–13, 115;
subjective freedom versus worldly agency,
111–17, 134
Okakura Tenshin, 17
Orientalism (Said), 11

Pabna, 204–5, 206, 207
Pagden, Anthony, 70
Paine, Thomas, 94
Pakistanism, 219–23
Pal, Bipin Chandra: "Bhawani Mandir,"
255n36; in boycott in response to partition
of Bengal Presidency, 137, 162; on composite patriotism, 198–99; on development
of modern industry, 172; as disciple of
Bijoy Krishna Goswami, 148, 255n44; on
economics and politics, 163; Emerson as
influence on, 255n44; on equality, 157; on
essential divinity of man as central conception of Hinduism, 149; on Hinduism's
underlying nondualism of self and not-self,
144, 165; on human unity, 156; on liberal
reformers, 142–43; on new politics based
on history of the nation, 171–72; on organic
constitution of society, 144; on rational
unfolding of Idea in history, 149–50; on
society, 151–52
Palit, Taraknath, 191
panchayat system, 196–97
pantheism, 112, 113
Parsons, Talcott, 38
patrilineage, 124, 125
patriotism, 125, 140, 172, 192, 193, 198–99
peasant society: Blue Mutiny, 55, 97; capitalism in, 51–60; Bankimchandra Chatterjee's
"Bengal's Peasants," 106, 108; commercialization of peasant agriculture, 71, 98;
in dual economy of India, 97; Muslim
peasants, 203–8, 212; peasantization, 53,
69, 191; M. N. Roy on, 229; Rammohun
Roy on the peasantry and British rule, 87;
self-interest associated with, 205; two axes
of organization of, 51–52, 137–38
Peirce, Charles Sanders, 46
Permanent Settlement, 69, 84, 85, 93–94, 97

Pincus, Steve, 73-74, 246n8

Pletsch, Carl, 38

political economy: Bankimchandra Chatterjee on, 108, 135; Comte's opposition to, 130; "drain of wealth" theory, 100, 158, 190; generalized pursuit of pleasure underpins logic of, 30; Malinowski on "primitive economic man," 39-40; nationalist, 100-101, 139; native custom contrasted with universalistic, 97-99, 137; Swadeshi, 155-70, 212. *See also* free trade; industrialism; protectionism

Pollock, Sheldon, 257n68

positivism, 129-30

postcolonialism: elements of, 236n29; ethical language of self-determination of, 70; European evolution of modernity rejected as general model by, 20; post-Swadeshi ideological trajectories as postcolonial, 230-32; primacy of colonial discourse in literature of, 16

Postone, Moishe, 66, 153, 257n68

poverty, in Rabindranath Tagore's educational philosophy, 182-83

Pracar, 252n32

"Primitive Economic Man," 39-40

Producing India (Goswami), 15

proletariat: Aurobindo on, 141; as identical subject-object for Lukács, 63-66; M. N. Roy on, 229

protectionism: Pramatha Nath Bose as advocate of, 190; Bankimchandra Chatterjee's opposition to, 106, 134-35; List on, 163; Moderate Congress support for, 101, 163; Swadeshi advocacy of, 162-63, 167

psychoanalysis, 37

Pufendorf, Samuel, 27

purdah, 59

race: Bankimchandra Chatterjee on inequalities of, 105; demands for equality, 108; Pal on liberal reformers on, 143; sharpening racial lines in second half of nineteenth century, 96-97, 99; in Swadeshi political vision, 173

Radha, 121, 147, 148

railways, 56

rakhi bandhan, 199

Ramakrishna Paramhansa, 144, 151, 152

Rasul, Abdur, 199, 202

Ray, Niharranjan, 3, 252n36

Ray, Prithvishchandra, 262n35

Ray, Rajat, 54

Ray, Satyajit: Apu trilogy, 1-2; cosmopolitan humanism of, 1, 5, 230, 236n16; *Ghare-Baire,* 2-3; *Jalsaghar,* 2; *Jana Aranya,* 2; political disillusionment of, 2

Raychaudhuri, Tapan, 248n41

reductionist determinism, 38-39

Reform, Age of, 68-69, 90

Reform Bill, 86, 87

religion: Ahmad on relation of culture to, 220; Buddhism, 112, 121, 150; as moral integration to Bankimchandra Chatterjee, 131-32; natural, 121-22, 127-28, 133, 199. *See also* Christianity; Hinduism; Muslims

Religion of Humanity, 131

rents, 54, 56, 57, 94, 98, 105

Resolution on Muslim Education, 201

Ricardo, David, 94, 98

Rickert, Heinrich, 38-39

Robertson, Bruce, 82

Robson-Scott, W. D., 27

Rousseau, Jean-Jacques, 28, 30, 33, 64, 65

Roy, M. N. (Narendranath Bhattacharya), 225-29, 230, 231

Roy, Ramkanta, 88

Roy, Raja Rammohun, 77-89; in Bengal Renaissance, 6; as Bengal's first modern, 77; Chandranath Bose's call for manufacturing development and, 100; within bounds of Brahman respectability, 95; and Buckingham, 86; criticism of luxurious indulgences of, 102; death of, 89; European influences on, 71; family's prosperity and status, 88; as free trader, 84; on India as empire, 247n19; on India's ancient constitution, 87; on indigo production, 84-85; liberalism of, 74, 77, 87, 88, 113; loyalty to British rule, 86-88; monotheism of, 78-84; motivation of modernism of, 70; new generation influenced by, 101; nondualism of, 78-79, 112-13, 115; Pal on reformism of, 143; pantheism rejected by, 113; on the Permanent Settlement, 84, 85; on property rights, 83-84, 85-86, 88; on the Reform Bill, 86, 87; as a republican, 86; on sati, 82, 83; Debendranath Tagore's theological reformism compared with that of, 113-14; and Tantrism, 251n7; on tenancy reform, 85-86, 98; Young Bengal's criticism of, 92

Roy, S. C., 263n61
Russia, 44

Sahebdhanis, 72–73
Said, Edward, 11
salaried employment: Aurobindo on return to land for Hindus, 211; Aurobindo on squabbles about positions, 141; educated middle class increasingly dependent on, 51; sense of marginalization and subordination in, 107; Swadeshi agenda challenged by, 197–98; Swadeshi criticism of, 157–58, 160; trope of femininity and, 104
Salimullah, Nawab, 199, 200, 202, 203, 210
Samiruddin, Maulvi, 204
Sandhya, 146, 164, 167, 169, 208, 260n34
Sankaracharya, 74, 80, 81, 112, 114, 145, 148
sanskriti: and identification of culture with life of the people, 177; purification associated with, 3, 176; Rabindranath Tagore's campaign to translate culture with, 3–4, 176, 189
Sarkar, Benoy Kumar, 171, 199
Sarkar, Sumit, 10, 69, 70, 71, 75, 164, 210, 256n64, 267n147
Sarvadhikary, Deva Prasad, 216, 217
sati, 82, 83
Saussure, Ferdinand de, 45, 46
Schiller, Friedrich, 64–65, 245n142
Schopenhauer, Arthur, 255n54
Seal, Anil, 10
Seal, Brajendranath, 109, 110, 150, 256n57
Seeley, Sir John, 127–28, 129, 131
self-interest: Arnold on, 30; Pramatha Nath Bose on, 197; British concern about, 239n26; Bankimchandra Chatterjee on cultivation versus, 23, 43, 108, 120, 134; civilization and, 28; dharma contrasted with, 136; Akshay Kumar Dutt on, 116; Extremist negation of, 165; Indian spirituality contrasted with Western, 174; liberalism on, 82; Marxist collective interest versus, 228; Muslim, 218; peasants associated with, 205; of "primitive economic man," 39; and Swadeshi criticism of British rule, 157, 159
self-preservation, 125
self-realization: Pakistanism as, 219; of the Sudra, 171; Swadeshi ideal of, 172, 196; Rabindranath Tagore on, 183, 186, 187, 188;

Tantrism on, 146; Swami Vivekananda on, 151
Sen, Asok, 69, 70, 71, 75
Sen, Nabinchandra, 209
shakti, 145, 147, 148, 150, 151
Shantiniketan, 4, 180, 181, 182, 188
Shiva, 145
Shore, Sir John, 93
Shudras. See Sudras (Shudras)
Simla deputation, 199
Skinner, Quentin, 10–11, 67
Slavophilism, 44
Smith, Adam, 48, 73, 107, 242n87
society: commodity exchange in liberal conception of, 73; Comte's view of, 133; culture versus, 42–43; Pal on organic constitution of, 144; in Swadeshi ideology, 151–52, 155, 156–57; in Rabindranath Tagore's educational philosophy, 183–84; transhistorical application of concept, 257n68; Swami Vivekananda on, 151. See also civil society; sociology
Society for the Acquisition of General Knowledge (SAGK), 92, 93
Society for the Diffusion of Essential Truth, 114, 116
Society for the Propagation of Technical Education, 191
sociolinguistics, 46
sociology: Brahmo, 143; Bankimchandra Chatterjee and Comte's, 129; Hindu, 149–55; indigenist, idealist, 147
Som Prakash, 205
Southard, Barbara, 153, 257n67
Spencer, Herbert, 125
spiritualism: India's spiritual predisposition, 174–75; late-nineteenth-century debate over materialism and, 111–17; Western materialism versus Indian spirituality, 195
"Spiritual Realization through Action" ("Karmayog") (Tagore), 184
Stocking, George, 36, 39
structuralism, 38
subjectivity: and anthropological culture, 38, 39, 40; Bankimchandra Chatterjee grounds in Hinduism, 118, 134; Bankimchandra Chatterjee on liberal, 108; commodity production and exchange as determining subjective propensities and objective circumstances, 60–61; as consequential, 61,

subjectivity (*continued*)
244n128; cultural specificity of forms of, 11; culture as subjective moment of capitalist society, 232–33; culture concept and underdeterminedness of, 21–22, 26, 47, 67; global resonance of subjective autonomy, 67; Hindu nationalism on subjective freedom through labor, 139; as necessarily and irreducibly mediated by objectivity, 61–62; Rammohun Roy on subject/object mediation, 112–13, 115; subjectivism articulated by culture concept, 63; Rabindranath Tagore on appropriation of nature and, 183; worldly agency versus subjective freedom, 111–17, 134, 135. *See also* autonomy

Sudras (Shudras): Rammohun Roy on materialism of, 228; Rabindranath Tagore on, 186–87, 188; Vivekananda on, 171, 186, 188, 212

surplus value, 50, 57, 58

svajati movements, 208

Swadeshi movement, 136–75; Bengali Marxism's genealogical links to, 24, 223–25, 228; and *bhadralok* communalism, 214, 216, 218, 219; Pramatha Nath Bose and, 192, 193, 194–95, 197, 198, 210–11; boycott of British goods of, 162–64, 178–79; and Brahmoism, 147; and Bankimchandra Chatterjee's neo-Hinduism, 110; on civil society, 154, 156, 162, 165, 168, 171, 173, 228; collapse of, 23–24, 176, 177, 193, 226; communal imagination as challenge to, 222; conception of the nation of, 155–56, 172, 183; concept of culture of, 173–74; critique of consumption of, 168; educational program of, 161–62, 181, 192, 225; failure to win broad-based support, 153, 178–80; on handicraft industries, 191; Hegel's influence on, 23, 170, 184; heteronomous forces negated by, 173; Hindu sociology of, 149–55; idealism of, 151, 154–55, 192, 198, 215, 225, 226; Muslim culture grounded in values of, 223; Muslim opposition to, 178–79, 187, 199, 203–4, 208, 210–11; on Muslim rule, 159, 208–10; Namasudra resistance to, 178–79, 212; national history in politics of, 23, 170–75; need for salaried employment challenges agenda of, 197–98; political economy of, 155–70, 212; political turn to religious idioms in, 152, 153, 256n64;

politics of popular mobilization elaborated from conceptual logic of, 138, 198, 210, 224; post-Swadeshi ideological trajectories as postcolonial, 230–32; and Salimullah party, 202; Sarkar on, 10; secret-society terrorism of, 176, 179, 187, 210, 225; Shantiniketan and ideal of ethical community of, 188; on society, 155; Tagore family as supporters of, 177; Rabindranath Tagore breaks with, 182, 187; Rabindranath Tagore on failure of, 177–80

Swadeshi Samaj (Tagore), 187

Ta'aiyuni movement, 207

Tagore, Debendranath: and Akshay Kumar Dutt, 116; on spiritual subjectivity of material world, 134; theological reformism of, 113–16

Tagore, Dwarkanath, 89–92; in antimissionary mobilization, 102; Black Act opposed by, 91, 99; on British rule, 90; criticism of luxurious indulgences of, 102; failure of company of, 115; inclination to compromise of, 95; indigo production advocated by, 91; and Landholders Society, 91, 95; liberalism of, 90–91; liberal leadership assumed by, 89–90; participation in British commercial activities, 75; religious views of, 90, 248n50; son Debendranath, 113; and Thompson, 91–92; and Turton, 89; and Union Bank, 90, 91

Tagore, Rabindranath: Bengali-Muslim literature influenced by, 8, 221; on Bengalis inverting natural relation between home and outside world, 167–68; in Bengal Renaissance, 6; at Bose-Dutt wedding, 263n46; breaks with Swadeshi movement, 182, 187; culture aestheticized by, 3, 176–77, 188–89; educational philosophy of, 180–84, 188; on failure of Swadeshi movement, 177–80; *Ghare-Baire* (*The Home and the World*), 2–3, 187; *Gora,* 187, 262n38; on Hindu-Muslim brotherhood, 199; on Japanese capacity for self-sacrifice, 166; kinship relations as Indian national genius, 143; Nobel Prize for, 189; and Okakura Tenshin, 17; on *rakhi bandhan,* 199; on *sanskriti* versus *krishti,* 3–4, 176; social status of, 8; Swadeshi movement's failure as watershed for, 210–11; *Swadeshi Samaj,* 187; on terrorism, 261n9; universalistic humanism of, 5, 24; Visva-Bharati university, 4; wealth accumulation of family of, 51

Tantrism, 145-48; in Hindu system of culture for Bankimchandra Chatterjee, 122; new type of gurus promote, 144; Rammohun Roy and, 251n7; on *shakti*, 145; Sivachandra Vidyarnava's defense of, 254n31; and Vivekananda's mediating category of society, 151

Tariqah-i-Muhammadiyah movement, 206-7

Tattvabodhini Patrika, 112, 114, 116

Tattvabodhini Sabha (Society for the Diffusion of Essential Truth), 114, 116

Tenancy Act of 1885, 204, 207-8

Thomas, Paul, 42-43, 63, 245n143

Thompson, George, 91-92, 94

Tilak, Bal Gangadhar, 111, 208

Time, Labor, and Social Domination (Postone), 66

tobacco, 56

Tractarians, 127

transportation: improvements in, 96, 98, 156; railways, 56

Treitschke, Heinrich von, 28

Turton, T. E. M., 89, 95

Tylor, Edward Burnett, 36-37, 39, 122-23

Unbehagen in der Kultur, Das (Freud), 27

Union Bank, 90, 91, 95, 96

universalism: of aesthetic appreciation for Tagore, 188-89; of Arnoldian conception of culture, 142; Bankimchandra Chatterjee on superiority of Hindu, 123-24; Bankimchandra Chatterjee's new Hindu, 23, 117-22; Partha Chatterjee on, 15-16; Eurocentric, 11; of Herder's conception of humanity, 36; of Krishna for Bankimchandra Chatterjee, 132; of laboring subject in Swadeshi political vision, 173, 174; liberal, 129; Marxist, 224; modernizing, 70; of political economy contrasted with native custom, 97-99; universalistic categories of capitalist modernity, 231; the West associated with, 9

Upadhyay, Brahmabandhab: in boycott in response to partition of Bengal Presidency, 137, 163-64; character in Tagore's *Swadeshi Samaj* based on, 262n38; on Divine Mother, 146; as educational innovator, 180

Urban, Hugh, 72

Urdu, 266n129

utilitarianism, 29, 107, 129, 140, 172, 186

Vaishnavism. *See* Gaudiya Vaishnavism

value: exchange value, 49, 50, 242n87; Marx's category of, 48-50; surplus value, 50, 57, 58

Vedantism: and Hegelianism, 150, 154, 184, 196; Rammohun Roy on need to reconceptualize, 74. *See also* Advaita Vedanta

Vedas, 118, 188

Vidyabagish, Ramchandra, 113, 114

Vidyalankar, Mrityunjay, 80, 81

Vidyalankar, Nandakumar, 251n7

Vidyarnava, Sivachandra, 254n31

vishishtadvaita, 149

Visva-Bharati university, 4

Viswanathan, Gauri, 237n31

Vivekananda, Swami: on age of Vaishya, 173; Pramatha Nath Bose on tradition of, 193; Sister Nivedita as disciple of, 17; on social work, 151, 152, 256n61; on Sudras, 171, 186, 212; and Tagore on spiritual realization, 184

Volk, 35

Voloshinov, Valentin, 46

wage labor, peasant, 54, 55, 57, 58

Washbrook, D. A., 72

wealth, 183

West, the: Asian and Western civilization contrasted, 45; *babu*'s embrace of Western learning, 104, 107; culture concept development beyond, 43-47; culture concept's genealogical roots in, 17; East is to culture as West is to commerce, 222; educational model of, 181; Eurocentric privileging of subjectivity of, 13; imposition of its categories on rest of world, 11; versus India as political economy versus custom, 98-99, 137; Indian spirituality contrasted with Western self-interest, 174; and India seen as incommensurable, 118; modern universality associated with, 9; non-Western histories seen as flawed reiterations of, 20; Pal on cosmopolitan religious reformers and, 143; provincializing Europe, 47; the subaltern becomes a horizon to Western modernity, 12; Western materialism versus Indian spirituality, 195; Western theory and Indian difference, 231-32

Westernization: Pramatha Nath Bose on, 193; and colonizer's claim to monopoly of truth, 11; Extremist opposition to, 165; Japanese

Westernization (*continued*)
and Chinese intellectuals' resistance to,
44; reformism, 69; social relationships as
utilitarian in, 143
Whiggism, 74, 84, 86, 91, 93
Williams, Raymond, 19, 42–43, 47, 60, 63, 67,
240n44
women: Bankimchandra Chatterjee on confinement of, 106; "new" versus "old-style,"
103, 106; *purdah,* 59; Roy on equality for,
82–83; Tagore on gender discrimination,
187; unpaid agricultural labor by, 58–59;
Young Bengal on education for, 93

Wood, Sir Charles, 97
worship, 127–28

yavana, 209, 210
yoga, 122, 215, 252n37, 255n38
Young Bengal, 92–95; on British rule, 93;
liberalism of, 92–93; on property rights,
93–94; radicalism of, 70–71; satirizing the
babu, 101–3
Yugantar, 157, 169
Yugantar group, 225

Zivilisation, 28, 31–32, 45, 241n71